DEVOTIONAL POETRY IN FRANCE
c. 1570–1613

DEVOTIONAL POETRY
IN FRANCE

c.1570–1613

TERENCE C. CAVE

CAMBRIDGE
AT THE UNIVERSITY PRESS
1969

Published by the Syndics of the Cambridge University Press
Bentley House, 200 Euston Road, London N.W. 1
American Branch: 32 East 57th Street, New York, N.Y. 10022

© Cambridge University Press 1969

Library of Congress Catalogue Card Number: 68–23177
Standard Book Number: 521 07145 3

Printed in Great Britain
at the University Printing House, Cambridge
(Brooke Crutchley, University Printer)

FOR MY MOTHER AND FATHER

CONTENTS

vii

Contents

PREFACE

One of the fundamental religious trends of the sixteenth century, whether one is considering the 'pre-Reformation', the Reformation itself, or the Catholic revival, is the attempt to rediscover an inner, personal value for a religion which had become too concerned with externals on the one hand and with an abstruse, impersonal theology on the other. Towards the end of the century, this 'inwardness' is manifested in the increasing popularity of vernacular devotional literature: and it is the first object of this study to show to what extent the contemporary rise of the religious lyric in France may be seen as part of the same historical and literary development.[1]

Until the emergence of specialist studies of the 'baroque' period in France, the existence of the substantial quantity of religious poetry which appeared during and after the wars of religion was acknowledged only with some embarrassment. Overshadowed by Ronsard's *Discours*, by d'Aubigné's *Tragiques*, by Du Bartas and to a lesser extent by the religious drama, the lyric poets were often given summary treatment; little attempt was made to consider the poetry of prayer and meditation as an organically coherent *genre*.[2] However, Henri Bremond demonstrated that such poetry could be placed in the context of the devotional revival; and his sympathetic and perceptive reading of La Ceppède, to mention only one poet among many, has formed the basis of much of the recent work on this period.

Since Bremond, and since Professor Boase's pioneer work on Sponde, the attempt to reassess the literature of the post-Pléiade era in positive terms has attracted the attention and energies of numerous scholars in

[1] See the conclusion of my article, 'The Protestant devotional tradition: Simon Goulart's *Trente tableaux de la mort*', FS, 21 (1967), pp. 1 ff. This article establishes one of the starting-points of the present study; I am most grateful to the Editorial Board of *French Studies* for allowing me to reproduce parts of it here (in particular the first two sections, which are placed in a wider context in chs. 1 and 2 below).

[2] See for example R. Lebègue, *La Poésie française de 1560 à 1630*, 2 vols. (Paris, 1951); M. Raymond, *L'Influence de Ronsard sur la poésie française, 1550–1585* (Geneva, 1965) (*THR*, 73), 2nd ed., chs. 13–15, 26; J. Vianey, *Le Pétrarquisme en France* (Montpellier, 1909), ch. 4, especially pp. 293–4, 297–303. The view that most of the successes in the field of religious poetry must be attributed to Protestants (Du Bartas, d'Aubigné, Sponde) is maintained (with some regret) by A. Müller, in *La Poésie religieuse catholique de Marot à Malherbe* (Paris, 1950).

Preface

Europe, North America and Australia. As a result of this activity, a certain amount of religious poetry is now readily accessible;[1] furthermore, the impact of the Counter-Reformation has been recognised as one of the most significant factors determining the general literary character of the period.[2] Nevertheless, the consideration of Sponde, La Ceppède and their contemporaries as 'metaphysical', 'baroque', or (more recently) 'mannerist' poets has tended from the outset to focus attention on problems of terminology.[3] Furthermore, the inclination to derive general historical concepts largely from the internal analysis of literary works has produced a dangerous area of abstraction; I have been disturbed, in my reading of the 'second generation' of critics, by the assumption that the word 'baroque' (and to a lesser extent its satellite terms) now has an agreed content and corresponds to a historical and stylistic fact. For the same reason, there has been a certain inbreeding of literary analysis and evaluation: since Sponde and La Ceppède are held to illustrate the baroque, their work continues to be assessed in terms of 'baroque characteristics'.[4]

[1] For Sponde, see the editions of Professor A. M. Boase; for Chassignet, see the selection by A.-M. Schmidt in *Poètes du xvie siècle* (Paris, 1959) (Bibliothèque de la Pléiade), or A. Müller, *Le Mespris de la vie et consolation contre la mort. Choix de sonnets* (Geneva, 1953) (*TLF*), together with the same author's *Un Poète religieux du xvie siecle: J.-B. Chassignet, 1578?–1635?* (Paris, 1951); for La Ceppède, see Professor J. Rousset's photographic edition of the *Théorèmes* (Geneva, 1966) (*THR*, 80), which supersedes the selection of F. Ruchon in *Essai sur la vie et l'œuvre de Jean de La Ceppède* (Geneva, 1953) (*THR*, 8). See also Rousset's *Anthologie de la poésie baroque française*, 2 vols. (Paris, 1961). Boase's anthology, *The Poetry of France*, vol. 1, *1400–1600* (London, 1964), contains two well-chosen sonnets by La Ceppède (p. 191).

[2] See for example I. Buffum, *Agrippa d'Aubigné's Les Tragiques* (Paris, 1951), pp. 83–8; J. Rousset, *Anthologie*, vol. 1, pp. 18–19, and *La Littérature de l'âge baroque en France* (Paris, 1954), pp. 236–40; O. de Mourgues, *Metaphysical, Baroque and Précieux Poetry* (Oxford, 1953), ch. 6 (especially sect. 1); Boase, *The Poetry of France*, vol. 1, *Introduction*, pp. xcix ff. A recent article by F. L. Lawrence, 'La Ceppède's *Théorèmes* and Ignatian Meditation', *CL*, 17 (1965), pp. 133 ff., makes a number of important points, but suffers from lack of reference to a complete edition of the *Théorèmes*, and from the consideration of Loyola as a principal source of La Ceppède's technique.

[3] See for example the studies by Rousset, Buffum and de Mourgues mentioned above; Buffum's *Studies in the Baroque from Montaigne to Rotrou* (Yale, 1957); a group of articles on the baroque published in *L'Esprit créateur*, 1 (1961), no. 2 and a similar group on mannerism in *EC*, 6 (1966), no. 4; and of course the work of Boase, including 'The Definition of Mannerism', in *Proceedings of the IIIrd Congress of the International Comparative Literature Association* (The Hague, 1962), pp. 143 ff. (see also *The Poetry of France, Introduction*, p. xcvii). Owing to the proliferation of such studies, it would be impossible, and irrelevant, to attempt anything approaching an *état présent* study here.

[4] Some of the articles in the first volume of *L'Esprit créateur* mentioned above seem to me to represent these tendencies; see for example Jesse Zeldin, '*Les Tragiques* and the

Preface

It seems advisable, therefore, to develop the study of this period through the isolation of areas of literature which have a close inner coherence both thematically and historically; and the coincidence of the devotional revival with the popularity of religious poetry provides a convenient way of delineating one such area.[1] The validity of this pattern has already been established for English poetry by Louis Martz, who, in his *Poetry of Meditation*, considers close parallels between techniques of meditation in contemporary translations of devotional treatises and the work of poets such as Southwell, Crashaw, Donne and Herbert.[2] Since most of the handbooks which Martz mentions had appeared in French editions some years earlier, there are clearly grounds for a comparative study of the French and English poets in devotional terms. Yet the special conditions of French poetry and of French religious history in the later sixteenth century demand an independent treatment, in the first instance at least: I have therefore made very few allusions to non-French poetry.

In delimiting the materials of this study, I have preferred to talk of a 'devotional poetry' rather than of a 'poetry of meditation', since the term devotion is more specifically religious: I have not followed Martz in his wider discussion of meditative poetry, for the affinity which links, say, Donne and Eliot has no counterpart in France. In the second place, as 'devotion' implies the private religious attitudes of meditation and prayer, the term will exclude a great deal of 'moral' poetry along the lines of Pibrac's *Quatrains*, of partisan poetry in the vein of the *Discours* and the *Tragiques*, and of epic, dramatic and 'scientific' poetry. I shall therefore be considering primarily 'lyric' poetry, a poetry of self-examination and prayer; but since the modes of medita-

Baroque', pp. 67 ff., or Ilona Coombs, 'Baroque Elements in Jean de Sponde's *Stances de la mort*', pp. 86 ff. See also V.-L. Tapié, *Baroque et classicisme* (Paris, 1957), where Sponde and Théophile are described together as poets who 'n'avaient point mis de frein à leur imagination, ni au plaisir de leur fantaisie' (p. 25); such a distorted judgement of Sponde suggests that the term baroque has created a barrier between the critic and the poetic text.

[1] Others could no doubt be found, for example in the realm of prose style (one or two suggestions on this topic are made below, chs. 2, 3 and 7).

[2] L. Martz, *The Poetry of Meditation* (Yale, 1962). See also Rosemond Tuve, *A Reading of George Herbert* (London, 1952), for Herbert's relation to the devotional and liturgical traditions (including some important observations on the ways in which Counter-Reformation devotional 'styles' were anticipated by the Middle Ages); Miss Tuve's critical approach is also relevant to the present study.

tion and sermon are often inseparable, Sponde's *Sonnets de la mort* and similar material may, I think, legitimately be considered under this heading. In order to illustrate the methods and matter of devotion, and thus to provide a context for this poetry, I have drawn on both medieval and sixteenth-century prose; but as the medieval tradition is to a large extent subsumed in the treatises of the Counter-Reformation, greater emphasis will be laid on the latter. Translations into French of foreign and Latin works will be used in nearly every case, since the whole argument depends on the movement of devotion into vernacular *media*; furthermore, verse paraphrase, both of Biblical texts and of medieval hymns, will be taken into account as an essential factor in this movement, although a full study of this vast field could clearly not be undertaken.

If one is to deal with such a rich period of literature, it is essential to be selective, particularly as the majority of primary sources are not easily accessible. I have omitted at least one important group of themes —those associated with the description and praise of Creation—on the grounds that it was not possible to do justice to such a wide-ranging topic without seriously disturbing the balance and unity of the book; similarly, there are many more minor poets of this period whose work could have been included, but who seemed superfluous to the demonstration of my thesis. At the same time, I have included a substantial number of quotations (often of whole poems), and have added an Appendix containing supplementary illustrations too long to include in the text, since much of this poetry is likely to be unfamiliar to the reader.

The dates I have chosen to limit the period are intended only as an approximate indication and are somewhat arbitrary. Most literary historians agree in placing the beginning of the vogue of religious lyrics in the 1570s: Jacques de Billy's *Sonnets spirituels* were first published in 1573, in 1574 appeared the Geneva *Poèmes chrestiens*, and from 1575, the works of Desportes were beginning to include religious poems. Several important devotional works were published in the years immediately preceding the accession of Henri III, so that 1570 seems to represent a significant moment in the rise of vernacular devotional literature; nevertheless, some account will be given of works published prior to this date. The terminal date, 1613, is more specific in that it marks the appearance of the first complete volume of La Ceppède's *Théorèmes*. By this time, the character of the various modes of devotional poetry was fully established, while the naturalisation into French of the devotional tradition had reached its first climax in the *Introduction à la vie dévote* of St François de Sales. This period of forty years, though organically related to developments both before and after, thus allows one to examine the beginnings and establishment of an independent devotional poetry.

The structure of the present study is based on the attempt to combine historical documentation with internal analysis and evaluation. The first chapter provides a broad historical sketch of the devotional revival; the second indicates certain relevant aspects of devotional themes and techniques as they appear in the handbooks themselves; and the third attempts to establish, in a historical perspective, the grounds for believing that the growth of the religious lyric is intimately linked with the devotional revival. The remaining four chapters are concerned almost exclusively with poetry. The material has been distributed according to thematic and formal criteria, since I felt that a purely chronological analysis would have resulted in excessive fragmentation; considerable emphasis has nevertheless been placed on the evolution of poetic attitudes and techniques. Chapters 4 and 5 deal with the themes of affliction and death, chapters 6 and 7 with meditation on the life of Christ. This division is justified on the grounds of emotional unity: the mood of penitential self-abasement which arises from the consideration of man's unredeemed nature is resolved in the contemplation of the Redemption. As we shall see later, the same pattern is used by many of the devotional masters, and it reflects the contrast between the Old Testament and the New. Within this broad thematic framework, the material has been grouped in terms of forms rather than of themes: the distinction between the devotional sonnet on the one hand and more expansive forms such as the psalm-like *stances* on the other is an essential one, since it is often the sign of a fundamental difference in poetic temperament. However, I have not excluded more specific thematic groupings, such as that suggested, for example, by the poetry of the Eucharist. Above all, the work of leading poets such as Desportes, Favre, Sponde, La Ceppède and César de Nostredame has been allowed to dominate the shape of individual chapters.

My aim is therefore threefold. In the first place, I have tried to show how far the devotional poets were able to create a valid and independent mode of poetic expression; in the second place, I have sought to indicate a pattern of themes, language and technique which is central to the devotional literature of the sixteenth and early seventeenth centuries as a whole; and finally, I hope to have shed new light on the work of poets already familiar—Sponde, Desportes, Chassignet, La Ceppède—and of others, like Favre and César de Nostredame, who deserve more attention than they have yet received.

A NOTE ON THE TEXTS

The scope and purposes of this book have made it impossible to account for the variants of a text in more than a small proportion of cases, especially as there is an almost total lack of modern variant editions even of such central poets as Desportes and Bertaut. I have referred to modern editions where possible, for reasons of accessibility, even where the presentation of the text is far from satisfactory (Michiels's Desportes, Chenevière's Bertaut). In the case of Desportes, this has resulted in a degree of inconsistency, since the prose prayers and meditations and many of the paraphrases are not included by Michiels: for these texts I have used one of the earliest contemporary editions in which all the religious work of Desportes appears.

When I have quoted from editions of the sixteenth and seventeenth centuries, I have retained the spelling and punctuation of the original and only corrected misprints where the true reading is in no possible doubt. In one or two cases, I have added punctuation suggestions in square brackets to clarify the sense, but I have been as economical as possible in this respect. Where there were *lacunae* in the original, I have also supplied a conjectural reading in square brackets. Consonantal 'i' and 'u' have throughout been rendered as 'j' and 'v' respectively, and all ampersands and abbreviations resolved. The arrangement of sonnets and extracts from sonnets has been standardised without separation of quatrains or tercets.

ACKNOWLEDGEMENTS

This book originated as a doctoral thesis. The definition of my subject, and most of the preparation of the thesis itself, was supervised by Professor I. D. McFarlane, of the University of St Andrews, to whom I should like to express my warmest thanks for his scholarly advice and criticism throughout this stage. I am similarly indebted to Professor A. J. Steele, of Edinburgh University, for his close reading of the completed thesis and of the version revised for publication. Both have contributed more to the fabric of this book than could possibly be acknowledged.

I am most grateful to Dr O. de Mourgues, Dr G. Castor, and M. M. Jeanneret, of Cambridge University, for the comments and suggestions which they supplied at important stages in the preparation of the manuscript. M. Jeanneret has further enriched my book by making available to me, in conversation and by correspondence, his close knowledge of fields related to my own; and since the title of his forthcoming book was not available to me when I compiled my footnotes, I am glad to be able to announce it here: *Poésie et tradition biblique au seizième siècle.*

Dr H. G. Hall and Professor D. G. Charlton, of the University of Warwick, were kind enough to read and comment on portions of the final draft; and many other friends and colleagues have from the earliest stages given me their help and encouragement.

I am grateful to the Trustees of the Jebb Studentship at Cambridge University, to Gonville and Caius College, Cambridge, and to the Universities of St Andrews and Warwick for making available to me scholarships and grants which enabled me to conduct my research, both in England and in France, unhampered by financial problems.

Finally, I should like to thank my wife Helen for helping me with proofs and Index, and for her patience and tactful encouragement throughout the revision and final preparation of the book.

T. C. C.

University of Warwick, 1968

ABBREVIATIONS

The following abbreviations have been used, both in the text and in the Bibliography:

Ann. hist. soc.	*Annales d'histoire sociale*
BHR	*Bibliothèque d'humanisme et renaissance*
BSHPF	*Bulletin de la société de l'histoire du protestantisme français*
CAEF	*Cahiers de l'association internationale des études françaises*
CL	*Comparative Literature*
DSS	*Dix-septième siècle*
EC	*L'Esprit créateur*
FS	*French Studies*
HTR	*Harvard Theological Review*
JWI	*Journal of the Warburg Institute*
MLN	*Modern Language Notes*
MLR	*Modern Language Review*
RB	*Revue des bibliothèques*
RHLF	*Revue d'histoire littéraire de la France*
RLC	*Revue de littérature comparée*
RSH	*Revue des sciences humaines*
RSS	*Revue du seizième siècle*
SF	*Studi francesi*
STFM	*Société des textes français modernes*
THR	*Travaux d'humanisme et renaissance*
TLF	*Textes littéraires français*
ZFSL	*Zeitschrift für franzözische Sprache und Literatur*

CHAPTER I

DEVOTIONAL TRADITIONS

The character of the Renaissance is frequently dependent on the convergence of different traditions; renewal begins in religion, philosophy and literature with an attempt to reassess and to synthesise the experience of past centuries. In this way, medieval modes of thinking and writing may persist in the new era, but no longer as the sole authority; the concept of tradition has been broadened, and by a process of comparison and reconciliation a rapid evolution becomes possible. Much the same is true of the history of devotional practice, at least in its codified, 'literary' form. There were already considerable differences of purpose and thus of emphasis in the works of the medieval masters, differences involving the whole range of possibilities between mystical theology and practical piety, between the formal treatise on the one hand and the liturgical hymn or the vernacular sermon on the other. The sixteenth century reviewed and developed most of these possibilities; at the same time, a variety of new factors came into play. Devotion

---

[1] The following outline of the devotional tradition and its revival in the sixteenth century is of necessity highly compressed. For a more detailed picture, consult, for example, H. Bremond, *Histoire littéraire du sentiment religieux en France depuis la fin des guerres de religion jusqu'à nos jours*, vols. 1–2 (Paris, 1929–30); L. Cognet, *De la Dévotion moderne à la spiritualité française* (Paris, 1958); J. Dagens, *Bérulle et les origines de la restauration catholique (1575–1611)* (Brussels, 1952), and *Bibliographie chronologique de la littérature de spiritualité et de ses sources (1501–1610)* (Paris, 1952); E. Gilson, *History of Christian Philosophy in the Middle Ages* (London, 1955), and individual studies on for example St Bernard and St Bonaventura in the *Études de philosophie médiévale* series; P. Pourrat, *La Spiritualité chrétienne*, 4 vols. (Paris, 1918–28). On more specific topics: M. Bataillon, *Erasme et l'Espagne* (Paris, 1937), and 'De Savonarole à Louis de Grenade', *RLC*, 16 (1936), pp. 23 ff.; C. Dejob, *De l'Influence du Concile de Trente sur la littérature et les beaux-arts chez les peuples catholiques* (Paris, 1884); L. Gillet, *Histoire artistique des ordres mendiants* (Paris, 1939); W. G. Moore, *La Réforme allemande et la littérature française* (Strasbourg, 1930); J.-M. Prat, *Maldonat et l'Université de Paris* (Paris, 1856); A. Renaudet, *Préréforme et humanisme à Paris pendant les premières guerres d'Italie (1494–1517)* (2nd ed., Paris, 1953); F. A. Yates, *The French Academies of the Sixteenth Century* (London, 1947).

made contact with humanist scholarship, and thus with the philosophy of antiquity: the themes of self-examination, spiritual progress and meditation on death were now remembered in the context of the schools of thought (predominantly Platonist) which had originally helped to form them. Furthermore, the increasing contact between monastery and lay society created a demand for treatises which were not only comprehensible to a wide public, but also attractive to read; thus devotional writing began to use the devices of profane rhetoric, finding its way before long into the ode, the sonnet, and narrative prose. The mingling of so many currents and influences produces a diversity which can at times seem as bewildering as that of other areas of Renaissance activity. On the other hand, it was the aim of both the Reformation and the Counter-Reformation to restore, in terms of personal religious practice as well as of theological reasoning, the sense of a fundamental, authoritative tradition. In the devotional manuals of the period, this aim is evident in the constant acknowledgement of Biblical and patristic sources. Furthermore, and in part because of the way these sources were used, there is a central core of devotional method and matter which is passed on from work to work, sometimes almost verbatim, so that writers of different religious orders or even of different confessions will often seem to echo one another and their medieval predecessors. This core gives the tradition a unity and a consistency amid many vicissitudes. Its main constituents (thematic, methodological, stylistic) will be considered in greater detail in chapter 2 and elsewhere; for the present, it will be sufficient to sketch the broader outlines of the tradition, laying particular emphasis on the forms it assumes when it reaches the post-1570 period in France.

It is convenient, if at times misleading, to think of devotion as existing in opposition to theology. In its most extreme form, this dichotomy would be represented on the one hand by the formalised reasonings of the scholastics, constructing faith on the basis of an authoritarian logic, and on the other hand by the simple, personal approach of, say, the *Imitation*, relying on imagination and emotion. The early Church Fathers were aware of no such distinction: theology and private prayer were both essential and complementary aspects of a Christian way of life. This was no doubt in part due to the Neoplatonist affinities of patristic theology. One of the central elements of

The devotional tradition and its revival

Augustine's religious thought was the concept of a meditative ascent towards knowledge of the Divinity, a spiritual progress which expressed itself naturally in Neoplatonist language; and in this system there is complete concord between the intellectual structure and the need for a personal faith. Much of what the Middle Ages knew about Platonism was transmitted through Augustine, and the devotional tradition was throughout to remain conscious of his influence. But with the emergence of scholasticism in the twelfth and thirteenth centuries the picture begins to change. The mystic Bernard of Clairvaux is opposed to the logic of Abelard, and in the following century the teaching of Bonaventura and the Franciscan school, although not incompatible with the theology of Aquinas, marks the starting-point of a divergence which within a century or so will become acute. The mystics of Germany and the Low Countries—Tauler, Suso, Ruysbroeck—maintain a direct link, through Bonaventura, with Augustine and the language of Platonism; their doctrine is scarcely on the level of 'simple piety', indeed it involves a considerable complexity of thought, but it is the principal generating force in the foundation of the Windesheim community, and later of the concept of a *devotio moderna*. Ruysbroeck and his disciples at Windesheim were increasingly concerned with the dissemination of devotional practice beyond the walls of the cloister, and it is this aspect of the group's activities which is represented by the *Imitation of Christ*; here the principles of meditation are laid down simply enough to make them accessible to the widest audience.

Once this movement in the direction of an organised devotional practice for the laity has become established, it is sustained in one form or another into the Counter-Reformation period; editions of the *Imitation*, both in Latin and in French translation, proliferate throughout the sixteenth century. On the other hand, the swing in favour of a simple, affective piety was later to be corrected, in some circles at least, by a revival of 'intellectual' meditation. Erasmus, who owed a great deal to Windesheim, was also deeply suspicious of the excessive externality of popular religion and its emphasis on pathos, on the easy flow of tears. His *De praeparatione ad mortem* brought to the *ars moriendi* tradition, with its simple, pictorial approach, a new element of intellectual argument; likewise, the *Enchiridion militis christiani* conceives of 'inward prayer' in terms of controlled thought rather than of quasi-mystical effusions. The latter work, as an authoritative formulation of the 'spiritual combat' concept, was to have a profound influence in the Counter-Reformation. The piety of Erasmus thus gives a new direction to the anti-theological nature of devotion; the method of the Sorbonne theologians is rejected, but the intelligence of the Church Fathers, of Augustine and Jerome, is re-invoked, and the New Testament is to be approached with the scholar's understanding. In France, the greatest direct influence of Erasmus concerns the circle of Evangelists associated with Marguerite de Navarre, converging there with the infiltration of Lutheran ideas and with a mysticism of Neoplatonist extraction. After his death, he was suspected of having opened the door to the Protestants; nevertheless, many of his ideas found their way (often anonymously) into the doctrine of the leading devotional movements, and his attempt to reconcile devotion with humanism anticipates a period in which these two traditions will be allowed to mingle in a number of ways.

Among the most vigorous opponents of Erasmus were the Carthusians of Cologne, who were responsible for publishing and disseminating the works of the Dutch and German mystics—Harphius, Tauler, Ruysbroeck and so on—as well as adding original contributions to the same tradition. The leading figure of the Charterhouse, up to his death in 1539, was Landsberger (Johann Justus), one of whose chief preoccupations was to stem the rising tide of Protestantism. His *Enchiridion*, like the *Imitation*, is directed towards a lay audience; but the degree of austerity and of abnegation it recommends would seem more suited to the cloister. The influence of Erasmus is suggested by the dislike of facile emotion and by the attitude to prayer, which should be 'inward' but controlled; Landsberger's ascetic ideal would however certainly have been too extreme for Erasmus. The work of the Charterhouse as a whole—and of the Benedictine Louis de Blois, whom the Carthusians were later to edit—is monastic, and its cultivation of an austere and highly-developed mysticism makes its influence a specialised one. It supplies an essential link in the tradition of mystical devotion, resuming and passing on with renewed impetus the work of the Dutch and German school, and its achievements will be remembered well beyond the turn of the century. But when the 'invasion mystique'

The devotional tradition and its revival

begins in France, it will be due equally to sources of inspiration transmitted from the south, particularly from Spain; and it is Spain, too, which will set many of the trends in the more popular forms of devotion with which we are concerned here. The history of devotion in Spain in the sixteenth century is full of tensions. On one hand there is from the early years of the century a powerful mystical current, represented particularly by the *alumbrados*; on the other hand, the terror of the Inquisition soon began to inhibit any public expression of these tendencies. Hence the somewhat ambiguous position of the Dominican Luis de Granada. His stress on interiority, and also on the need to make devotion accessible to all kinds and classes of people, earned him the censure of the Inquisitors;[1] but for the same reasons his works became very widely disseminated both in Spain and in Europe as a whole. Indeed, there is little doubt that, in France at least, their impact was initially far greater than that of Loyola's *Spiritual Exercises*; and this point needs to be emphasised if one is to consider the relationship between devotional method and literature. Much the same could be said of his contemporaries Alonso de Madrid and Antonio de Guevara. Granada's devotional method was influenced by Cisneros, one of the great precursors of Counter-Reformation methodology, but also by Erasmus's *Modus orandi*; indeed, Erasmus was acknowledged as a master in many Spanish circles before his death, particularly at Alcalá.

Loyola himself was intimately involved in the same atmosphere. His formation was influenced by the piety of the Dominicans and Franciscans, and his *Spiritual Exercises*, the focal point of devotional method in the sixteenth century, were doubtless modelled to some extent on the *Exercises* of Cisneros, published in 1500. Loyola's work appeared at a crucial moment. Inward prayer had become a highly controversial issue, since the undisciplined appeal to faith and to 'illumination', the reliance placed on the individual in his relationship to God, could and did produce dangerous approximations to Reformation doctrine. Loyola's task was to place prayer and meditation on a securely orthodox footing, to provide a clear-cut framework, and thus to justify personal reflection as one of the central aspects of Christian life in both

---

[1] His *De la Oracion y Meditacion* and his *Guia de peccadores* were nevertheless condemned (temporarily) by the Valladolid Index of 1559.

monastic and lay circles. Considered as a group, the Spanish prayer-
methods were extremely influential in France, and dominated the
devotional atmosphere there in the last third of the century; but with
the beginning of the new century, other influences began to make
themselves felt, especially that of St Teresa's Carmelite reform and
thus of a feminine, emotional mysticism. In this way, the achievements
of Spain continued to contribute to those of France long after the end
of our period, and tended to replace the straighforward devotional
exercise with a more ambitious progress towards the mystical experience.

This is a century in which influences travel far and fast; and the
internationalism of the Jesuits is the outstanding example of the way
in which contacts were made and new ideas promulgated. Loyola had
been nurtured in a Spain where the influence of both Erasmus and
Savonarola was strong; between 1528 and 1535 he studied at Paris—
at the Collège de Montaigu, the Collège de Sainte-Barbe, and the
Sorbonne; and he also maintained a close contact with the Cologne
Charterhouse. Certainly, in the preparation of an atmosphere which
fostered the wave of devotional translations in the later sixteenth
century, the influence of the Jesuits was decisive. Their optimism, soon
to become notorious, was largely successful in overcoming ascetic
trends in the devotional tradition. They met the attacks of Erasmus
(and of the Calvinists) on excessive 'externality' in popular religion
by an affirmation of the value of external aids to complement a
thorough-going revival of 'interior' devotion; thus painting and
rhetoric were confidently exploited to arouse religious fervour. Meanwhile, the Council of Trent was slowly reconciling itself to a similar
course of action: its final ratification only added impetus to a movement
already firmly established.

It will by now be clear that the major devotional movements of the
sixteenth century are not of French origin; the circle of Marguerite de
Navarre is perhaps the nearest approach to an organised effort in the
earlier part of the century, and the term 'devotion' can only be
applied to it in a rather special sense. However, after the outbreak of
the wars of religion, with the multiplication of external influences,
interest in devotion begins to gather way. The most important single
factor in this change of climate is the increasing use of the vernacular,

both in translations and in original compositions. For more than a century, the French language had gradually been gaining authority as a vehicle for religious doctrine and worship: French translations of devotional literature had appeared occasionally in the fifteenth and early sixteenth centuries, together with picture-Bibles and other aids for the unlearned. But it was only in the second half of the century that such translations became numerous and finally outstripped Latin editions.[1] At the same time, original treatises in French and collections of sermons became commonplace. The importance of this wave of French devotional literature is stressed by both Bremond and Dagens:

Avant François de Sales on a vu des centaines d'introductions à la vie dévote, écrites en français et qui s'adressaient à tout le monde. Pendant les trente dernières années du XVIᵉ siècle et les toutes premières du XVIIᵉ, des prêtres, des religieux...des laïques enfin ont mis en notre langue presque tous les grands mystiques, de saint Denis à sainte Thérèse.[2]

This movement, dissociating itself from the cloister and penetrating deeper and deeper into lay circles, was to culminate in the *Introduction* itself, which St François intended as a replacement for the translations which he had had to recommend hitherto.

The 'popularisation' of devotion may be seen as one element of an overall attempt to meet the Calvinist challenge, with its direct, vernacular appeal (the *Institution chrestienne* became the first French theology in 1541). Catholic translations of the Bible began to appear almost as regularly as Calvinist ones, and translation changed the whole nature of the Bible: it had been part of a distant, immutable ritual, now it was available for personal meditation. At the same time the potentialities of its language were released into the vernacular, and here again the achievement of the Calvinists—the Marot-Bèze Psalter, the Calvinist drama, and the prose of Calvin himself—was formidable and invited rivalry. Before 1550 there were few enough popular Catholic treatises— one or two works by Gerson, lives of Christ in the picture-Bible tradition by the Carthusian Guillaume de Branteghem, and several of the oddly-titled productions of the Dominican Pierre Doré (Rabelais's Doribus). Between 1550 and 1570 the publication of handbooks in

---

[1] At the level of European communication, the vernacular was on the other hand often a barrier; thus translations were made in both directions, according to the audience for which a particular work was destined.

[2] Bremond, *Humanisme dévot*, p. 19; cf. Dagens, *Bibliographie*, 'Préface', p. 9.

French increases steadily: Doré still proliferates, but he is joined now by René Benoît (translator of the Bible and later to become the confessor of Henri IV), the Jesuit Edmond Auger, Dupuy-Herbault, and translations of Vives and of Louis de Blois. But it is not till after 1570 that the full range of foreign and Latin devotional works—those of the Cologne Charterhouse and their mystical forebears, of the Spanish mendicants and Jesuits, of Italians like Panigarola and Serafino da Fermo, as well as the patristic and medieval treatises of Augustine, Bernard, Bonaventura and so on—becomes available in French. In the four years immediately preceding Henri III's accession, versions were published of Augustine, Anselm, Bernard, the *Imitation*, Dionysius de Leuwis, Landsberger, Louis de Blois, Vives, Guevara, Luis de Granada, Serafino da Fermo and Borromeo, not to mention original works by Auger, Dupuy-Herbault, Benoît and others.

At the same time a new trend becomes increasingly evident: the work of lay translators, often better known in other fields. The historian François de Belleforest is first mentioned in Dagens's *Bibliographie* as the translator of St Cyprian's sermons (1565), but his first great success was undoubtedly his version of Guevara's *Livre du Mont de Calvaire* (1571), which was being reprinted up to the end of the century; the following year he produced Granada's *Devotes contemplations*. In the dedication of the Guevara work, he stresses repeatedly the unusual nature of his translation, composed by a layman, for a layman: 'plusieurs s'estonneront autant de voir à qui je le dedie, comme qui est celuy qui le traduit'.[1] He says that he is accustomed to 'tracer l'histoire', not to 'boire à plaisir de ceste surnaturelle liqueur de Theologie' (notice that he calls 'theology' this devotional work with its detailed description of the sufferings of Christ and its symbolic interpretations of each episode in the Passion story). But he points out that Guevara addressed his works to laymen as much as to priests:

...sommes tous Chrestiens, ayans besoin de sçavoir le chemin de nostre perfection, et les moyens de parvenir à icelle...Cecy estant le devoir du Chrestien (je dis de tous, afin qu'on ne pense que les seuls hermites et devotieux doivent mediter la passion de nostre Seigneur) que de chercher la voye de felicité: et n'en y ayant d'autre que la mort du Sauveur du monde nostre Dieu, et le fils de l'homme crucifié.

[1] A. de Guevara, *Livre du Mont de Calvaire*, trans. F. de Belleforest (Paris, 1589; 1st ed., Paris, 1571), dedication, *non pag.* (dated July 1571).

The devotional tradition and its revival

Much the same attitude is outlined in his translation of Granada's *Vray chemin*, where he speaks of 'le soing que ce religieux avoit de faire voir et entendre aux rudes, et petits (car c'est à eux à qui il adresse cest œuvre) le moyen de se preparer à la devotion, et meditation'.[1] This explicit popularising aim is frequently found in the works of the Spanish school, and although the Germanic tradition plays an important part in this wave of translations, the Spaniards are more popular with lay translators. Belleforest and his contemporary Gabriel Chappuys are principally concerned with the treatises of the Spanish mendicants, never with the Cologne Carthusians, whose ascetic tendencies would certainly make them less acceptable to a lay audience.

The coincidence of the devotional revival with the wars of religion is doubtless also due in part to the universal need for 'consolation' at a time of national affliction. The words *consolation* and *affliction* (often *consolation des affligés*) appear regularly in the titles listed in Dagens's *Bibliographie*. At the same time, contemporary evils were frequently seen as a punishment for sin. Tamisier's dedication of his meditations in verse on the Penitential Psalms speaks of 'oraison et meditation' as the remedy for 'les extremes calamitez et afflictions, desquelles Dieu a visité nostre pauvre patrie'; this is typical of many other contemporary dedications and prefaces to devotional works.[2] It was the same attitude that motivated Henri III's conviction that the best cure for the civil wars lay in the appeasement of God's wrath through penitence and devotion. Henri III's religious attitude is in itself an outstanding example of the devotional revival. He felt himself singled out for a high spiritual destiny, symbolised by the emblem of the three crowns, and his wife Louise de Vaudémont was famous for her piety. Champion has collected an impressive array of testimonials for Henri's devotional ardour, by Louis Le Roy, Du Perron, and Pierre Crespet among others:

Henri est le contemplateur fait pour la vie paisible ou tourmentée de l'âme. Il n'est pas un homme d'action...Le fond de l'esprit du roi demeurait la

---

[1] L. de Granada, *Le Vray chemin et adresse pour acquerir et parvenir à la grace de Dieu... par le moyen et compagnie de l'Oraison et Contemplation en la Loy et amour de Dieu,* trans. F. de Belleforest (Paris, 1579; 1st ed., 1576), 'Advertissement au lecteur, sur la traduction du present livre', *non pag.*

[2] See, for example, J. Guytot, *Les Meditations des zelateurs de pieté* (Paris, 1582), 'Conclusion du traducteur sur le profict de la presente version', *non pag.* The dedication of this edition is dated 1568, the *privilège* 1580. Dagens lists a 1571 edition.

piété; et il ne fait aucun doute...que sa grande idée a été la réforme du royaume par la douceur, la foi, la pénitence, la restauration des mœurs.[1]

From the beginning of his reign he was subject to the influence of the Jesuits: he defended them in their struggle at the Collège de Clermont (where Maldonat had taken over the chair of theology in 1564), and his confessor Auger was the first Jesuit confessor of a French king. Auger composed a number of treatises, as well as a translation into French of the *Imitation*, published in 1578; and that this translation was intended for the widest possible audience is suggested by the vignette on the title-page of the first edition, showing a labourer, a woman, and a child carrying the Cross.[2] Auger was familiar with the Italian penitential orders, and had encouraged parallel orders in the south of France; thus he was no doubt largely responsible for the king's creation of a series of penitential *confréries*. The *Confrérie des pénitents de l'annonciation de Notre-Dame* (the 'white penitents'), formed in 1583, were associated with the need for an heir; it was this order that held the famous procession in the rain in which Henri and the *mignons* took part. In December of the same year, the *Confrérie d'Hiéronymites* was founded at Vincennes. The Hieronymites were related to the Blue Penitents of St Jerome;[3] among their number was Henri de Joyeuse, comte de Bouchage, once a *mignon* and later to become the Capuchin Père Ange de Joyeuse. Finally, in 1584, Henri formed the *Congrégation de l'Oratoire de Notre Dame de Vie Saine*, to which were attached first a number of Cordeliers, later of Minims. The character of this institution, representing a devotional parallel to the *Académie du Palais*, was certainly influenced by Borromeo's *Accademia delle Notti Vaticane*; the Italian saint, renowned for his asceticism and his reformation of religious orders, had made a great impression on Henri from the time of the new king's passage through Italy in 1574. This Vincennes 'Academy' brought together a wide variety of political, religious and literary figures, and the combination is particularly interesting in that it suggests a close connexion between devotion and the humanist tradition:

[1] P. Champion, 'Henri III et les écrivains de son temps', *BHR*, 1 (1941), pp. 65, 104.
[2] See *ibid.* p. 107.
[3] The 'white penitents' had been established at the Couvent des Augustins, and thus both orders were associated with the 'humanist fathers', Augustine and Jerome. This may be of significance when seen in relation to the atmosphere of the two Academies.

The devotional tradition and its revival

The Palace Academy, with its humanist debates and 'profane' images, merged into the Congrégation de l'Oratoire de Notre Dame de Vincennes, where the current which has been traced through the Pléiade, through Baïf's Academy, through the Palace Academy, takes on the intensely pietistic colouring of the new age.[1]

Miss Yates has analysed at some length the fusion of profane and sacred oratory that is at the centre of Du Perron's sermon-technique;[2] and it is clear that such an atmosphere would be liable to encourage in the same direction poets who were in some way attached to the court—not only Desportes, but also Amadis Jamyn, Joachim Blanchon, Jean de Boyssières, Isaac Habert, and the young Malherbe.

Important indications of Henri's reading preferences are given by dedications and similar documents. Champion quotes Vigenère's dedication to Henri of his translation of the pseudo-Bonaventuran *Aiguillon*:

Sire, où il est question de zele, pieté et religion, de devotes et ferventes prieres, de solitaires et contemplatives abstractions de soy mesme, et semblables exercices spirituels pour eslever son cœur à Dieu, et le despouiller de ce monde, il n'est point autrement besoin vous user de longs preambules... car Vostre Majesté n'y est qu'assez inclinée. Et pourtant, Sire, ce petit labeur y pourra aisement trouver place, sans autre plus particuliere recommandation. Outre de ce qu'il vient de son expres commandement, luy ayant pleu me faire cest honneur que de me l'ordonner et commettre.[3]

Corbinelli's correspondance contributes some equally valuable, if less direct evidence: he says he is working on a translation of Fra Jacopone for Henri, and mentions mystics such as St Catherine, St Bernard, and Hugh of St Victor.[4] The dedication of Chappuys's translation of Diego de Estella's *Livre de la vanité du monde* speaks of

nostre tres-magnanime Prince tant amoureux de Dieu, et tant addonné à son service, que volontiers il soumet ses couronnes et sceptres, au royaume divin, duquel il procure sans cesse l'avancement, par une guerre continuelle qu'il fait aux sens humains et au monde, emportant de plus belles et triomphantes victoires sur tels ennemis, que ne font les autres Rois et Princes, qui s'efforcent par le trenchant de leurs espees, d'accroistre leurs estats, qui ne font que passer comme choses vaines, et d'usurper ceux-là d'autruy. A raison dequoy il n'y a livre, que sa Majesté manie presque plus souvent, que ce petit livre de la vanité du monde, qui s'est plusieurs fois imprimé cy devant.[5]

[1] F. Yates, *The French Academies*, p. 151.   [2] *Ibid.* chaps. 7, 8, 9.
[3] Champion, *op. cit.* p. 120.   [4] See Yates, *op. cit.* p. 175.
[5] Diego de Estella, *Livre de la vanité du monde*, trans. G. Chappuys (Paris, 1587), dedication, *non pag.* Cf. Yates, p. 175: 'The binding of a copy of a French translation of Diego

Devotional traditions

Various other works give a clue to the devotional reading in and around the Vincennes circle: Chappuys's translation of Panigarola's *Cent sermons sur la Passion de Notre Seigneur*, which was dedicated in 1586 to the 'tres-insigne.. Compagnie et Societé des Penitents de l'Archi-Congrégation Royale de l'Annonciation de nostre Dame'; the translation, also by Chappuys, of Alonso de Madrid's *Methode de servir Dieu*, dedicated in 1587 to Ange de Joyeuse; Tauler's *Institutions divines*, translated by the Minims of the Oratory of Vincennes, and dedicated also to Ange de Joyeuse by Antoine Estienne;[1] and Belleforest's translation of Granada's

de Estella's meditations on the love of God in Henri's possession suggests the spiritual atmosphere in which he lived. On the back is the royal arms surrounded by the monograms and pendant of the Order of the Holy Spirit on which he founded such hopes. Above it is a grinning skull, and a chaplet of skulls surrounds the medallion of the Crucifix on the cover.' The binding of a contemporary psalter is described in the catalogue of the exhibition for the fourth centenary of the birth of Malherbe (*Malherbe et les poètes de son temps* (Paris, 1955), p. 18, no. 63): 'Reliure maroquin brun clair. Décor montrant des traces d'argent, composé d'ornements représentant des emblèmes funèbres: larmes, ossements, cercueils, croix, faux, pelles, candélabres, sonnettes, torches, flèches, encensoirs; au centre, un squelette sur un semé de larmes. Dos long orné d'un semé de larmes et d'un cercueil, entre deux candélabres. Sur: *Le Pseaultier de David...*, Paris, chez Iamet Mettayer, 1586. in-4o. BN, Collection Rothschild, I. I. 29. Cet exemplaire qui passe pour avoir appartenu à Henri III fut vraisemblablement exécuté pour un des membres de la *Compagnie des confrères de la Mort*.'

[1] Estienne's dedication of the translation to 'Monseigneur le Conte de Bouchage' shows how the Germanic mystical tradition is taken up in the context of the new devotional revival: 'Monseigneur, il y a long temps que j'avois grand desir de traduire de Latin en François le œuvres du Reverend Pere Jean Thaulere, en son vivant grand Theologien, grand contemplatif, et heureusement versé en la Theologie mystique: afin que les ames, qui ont faim et soif de justice, et qui sont alterees d'une bruslante soif de l'amour de Dieu, peussent se rafraichir et boire à grans traicts à la fontaine de ses doctes escrits, de laquelle sont sortis, pour la plus part, les clairs ruisseaux d'eauë vive, dont elles ont gousté par le passé, en la lecture des œuvres de ce bon pere Loys de Grenatte.' The 'Advertissement du Libraire au Lecteur' explains the dedication: 'Amy Lecteur, je te prie, ne trouver estrange si cest œuvre est dedié à ce bon Seigneur, lequel nagueres on nommoit le Conte du Bouchage, et maintenant le Reverend pere frere Ange. Car le pere provincial de la province en France, de l'ordre des freres Minimes, qui a reveu et corrigé ceste traduction, m'avoit envoyé l'epistre dedicatoire pour mettre au frontispice du livre, long temps auparavant que ledit Sieur eut pris l'habit de ces bons peres, de l'ordre de sainct François, dits vulgairement, Cappucins: de maniere que le livre dessusdit estoit des-ja fort advancé d'imprimer, quant ledit Sieur quitta du tout le monde pour entrer en religion, et se mettre au service de nostre Seigneur.' The publisher goes on to say that Estienne had been inspired to bring about this translation so that the book might serve Ange 'comme de manuel, en l'annee de son noviciat' (all this liminary material is without pagination). The work begins (fols. 1–2) with Louis de Blois's defence of Tauler against Eck (cf. below, p. 19); he recommends Tauler by saying 'pleust à Dieu, que Thaulere fut cogneu par tout, et receu en tous les monasteres des Religieux qui sont par l'univers'. Thus the atmosphere in which this

The devotional tradition and its revival

Devotes contemplations, a copy of which was in the library of Henri III
(1583 edition).

It is clear, then, that this extraordinarily heterogeneous spate of
devotional works in the vernacular, set in motion by no single organised
campaign, crystallised itself about the person of Henri III. The quality
of Henri's own religious temperament has often been questioned, if not
ridiculed, by Catholics as well as Protestants from his day to ours; but,
as Miss Yates remarks, Henri's 'extravagant devotionalism' is an
essential preparation for the devotional atmosphere of the early
seventeenth century. Henri and the Vincennes Academy did not create
the French devotional movement, any more than they initiated the
convergence of devotion and humanist rhetoric; but in both spheres
they represent an important landmark, and give the first cogent impulse
necessary for later achievements.

Henri's example was decisive in the encouragement of lay writers to
turn to sacred subjects particularly associated with the devotional
atmosphere of the *Confréries* and of the Vincennes Academy. Belleforest, Chappuys and Vigenère mixed secular and sacred translation;
Biblical paraphrase became a commonplace exercise for poets; and
Desportes, besides producing his own version of the Psalms, wrote
prayers and religious poetry that often takes the form of prayer. Just
as the 'philosophical' or 'scientific' poetry of the Pléiade and its successors had been diverted—chiefly by Guy Le Fèvre and Du Bartas—
into religious channels, so lyric poetry was being deeply modified by
contact with a tradition of prayer and meditation beginning with the
Bible and continuing through the Middle Ages and the early Renaissance
to its vernacular climax in the latter part of the sixteenth century. This
contact had only briefly and spasmodically been achieved before the
1570s; but in the ambiguous atmosphere of Henri III's reign, its
potentialities first began to be properly exploited.

The progress of the devotional revival is by no means dependent on
Paris. Several local towns and regions established their own orders
and brotherhoods, and it is frequently against this kind of background
that the most interesting devotional poetry is produced. Perhaps the

translation was produced is markedly monastic: the lay audience which Granada is
aiming at is not mentioned. This is in keeping with the ascetic mysticism of the Germanic
group, and with the predominant attitudes of the Cologne Charterhouse and Louis
de Blois.

13

most striking example is Aix-en-Provence, which we shall be considering in more detail later, but there are signs of similar activity in Savoy, in Rouen, and in Douai. Douai was the centre of a region in which the Jesuits were firmly entrenched, and its presses produced an impressive series of editions of devotional works. Coster and Arias, Bruno and Androzio—the number of leading Jesuits whose meditations were published there is formidable, and in 1594 Pierre Maffée's *Trois livres de la vie du P. Ignace de Loyola*, translated by Michel d'Esne, provided a further advertisement for the Jesuit cause. The Jesuit influence naturally did not exclude the translation and publication of works by other devotional masters, by Granada, Alonso de Madrid, Guevara, Savonarola, Dionysius de Leuwis. Paul Du Mont appears to be the central figure in the domain of translation,[1] but the translators were not always local men; the town was clearly a centre for the distribution of works by any hand, provided they served the cause of Catholic devotion. And if one takes account of all the treatises published at Louvain, Arras and Antwerp, it becomes clear that the Low Countries were a hive of devotional activity in the last thirty years of the sixteenth century. It was in this area also that a *Confrérie de la très-heureuse Vierge Marie*, related to Henri III's oratory of the Virgin Mary, was promoted. This foundation was due largely to the Jesuit François Coster, under whose name the *Institutions* of the company first appeared in Latin at Antwerp in 1587 (also at Douai, 1605), and in French in 1588.[2] The work begins with an extract from the Papal Bull granted in 1577 by Gregory XIII, approving the *confrérie*, and continues with a dedication 'A toute la Confrerie de la tresheureuse Vierge Marie'. In this dedication, Coster outlines the formation of the order:

Pour ces causes ceste Confrerie ayant esté establie sous le tres-auguste nom de la tressacree Vierge Mere de Dieu, premierement à Rouën, puis à Paris,

[1] Translations by Du Mont include: L. de Granada, *La Guide des pescheurs* (Douai, 1574, 1577); Antonio de Guevara, *L'Oratoire des religieux et l'exercice des vertueux* (Douai, 1577, 1583, 1599); Dionysius de Leuwis, *Le Décrotoire de vanité* (Douai, 1581), and *Les Lunettes spirituelles* (Douai, 1587; also Paris, 1597 and Lyons, 1598); Théodoric de Herxen, *La Sepmaine chrestienne pour mediter sur la mort et passion de Jesus Christ* (Douai, 1592). See also below, p. 21.

[2] For other works by Coster, see below, p. 49, n. 2. The first edition of the *Vierge Marie* meditations was dedicated to Henri III, the 1590 edition 'à la sodalité de l'heureuse Vierge Marie au College d'Anchin en l'Université de Douay'. The *Traité de l'imitation de Notre-Dame* of the Jesuit François Arias (Paris, 1595; Douai, 1611) may well be connected with the same movement; cf. also Pierre Crespet, *Triomphe de Marie Vierge* (Lyons, 1594; Paris, 1600).

et qu'elle en rapportast de tres-beaux fruicts, le College de la Compaignie du nom de Jesus à Douay, fondé par le religieux et celebre Convent d'Ancien, a jugé qu'il falloit ramener la mesmes (*sic*) Confrerie entre ses nourissons. Si tost qu'elle a esté encommencee, on a veu un si grand changement soudain és mœurs d'un chacun, une si grande diligence et ferveur és estudes, un si grand avancement és lettres, que la renommee du College s'est espandue presque par toutes les contrees de l'Europe, et les autres Colleges de l'Academie de Douay ont pris envie de suyvre ceste Confrerie.[1]

Coster then goes on to describe how the *Institutions* were first written for the students of Cologne:

...ayant receu le gouvernement de ceste Confrerie à Coloigne, j'ay commencé proposer aux jeunes hommes quelques poincts du moyen de se confesser, de communier, de prier, et de mediter... que j'avais en partie appris d'aucuns personnages, et sçavans, et devotieux, du corps de nostre Compaignie; en partie aussi j'avois recueilly des Peres anciens, et nouveaux escrivains Catholiques.

The *Institutions* are in fact a comprehensive devotional method, designed to carry out the programme of the Council of Trent: the main body of the work begins with a 'Profession de foy Orthodoxe, faite suyvant l'ordonnance du Concile de Trente'. It is fascinating to see how this devotional programme, framed explicitly in Counter-Reformation terms, is in the hands of the Jesuits integrated with a university reform which is both moral and educational; the fact that 'un si grand avancement és lettres' is attributed to the establishment of a cult of the Virgin Mary may be something of a hyperbole, but it is nevertheless suggestive of the way in which devotion is becoming connected with the liberal arts. Further study of the devotional, educational and literary climate of this area would almost certainly be rewarding: more information about the Jesuits' attitude to rhetoric could well emerge, and poetry both Neo-Latin and French was published at Douai.[2]

The reign of Henri IV is a period of pacification. The wars of religion had left behind them a great deal of ill-feeling and misunderstanding: the Jesuits, for example, were often identified with Spain and the Ligue,

---

[1] F. Coster, *Le Livre de la Compaignie, c'est-à-dire les cinq livres des Institutions chrestiennes: Dressees pour l'usage de la Confrerie de la tres-heureuse Vierge Marie* (Antwerp, 1588), dedication, *non pag.*

[2] See below, pp. 65–6; and, for example, Robertus Obrizius' *Eidyllia sacra in utrumque Testamentum* (Douai, 1587).

and when in 1595 a former pupil of theirs was involved in an attempt to assassinate the king, the whole Company was banished. The period of their exile was relatively short; thanks to the diplomacy of Jesuits like Louis Richeome and above all Pierre Coton (later to become the king's confessor), they were allowed to return in 1603. By this time the tide was turning in favour of co-operation between the different religious orders: Jesuits, Carthusians, Benedictines, Carmelites and Capuchins mingle in an atmosphere from which the tensions of the later sixteenth century are largely absent and which was highly favourable to the reform of existing orders and the creation of new ones. Devotion at court, under the ascendancy of Coton, was on the whole less extravagant and obtrusive than it had been in the 1580s; Coton's *Intérieure occupation d'une âme dévote* set the pattern for a simple lay devotion in which everyday actions could become the subject of prayer. At the same time, the Ignatian method was still being disseminated through Coton's sermons, later to be published in the form of meditations.

Paris was by now becoming the centre of a movement which was to determine the direction of much of the religious practice of the earlier seventeenth century. It was a movement which was not restricted to any one order, although the Capuchins, recently established in France, and the French Carmelites were to provide much of its initial impetus. One of the most influential figures in its formation was Madame Acarie, who was largely responsible for the creation in France of the equivalent of St Teresa's Carmelites. She is thus directly linked with Spanish mysticism in one of its most extreme forms; but at the same time, her few published works show that she was familiar with the mystical devotion of Germany and the Low Countries, and in particular with Louis de Blois.[1] Although she seems to have been subject to frequent mystical *extases*, much of her life was spent in promoting the reform of spiritual communities of all kinds. She worked in close co-operation with the Carthusian Dom Beaucousin and with the Capuchin Benoît de Canfeld, whose *Règle de perfection*, first published in 1609 but written much earlier, was to become one of the principal native sources of seventeenth-century French mysticism. The full impact of this movement was however scarcely felt in the first decade

---

[1] Antoine Estienne, the Minim who directed the translation of Tauler's *Institutions* for Ange de Joyeuse, may well have guided her towards this kind of mystical devotion; cf. Dagens, *Bérulle*, p. 119.

of the seventeenth century, particularly if one is thinking in terms of poetry: Claude Hopil is at this time writing verse which is decidedly devotional, but his mystical poetry will not appear until much later. The need for a fully laicised devotion, already emphasised by Coton and indeed implied by the whole devotional revival of the preceding thirty years, reached its culminating point in St François de Sales, who began his activities as devotional adviser while he was in contact with Madame Acarie at Paris. Later, he too was to become involved in the mystical movement, but in 1608 he is still chiefly concerned with the practice of devotion among the laity:

Ceux qui ont traitté de la devotion ont presque tous regardé l'instruction des personnes fort retirees du commerce du monde, ou au moins ont enseigné une sorte de devotion qui conduit a cette entiere retraitte. Mon intention est d'instruire ceux qui vivent es villes, es mesnages, en la cour, et qui par leur condition sont obligés de faire une vie commune quant a l'exterieur, lesquelz bien souvent, sous le pretexte d'une pretendue impossibilité, ne veulent seulement pas penser a l'entreprise de la vie devote.[1]

And again, in Book 1, chapter 3:

C'est un erreur, ains une heresie, de vouloir bannir la vie devote de la compaignie des soldatz, de la boutique des artisans, de la cour des princes, du mesnage des gens mariés. Il est vray, Philotee, que la devotion purement contemplative, monastique et religieuse ne peut estre exercee en ces vacations la; mais aussi, outre ces trois sortes de devotion, il y en a plusieurs autres, propres a perfectionner ceux qui vivent es estatz seculiers. (pp. 20–1)

St François's devotional teaching, echoing at thirty years' distance Belleforest's comments on the aims of Guevara and Granada, is thus directed towards an extremely wide audience. Nevertheless it seems that he had a special interest in the literate classes, and even in those with a degree of learning, since his devotional writing is calculated to appeal to a public accustomed to the pleasures of secular literature. This aspect of his work is also borne out by his foundation of the *Académie florimontane* at Annecy in 1607, and by his relations with Antoine Favre, who was a scholar and a poet of some distinction.[2]

Thus in this period as a whole one has to consider a broad range of devotional approaches. At one end of the scale one might find Granada's

---

[1] St François de Sales, *Œuvres*, vol. III, *Introduction à la vie dévote* (Annecy, 1893), p. 6.
[2] For the *Académie florimontane*, see Yates, *The French Academies*, p. 283; also below, pp. 61–2, 81–4.

'rudes et petits', the illiterate and the young, who would presumably learn their devotional method orally, simplified as necessary by the priest; at the other, the humanism of the Jesuits, the linking of devotion with university study, or Du Vair's combination of Biblical meditation with apologetic philosophy.[1] Devotion may be equivalent to simplicity, to unsophistication, and therefore perhaps encourage certain poets towards an unadorned style like that of many medieval hymns; or (more commonly) it may assume a social or literary sophistication, exploiting the themes and figures of profane rhetoric. In all its forms, it seeks to familiarise the public at large with the perennial themes and modes of meditation, with the consideration of death and the sinner's corruption, of Christ's life and Passion, and of the beauty of the created world.

'CATHOLIC' AND 'CALVINIST'

The nature of the Catholic devotional revival might at first sight seem to preclude any close parallels in the religious literature of the Calvinists. The optimism, the reliance on the senses, which characterise Loyola's *Spiritual Exercises* and many treatises of the later sixteenth century, would appear to be foreign to the austerity of Calvin or Bèze. Certainly there is nothing in Calvinist literature to match the sheer quantity of devotional handbooks produced by Jesuits, Mendicants, Carthusians and the rest; nevertheless, parallels do exist, and their existence is important not only for religious history but also for the understanding of a significant body of poetry by both Catholics and Calvinists.

Protestant doctrine did not rely exclusively either on the original thinking of Luther and Calvin or on a new interpretation of the Bible. One of its most profound sources was the group of Dutch and German mystics centred on Windesheim, for it was on their mystical theology

---

[1] Du Vair published a short meditational method (*De la Prière*), and meditations on the Penitential and Consolatory Psalms, the Lamentations of Jeremiah, the *Cantique d'Ezechias* and Job, as well as the *Saincte philosophie* and other apologetic treatises; likewise Duplessis-Mornay. In such writers, the traditional concepts of devotion often mingle with a syncretist philosophy, but to analyse the precise nature of these over-lappings is scarcely relevant to the purposes of the present study. It is certainly important to be aware that devotional themes and figures may move into an area in which they coincide with equivalent humanist *topoi*, and that these *topoi* may be very different from those one associates with Pléiade poetry; but the details of the apologists' arguments are seldom of direct concern for a study of devotional poetry. See also below, pp. 46–7.

that Luther based his *Deutsche Theologie* of 1516; and in his disputations with Luther, Eck deplored the writings of Tauler as contributing to the Protestant heresy. Thereafter, Catholic orthodoxy was to become increasingly suspicious, in retrospect, of the later medieval mystics, and editions of Tauler and his contemporaries were frequently accompanied by an introductory justification. The stress laid by the whole *devotio moderna* movement on the need for a renewed inwardness of religious experience became one of the principal foundations of Reformation thinking; thus the devotional tradition is at one point (a central one) intimately linked with both the Reformation itself and the Catholic reform movements. Hence, too, the ambiguous position of the piety of Erasmus, which resumes the achievements of the *devotio moderna* and at the same time anticipates much that is essential to the devotional attitudes of both confessions.

The affinity between Protestant faith and mystical devotion is demonstrated in another way by the apostasy of the Italian Capuchin Ochino, which caused a considerable stir among Reformation leaders. Ochino was welcomed by both Calvin and Castellion; he visited Basle in 1545, and Castellion later translated into Latin his *Espositione sopra la Epistola di Paolo alli Romani.*[1] It should be remembered that in making the change from the Franciscan to the Capuchin habit, Ochino had already shown an inclination towards the Bonaventuran tradition of mystical devotion, and in the Calvinist context, this inclination reveals itself in its insistence on the illuminating power of faith:

La foy humaine est comme une flamme peinte, que (*sic*) ne luist ne illumine ne ard et n'enflamme point. Mais l'infuse est une lumière de feu divin qui, en ardant, illumine. La foy acquise ne fait aucunement changer de vie ne de mœurs comme fait celle qui est infuse, laquelle te fait renaître et devenir filz de Dieu.[2]

Calvin himself was no mystic (he was highly suspicious of the *Deutsche Theologie*), nor was he much concerned with arousing devotional fervour, except in so far as he approved the French Psalter and religious drama. His aim, in the *Institution* and elsewhere, was to present a coherent corpus of theology, particularly designed to guarantee the proper interpretation of the Bible; at the same time he

---

[1] See F. Buisson, *Sebastien Castellion* (Paris, 1892), vol. I, p. 227.
[2] Quoted by Buisson, *ibid.* p. 228; the same ideas reappear in Castellion's own works. Castellion also translated the *Deutsche Theologie* into Latin.

Devotional traditions

had to solve the problem of religion in society. On the other hand, the influence of Augustine, and of patristic sources in general, accounts for a great deal that is central to his thinking,[1] and the *Institution* itself is frequently phrased in such a way as to make its themes accessible for personal reflection. Listen, for example, to this passage from the first chapter of the second book:

> Car nous ne pouvons penser ny à nostre première origine, ny à la fin à laquelle nous sommes créez, que ceste cogitation ne nous soit comme un aguillon, pour nous stimuler et poindre à méditer et désirer l'immortalité du royaume de Dieu...il ne nous reste rien, sinon qu'après avoir réputé nostre misérable condition, nous gémissions, et en gémissant, souspirions après nostre dignité perdue.[2]

Here a traditional penitential theme is clothed in a language which is explicitly devotional, both in its incitement to emotion, to groaning and sighing, and in its suggestion of the *Stimulus amoris* ('un aguillon, pour nous stimuler et poindre à méditer'). At the same time, Calvin was a great preacher; parts of the *Institution* have the tone of a sermon, and many of his sermons proper were written down and published. Preaching and meditation are never very far apart,[3] and these sermons would often take the form of an exhaustive series of meditations on a book of the Bible. Likewise, his commentaries on the Psalms tally with the tradition of Augustine's *Enarrationes in psalmos* which was popular with sixteenth-century devotional authors of both confessions.

Psalm-meditation was particularly favoured by Calvin's disciples in the later sixteenth century. Bèze's *Chrestiennes méditations sur huict pseaumes*, first published in 1582, were followed within the space of seven or eight years by the meditations of Duplessis-Mornay, Pellisson, and Sponde, and later by those of d'Aubigné; these works represent one of the high-water marks of Calvinist devotional practice.[4] A link with patristic tradition is suggested by the penitential *Priere extraite des Meditations de S. Augustin* which accompanies the medita-

[1] See F. Wendel, *Calvin: Sources et évolution de sa pensée religieuse* (Paris, 1950), and L. Smits, *Saint Augustin dans l'œuvre de Calvin* (Assen, 1957).
[2] J. Calvin, *Institution de la religion chrestienne*, ed. J.-D. Benoît, vol. II (Paris, 1957), p. 10.
[3] See below, pp. 36–7.
[4] See, in particular, A. M. Boase's introduction to his edition of Sponde's *Méditations*, and M. Richter's introduction to his edition of the meditations of Bèze. Richter's useful articles and editions constitute the most important recent contribution to the study of Protestant devotion (reference to these will be made where relevant).

tions of Duplessis-Mornay and Pellisson; likewise, Goulart's edition of Jean de L'Espine's *Excellens discours . . . touchant le repos et contentement de l'esprit* contains an extract from the meditations attributed to Augustine, as well as St Bernard's twenty-second sermon on the Song of Solomon.

One of the most interesting phenomena of this period (and this points in the same direction) is the part played by Savonarola. His theories on prayer had influenced Granada's *Libro de la Oracion*, and, like Granada, he was put on the Index in 1559 because of his emphasis on justification by faith. His two psalm-meditations appeared together with the 1584 edition of Duplessis-Mornay's *Discours de la vie et de la mort*, while three years later his *Verité de la foy* was translated by Du Mont as a counter-attack on Duplessis-Mornay's *De la Verité de la religion chrestienne*. Du Mont feels it necessary to justify his author by invoking as witnesses of Savonarola's orthodoxy Commines, Pico della Mirandola, Guicciardini and others; whereas Tamisier paraphrased the Psalm 51 meditation with apparent unconcern.[1] This ambiguity (like that of Tauler and Erasmus) is due to Savonarola's dislike of the external apparatus of religion, and to his doctrine of faith: both the Calvinists and the Catholic illuminists could see him as a precursor of their theories. Tamisier, on the other hand, by choosing verse for his translation, could more easily avoid the controversial issues.

Savonarola's meditation on Psalm 51 also appeared with Duplessis-Mornay's *Meditations chrestiennes* in a translation by Simon Goulart, who was one of the most prolific Calvinist writers of the late sixteenth and early seventeenth centuries. Towards the turn of the century, Goulart's literary activity seems to have centred increasingly on works of meditation, including for example a collection of *Exercices et combats de l'ame chrestienne, contre Satan, la Chair, et le Monde* and *Vingt-cinq meditations chrestiennes*.[2] Perhaps the most interesting work of this period is the *Tableaux de la mort*, of which a first edition, containing

[1] For Du Mont's translation, see below, p. 65; for Tamisier, see p. 80.

[2] See L. C. Jones, *Simon Goulart (1543–1628)* (Geneva–Paris, 1917), 'Bibliographie', nos. 56 and 64. Cf. also nos. 34, 35, 65, 66, 71, 73. Even a brief glance at this bibliography gives one an idea of the impressive range of Goulart's scholarship, including humanist edition and translation (notably of the works of Seneca), editions of the music of Lassus and other composers, as well as the edition, translation or composition of a wide variety of works of religious instruction, apologetics, and meditation, of patristic and other treatises, martyrologies, and a number of religious odes and sonnets.

eighteen tableaux, probably appeared in 1601, to be followed soon after by expansions first to thirty and then to forty tableaux.[1] The dedication of the second edition establishes immediately that the work is intended for the general public; it has been put together 'pour servir... à ceux qui n'ont ni n'entendent les livres Latins, ains seulement nostre langue vulgaire'.[2] This intention represents a familiar aspect of Calvinist propaganda (indeed of Protestant belief in general), but it may nevertheless be seen, in the devotional context, as a parallel to the Counter-Reformation programme which reaches its climax in St François. The work as a whole is very much in the tradition of the *ars moriendi*, with its concrete visualisations of death and the tomb and its tendency to move into the tone of the sermon; at the same time, Goulart seems to have borrowed from the Counter-Reformation handbooks the clarifying device of dividing each tableau into 'points'. Sometimes there are even subdivisions, as in the twelfth tableau, the fourth point (*Que font les ames, sorties des corps, jusques au dernier jour*):

> 1. Elles sont en la compagnie des Anges maudits, qui les tourmentent et sont incessamment tourmentez avec elles en enfer, liez de chaines d'obscurité, et reservez à ceste redoutable condamnation du dernier jour.   2. Pier. 2. 4.
> 2. Elles y souffrent de grands tourmens...   (p. 248)

This resemblance (even if it is accidental) proves once again that the elements of devotional practice were flexible enough to be used by Calvinists as well as Catholics.

All this evidence suggests that it is legitimate to speak of a Protestant devotional tradition running parallel to the Catholic one and encouraging private prayer and meditation. Certainly, it was more limited in its range, and there is a major difference of emphasis in so far as the Protestants had no equivalent for meditation on the life of Christ or the saints, but there is still a great deal of common ground between the two traditions. Much the same characteristics are reflected in the religious poetry of this period, which (if one excludes satirical or 'committed' poetry) was far from being sharply defined by the convictions of the poet. The only really satisfactory way of defining the difference between the two confessions, in poetry as in prose, is a

---

[1] Jones, no. 55. See also no. 59.
[2] Goulart, *Trente tableaux de la mort, ou discours chrétiens sur nostre preparation au depart de la vie presente, 2eme ed. augm. de douze tableaux* (*s.l.*, 1602), dedication, *non pag.*

negative one: it is unlikely that a Calvinist would produce Passion poetry on the scale of La Ceppède's *Théorèmes*, still less an effusive poem on Mary Magdalene like César de Nostredame's *Perles*. But if one compares Calvinist poetry on penitential themes with its Catholic equivalent, it becomes much harder to find a line of demarcation between the two. In theology, there is a wide chasm between the Calvinist and the Catholic view of sin and redemption; but the demands of poetry tend to minimise the gap. The tendency to identify sin and sickness, which is one of the most important points of departure for penitential poetry, is perfectly valid for both faiths; likewise the themes of death and God's mercy ('grace' need have no partisan colouring in a poem) and the contrast between God and the sinner.[1] Both can use Biblical material, with only a slight shift of emphasis. In the Maisonfleur anthology, Catholic and Calvinist poets stand shoulder to shoulder; Du Bartas, whose religious attitude was moderate and conciliatory, influenced poets in both camps; and Sponde's *Stances et sonnets de la mort* bear no clear mark of Calvinism. For these reasons I shall make no attempt to draw *a priori* distinctions between poetry of one and the other confession; individual instances will be considered as they arise, in terms of their own specific context.

[1] See below, chaps. 2, 4 and 5, also pp. 79–80, 84.

23

CHAPTER 2

THE DEVOTIONAL TREATISE: METHOD AND MATTER

TECHNIQUE AND STYLE

In a preface to Granada's *Le Vray chemin et adresse pour acquerir et parvenir à la grace de Dieu*, one of the most popular devotional handbooks of the later sixteenth century, the Bishop of Cuenca summarises thus the principal difficulties facing those who attempt the exercise of devotion: 'L'une desquelles est faulte de matiere en laquelle occupe[r] leur pensee et contemplation: et l'autre est defaut de devotion...d'où leur advient une sterilité de cœur et une grande guerre et diversité de pensees'.[1] The handbook itself begins with a theoretical 'sommaire de la méditation' and then provides a standard application: hence it sets out not to give doctrinal instruction but to stimulate controlled individual reflection. Granada is concerned with overcoming the 'sterilité de cœur' and 'diversité de pensees' of the reader by providing him with both material and technique. Meditation is a discipline, a way of 'practising' love: '...en pratiquant l'amour, l'homme se fait vray amateur des choses sainctes';[2] devotion, like logic or rhetoric, can be learned methodically. The implications of this notion are important: any technique for organising and at the same time stimulating emotional reactions is likely to have significant consequences if it is applied to literary creation, and as will be seen later many of the Counter-Reformation treatises themselves have overtly literary pretensions. One should point out however that the systematisation of devotion was not a new idea: it was already well advanced in the *devotio moderna* of the fifteenth century, in Gansfort's *Scala meditationis* for example,[3] and most of the basic ingredients of later methods were apparent in the Church Fathers, from Augustine to Bonaventura. The methodology of the Jesuits and Mendicants was thus a resumption and a consolidation

---

[1] Luis de Granada, *Le Vray chemin*, 'Exhortation', *non pag.*
[2] *Ibid.* fol. 6.   [3] See below, pp. 298–9.

of a long tradition: Granada acknowledges his debt to Bonaventura for the laying down of the principles of daily meditation.[1] What is more, the Counter-Reformation theoreticians usually made it clear that their systems, once assimilated by the reader, need not be followed strictly. Thus it will not be necessary here to deal with all the refinements of the devotional handbooks; the relevant techniques will be those which are common to a wide range of treatises, and more especially those which can be seen in relation to a literary style.

The fundamental principle of devotional method is a division into thematic categories. In the first place, the progress of meditation should reflect the twofold nature of the Bible: beginning with a consideration of the fallen nature of man in general, and with his own sins in particular, the *dévot* should pass on to the contemplation of Christ's redemptive act. With a characteristic reliance on Biblical authority, Guytot interprets the Psalmist as anticipating this pattern in Psalm 3: 'Le Prophete royal montre qu'il y a deux especes de meditation, L'une qui contemple la divine nature de Jesus-Christ, et l'autre l'humaine.'[2] Not all devotional writers give equal weight to both themes: Loyola recommends four 'weeks' of daily meditation, the first dealing with the penitential themes, the remaining three with the life of Christ. The concept of two parallel sequences, however, is best illustrated by the principle of 'evening' and 'morning' meditation, popularised by Granada and Loarte:

> The usual procedure was to set forth two sequences of seven meditations each: one, normally followed in the evening, was devoted chiefly to self-knowledge and the fear of God...Such a sequence obviously accorded very well with the nightly practice of examining the conscience. The seven morning meditations then dealt with the life of Christ from the washing of the apostles' feet to the Resurrection. (Martz, pp. 26–7.)

Although there is some overlapping of the evening and morning themes, the distinction between the two sequences, reinforced by a contrast between Old and New Testament, is relatively clear-cut: and this distinction tends to be carried beyond the comprehensive handbook

---

[1] Granada, *Le Vray chemin*, fol. 18 (misprinted as 17).

[2] J. Guytot, *Les Meditations des zelateurs de pieté recueillies de plusieurs et divers livres des saincts et anciens Peres. Avec autres Meditations prinses en la librairie sainct Victor lez Paris* (Paris, 1582), 'Sommaire advertissement', *non pag*. Cf. Marguerite de Navarre's vision of the two testaments, *Les Dernières poésies*, ed. A. Lefranc (Paris, 1896), pp. 239–40.

into devotional literature in general. A verse of the Psalms may be seen to prefigure the atonement of the Passion, and the *dévot* who contemplates the Cross may recall the corresponding symbols of the Old Testament, but in each case the emotional view-point is different. The penitential sequence involves primarily a downward movement into a consideration of the sinner's corruption, of his death, and of the torments of Hell; the Passion sequence, on the other hand, moves upwards towards absolution, redemption, and the all-embracing love of God. In this way, the devotional methodologists, by systematising a dichotomy basic to the Christian concept of man and his salvation, encourage a pattern of meditation which will be clearly recognisable also in the poetry of the coming generation.[1]

Within the overall structure of the sequence, each meditation has its own individual structure. Largely thanks to the work of Martz, the three basic elements of this structure are already becoming familiar to us: 'composition', 'analysis', and 'affective prayer'. In the first of these, one brings all the senses to bear on the object of meditation; in the second, the intellect is summoned to reflect on the problems involved (often of a theological nature); in the third, the 'affections' are poured out in thanksgiving and prayer. That these three phases do not merely represent a convenient categorisation but imply a conception of the function of the mental faculties is demonstrated by two passages from Granada:

...ceste meditation se fait quelquefois des choses qui se peuvent figurer en l'imagination, ainsi que sont tous les passages de la vie et passion de nostre sauveur Jesu-Christ: y a d'autres choses qui appartiennent plus à l'esprit, qu'à l'imagination, comme lors que pensons és benefices de Dieu, ou en sa bonté et misericorde, ou en quelque autre de ses perfections: et telle maniere de meditation s'appelle intellectuelle, et l'autre imaginaire.

A fin donc que nostre volonté incline vers l'amour de son Dieu, il faut que l'entendement la guide et precede.[2]

---

[1] As was indicated in the Preface, I have omitted in this study any extended reference to meditation on Creation; this aspect of devotional practice will however be mentioned occasionally where the context demands it.

[2] Granada, *Le Vray chemin*, fol. 180 and fol. 5. The assumptions made by devotional writers of this period about the respective functions of the mental faculties might prove an interesting topic. It is relevant, for example, to the problem of illumination by faith: Granada, although an *alumbrado*, seems in this passage to hold the Thomist view that knowledge must precede love—'nihil volitum nisi praecognitum' (cf. A. H. T. Levi, *French Moralists* (Oxford, 1964), p. 33).

Technique and style

Composition is thus the function of *imagination*, analysis of *entendement* or *esprit*, and affections arise from the *volonté*. As well as being a prescription for the ordering of religious reflection, this application of the faculties could be seen as a kind of embryonic literary theory (though there is little evidence that lay writers ever consciously adopted it as such): it might provide a poet with a ready-made structure, or at least suggest various possible modes of development. At the same time, the contrast between sensual imagination and intellectual understanding recalls the traditional theory of 'clothing' and 'body', of 'le livre du Prophete envelopé des mysteres, escrit dedans pour les doctes, et dehors pour les ignorans'.[1] The simple or the illiterate must be taught through concrete representation (stained-glass windows, the *Bible des Pauvres*, the stations of the Cross); the initiate can penetrate beyond this outward show to the meaning hidden beneath. Similarly, in order to appeal to a wide audience, the devotional writer sets out to provide straightforward description and narration on the one hand, and quasi-theological reflection on the other. Hence the implications of this sequence of devotional 'moods' or 'styles' are extremely rich and can be realised in a wide range of different situations.

The object of the devotional writer in the composition section of the meditation (or its equivalent) is to make a concerted attack on the reader by a cumulative effect of horror, designed to awaken his conscience through his senses; or to involve him emotionally and almost physically in a situation such as the Nativity or the Passion. Loyola's famous 'application of the senses' is a striking example of this intention; but many writers prefer a more flexible scheme, which from a literary point of view could be an advantage, since the enumeration technique frequently results in fragmentation. Goulart's description of the corruption of the body after death outdoes Loyola in virtuosity:

Si nous ouvrons la fosse d'un trespassé, nous verrons un corps puant, un pasté de vers, un fumier infect, un caque de pourriture, effrayable, insupportable, miserable en toutes sortes. Pourquoy donc la cendre et la terre infecte s'esleve elle ainsi superbement? Le plus grand du monde, pourra estre entre ci et demain, heritier des crapaux et des vers...Entrons es sepulchres et aprenons quelque chose de ce que nous y trouvons. Et quoy? des testes où nous verrons des crapaux sautellans engendrez de la cervelle, des serpens es

---

[1] J. de La Ceppède, *Les Théorèmes* (Toulouse, 1612–13), 'A la France', p. 8.

27

reins, des vers au ventre, produits des entrailles. Voila ce que nous serons bien tost...Amassons et entassons richesses sur richesses: mais pour qui? pour le corps qui n'en a plus que faire apres que l'ame en est separee, et l'ame encore moins...Toutes ces choses ne servent qu'au bien du corps, et pour un peu de temps; c'est à dire à l'entretenement d'un sac d'ordure et de puantise, dont naissent crapaux, vers, et serpens. Ce sont nos nourrissons, que nous engraissons soigneusement, en farcissant nos corps de mangeaille, de bruvage desmesuré, de friandises et delices.[1]

Meditation on this theme naturally tends to stress the sense of smell: Loyola uses a similar range of words in his consideration of Hell ('fumee, soulphre, infection...cloaque, fumier, voirie').[2] Description of the Passion, on the other hand, is primarily visual, as in the following passage from the meditations of the pseudo-Augustine:

Regardez vostre doux et debonnaire enfant en la croix estendu, jettez vostre veuë sur ses innocentes mains descoulans de toutes parts sang pitoyable... Considerez son nud et precieux costé, percé d'une lance cruelle, et me lavez de ceste tressacree fontaine...Contemplez ses pieds immaculez d'horribles cloux navrez...Regardez je vous supplie sa poitrine nuë blanchissant, son sanglant costé rougissant, ses seiches entrailles estenduës, ses beaux yeux languissans, ses royales levres pallissans, ses bras haut eslevez roidissans, ses blanches cuisses allongees, et ses pieds percez arrousez de son tresprecieux sang.[3]

Here the colouring of the scene is provided principally by a massing of adjectives and adjectival participles, and is based on contrasts between red and white: the thematic emphasis on blood is reinforced by words like *sanglant* and *rougissant*, which reduplicate one another in order to saturate the atmosphere with redness. The methodical description of Christ's body, akin to the rhetorical procedure of *descriptio*, anticipates Counter-Reformation method; incidentally, it tends to rule out any organisation of the scene, the kind of 'composition' demanded by the visual arts.

Physical representation, even where it is not explicitly referred to as 'composition', is a widespread practice in devotional handbooks of all kinds. It is worth remembering, however, that the Ignatian formula is in Granada's *Vray chemin* replaced (partially at least) by *lecture*:

[1] S. Goulart, *Trente tableaux de la mort*, pp. 314–15.
[2] St Ignatius de Loyola, *Les Vrais exercices spirituels* (Paris, 1620), p. 85.
[3] Guytot, *Les Meditations des zelateurs de pieté*, fols. 17–18.

'Il faut plus-tost preparer nostre cœur pour cest exercice, puis lire ce dequoy nous voulons mediter...'[1] This is only a shift of emphasis: the 'reading' will frequently involve physical depiction, whether of man's corruption or of Christ's sufferings, and the use of an authoritative text or quotation at a key point in the meditation is a common practice with Loyola as with most other devotional writers. But the stress on *lecture* should be given its full value, since the nature of the text chosen will frequently determine the character of the subsequent 'improvisation' in regard to style, as well as theme. Indeed, one particular aspect of devotional style, both in the composition and elsewhere, is directly related to this aspect of meditation: the augmentation and intensification of a theme by a series of quotations or allusions. All the devotional writers, Catholic and Calvinist, were naturally steeped in their Biblical and patristic source-material, and frequently supplemented their development of a text with a similar one from elsewhere. Duplessis-Mornay elaborates the parallel of Moses and the rock, and Peter penitent:

M'as-tu pas regardé de l'œil de tes misericordes, puis que mon cœur est fondu en larmes? Autrement, Seigneur, qui eust tiré ces ruisseaux de ce rocher? tant de larmes de la dureté de mon cœur? Ainsi, Seigneur, quand Pierre ton serviteur eut peché contre toy, tu le regardas, et il pleura, il pleura jusques à l'amertume de son ame: il pleura, et se retira d'entre les persecuteurs. Seigneur, donne à ceste pierre de pleurer de mesmes, non point le pleur d'Esau, mais le pleur de Pierre: non point les heritages de ce siecle, mais l'eslongnement de ta bonne grace. Et qu'alors je puisse triompher avec ton serviteur David, et dire, Arriere, ma chair: Arriere, Diable: Retirez-vous, tentations, Retirez-vous, tentateurs.[2]

D'Aubigné quotes so often, and at such length, from other parts of the Bible, that his meditations are often in danger of losing their individual shape and tone.[3] Elsewhere, direct allusion may be hard to pin down: the writer is recreating a dense Old Testament style for himself: 'Ta

[1] Granada, *Le Vray chemin*, fol. 19.

[2] P. Duplessis-Mornay, *Meditations chrestiennes sur quatre Pseaumes du Prophete David. Composees par Philippe de Mornay, seigneur du Plessis Marly. Meditation sur le Pseaume CXXVII par P. Pellisson, P. Meditation sur le Pseaume LI. traduite du Latin de Jerosme Savonarole, par S.G.S.* (*s.l.*, 1591), pp. 22–3.

[3] A. d'Aubigné, *Œuvres complètes*, ed. E. Réaume and F. de Caussade, vol. 2 (1877); see for example the meditation on Psalm 73 (pp. 155–73), especially the long quotation from Job (p. 161); also the meditation on Psalm 51, where there is a series of quotations from Jeremiah and elsewhere (pp. 184–86).

main s'est apesantie sur moy, et veut que je parle. Ta main a pressé mon apostume, et faut que je crie. Ta bouche a sufflé sur mon humeur, et sur ma seve, si que je suis brouy comme d'un hasle d'esté'.[1] Although this characteristic is most striking in meditation involving the Old Testament (especially the Psalms), there are analogous techniques in the morning meditation. The impact of the sufferings of Christ is increased by a juxtaposition of all the available details from apocryphal sources: an author like Guevara will refer again and again to the Church Fathers for authority on a specific point.[2] Or elsewhere, a series of symbols from the typological tradition will be introduced to give body to the meditation. In whatever form it occurs, however, the inbreeding of allusion produces a characteristic effect of saturation. The multiplication of allusion is common enough in sixteenth century treatises, both sacred and profane. But there is not only a massing of commonplaces: the horror of the sickness theme may for example be intensified by a combination of Job's sickness with David's. The meditation thus acquires a greater density and richness of texture, as well as a certain 'physicality'; and it is this technique which gives contemporary poetry what Weber calls its 'caractère plus biblique que la *Bible*'.[3]

If detailed description is a logical consequence of 'composition', it is also true that, in general, the analytic section (which many devotional writers would consider to be the meditation proper) is accompanied by a high degree of imagery—figures, *exempla* and the like. The extent to which these images are developed in a particular text may vary very widely; it may also depend to some extent on the dominant theme. In the Tuesday meditation ('Ce jour tu dois penser aux miseres et conditions de ceste vie', according to Granada), and in other expositions of the *vanitas* theme, the principal technique is one of accumulation: the author relies on bombardment, on quantity rather than quality. Little attempt is made to expand the image, to give it sensual detail:

A moy, Seigneur, helas! qui suis un vent, bien moins que vent, que vent emporte: à moy moins que vapeur, qu'une vapeur enorgueillit: moins que la parole qui se perd en l'air, qu'une parole douce enchante: une parole de louange enfle et assotte: donne, bon Dieu, de considerer à bon escient la vanité du monde, et de moy-mesme.[4]

---

[1] Duplessis-Mornay, *Meditations chrestiennes*, pp. 79–80.   [2] See below, p. 53.
[3] H. Weber, *La Création poétique au XVIᵉ siècle en France*, Paris (1956), vol. II, p. 708.
[4] Duplessis-Mornay, *Meditations chrestiennes*, p. 46.

Much the same applies, in the morning meditation, to the typological symbols through which the events of the New Testament are foreshadowed in the Old—symbols, for example, of the Crucifixion:

Vous qui desirez de l'eau de vie, voici la pierre mistique, frappee avec la verge de Moyse au desert, de laquelle ruisselerent les eaux en abondance pour le rassasiement de tout le peuple alteré...Vous qui desirez du vin pour guerir voz playes, voici le raisin porté de la terre de promission en ce val de misere, lequel est ores pressé et espraint au pressoir de la croix pour nostre remede.[1]

At the opposite end of the scale from these 'grapeshot' images is the extended *similitude*, which may well cover several pages. The Calvinist Pellisson bases the whole of his only meditation on images of this kind. He begins with the *palais* built by presumptuous humans, and continues with a long development on 'le juste bastiment de ton indignation'; each part of the image is given its literal, abstract equivalent.[2] Two or three pages later, there is another 'architectural' image—Christ as the 'pierre angulaire', accompanied by the 'esquierre de sa verité' and the 'plomb de sa justice'; all this is justified by the psalm-text 'Si le Seigneur n'edifie la maison, en vain travaillent ceux qui l'edifient'. One might compare Pellisson's elaboration with Tauler's 'gibbet' image; the *Institutions*, which are far more theological than the average Counter-Reformation meditation, being intended for monastic use, are full of extremely long and detailed *similitudes* of this kind:

Job 7: mon ame...a esleu d'estre pendue. Mais on peut icy demander, quelle est ceste croix, et gibet amoureux, auquel l'ame est attachee? On respond à cela, qu'il y a deux sortes de gibets. L'un est la creature qui se presente à l'ame, mais elle le refuse, et n'en veut point du tout: L'autre est la vision et la fruition de Dieu, qu'elle desire obtenir de tout son cœur, mais elle ne peut encore. La corde dudit gibet se fait de trois filets. Le premier est le pur amour de Dieu, et le second, les divins et fervents desirs. Le troisiesme est une pure intention en toutes noz actions. Il y a aussi trois colonnes et pilliers en ce gibet, à sçavoir est, le Pere, le Fils, et le sainct Esprit. Et tout ainsi, qu'un larron estant pendu au gibet, ne peut prendre ny embrasser l'un des pilliers, ainsi ne peut nostre entendement comprendre pas une des trois personnes, sinon par la foy: Et comme on couvre d'un voile les yeux d'un brigand et voleur, sans luy lier la langue: Ainsi sont voilez les yeux de nostre entende-

---

[1] Granada, *Le Vray chemin*, fol. 56.
[2] Duplessis-Mornay, *Meditations chrestiennes*, pp. 191–2.

ment, afin qu'il ne puisse veoir appertement. Mais la volonté peut servir à Dieu, sans que rien l'en empesche.[1]

These extended images have the functional character of emblems: each detail of the description has its own label of significance. A further essential characteristic of the emblem, its connexion with a maxim or proverb, is exemplified again by an image of Pellisson: a tree, once used by all as protection against the weather, is destroyed by lightning and hail and becomes an object of scorn; then follows the moral: 'L'ami, Seigneur, aime le temps: aussi tost que le temps se change, l'ami se change aussi.'[2] This maxim is a favourite one of emblem-books, where it is frequently connected with the story of Actæon being destroyed by his dogs.

However extensively they may be elaborated, or however densely they may be packed (and an author may illustrate a single idea over several pages of different *similitudes* or *exempla*),[3] one would seldom be tempted to describe any of these kinds of image as producing a 'concrete' style like that of the 'composition' phase of meditation: they are an instrument of analysis, a device for conveying an important abstract concept. They are not intended primarily to evoke a scene, or a real physical object, since the visual element may be purely schematic. This is in marked contrast to the composition passages, where every effort is made to appeal to the reader's sensual awareness through direct description, but where metaphors tend to be rare. Using Granada's terminology, one could say that in composition, the *imagination* is allowed free rein, whereas in analysis, which is the meditation of the *entendement*, abstraction is predominant, and the *imagination* fulfils only the intermediary function of presenting abstract material in a palatable form. This distinction between description and

[1] J. Tauler, *Les Institutions divines, et salutaires enseignemens du Reverend pere frere Jean Thaulere grand Docteur contemplatif, en son vivant religieux de l'ordre de S. Dominicque . . . le tout nouvellement traduict de Latin en François par les peres Minimes de l'Oratoire nostre Dame de vie-Saine* (Paris, 1587), fol. 198. Notice that Tauler, unlike Granada, here maintains that the *volonté* can operate even though the *entendement* is 'blindfolded': faith is the sole means of illumination.

[2] Duplessis-Mornay, *Meditations chrestiennes*, p. 225.

[3] Devotional writers often list *similitudes* separately (cf., for example, Goulart, *Trente tableux de la mort*, pp. 318–19), or indicate them in the margin. Jacques de Billy's *tables des similitudes* are perhaps the most developed examples of this tendency: see below, p. 45, and Billy's *Sonnets spirituels, Livre second* (Paris, 1578), which is prefaced by a similar *table*.

image is of some importance in the interpretation of devotional poetry, for the individual character of Sponde, La Ceppède or César de Nostredame is partly determined by the weight they give to one or the other. It may often happen that a poet will be tempted to give his 'emblem' a certain physical presence; and that even the brief, undeveloped images of the *vanitas* meditation may make a concrete impact by means of alliteration, rhythm, and sheer accumulation. But it is wrong to assume, in the devotional context, that a wealth of imagery in this poetry implies sensual representation: on the contrary, the presence of *similitudes* or other analogies is frequently a sign that the author is trying to make an impact on the reader's *entendement*.

In the meditational structure which we have been examining, the final phase of prayer, being associated with the 'affections' and the *volonté*, is clearly intended to provide an emotional climax. However, the devices used for this purpose are often introduced at other points in the meditation, particularly where the framework is a flexible one. Prayers may be woven into the composition, or the analysis may take the form of an emotive 'questioning' of God. Furthermore, since the principal intention of the devotional writer is to evoke in the believer a sense of horror and self-loathing, or to persuade him to identify himself with the sufferings of Christ, the need for stimulation to emotion is felt throughout the sequence. From this need there arises a wide range of 'tones of voice'—interrogative, exclamatory, imperative, demonstrative—through which the mechanics of meditation can be brought to life. Fervour and persuasion are after all fundamental to the whole concept of devotion.

Consider first Granada's invitation to the soul to enter the emotional atmosphere of the Passion meditation, using the traditional devotional aid of the stations of the Cross:

Tu as (ô mon ame) plusieurs choses à contempler à ce jour, et faut que face plusieurs stations en la compagnie de ton Sauveur, si ne veux t'enfuir avec les disciples. . . Regarde si ces stations ne meritent pas qu'on y aille pieds nuds, et le sang en decoulant, et si ce n'est pas pour nous crever le cœur, et nous induire à compassion?[1]

---

[1] Granada, *Le Vray chemin*, fol. 40. A French meditation on the Passion, published at Paris as early as 1550, is planned with the stations of the Cross in mind: *Devote Meditation sur la mort et passion de Jesus Christ, et de place en place ou nostre Sauveur a souffert pour nous.*

The dominant tone here is one of gentle insistence: the imperative is persuasive rather than aggressive, the use of second person singular and first person plural creates immediately a mood of intimacy. To sustain this mood, the devotional writer will use the full range of vocatives: Granada addresses his own soul in this instance, but it might equally have been the soul of the believer—'O ame amoureuse', 'ô ame devote', says Bonaventura—or Christ, or God, or in a hyperbolical application of the same device, the flesh of Christ:

...tu es toute meurtrie et enflee par le renouvellement de tes playes et ulceres si souvent rafraischies, les ruisseaux de sang corrompu et meurtri te couvrent toute...tu arrouses de sang tout le pavé qui te soustient tellement que de toutes parts on ne voyoit que du sang.[1]

As the sense of identification increases, the insistence becomes greater, the tone more demonstrative, as in the pseudo-Augustine passage already quoted, where, in a mingling of composition and prayer, the meditator calls directly on God to contemplate the sacrifice of his Son:

Regardez je vous supplie sa poitrine nuë blanchissant...

For the same purpose, a series of emphatic demonstratives may be used:

Considere ce chef couronné d'espines, ces membres si violentement estendus, et tous les endroits de ce corps precieux, tu n'y trouveras que playes et sang.[2]

And at moments of climax, the tone will often break out into exclamation:

...estant nud il apparoissoit comme un homme escorché, O tres-delicat Jesus! O tres-bon Jesus! O tres-excellentement beau Jesus, quel se represente maintenant ton elegant et beau visage?[3]

This range of tones, as will be seen from the last quotation, is supplemented by a frequent use of interrogatives, usually in the form of rhetorical question. Even where the answer to the question is perfectly clear, the questioning tone, like the imperative and the demonstrative,

---

[1] St Bonaventura, *Les Meditations...sur la Passion de nostre Seigneur Jesus Christ*, trans. Gilbert de La Brosse (Lyons, 1616; 1st ed., Paris, 1580), pp. 206-7.

[2] P. Desportes, *Quelques prieres et meditations chrestiennes* (Paris, 1603), fol. 3 (bound with *Les CL Pseaumes de David...Avec quelques Cantiques de la Bible, Hymnes, et autres œuvres et Prieres Chrestiennes* (Paris, 1604)). See below, pp. 50, 54-5.

[3] Bonaventura, *op. cit.* p. 252.

is designed to arouse the reader's attention and induce his participation in the meditation which is being sketched out for him:

De quel homme est-ce que je voy l'image sanglant par tout le corps, de toutes parts meurtry et marqué de coups, par tout enflé, boufy, et griefvement offensé, pendant le chef sur son espaule, à cause de son imbecillité, coronné d'espines qui luy percent le crane et teste jusques au cerveau, et attaché en la croix avec des clouds?[1]

In the analysis section, the interrogative may have a function much closer to enquiry. Granada's depiction of the Flagellation scene is followed by a reflective or analytic passage in which a number of questions are asked ('what is it that brought about the Incarnation?' and so on), all leading to the single answer, 'l'amour'. It will be noticed that the role of the *entendement* is here purely nominal: there is no question of a difficult problem being posed and worked out. The reader is being persuaded by rhetoric rather than by a formal theological argument. This use of a rhetorical device as the mainspring of 'analysis' is characteristic; it is also of some importance as a literary aspect of the devotional treatise, since it is one of the most common techniques used in the poetic equivalent of analytic meditation.

All the examples so far quoted have been taken from the morning meditation, the tone of which, in spite of an accumulation of horrific details, has a certain *douceur*; indeed at times the atmosphere of intimacy and fervent emotion anticipates the love-union of the mystics. The evening cycle makes use of similar rhetorical devices to stimulate involvement, laying particular stress on the interrogative mode, but owing to the change of context the resulting range of tones is now predominantly restless, pleading, or aggressive. The difference is immediately apparent in the following passage from one of Duplessis-Mornay's psalm-meditations, exploiting and extending the impatience, the questioning of God, which normally accompanies Old Testament affliction:

Seigneur, est-ce point donc assez? Et quelle autre conversion requiers-tu de moy? T'es-tu pas à bon escient converti à moy? M'as-tu pas regardé de l'œil de tes misericordes?[2]

---

[1] Alonso de Madrid, *La Methode de servir Dieu divisee en trois parties: avec le Miroir des personnes Illustres. Augmentée du Memorial de la vie de Jesus Christ: contenant sept belles Meditations pour tous les jours de la Semaine*, trans. G. Chappuys (Douai, 1600; 1st ed., Paris, 1587), p. 352 ('Oraison devant l'image de Jesus-Christ crucifié').

[2] Duplessis-Mornay, *Meditations chrestiennes*, p. 22. For the continuation of this passage, see above, p. 29.

This is a central example not only of Calvinist psalm-meditation, but also of evening meditation in general, where the sinner is constantly analysing his suffering and its significance in relation to God's mercy. The movement, and the emotional impact, of nearly all these meditations is sustained by a constant use of interrogatives, sometimes resolved, sometimes left unanswered:

Que craindrons-nous, Seigneur? Le monde? la bouë ne peut salir ton ouvrage. La chair? qui coule et s'escoule comme eau. Le diable? l'air obscur ne peut rien contre ta lumiere.[1]

We shall hear this tone of voice again, allied to the same theme, in the poetry of Chassignet and his contemporaries. In the meditations of Bèze and of Sponde question-marks seem almost as frequent as full stops:

Où iray-je donc? que diray-je? que feray-je? j'iray droit à toy, ô Eternel, car que me servira-il de fuir devant celuy qui est partout? Qui me pourroit cacher devant celuy qui void mesmes ce qui n'est point? Et quelle creature, quand elle pourroit, oserait entreprendre ma querelle contre toy?...[2]

With Sponde, we are moving into an area where the interrogative is used with an aggressive, attacking tone of voice, the tone which reappears in Goulart's ironic 'Et quoy?' and 'mais pour qui...?' (see above, pp. 27–8). At this point, one can hardly avoid the conclusion that meditation has become sermon: the devotional writer spends so much of his time addressing his reader with insistent interrogatives and imperatives that he cannot fail to give the impression that he is preaching. This applies to Granada as much as to Sponde: indeed, it is Granada who says of his own meditations:

Et à dire la verité on peut dire que ces quatorze meditations sont autant de sermons, par lesquels on faict comme une baterie au cœur humain pour le rendre et livrer és mains de son vray et legitime Seigneur.[3]

And in his first chapter:

...il n'y a autre difference entre la predication et contemplation, que entre la lecture et consideration de ce qu'on lit: ou qu'entre la viande mise en un plat, et la mesme cuite, et digeree en nostre estomach.   (fol. 1.)

---

[1] Pellisson, in Duplessis-Mornay, *Meditations chrestiennes*, p. 196.
[2] Théodore de Bèze, *Chrestiennes méditations*, ed. M. Richter (Geneva, 1964) (*TLF*), p. 53.
[3] Granada, *Le Vray chemin*, 'Prologue et argument de ce livre', *non pag.* The image used by Granada here bears a close resemblance to that of Donne's sonnet 'Batter my heart, three person'd God'.

Technique and style

Dedicating Alonso de Madrid's *Methode de servir Dieu* to the Capuchin Paul de Mol, the publisher mentions that de Mol had sometimes used material from the *Methode* for his sermons; a generation later, Goulart was to base his *Trente tableaux de la mort* on funeral oration:

> Il y a dixhuict mois qu'ayant recouvré plusieurs harangues funèbres de quelques doctes Theologiens, je m'estudiai d'en recueillir et dresser en françois certaines [pieces] pour servir en ce petit labeur à ceux qui n'ont ni n'entendent les livres Latins, ains seulement nostre langue vulgaire.[1]

Both meditation and sermon involve argument and persuasion, illustration and analysis: it makes very little difference whether the apostrophe is directed outward or inward. Both may use a 'text', usually Biblical, as a starting-point, bringing in others where relevant (hence the importance, once again, of *lecture*); both end in a prayer which is related thematically to the preceding argument. A series of sermons on a particular subject, published together, may well look like a collection of meditations—especially if the subject is the Passion, where the sermons may follow the chronological order of the narrative.[2] One important reservation should, however, be made: the devotional writer is unlikely to adopt the manner of the formal, 'Ciceronian' sermon (as preached, for example, by Du Perron), but rather the intimate personal manner of the Jesuit confessor or the urgent familiarity of the Calvinist preacher. Moreover, the highly emotive tone of the best meditation is often produced precisely by a combination of what is essential to both modes, by an alternation between reflection and apostrophe, first and second person, as in the meditations of Sponde.[3]

Clearly, the range of rhetorical devices and principles which we have been examining is potentially capable of making a considerable literary impact. They are not, of course, the exclusive province of devotional literature, but their use in specific combinations and in the context of certain themes (which will be discussed in the remainder of this chapter) makes it possible to speak of characteristic devotional modes or styles. The success of St François's *Introduction* owes much

[1] Goulart, *Trente tableaux de la Mort*, dedication, *non pag.*
[2] See, for example, F. Panigarola, *Cent sermons sur la Passion de nostre Seigneur*, trans. G. Chappuys (Paris, 1586).
[3] See also St François de Sales, *Œuvres*, vol. III, *Introduction à la vie dévote* (Annecy, 1893), pp. 41–2.

the personal penitence of Henri de Navarre; while Sponde's group seems to combine all these functions in a particularly rich way.[1]

The foundation of all penitential meditation is the self-examination recommended by Granada for the first day's reflection. What the devotional masters meant by this exercise was principally self-deprecation in the light of one's sins. The model was to be St Augustine or David rather than Socrates, and the glorification of man proposed by certain 'philosophers' was to be rejected.[2] Granada suggests that the sinner should consider in turn the corruption of each of the senses and ask himself which of the seven deadly sins he had committed, which of the ten commandments he had transgressed: the Old Testament Law should be his mirror, in which he would see himself to be imperfect, if not utterly corrupt. The Calvinists liked to stress in particular the sharp antithesis between the humiliation of the sinner and the glory of God: 'M'eslever à toy, Seigneur', says Duplessis-Mornay, 'c'est m'abaisser en moy-mesme';[3] Sponde expands this with a characteristic antithesis of smells:

Nous sommes toute ordure, et tu és toute pureté; nous ne sommes que mort, et tu n'es que vie... Ces charongnes empuanties d'iniquité entreront-elles dans le flairant pourpris de ton héritage?[4]

Indeed, the predominant image of all this literature is that of evil smell, the *puanteur* which is the physical manifestation of sin. It is accompanied by a whole range of imagery derived eventually from the Old Testament and suggesting an intimate relationship between physical and moral corruption, between sin and sickness:

Meditation des dommages qu'apporte le peché mortel. Le 1. Prelude sera, de se representer le spectacle pitoyable de l'homme, auquel depuis la plante des pieds jusques au sommet de la teste, ne se retrouve santé aucune, ains par tout son corps meurtry, et n'a que blessure, playe et tumeur.[5]

[1] Bèze, *Chrestiennes méditations*, pp. 39–40; d'Aubigné, *op. cit.* p. 174. On Sponde, see the lucid article of F. Higman, 'The *Méditations* of Jean de Sponde: A Book for the Times', in *BHR*, 28 (1966), pp. 564 ff.

[2] One of the most explicit statements on this subject is to be found in the *Institution* of Calvin, at the beginning of the second book (*ed. cit.* book II (Paris, 1957), pp. 7–8, 10).

[3] Duplessis-Mornay, *Meditations chrestiennes*, p. 101.

[4] Sponde, *Méditations*, p. 67. See also d'Aubigné, *Œuvres*, vol. II, p. 314.

[5] Loyola, *Les Vrais exercices spirituels*, pp. 65–6. See also *ibid.* p. 50, and d'Aubigné, *Œuvres*, vol. II, pp. 179–80. This theme will be discussed more fully in the context of Old Testament paraphrase in ch. 4.

In Granada the same idea is reinforced by the theme of the dead and decaying Lazarus:

...aye la moindre opinion de toy que faire se pourra...Pense que tu es un Lazare mort, il y a ja quatre jours, et un corps puant et abominable plain de vers, lesquels tous passans detestent et estoupent et yeux et nez pour ne les voir ny sentir.[1]

This theme is complemented and to some extent resolved by that of the penitent's tears. In Psalm 6 they appear chiefly as the mark of an extreme penitence:

O nuicts tesmoings de mille pensees tres mal pensees et de ce qui s'en est ensuivi, soyez maintenant tesmoings de mes regrets: et toy mon lict, lict jadis de repos tres-mal employé, sois trempé maintenant et noyé en mes larmes.[2]

But the theme is frequently extended to the point of becoming an image: the tears will perform the function of washing the penitent of his corruption. Savonarola's lengthy analysis of the 'hyssop' verse of Psalm 51 exploits precisely this figurative sense, referring back at the same time to Psalm 6:

L'hyssope, herbe basse, chaude, et odoriferente, me represente ton Fils mon Seigneur Jesus Christ, qui se est abaissé soy-mesme jusques à la mort, voire la mort de la croix, qui par l'ardeur de son immense charité nous a aimez, et nous a lavez de nos pechez en son sang, qui de l'odeur de sa benignité, de son obeissance, et de sa justice a rempli tout le monde. Alors je serai net de toutes mes ordures: lors tu me laveras de mes larmes descoulantes de l'amour de Christ: lors je ahannerai en mon gemissement, toutes les nuicts ma couche baignera en larmes: lors tu me laveras, et je serai plus blanc que neige.[3]

This is one of the most fertile combinations of theme and image in the whole evening cycle, anticipating as it does the redemptive washing in the blood of Christ of the morning sequence.

Allusions to the corruption of the body in death occur throughout the evening sequence; but the meditation on death proper—that of the Wednesday meditation, or of the *ars moriendi*—has its own well-defined characteristics. Fundamentally, the penitent is invited to reflect on two scenes, the moment of his own death and the corruption of his

---

[1] Granada, *Le Vray chemin*, fol. 81.
[2] Bèze, *Chrestiennes méditations*, p. 56.
[3] Duplessis-Mornay, *Meditations chrestiennes*, pp. 260–1.

41

body in the tomb. Loyola's *Exercice de la Mort* begins with a characteristic 'composition':

Que je m'imagine vivement, de me voir couché dans un lict abandonné des Medecins, sans aucun espoir de vivre plus long temps.[1]

The subsequent development insists strongly on the element of physical corruption, while constant reference to Job and others assures that death is always seen as the image of man's debasement and sinfulness:

Le 2. Poinct...la mort est la peine du peché...Le 4. Poinct est, considerer ce qui doit arriver au corps, tant devant qu'apres la mort. 1. Une incomparable douleur luy surviendra, causee par la longueur et griefveté de la maladie, et de la separation proche de l'ame d'avec le corps. 2. Les sens ne feront plus leur fonction. 3. L'horreur du tres puant sepulchre (representé aux yeux de l'esprit) auquel doit estre mis bien tost son corps par ses plus cheris, à fin d'estre mangé des vers, et de peur que par sa puanteur il n'infecte point l'air. Ce que le sainct Job recognoissoit fort bien, disant: *J'ay dit à la pourriture, Tu es mon pere et ma mere; et aux vers, Vous estes ma sœur.*[2]

The elements of this scene had been laid down in the Middle Ages, in works such as Damian's *Admirable discours...touchant l'heure de la mort.* Damian pictures the dying man surrounded by devils and angels waiting to dispute his soul; he emphasises both the future sufferings of the damned soul and the present sufferings of the body:

Et ce pendant que les yeux corporels sont ja à demy fermez et presque esteints et tariz, que l'estomac panthois ne peust quasi plus poulser, le gosier est tout enroüé, les dents commencent petit à petit à se noircir, et attirent je ne sçay quelle roüilleure, le visage paslist, les membres se roydissent et retirent.[3]

Granada's description has remarkable verbal similarities, demonstrating once again the unity of the devotional tradition:

...Veu que l'estomach deffault, la voix s'enroue, les pieds meurent et s'enroidissent, les genoux deviennent froids comme glace, le nez s'estressit, les yeux sont enfoncez en la teste, la face a signe de mort, et la langue ne peut plus faire son office.[4]

---

[1] Loyola, *Les Vrais exercices spirituels*, p. 74.
[2] *Ibid.* pp. 75–7. See also St François's fifth meditation, *De la mort, Œuvres*, vol. III, pp. 43–5.
[3] Guytot, *Les Meditations des zelateurs de pieté*, fol. 445. Peter Damian (d. 1072) was also a Latin poet of some importance.
[4] Granada, *Le Vray chemin*, fol. 110.

Penitence: the evening meditation

The *ars moriendi* branch of the tradition follows broadly the same pattern, though with certain elaborations. The *genre* seems to have taken shape in the early sixteenth century with the *De scientia mortis*, attributed to Gerson. Subsequently, both Latin and French texts appear at regular intervals; the tradition was subscribed to by Savonarola and Erasmus and continued beyond the end of the sixteenth century.[1] In most instances, the angels and devils are again portrayed at the death-bed, and their dispute passes through several episodes which correspond to Satan's temptations of the dying man. For example, the *Ars moriendi* of 1470 has this sequence: *Temptacio dyaboli de fide; de desperacione; de impaciencia; de vana gloria; de avaricia*, each one being followed by the angel's reply.[2] In the temptation of despair, Satan enumerates the man's sins: how can he hope for salvation? The angel replies by reminding him of the New Testament penitents— St Peter, the penitent thief, Mary Magdalene. This battle is in effect a dramatised form of internal debate or meditation, one of the variations on the spiritual combat; and it is implicitly related to the 'questioning' theme of the Old Testament, since the virtue of Job is that he succeeds in suppressing *impaciencia*. One of the distinguishing features of the tradition, particularly in the fifteenth and early sixteenth centuries, is that the *ars moriendi* is often illustrated with wood-cuts;[3] it thus anticipates in a striking way the Counter-Reformation emphasis on both pictorial representation and visualised meditation.

Before leaving this aspect of devotion, it will be as well to indicate that Calvinist parallels are not lacking, although the psalm-meditations of the 1580s tend to avoid extended description of death and decay. The outstanding example is Simon Goulart, who at the turn of the century was to do a considerable amount of work in the *ars moriendi* field, including a translation of William Perkens' *Salve for a sicke man*, as well as his own *Trente tableaux de la mort*: the passage already quoted from this last work is an ample illustration of Goulart's concrete

[1] Cf. Mary C. O'Connor, *The Art of Dying Well* (New York, 1942); Martz, *The Poetry of Meditation*, pp. 135 ff.; L. Réau, *Iconographie de l'art chrétien* (Paris, 1955–9), vol. II, 2, book III, ch. 1; and Dagens, *Bibliographie*, especially under the years 1580, 1584 and 1607.

[2] See R. Klein, 'La Dernière méditation de Savonarole', *BHR*, 23 (1961), pp. 441 ff. Klein discusses Savonarola's meditation against the background of the *ars moriendi* tradition, and in the context of the 'justification' debate.

[3] See Réau, *Iconographie*.

awareness of death. Finally, d'Aubigné's treatise *De la Douceur des afflictions* contains a deathbed scene which is clearly related to the *ars moriendi* tradition:

> Je ne craindray point après les qualités de la vie, de vous faire encore appréhender celles de la mort. Bienheureux qui meurt au Seigneur en la maison de Dieu, entre des mains fidelles, pleurs et larmes sans feintes, et qui, aggréable flambeau de l'Eglise, s'esteindra au regret des bons, et ne laisse pas une puante fumée au nez de la postérité. Au contraire, malheur de mourir sur le précipice de l'enfer, dans un lict assiégé d'idoles, environné de bouches blasphémantes, d'un concert de démons, et voir les ennemis de Dieu, et de vous, qui avec souspirs contrefaicts, préparent leurs impures mains à vous fermer les paupières.[1]

Here the traditional scene has been rephrased to suit d'Aubigné's technique of making a point by violent contrast; piety and beauty are seen in diametrical opposition to grotesque horror, very much as in the martyrdoms of *Feux*.

The Thursday and Friday meditations, on the Last Judgement and Hell respectively, have less direct connexions with poetry, except in so far as they expand the themes already discussed. The Tuesday meditation, however, which deals with the vanity of the world and of human life, is of great importance. Although it is closely related to the other penitential meditations in that it involves self-deprecation and frequent reference to human fragility and death, the perspective is here rather different. Sicknesses may sometimes be listed to prove the imminence of death, but they are not described in detail as an outward manifestation of man's sin. Similarly, death is not visualised as a physical circumstance: it is an abstraction, a negation of human life, one term of a 'paradox': 'vie...qui ne doit estre appellee vie, mais plustost mort'.[2]

This meditation, and parallel treatises on the same theme, may consider the subject either from the point of view of the preacher issuing a moral warning, or as a 'consolation' against affliction. The first tone —and the predominant one—is that of Ecclesiastes. Chappuys's translation of Estella's *Livre de la vanité du monde* opens with a 'vanity'

---

[1] A. d'Aubigné, *De la Douceur des afflictions*, ed. F. Chavannes and C. Read (Paris, 1856), p. 25.

[2] Guyot, *Les Meditations des zelateurs de pieté*, fol. 52 (from the pseudo-Augustine meditation, ch. 21, 'De quantes amertumes ceste vie humaine est remplie').

sonnet, and with a liminary emblem portraying Christ on the Cross, with Mary and two disciples: underneath is the motto 'Vanitas vanitatum et omnia vanitas praeter amare Deum'; and the whole work is riddled with references to Ecclesiastes and to Job.[1] The *Epistre a la Royne* which introduces Abelly's sermons on the Lamentations is based on the *vanitas* theme and on the image 'omnis caro faenum' from Isaiah 40;[2] and this image is the centrepiece of the battery of figures with which the *vanitas* preacher can reinforce his theme. The stock appears to be inexhaustible, and yet never to break new ground; its principal source is the Old Testament, but the allusion is seldom precise and the overall impression is often one of anonymity. Pellisson has 'plume, poussière, rien', 'vent, soufle, festu', 'chemin glissant de ce monde'; Savonarola: 'bouë, fiente, rien', 'poudre, foin';[3] Sponde: 'des roseaux, des fueilles, de la plume, du vent, un Rien'.[4] Jacques de Billy is particularly obliging in prefacing his *Recueil des consolations* with a *table des similitudes* ('de la nuict, et de cette vie'; 'du torrent, et de ce monde'; 'de la glu, et de l'amour du monde'); one could hardly have a better illustration of the tendency of the *vanitas* theme to attract vast numbers of commonplace similes.[5] Much of this material can become tedious to the modern reader. But Sponde's *mise en valeur* of the whole range of *vanitas* commonplaces (particularly in his first meditation) is extremely elaborate and would bear detailed examination, both thematically and stylistically; indeed, all the Calvinist meditations contain passages where a point is suddenly driven home by the use of interrogation, assonance or ellipsis:

La mort de ce monde n'est rien qu'un nom, qu'un son vain, qui bat l'oreille des fols, mais qui coule doux en celle des sages: rien qu'un effroy d'enfans, un espouvantail d'oiseaux, masque plaisant aux bons, hideux à la conscience cauterisee: ce n'est qu'un passage, Seigneur, nostre vie qu'un voyage, chaque pas d'icelle est une mort: du premier le second, et le dernier, de tous.[6]

---

[1] See also below, p. 64.

[2] A. Abelly, *Sermons sur les Lamentations du sainct prophete Hieremie* (Paris, 1582), 'Epistre a la Royne', *non pag.*

[3] Duplessis-Mornay, *Meditations chrestiennes*, pp. 190, 219, 223, 277, 250.

[4] Sponde, *Méditations*, p. 155. See also Granada, *Le Vray chemin*, fol. 81.

[5] J. de Billy, *Recueil des consolations et instructions salutaires de l'ame fidele, extraict du volume de S. Augustin sur les Psalmes* (Paris, 1570).

[6] Duplessis-Mornay, *Meditations chrestiennes*, pp. 216–17 (Pellisson's meditation). See also Duplessis-Mornay's own meditations, *ibid.* pp. 127 and 158.

Throughout his *Méditations* Sponde shows concern for the theme of 'form-changing', the fluctuation and unreliability both of man and of the physical world. The theme is again central to this *vanitas* meditation as a whole, but Sponde handles it with greater penetration and intellectual control than most of his contemporaries. In the meditation on Psalm 13, he is attacking the explanation of the world's inconstancy by reference to *fortune*: 'La fortune? Quoy? Ordre si ferme, de chose si mouvante?' Fortune embodies inconstancy, and is therefore more inconstant even than the epitomes of inconstancy,

moindre que toy-mesme, qui en parles, moindre que les Abeilles, que les Formis, que les Cirons, voyre moindre que les mesmes Atomes, qui par leur mouvement monstrent encore je ne sçay quoy de réglé, je ne sçay quoy de mesuré...car chaque subject a sa nature, et par conséquent sa fortune, diverse d'une autre nature, diverse d'une autre fortune. Te voilà en fin dans le gouffre de la pluralité.[1]

The Psalm 50 meditation includes another range of allusions, this time designed to attack man's tendency to polytheism: 'Monde d'Atomes', 'Ces Hydres', 'Ces fleuves, ces Protées [qui] ne se peuvent lasser de changer de formes' (p. 87); and the same view of the world is transformed into a consolatory theme in the *Recueil des consolations* compiled from Augustine's psalm-commentaries by Jacques de Billy and published in 1570. The principal argument invoked to counter the notion of inconstancy is that everything happens in a necessary and natural order—what Montaigne would call, in a profane application of the same idea, 'l'encheinure des causes Stoïques':[2]

Tout homme qui est né, faut par necessité qu'il face place à celuy qui naist apres: et tout l'ordre des choses caduques et corruptibles est comme un fleuve.[3]

The generations of man are like leaves: death is followed by regeneration, a constancy underlies the apparent fluctuation.

As I have suggested by referring to Montaigne and to Sponde's 'philosophical' allusions, the *vanitas* meditation has overt connexions

---

[1] Sponde, *Méditations*, p. 16.
[2] M. de Montaigne, *Œuvres complètes*, ed. A. Thibaudet (Paris, 1962) (Bibliothèque de la Pléiade), p. 793.
[3] *Recueil des consolations*, fol. 79.

with a debate whose ramifications go far beyond the realms of devotional literature. The theme of change and instability in the material world coincides broadly with a number of pagan philosophical approaches—Stoic, Sceptic, Epicurean—all of which were current in the later sixteenth century. Estella, for all his reliance on Ecclesiastes, is aware too of a debt to the philosophy of antiquity: 'la vie dit le Sage' (and he gives the reference 'Plat. in Phaed.'), 'est meditation de la mort', and 'La tres-haute philosophie est la meditation frequente de la mort';[1] while Borromeo, Du Vair, Duplessis-Mornay, Goulart, and Sponde all had avowed leanings towards Stoicism. On the other hand, to attempt a thorough-going reconciliation of Christian and pagan philosophy was not the primary aim of the devotional writer as it was for Du Vair and Lipsius. There is a general tendency in most of these handbooks away from complex thought, a tendency towards commonplace formulation and facile paradoxes; thus the *vanitas* themes, like their accompanying images, tend to move into an area of anonymity, a no-man's-land in which humanism and devotion can overlap without the need for reasoned justification.

In reading the evening cycle of meditations, one is struck first by the spectacular physicality of the death-bed scenes, of the leprous sores of the penitent, of the worms in the tomb. The atmosphere is pervaded with the terror of a 'fire and brimstone' sermon; and one is constantly reminded of the concrete violence of the Old Testament, the smell of flesh and decay, the intimacy with corruption: 'J'ay dit à la pourriture, Tu es mon pere et ma mere; et aux vers, vous estes ma sœur'. But although the shock-tactics of 'composition' seem to predominate, the reflection of the penitent plays an equally important part. These meditations are about the relationship of the individual sinner to God, and are full of uncertainties and questionings. What is the connexion between physical suffering and sin? Is affliction a punishment, or an outward sign, or a 'test'? How can one protect oneself against the fear of death? How can man, who is all corruption, communicate with God, who is all purity? Many of these questions had been posed and reflected on in the Old Testament; the task of the devotional writer is to rephrase

[1] Estella, *Livre de la vanité du monde*, fols. 193, 194. Montaigne makes the same point from the other side of the fence when he remarks in a more or less Stoic context: 'Nostre religion n'a point eu de plus asseuré fondement humain, que le mespris de la vie' (*op. cit.* p. 90).

them and to suggest if not to impose an answer. Hence 'analysis'—question, argument, paradox, antithesis—arises out of the physical situation. Finally, the tones of sermon and self-examination are interwoven with that of prayer. Unable to resolve his anxieties on his own account, the penitent seeks resolution from God. The penitential cycle ends with the hope of redemption, a hope which is already present in embryo in the Psalms and the Old Testament as a whole, but which will not be fully realised until the New Testament.

THE LIFE OF CHRIST: THE MORNING MEDITATION

Although the evening cycle of meditations draws on New Testament material to develop penitential themes, references to the life of Christ are limited: contemplation of the Nativity or of the Passion is reserved for the more optimistic morning meditation. The theme of penitence does, however, provide the main link between the two sequences. The individual sinner shares the burden of responsibility for the Crucifixion of Christ; the 'imitation' of Christ's sufferings is a part of the ritual through which he seeks forgiveness; his tears mingle with those of the Virgin Mary, of Mary Magdalene, and of Christ himself, and are identified with the blood in which his corruption is washed away. It is thus the perspective which is different: no longer confronted by the wrath of an Old Testament God, the penitent can now contemplate the instrument of his redemption, and the *puanteur* of sin begins to give way to the *douceur* of Christ's love and of the meditator's compassion. Just as the New Testament was occasionally foreshadowed in the images of the Old, the history which leads up to the coming of Christ is here seen in retrospect and given its full symbolic meaning: Adam's tree has become Christ's Cross.

Meditation on the life of Christ forms a much more coherent cycle than the evening group of themes. Many treatises restrict themselves to the dominating Passion episode, and although pride of place may be given to one of the Marys (for emotive reasons), the central narrative remains the same. Indeed, it is primarily because of the narrative character of the sequence that consistency is maintained. Likewise, meditations and sermons on later saints and martyrs merely exemplify how the Passion should be imitated, giving continuity to the tradition

of suffering and sacrifice. In this area of devotion, the Catholic mono-
poly remains more or less uncontested. For the Calvinist, the Incarnation has to remain abstract, any appeal to the senses being suspect;
and the martyrologies which provide some kind of remote parallel
with Passion meditations belong to the history of polemical rather than
devotional literature.

Although the Gospels naturally provide the basis for this cycle, one
cannot speak of a separate *genre* of Biblical meditation in this instance,
parallel to the psalm-meditation. As we have seen, nearly all the later
devotional writers elaborate the narrative and its significance according
to material laid down by the Fathers, and this again leads to standardisation both of matter and of method. The sermons and meditations of
Bernard, Bonaventura and the pseudo-Augustine are frequently re-
edited and translated in the later sixteenth century, while the whole
tradition is resumed in anthologies such as that of Guytot, or of Antoine
Estienne, whose *Dévot discours sur la Passion* comprises works from
the Middle Ages, the *devotio moderna* movement, the Cologne Charterhouse and the Spanish Friars.[1] The programme of the Jesuits and the
Mendicants reaches one of its culminating points in this area of meditation, and editions of works on the life of Christ by Loarte, Granada,
Guevara and Alonso de Madrid are abundant throughout the period;
but apart from their greater systematisation and their attempts to flatter
the literary tastes of a lay audience (an important reservation), they
remain extremely close to their predecessors. In certain circles one
does however notice a marked preference for meditation on the Virgin
Mary and to a lesser extent on other saints. The part played by François
Coster in founding a sodality of the Virgin and in producing treatises
of his own is strongly indicative of a movement designed to counter
the Protestant iconoclasm, while a link with the Middle Ages is preserved through meditation on the *Salve regina* and the *Stabat mater*.[2]

---

[1] A. Estienne, *Dévot discours sur la Passion... où sont comprises plusieurs méditations recueillies des œuvres de S. Bernard, Tauler, Lansperge, Grenade, et autres auteurs* (Paris,
1582). In the same year Guyot published a separate translation of St Bernard's sermons
and meditations.

[2] See F. Coster, *Cinquante meditations de la vie et louanges de la Vierge Marie* (Antwerp,
1587); *Cinquante méditations de toute l'histoire de la Passion de Nostre-Seigneur* (Antwerp,
1587) (both these works are translations by G. Chappuys from the Latin); *De cantico
Salve regina septem meditationes* (Antwerp, 1589); also L. Richeome, *La Sacree Vierge
Marie au pied de la croix* (Paris, 1603) (based on the *Stabat mater*).

Likewise, Crespet's treatises on the saints, echoing the medieval tradition of 'lives of the saints', anticipate also the glorification of Counter-Reformation saints such as Teresa and Ignatius.[1]

Most of these treatises were written by renowned devotional authors and were read from one end of Europe to the other. If one is concerned with possible influences on poetry, however, a work such as Desportes's *Quelques prieres et meditations chrestiennes* (published first in 1594) is of more direct significance. Although Desportes was in holy orders and intimately connected with the Vincennes circle and the penitential orders, one would scarcely consider him as being in the same category as Granada or Coster. Here, nevertheless, is a major poet writing his own devotional prose, an example which can scarcely have gone unnoticed; and among these prayers and meditations is a *Meditation devant la Croix de nostre Sauveur Jesus-Christ*, an *Oraison à la Vierge Marie*, and a *Priere aux Saincts*. Fifteen years later, a less familiar figure, Henry Humbert, produced his *Sepmaine saincte*, where prose meditation alternates with poetry: the laicisation of the morning meditation and its convergence with poetry are now fully established.

The principal themes associated with the morning meditation are easily classified, since they are merely the episodes of the life of Christ, together with the reflections which these may arouse in the mind of the meditator. The Nativity and the Passion are the most popular episodes, presenting the writer with innumerable opportunities for colourful dramatisation and pathetic appeal. The Passion has the added advantage of fitting the seven-day plan of the morning meditation proper; whether or not the *dévot* was actually meditating during the Easter week itself, the sequence of events leading up to the Passion provided him with a ready-made division of material as well as a wide variety of themes. The fourteen stations of the Cross are convenient in much the same way. One should not forget that the ritual of meditation was very often a preparation for the Church rituals rather than an end in itself: the layman might use contemplation as an approach to a mystical *extase*, but more often it would be a way of deepening his participation in the Christmas or Easter Communion. Hence St François de Sales recom-

---

[1] P. Crespet, *Triomphe des saincts*; *Traictez de...Tertullian, de la vertu de patience en affliction, et aux saincts martyrs* (Sens, 1577); *Discours sur la vie et tragique passion de la glorieuse vierge et martyre S. Catherine* (Sens, 1577). For works on Ignatius and Teresa, see Dagens, *Bibliographie*, for example under years 1594 and 1601.

mends Passion meditation as part of the confessional, thus making explicit the link with the sacramental value of the evening cycle: '...imaginés-vous d'estre en la montagne de Calvaire sous les pieds de Jesus Christ crucifié, duquel le sang precieux distille de toutes partz pour vous laver de vos iniquités.'[1] Likewise, the raising of Christ on the Cross is symbolized for Guevara by the raising of the Host (*op. cit.* fol. 178). Indeed, glosses which associate the Passion with the Eucharist abound in the devotional treatises of every period, stressing the physical presence of Christ's body and blood in the context of the sinner's need for sacramental purification. This merging of Passion meditation with the Eucharist ceremony is to have its own parallels in religious poetry.

Contemplation of the Nativity scene has two salient characteristics, one associated with 'composition', the other with 'analysis': both are well illustrated by Granada's meditation *De la Nativité glorieuse de nostre Sauveur Jesus Christ*. The first is the tendency to sentimentalise, to seek out the most extreme hyperboles to describe the Christchild. The atmosphere is full of *douceur* and *miel*, the very tears of Christ are sweet:

En ce jour...que le ciel distille goutes de miel par tout le monde, nous a esclairé le jour d'une nouvelle redemption.

Donne toy donc garde, mon amy, de ne t'esloigner de ceste estable, où la parole de Dieu plore en se taisant: mais ce pleur est plus doux que toute l'eloquence Ciceronienne, voire plus agreable que n'est la mesme musique des Anges és cieux.[2]

Here already there is a hint of the picturesque contrast between the humility of the setting (the stable, the cattle, the swaddling-bands) and the majesty of Christ, a contrast which provides the main impetus of the analysis section and which is stated in its simplest form by Granada in a single antithetical sentence: 'Qui est cestuy si hault, et si bas, si grand, et si petit?'[3] The elaboration of this question involves all the elements of physical composition; indeed, composition and analysis

[1] St François de Sales, *Œuvres*, vol. III, pp. 57–8.
[2] Granada, *Devotes contemplations et spirituelles instructions sur la Vie, Passion, Mort, Resurrection, et glorieuse Ascension de nostre Sauveur Jesus Christ*, trans. F. de Belleforest (Paris, 1583; 1st ed. 1572), fols. 34–5, 40.
[3] *Ibid.* fols. 42–3. Cf. R. Tuve, *A Reading of George Herbert*, pp. 36 ff. and 53–4, for this and parallel themes in the medieval tradition.

4-2

merge as the meditator begins at once to marvel on the sight of the omnipotent king become helpless infant:

> Qui ne s'effroyera de voir le Roy de toute chose creé, estre couché au lieu où gisent les bestes?...Et comment a il fait eschange du Temple avec une estable, et du Ciel pour une creiche. (fol. 38.)

> La splendeur de la gloire du pere est emmaillottee en les langes et drapeaux, par laquelle faut que soyent nettoyees les taches et souilleures de noz pechez. Le rassassiement des Anges est icy sustenté d'un peu de laict...Le pain des Anges est converti en avoine. (fol. 40.)

The poets may emphasise one element or the other according to personal taste—Bertaut prefers symmetrical antithesis, César de Nostredame the sweetness of babyhood—but both remain characteristic of the Nativity meditation, whether in prose or in poetry.

The theme of Christ's sufferings, in the Flagellation scene, in the Crucifixion itself, or in subsidiary episodes such as St Peter's denial, runs through the whole of the Passion sequence of meditations and provokes similar combinations of pathos and paradox. In most cases, contemplation of the Passion implies first and foremost a lingering over each agonising moment.[1] According to Bonaventura, the executioners use nails without points, 'et fut si grande la douleur qu'il endura que incontinent tous ses nerfs s'en retirerent'; and the body has to be stretched with ropes to make it fit the Cross.[2] The Counter-Reformation devotional writers follow their models closely, at times word for word. Alonso de Madrid says that when the nail was hammered into Christ's hand, the pain was 'si grande, que tous les nerfs de son sacré corps se retirerent';[3] likewise for the stretching of the body: 'Ils luy atacherent une corde a sa delicate main, et tirerent tant qu'ils peurent avec icelle...' This is followed by a psalm-quotation used also by Bonaventura.[4] Alonso substantiates the detail by referring to

---

[1] In some devotional works, particularly the stricter monastic ones, this is not the case. The *Manuel du chevalier chrestien* of the Carthusian Landsberger (trans. Jean de Billy, Paris, 1571) gives no physical details of the Passion; the reader is encouraged to consider the moral and symbolic significance of the sacrifice. The principle of 'imitation' or 'identification' is however recommended here, much as in the less ascetic treatises (e.g. fols. 215, 218, 219; refs. to ed. of Rouen, 1609).

[2] Bonaventura, *Les Meditations*, pp. 253–5.

[3] Alonso de Madrid, *La Methode de servir Dieu*, p. 311 (the pagination is irregular).

[4] 'Foderunt manus meas et pedes meos et dinumeraverunt omnia ossa mea' (Vulgate, Ps. 21. 18).

'le grand Theologien Gregoire Nazianzene'; and in Guevara's *Livre du mont de Calvaire*, Anselm, Bede and Ubertino are made to testify to the renewal of Christ's agony by the jolt of the Cross as it falls into place.[1] The technique of attacking the imagination by an accumulation of horrors is thus precisely the same as in earlier works except that the new writers may try to outdo their predecessors.[2]

Likewise, both the medieval and the Counter-Reformation authors insist on the violent contrast between Christ's fragile and delicate beauty and the insults that are heaped upon him:

Ces assasinateurs et bourreaux estant agenoüillez devant sa majesté, font semblant de l'adorer, et l'appellent Roy à haute voix, et tout soubdain de leurs ordes sallives et immundes crachats ils difforment et salissent ses belles et delicates joües, sur lesquelles ils frappent de leurs mains meurdrieres et chargent lourdement son col tant honorable du trespesant fardeau de sa penible croix.[3]

In the pseudo-Augustine meditation, the same procedure is used, but at even greater length. This is a classic passage, which in Tamisier's version becomes one of the earliest pieces of fully devotional poetry of the period:

> Jette tes yeux sur ses mains innocentes,
> Ces belles mains livides et sanglantes,
> Voy en le sang goutte à goutte couller...
>
> Voy (ô bon Dieu) remarque, et considère
> Son costé nud, qu'une lance meurtriere
> Cruellement a poingt et transpercé,
> Et lave moy de celle onde sacree
> Avec le sang de ce costé tiree,
> Et par là soit le mien vice effacé.
>
> De ces deux pieds voy les plantes jumelles
> Oultrepercez avec poinctes cruelles...
>
> Voy de ton filz la poictrine aussi blanche
> Que le beau lys, ou que la rose franche,
> Voy son costé saigneux et rougissant,
> Voy desecher ses entrailles tendues,
> En pasle teint voy ses levres rendues,
> Et ses beaux yeux s'aller obscurcissant.

---

[1] Antonio de Guevara, *Livre du Mont de Calvaire*, ed. cit., ch. 33, fols. 177–8.
[2] See, for example, *ibid.* fol. 171.
[3] Guytot, *Les Meditations des zelateurs de pieté*, fol. 430 (from the *Sermon de S. Bernard de la Passion*).

> Voy (ô bon Dieu) ses joües paslissantes,
> Son chef percé par espines poignantes,
> Ses bras roidis, et en hault eslevez,
> Sa blanche cuisse efforcement tiree,
> Ses pieds trouez d'une poincte aceree,
> Et de son sang arrosez et lavez.[1]

The focal point of all meditation on the Passion is the blood of Christ. Its physical quantity is always expressed hyperbolically, at the Flagellation as well as the Crucifixion; and this is the starting-point of a *topos* in which the tears of the meditator, or more often of Mary, 'rival' with the blood of Christ. Granada warns his reader to have his tears ready,[2] and in this literature of tears opportunities for elaborate rhetorical conceits are always available. 'Plustost faillira le sang aux veines du fils, que les larmes aux yeux de la mere' is the *topos* in embryo;[3] from this, elaborations like Coster's:

Considere 3. de quelz yeux la mere auroit regardé son filz, quand la croix estoit eslevee en haut...les ruisseaux de sang, et les ruisseaux de larmes couloient des membres du filz, et des yeux de la mere...Quant à toy, prie la mere que ses pleurs et ses larmes, et le sang coulant de son filz, amollisse ton cœur à compassion, pour autant que la durté est emerveillable, laquelle et ne se fond ou liquefie par si grande chaleur du sang, et ne s'amollit par tant d'eau et de liqueur de larmes.[4]

This passage and the pseudo-Augustine paraphrase make it clear that the copiousness of the blood is only the outward sign of its redemptive qualities; when the *dévot* begins to analyse the mystery of the Passion, it will be of penitence that he thinks first. Desportes's *Meditation devant la Croix* provides a good illustration of the kind of variation possible within this aspect of 'analytic' contemplation; it also coincides conveniently with the thematic trends of Passion poetry written by the Louvre poets. After a brief composition ('Considere ce chef couronné d'espines...'), Desportes takes up the sufferings of Christ as an allegory; the Crucifixion is seen as a symbol instead of a historical event:

[1] P. Tamisier, *Les Meditations de sainct Augustin. Traduictes du Latin, et mises en vers françois* (Lyons, 1587), pp. 14–15. For the corresponding passage in the Guytot version, see above, p. 28.
[2] Granada, *Le Vray chemin*, fol. 45 ('aye des larmes toutes prestes').
[3] Guevara, *Livre du Mont de Calvaire*, fol. 181.
[4] Coster, *Cinquante meditations de la vie et louanges de la Vierge Marie* (Antwerp, 1590), p. 222.

Tu t'y es cloué pour nous attendre à penitence, tu estens les bras pour nous embrasser, ton sang ruisselle de tous costez, à fin de n'espargner à personne une si salutaire medecine.[1]

The remainder of the meditation follows much the same pattern, the increasing boldness of the paradoxes and inversions being matched by a new upsurge of pathos (the 'affections'):

Je perce ton cœur avec mes humbles et violentes prieres, te suppliant de distiler au moins une petite goutte de ton sang dedans mes playes...Je t'offre son sang au lieu de larmes qu'il me faudroit espandre, et ses prieres enflammees pour les miennes froides et languissantes. (fols. 4, 5.)

It will be seen from this last quotation that, in the context of the morning meditation, penitential self-deprecation may involve a sense of emotional sterility or 'coldness': Desportes here resolves it in terms of the warmth of Christ's own love and its vicarious function; and Favre will dwell on it more than once, particularly in his Rosary sequence. It is at this point that contemplation of the Passion begins to converge with the mystical allegory of love, as in Bonaventura's meditation on the 'sept flammes d'amour qui sortirent de la fournaise de l'amoreux Jesus gisant sur la croix'.

In spite of the connexions between the penitential cycle of meditations and the life of Christ sequence, there is a striking difference of atmosphere between the two. In the second, one moves out of the sombre evening tones, the deathly pallor and the funereal black, into a world where red is predominant: the crimson of blood or the royal purple, accompanied by the pure white of innocence and the delicate texture of Christ's skin. In this atmosphere, sweetness and suffering are mingled; an underlying optimism runs through the agony of Good Friday, for the sequence must resolve itself in the triumph of Easter Sunday. The shift of emphasis has a relevance which is also chronological. Meditation on death and vanity coincides approximately with the civil war period and may well have been encouraged by current events; this is after all the conclusion one would draw from the penitential activity of Henri III's reign, and from the popularity of Old Testament meditation in this period. In later years, and particularly from the turn of the century, interest in the life of Christ, the Virgin

---

[1] P. Desportes, *Quelques prieres et meditations*, fol. 4.

Mary and Mary Magdalene emerges as the focus of attention. The change is naturally not apparent in the comprehensive treatise (which is by this time becoming less popular, having fulfilled its instructive function); it bears principally on the individual, specialised treatises, and also on the general mood of devotion, which is now veering towards the gentler, more feminine approach of St François de Sales. A similar contrast can be seen in the non-devotional affinities of the two cycles. The *vanitas* meditation and its equivalents elsewhere frequently develop their themes along lines which coincide with pagan thought, consciously exploiting the ground they share with apologetic humanism. The morning meditation on the other hand is in certain respects orientated towards secular literature; as we shall see later, the narrative techniques, the ambiguities of the theme of love, and the appeal to a pathetic sensibility can easily produce a convergence with profane prose. This is not to say that penitential meditation is of a lower literary value: Sponde's *Méditations* are perhaps the finest piece of devotional writing in French prior to St François de Sales. What is important is that Sponde is not conscious of making a compromise with secular modes of rhetoric, whereas St François certainly is.

Although the range of available material in both cycles is very great, the force of tradition naturally creates a degree of standardisation: Granada and Damian, Alonso de Madrid and Bonaventura, even Goulart and Loyola bear a family resemblance to one another. As in other areas of sixteenth-century (and earlier) literature, certain dominant commonplaces emerge which are repeated from work to work, allowing for variations of individual manner and context. The linking of sin and sickness in an Old Testament atmosphere is one such *topos*, as is the theme of *vanitas* and its accompanying images. Then there is the complex of commonplaces associated with tears: the bed drowned in tears of Psalm 6, the hyssop-motif of Psalm 51, and thence the New Testament mingling of tears and blood. This characteristic makes a great deal easier the task of finding points of comparison between devotional prose and devotional poetry, since the *topoi* are usually specific enough to be recognisable. Furthermore, they do not suggest a relationship with any one source but rather with a whole tradition, and this is appropriate to the kind of material we are dealing with: evidence of direct contact between a poet and his source-material is relatively rare, although some important examples exist. On the whole, the themes of the morning meditation are more easily recognisable when transferred than some of their evening counterparts, since they are dependent on narrative detail rather than Old Testament allusion or abstract comment on human fragility. Both groups of treatises do however provide an abundance of preliminary data, thematic and stylistic, in terms of which the character of the poetry discussed in the following chapters may be more sharply defined.

CHAPTER 3

FROM DEVOTION TO POETRY

One cannot go far in sixteenth-century literature without coming across variations on the Horatian *utile dulci*. In the later part of the century it was applied in the new context of the Counter-Reformation. For the Pléiade, 'utility' had implied serious intellectual content—the allegories of Ronsard's *Hymnes* for example—and thus a wider relevance for the poetic vocation itself: the poet was to be not merely an entertainer but an interpreter of the world and of man. The Counter-Reformation added a religious direction to this concept: 'profit' now meant orthodox instruction and the stamping out of heresy and 'paganism'. The appropriation of the *dulce* element is a little more complicated and varies according to the individual author and his background; but if one is thinking in terms of the emergence of vernacular devotion, the general sense is clear enough. The cloister had evidently not encouraged or needed to encourage literary ornament in devotional works: propaganda was superfluous since the audience was already converted. The Counter-Reformation, on the other hand, demanded that such works be circulated amid the widest possible audience: hence translation into the vernacular, and the composition of new treatises which were designed to be palatable to a lay audience accustomed to the attractions of profane literature. The new orientation of devotion soon began to converge with the increased popularity of religious subjects in literature, encouraged first by the Calvinists and later matched by Catholic teachers and writers. Established literature, especially poetry, thus began to apply *utile* in its religious sense, while devotional works inclined towards the *dulce*. This convergence becomes apparent in a number of ways. The men who translate devotional works into the vernacular often indicate that they see their work in a literary perspective, and not merely as a pious labour; poets and other literary figures show their interest in these translations by writing liminary poems; and religious poets themselves begin to give explicit signs of devotional intention, or accompany their poetry with prose meditations and prayers. Meanwhile, devotional handbooks move closer and closer towards the attractions of profane literature; before the end of the century, interconnexions are already frequent and unmistakeable.

THE DEVOTIONAL TREATISE AS LITERATURE

If one is to consider devotional writing in literary terms, two important tendencies must be distinguished: the emergence of certain styles which result (as we saw in the foregoing chapter) directly or indirectly from the formal method of meditation and sermon, and the attempt to turn to the advantage of religion the popularity enjoyed by secular literature. No doubt these tendencies overlap to some extent, owing to the standardisation of rhetorical procedures: but the decision to launch a devotional literature which could compete with the secular on its own terms required very much longer to become established. It is not until the writings of Richeome and St François that one feels that the 'dépouilles d'Egypte' theory has been thoroughly assimilated in France; by then, a lay audience is beginning to form for whom devotion is a fashionable pastime (if an eminently respectable one). Meanwhile, in the university context, the Jesuit educators had been at work rephrasing humanist scholarship in Counter-Reformation terms and thus preparing the ground for future laicisation.[1]

The direct predecessors of the *Introduction* are however the translations of the 1570s and 1580s. Granada, like many of his contemporaries, is consciously aiming at a literary effect, which he feels to be essential if he is to please a wide enough audience: Christ's tears, he says, are sweeter than all the eloquence of Cicero, which suggests that for him the eloquence of Cicero is the epitome of sweetness.[2] His programme is made explicit in the *Exhortation* which precedes *Le Vray chemin*:

Et d'autant que l'auteur sçavoit bien le desgoust des hommes de ce siecle, et que plus ils sont affectionnez aux viandes d'Egypte, qu'au pain des Anges, c'est à dire aux livres mondains et prophanes, à cause de la douceur de leur stile, qu'à ceux qui contiennent doctrine spirituelle, esquels la simplicité est

---

[1] This is broadly speaking Bremond's distinction between *humanisme chrétien* and *humanisme dévot*. See also F. Dainville, *La Naissance de l'humanisme moderne* (Paris, 1940) (vol. II of *Les Jésuites et l'éducation de la société française*).
[2] See above, p. 51.

requise: il a desguisé si gentiment ceste viande, qu'escrivant avec un doux et plausible stile, il remet en goust les plus desappetissez, et leur donne appetit de taster de ces choses, lesquelles sont d'elles-mesmes, et choisies, et proufit-ables.[1]

Immediately after, Granada's work is referred to as 'ceste viande si mielleuse'. Hence all the images which normally surround the *utile dulci* theory (appetite, sweetness, honey, disguise) reappear in a context which is unambiguously devotional; furthermore, the *douceur* of Granada's style is offered to the reader without any reservations as a valid way of making 'doctrine spirituelle' more palatable. The application of this programme is somewhat uneven: the prose of *Le Vray chemin* (in French translation at least) tends to suffer from syntactical incoherence and lacks the controlled momentum of, say, Sponde's *Méditations*. Granada's work was however immensely popular, if one is to judge by the frequent re-editions, and part of this popularity may be due to its concessions to literary elaboration. At moments of climax, Granada will make full use of circumlocutions, of a rich vocabulary, of parallelisms which recall both the Old Testament and the Ciceronian period:

O miroir sans tache de la majesté de Dieu, qui t'a ainsi maculé et taché? O ruisseau coulant et surgeonnant du Paradis de delices, qui esjouis avec les flots de tes courantes la cité de Dieu, qui a troublé ces tiennes tant cleres et savoureuses eaux? Ce sont mes pechez (ô Seigneur) qui les ont troublees, et mes iniquitez qui leur ont osté leur splendeur.[2]

His contemporary Alonso de Madrid aims at similar effects of rhetorical brilliance; in this passage, the connexion with secular style is made explicit in a passing mythological allusion:

O midy de vostre ardeur et du Soleil qui jamais ne tend à l'Occident, monstrez nous ou vous paissez à myjour, ou vous chassez voz brebis, loin de toute froidure. O Aquilon des choses tresaspres et rudes, auquel tous les flots ont

---

[1] Granada, *Le Vray chemin*, 'Exhortation' (by the Bishop of Cuenca), *non pag.*

[2] *Ibid.* fol. 50. Cf. the following passage from Humbert's *Sepmaine saincte*, 'Jesus couronné d'espines', which is remarkably similar, but which is still more evidently concerned with rhetorical ornamentation: 'O Splendeur de la gloire celeste, quel eclypse s'est opposé à vos rayons? fontaine d'eau vive qui serpentés par les quarreaux fleurissants du parterre de la cité de Dieu, qui à (*sic*) troublé le cristal de vostre source? O miroer sans macule, quelles taches ont offusquée la pureté de vostre glace? Sortés, filles de Sion contemplés le vray Salomon qui faict espanoüir les roses de son sang dans les espines de sa couronne' (p. 133).

redondé en vous, je voudrois qu'il nous fut permis d'estre transformez en ceste croix.[1]

It was the work of the *humanisme dévot* movement to apply a similar method in a native French context: this is where Bremond's *Histoire littéraire du sentiment religieux* begins. Further analysis of the period leading up to the publication of the *Introduction* in 1608 might yield some important results for the development of prose style at the turn of the century, but for present purposes it will be sufficient to consider briefly the position represented by the *Introduction* itself.[2] Given that St François was even more preoccupied with the needs of a lay public than Granada, it is not surprising that much of his reputation should rest on his *douceur*, on the accessibility of his devotional manner. The preface to the *Introduction* could be more explicit as a statement of literary intention, but the clues it gives are significant:

Or, affin que le tout fust plus utile et aggreable, je l'ay reveu et y ay mis quelque sorte d'entresuite, adjoustant plusieurs advis et enseignemens propres a mon intention. Mais tout cela je l'ay fait sans nulle sorte presque de loysir; c'est pourquoy tu ne verras rien icy d'exacte, ains seulement un amas d'advertissemens de bonne foy que j'explique par des paroles claires et intelligibles, au moins ay-je desiré de le faire. Et quant au reste des ornemens du langage, je n'y ay pas seulement voulu penser, comme ayant asses d'autres choses a faire.[3]

The overall tone is that of humility; or rather, it is the tone of the humility *topos*, which, like that of the *utile dulci*, is reapplied in the context of the religious literature of the later sixteenth century and after. Some of the phrasing is like Montaigne's ('tu ne verras rien icy d'exacte, ains seulement un amas d'advertissemens de bonne foy...'); and indeed, an avowedly 'negligent' manner of composition is in both writers associated with a reaction against formalism of one kind or another, whether it be scholastic theology or Ciceronianism. The humility, as such, is scarcely justified; and the modern reader might find it strange that a writer renowned for his colourful style should disclaim the 'ornemens du language'. But what St François is aiming at principally is a less self-conscious form of rhetoric, one which will supersede his predecessors' often awkward attempts to reconcile the

---

[1] Alonso de Madrid, *La Methode de servir Dieu*, p. 354.
[2] Other aspects of this problem—in particular the modes of narrative prose—will be considered below in ch. 7.
[3] St François, *Introduction*, ed. cit., 'Préface', p. 7.

sacred and the profane. Certainly there is no doubt that the result was meant to be pleasurable: for St François the *utile* and the *aggreable* were as inseparable as they had been for the Pléiade. As Miss Yates puts it:

That vein of the *utile-doux*—the combination of poetic 'sweetness' and charm with 'useful' truth—which Ronsard and the Pléiade set before themselves as an object, turns up in its purely religious form in the *douceur* of the devotional style of St François. One might make an interesting study of the saint's language in relation to the imagery of the poets of the Pléiade and their academic speeches... [1]

On the other hand, the Pléiade's use of humanist allusion is attenuated in the prose of St François; it was after all hardly his intention to keep the *vulgaire* at arm's length. The imagery is adapted to the persuasive, flattering manner of the spiritual adviser:

L'ame qui remonte du peché à la devotion, est comparée à l'aube, laquelle s'eslevant ne chasse pas les tenebres en mesme instant; mais petit à petit. [2]

The *Introduction* appeared in a decade in which the history of the devotional treatise is closely linked with that of elegant courtly literature: the religious and the secular seem to merge into one another without the least contradiction. As we shall see later, this is particularly true of narrative literature, of the convergence of *roman sentimental* with *roman dévot*. It is a trend which depends on the full establishment of the French vernacular as a language both of literature and of personal religion, and thus has no earlier counterpart (except perhaps in the age of Marguerite de Navarre). Springing from the earliest of the movements associated with the Counter-Reformation, it first appears in France in the 1570s and is thoroughly naturalised and absorbed at a time when César de Nostredame's poetry is appearing and when La Ceppède is preparing for publication his first series of *Théorèmes*.

[1] Yates, *The French Academies*, pp. 283–4.
[2] St François, *op. cit.* p. 26. Recent interest in St François as a prose writer has centred on his 'baroque' characteristics; see I. Buffum, *Studies in the Baroque from Montaigne to Rotrou*, ch. 2; and A. Mor, 'François de Sales e il Barocco', *SF*, 4 (1960), pp. 74 ff. For a more general study of St François's imagery, see H. Lemaire, *Les Images chez Saint François de Sales* (Paris, 1962), and *François de Sales, Docteur de la confiance et de la paix. Etude de spiritualité à partir d'un choix important d'images* (Paris, 1963).

From devotion to poetry

TRANSLATORS AND POETS (1570–1589)

In the reign of Henri III, the interest of secular writers in the devotional revival suddenly becomes apparent in an unprecedented manner. A quantity of prefaces and liminary verse testifies to the change of atmosphere; and the fact that so many of the translators themselves were laymen familiar with profane literature of all kinds already establishes an important link between the realm of humanist letters and the hitherto cloistered world of devotion. Nor could one say that in turning to religious subjects, these translators assume an ascetic, monastic manner: François de Belleforest, while making a distinction between his secular works and his new translation of Granada, nevertheless implies that he has not abandoned the pleasures of literature:

> Ce ne sont des delices et folles mignardises que nous avons traicté jadis en noz livres, ny des subjects d'une vaine eloquence, ains y est le stile doux, coulant, et plain de saincte affection, ravissant les ames à la contemplation de leur Dieu.[1]

There is a certain amount of equivocation here: to substitute a 'stile doux, coulant' for 'delices et folles mignardises' is scarcely a conversion, at least stylistically speaking. For Ronsard, *mignardise* and *stile doux-coulant* were more or less synonymous, and Desportes's love-poetry was soon to become famous for a similar stylistic quality. Belleforest is evidently speaking of subject-matter rather than of what we should call style, or perhaps of both at once: 'des subjects d'une vaine eloquence' and the qualification 'plain de saint affection' are the key phrases. In fact, this 'programme' is very much the same as that put forward in the *Exhortation* of Granada's *Le Vray chemin*, which Belleforest had probably already read and which he was shortly to translate: the subject is devotional, but the manner is none the less attractive.

Here, then, Belleforest is identifying himself with Granada's intention of providing some kind of literary embellishment for devotion. Before this translation first appeared, Guyot had completed his *Meditations des zelateurs de pieté*, for which Belleforest wrote a liminary sonnet: 'François de Belle-Forest, Comingeois au Secretaire Guyot son bon amy.' The conclusion of this sonnet suggests that Belleforest

---

[1] Granada, *Devotes contemplations*, trans. Belleforest, 'Epître dédicatoire', p. iii.

attached importance to Guyot's work as a translation into French: the resolution to raise French to the level of a literary language on the antique scale (which the Pléiade claimed to have inaugurated) had not been forgotten:

> Si que l'on penseroit ou que Guytot est plein
> Des saincts qu'il a traduits, ou que dedans son sein
> Ils parlent à present tous purement François.   (*non pag.*)

More important still, Belleau himself had graced the *Meditations* with a liminary sonnet. Belleau, as much as any other member of the Pléiade and more than most, had worked in the field of Biblical translation and religious poetry;[1] at the same time, he had made a name for himself as a cultivator of *mignardise* (having helped to bring Anacreon into French poetry) and of rich pastoral description. Both of these characteristics stood him in good stead in his *Cantique des cantiques*; both appear in the liminary sonnet for Guyot's translation:

> Mais toy qui as et l'une et l'autre grace,
> Soit d'inventer, ou de suivre à la trace,
> Les pas de ceux qui nous guident le mieux:
> Tu vas suçant (ainsi que les avettes
> Au temps nouveau les odeurs des fleurettes)
> Les saincts tresors des peres les plus vieux.

The bee-image is too commonplace to have much significance on its own account, but it is developed with Belleau's usual fondness for diminutives: the Church Fathers appear to have made contact with one of the most hedonistic currents of Pléiade poetry. Similarly, Chappuys's translation of Estella's *Livre de la vanité du monde*, intended as a supplement to Henri III's devotional programme, contains a liminary sonnet which develops the *vanitas vanitatum* commonplace in the phraseology of profane poetry:

> Vain est le grand credit, vaine est la dignité,
> Vain est le beau parler, vaine est la tresse blonde,
> Vain est l'or et l'argent, vaine est la parenté,
> Bref, vain est tout l'enclos de la machine ronde.   (*non pag.*)

---

[1] The *Seconde journee de la Bergerie*, which appeared in 1572, a year after Guytot's *Meditations*, included the *Prieres et doleances de Job* and the *Amours de David et de Bersabée;* in 1576, there followed the *Eclogues sacrees, prises du Cantique des Cantiques* and the *Discours de la vanité, pris de l'Ecclesiaste*, published with the *Amours et nouveaux eschanges.*

Thus as soon as devotional works are translated in the 1570s, they begin to attract the commonplace apparatus of secular literature— liminary poems, expression of intention to please and so on.

The same tendency is apparent in a more elaborate form in the introductory material for Du Mont's translation of Savonarola's *La Verité de la foy*.[1] This work was published at Douai, and the liminary section has a distinctly local flavour: the dedication (to 'P. Jean Sarrazin Abbé de S. Vaast d'Arras') says that it is intended as a counter-attack on the *De la Verité de la religion chrestienne* (published in 1579) of Philippe de Mornay, who is better known in France than in 'ces Pays-Bas'. The contributions to the liminary section suggest the existence of a group of serious-minded gentlemen with unmistakably literary pretensions and apparently interested in the devotional revival: Du Mont speaks of '...les gens de lettres (desquels j'ay esté tousjours amateur)'.[2] The first liminary poem is a lengthy *Chant de Triomphe de la Croix*, 'par Philippe de Broide, licentié és droictz, Conseillier de la ville de Douay'. It is scarcely in the spirit of the ascetic Savonarola, for the allegorical 'triumph' theme is here clothed in a language which outdoes Du Bartas in pagan reference, weighty vocabulary and onomatopoeia:

> Endosse, mon DU MONT, ta cotte bigarrée
> Pourpointée de croix des Chrestiens la livrée:
> Comme Gonfanonier, et roy d'arme sacré,
> Desploye l'estandart, l'auriflambe pourpré,
> Chantant ïo MON CHRIST, en signe de victoire:
> Puis dresse un chapiteau d'eternele memoire,
> Où soit en lettres d'or azuré sur metal
> Le sainct nom de IESUS luisant comme un crystal
> Dans les rays d'un soleil, comparty par mesure,
> D'un art elabouré surpassant la nature...
> Trantranant de ta trompe, ou de ton cor d'ivoire
> Son ban et riereban, afin qu'il soit notoire.

Then appears '...la croisée banniere / Que tiendra l'almefoy Amazone guerriere', and a whole procession of allegorical 'dames d'honneurs',

> Belles comme le jour, blanches comme l'Aurore,
> Quand Phœbus au matin sa perruque redore...

[1] G. Savonarola, *La Verité de la foy, sous le triomphe de la croix de Jésus*, trans. P. Du Mont (Douai, 1588).

[2] *Ibid.*, dedication, *non pag*. The poem by Philippe de Broïde quoted below is also not paginated.

dragging after them a horde of monsters:

> Ces gobelins faës que d'un docte pinceau
> Fantastique depeint de Bosche en son tableau...

—these intended to represent philosophers, heretics, and so on. The atmosphere gradually changes to a pastoral, with

> ...l'œillet
> Ja ja s'espanissant en bouton vermeillet,
> Que les souefz Zephyrs d'une doulcette alaine
> Muguettent à l'envy...
> Et moy je chanteray d'un pipiant festu,
> D'un fifre chalumeau phireliritutu,
> Ou comme un Darinel, Corydon, ou Tityre,
> D'une muse-abruyant un petit lyrelyre,
> Lyre-lyra-lyré, lyra-lyre-lyron,
> Et puis blyre lyron blyre-lyra-blyron.
> S'on en rit, c'est tout un: mais les hautes buccines
> Enfleront les mieux nez à leurs voix argentines.

Christ is reintroduced, this time in his capacity as Shepherd; and finally de Broïde invites his 'Douysien' friends to join in a pastoral concert— Jean Loys,[1] the author of two of the liminary sonnets, and also of a *Saincte Christiade*, and 'Febvrot', who has sung the praises 'du grand Dieu Pan en sa Machabeïde'.

The character of this religious-literary circle at Douai, for all its absurdities, is of some importance. In the first place, it is clear that the provinces are at least as advanced as Paris in their willingness to connect devotional prose with poetry, if not in their sophistication. No doubt this is the result of a strong local religious influence (largely Jesuit), combined with an attempt on the part of local dignitaries to ape the literary trends of the day. Although they must have been familiar with a considerable amount of devotional literature in translation, Philippe de Broïde and his friends were unable to conceive of poetry in terms other than those of profane traditions. By this time, the idea of a 'muse chrestienne' was firmly established: the influence of Du Bartas had made itself felt among both Catholics and Calvinists. But it was an influence which was hardly favourable to the emergence

---

[1] For further information on the Loys family, and on the existence of a *Puy* at Douai, see below, pp. 194–6. See also, below p. 74.

of an independent devotional poetry. Chappuys's *Figures de la Bible,*
a set of Biblical emblems published in 1582, contains some liminary
stanzes by Antoine Du Verdier, acclaiming Du Bartas as the in-
augurator of the Christian Muse and Chappuys as his heir:

> Au passé jusqu'a huy soubz les plumes lascives
> Les Muses ont esté detenues captives:
>   Mais du Bartas les a mises en liberté,
> Quand d'un stile divin et admirable veine,
> Il a heureusement escrit ceste sepmaine,
>   Où l'ouvrage de Dieu, haultement est chanté.
>
> A l'imitation de ce Poëte grave,
> Chappuys qui tous les jours ses lebvres trempe et lave,
>   En Pirene, a choisi un subjet hault et grand,
> Assavoir, les tableaux de la Saincte escripture,
> Et une stanze a mis soubs chacune figure
>   Qui d'icelle le sens en brefs termes comprend...
>
>   Vive mon du Bartas eternellement, Vive
>   Chappuis mon cher esmoy, que l'un et l'autre escripve
>   Tousjours Poëmes saincts...[1]

Significantly, there is no mention of a possible *rapprochement* between
the Christian Muse and the character of the devotional revival:
Chappuys had not yet begun to publish his translations of the Spanish
devotional masters. Likewise, the anonymous editor of the *Muse
chrestienne* which appeared in the same year was forced to conscript
for the service of his Muse a considerable number of Pléiade poems
which had never been intended to have a religious sense (although he
does include Desportes's recent sacred poetry); and this anthology is
characteristic of a period in which few poets seem to have been aware
of the poetic potentialities of devotional themes and method.

One of the first signs of a different approach is the poetry of Jacques
de Billy. The brothers Jean and Jacques de Billy were among the most
productive advocates of the devotional revival in the early 1570s. The
Carthusian Jean, prior of the Charterhouse of Mont-Dieu, specialised
in the translation of authors associated with the Cologne Charterhouse
(Louis de Blois, Dionysius de Leuwis, Landsberger) whereas Jacques,

---

[1] G. Chappuys, *Figures de la Bible, declarees par stances...Augmentees de grand Nombre de figures aux Actes des Apostres* (Lyons, 1582); Du Verdier's *stanzes* are part of the liminary material for the extra emblems on the *Actes*, fols. AA 3–4.

the Benedictine abbot of Sainct-Michel de l'Herm, produced a variety
of translations and florileges, including the *Recueil des consolations*
already mentioned; and it is in terms of these preoccupations that one
should see Jacques's *Sonnets spirituels*. Each brother favoured the
other's works with liminary poems, usually in Latin, like this 'Ioannis
chatardi ad lectorem Tetrastichon' for his brother's *Recueil des consolations*:

> Sicut apis flores per prata virentia carpit,
> Mellifluos aliis condit et ore favos:
> Sic tibi mellificans struxit mira arte libellum
> Billius ex variis floribus Aurelii.
> Quae veluti sertum bene fragrans, arripe Lector,
> Et plenum gusta melle salutifero.
> Sic fies iucundus odor, sic lumina mentis
> (Ut Ionathae) fient lucidiora tuae.

This compliment coincides with the kind of presentation of translated
devotion we have already been considering; and the liminary sonnet in
French composed by Jean for Jacques's *Sonnets spirituels* is in the same
mood:

> Quelle estoit de David la harpe harmonieuse...
> Tel est de tes doux vers, Billy, la grace heureuse...
> Ainsi toy, rejettant toute lasciveté,
> N'as icy pour subject que toute honnesteté,
> Puisant des Peres saincts une onde salutaire.[1]

Profit and pleasure again, and a substitution of David for Orpheus and
the Muses. But in the second instance there is a difference, for this is a
collection of religious poetry, not a prose treatise; yet it is still linked
with the atmosphere of devotional translation not yet divorced from
the cloister. Indeed, Jacques's own dedication of his poems to his
brother refers to Jean as a paradigm of devotional virtue—'celuy,
duquel toute la vie n'est qu'une perpetuelle croix, et vraye meditation
de mort, ou plustost mort mystique'. What is still more important, the
same dedication, outlining the way in which the collection was conceived, bears out the claim in the title (and in the last line of the liminary
sonnet) that the poems draw on patristic sources. The author describes
a recent illness, during which, being unable to read a great deal, he

---

[1] Jacques de Billy, *Sonnets spirituels, recueillis pour la plus part des anciens théologiens, tant
grecs que latins, avec quelques autres petits traictez poëtiques de semblable matiere* (Paris,
1573), liminary material, *non pag.*

meditated on passages from the Fathers; and since he found this material somewhat indigestible, he decided to add 'par maniere de saulse la douceur de la poesie'. He chose the sonnet-form as being shorter and less tiring: 'ne prenant que brieves sentences, ores je faisois quelque petit sonnet, ores un autre'. The commentaries that follow the sonnets frequently specify the source, and although there is a strong admixture of classical antiquity—Plato, Aristotle, Homer, Virgil, Seneca, Pliny, Plutarch—and of more recent writers like Erasmus, Jacques supports his poems again and again with references to Christian sources (the Bible, Augustine, Gregory, Lactantius, Bernard). Many develop the theme of death, the misery of life and the corruption of the world in the manner of Billy's own *Recueil des consolations*; and if at times the phraseology tends to be too anonymous to be completely convincing, one can quote examples of a devotional connexion which is fully explicit. The sixty-second sonnet, *Des degreʒ d'illumination spirituelle*, elaborates an idea which according to the commentary was taken from Gerson:

> Si tost qu'on jecte au feu du bois plein de verdeur,
> Soudain on ne voit pas la matiere allumee.
> Premier on voit sortir une obscure fumee,
> Du feu n'estant encor assez forte l'ardeur.
> Apres venant plus fort à se cuire l'humeur,
> En sort quelque clarté, mais non guere enflammee.
> En fin estant du tout la vapeur consumee,
> Le feu, non ja fumeux, monte en haut de roideur.
> Ainsi qui de long temps aveugle et miserable
> Du ciel n'a contemplé la lumiere admirable,
> Clair soudain il ne voit que ses yeux sont ouvers.
> Premier comme de nuict se mect à tastonner,
> Puis les hommes il voit comme arbres cheminer,
> En fin il vient à voir tout à clair l'univers. (fols. 79–80.)

This exposition of a mystical theory in terms of an emblematic image has precisely the character of Tauler's 'gibbet' image. Its purpose is analytic and explanatory: it does not aim at the emotional involvement of the reader. The tone of Billy's poems is often on this level, and is thus only to a limited extent 'devotional', if devotion appeals to the *volonté* as well as to the *entendement*. On the other hand, the poem which concludes the cycle of sonnets (it is entitled *Conclusion, avec une priere à Dieu*), suggests a devotional application; at the same time, the familiar bee-image and the reference to patristic sources reappear:

> Ainsi qu'on voit l'abeille, au labeur diligente,
> Voler par cy par là, les fleurettes pillant:
> Ainsi des Peres vieux les escrits recueillant,
> Cet œuvre ay fait pour l'ame à son Dieu souspirante...
> O dieu de mon salut, ô source de douceur,
> Qui jamais ne taris, fais moy cette faveur,
> Que ma vie à mes vers en rien ne contrarie.
> Ne permets, ô Seigneur, que par un tel discord
> Je me juge moy-mesme, et en mode d'Urie
> Sur moy vienne à porter les lettres de ma mort.   (fol. 149.)

The remainder of the work, consisting of longer poems, sustains this atmosphere. *Des Tromperies de ce Monde*, for example, is a poem of personal confession and repentance, developing the penitential themes of corruption and *ordure*:

> Aussi j'avois un esprit si privé
> De tout bon sens, le goust si depravé,
> Que doux m'estoit l'amer, et chose pure
> Je reputois de vice estre l'ordure.
> L'obscur m'estoit pour la claire lueur
> Du Midy plein (ô estat fort estrange!)
> Mon malheur grand j'estimois à grand heur,
> M'esjouissant en mon horrible fange.[1]

Later there is an *Action de grâces à Dieu apres estre sorty d'une griefve maladie: où est aussi joincte une complaincte sur le trop grand desir de cette vie*, which anticipates a whole series of 'sickness' poems in penitential mood by contemporary poets.

Five years later, a second book of sonnets appeared. This volume is dedicated to Magdelaine de Savoie, and the *dédication* describes at some length the atmosphere of contemporary devotion and the part played in it by Billy's own works, explicitly connecting his sonnets with his other *escrits* (including, presumably, the *Recueil des consolations*):

Madame, voyant qu'en ce temps malheureux ou nous sommes de present, et qui tend ouvertement à un abominable Atheisme, se trouvant neantmoins par la grace de nostre Dieu maintes personnes, qui n'ont rien en plus grande recommendation que son honneur et le salut de leurs ames, entretenans en

---

[1] *Ibid.* fol. 158. This poem combines the tone of confession with that of admonition.

leur cœur, le mieux qu'il leur est possible, le feu de charité et saincte devotion, par la lecture de certains livres plains de pieté: cela m'induict y a quelque temps, entre autres escrits traictans de cette matiere, jetter en lumiere un petit Opuscule de Sonnets spirituels, dequel il me sembloit qu'il se pourroit recueillir pour les gens de bien quelque consolation et utilité.[1]

He goes on to say that St Augustine provided him with a model for this literary 'relaxation':

Que si un si sainct personnage, et qui avoit les nerfs assez roides, et les pieds assez forts, pour marcher tousjours par chemins aspres et raboteux, a neantmoins voulu par fois prendre la prairie, et recreer son esprit par la meditation des choses plus douces: combien plus ont besoing de tel remede ceux, qui sont autant esloignez de sa saincteté et doctrine, que le Levant est du Ponant?

These passages, with their imagery of accessibility and sweetness, stressing the need to provide, through the pleasures of poetry, for a lay audience unused to the stony paths of monastic or theological meditation, anticipate much that is to follow in later years and represent perhaps the most significant single aspect of Billy's work.

Although Billy makes little or no reference to the Incarnation, the Passion, or the saints, we have here already many of the elements which are necessary for the constitution of a devotional poetry. His contemporary Marin Le Saulx produced a work of much smaller dimensions but with a preface as extended and as explicit in its own way as anything in the *Sonnets spirituels*. The *Theanthropogamie* is a collection of sonnets based on the Song of Solomon, 'duquel j'ay pris quasi de mot à mot, la plus part de ce qui est contenu en tout ce mien petit traitté'.[2] The use of the word *traitté* suggests something other than a mere collection of religious poems, and the exposition of the allegory is in fact done in semi-theological terms, both in the poems themselves and in the preface, where Marin mentions for example the theory of the 'communication des proprietez' as explaining the mystery of the Incarnation (p. 29). The same is true of the sonnets where he deals specifically with the Redemption:

...j'adjouste le moyen par lequel ce sainct salut est advancé par iceluy Jesus Christ. Sur ce point je parle fort au long de la naissance, mort, sepulture,

---

[1] Jacques de Billy, *Sonnets spituels...Livre second* (Paris, 1578), dedication, *non pag.*

[2] Marin Le Saulx, *Theanthropogamie en forme de dialogue par sonnets chrestiens* (London, 1577), 'Au Lecteur', p. 7. The references to Marin's exile and his fear of condemnation in the preface suggest that he was a Protestant, or at least that he held suspect beliefs.

resurrection, ascension et dernier jugement de Jesus Christ le fils de Dieu. (p. 32.)

In these poems, the potential narrative element of the life of Christ is absorbed into the love-dialogue between Christ and his 'bride' (see below, p. 240, n. 1); the episodes are dealt with in figurative terms to such an extent that one has difficulty at times in following their sequence, unlike La Ceppède's meditations, where the phases of the 'story' are perfectly clear. Indeed, Marin admits that the appeal of his work is limited because of its complex allegorical nature:

...comme de vray il nest pas le plus utille de tous ceux que l'on pourroit bien mettre en avant, pour estre enveloppé de beaucoup de façons de parler figurees, ausquelles le vulgaire simple n'entend que le haut Alleman (ainsi que porte le proverbe) aussi n'est-il pas vuide de toute utilité. (p. 33.)

On the other hand, by referring to the 'vulgaire simple', he is perhaps hoping to flatter a more intelligent lay audience to whom the allegories would be comprehensible. Moreover, this is poetry, and the poetic form has been chosen because it is more attractive: once again, religious poetry is competing with profane,[1] and if Marin is careful to point out in his preface the hidden significance of his sensual imagery it is because he wishes to retain its sensuality in full. Furthermore, the mystical language of love, fire and *ravissement* is much in evidence in the sonnets, and is defended in the preface:

Ceste façon de parler peut sembler dure: O que d'amour divin la douceur est cruelle, mais il la faut prendre comme poëtique, et est a vray dire une façon de parler excessive, par laquelle l'Eglise est ravie en admiration de l'extreme bonté de Dieu, qui pour sauver l'homme pecheur, n'a point espargné son Fils innocent. (p. 31.)

Thus the *Theanthropogamie* combines physical detail both with allegorical interpretation and with affectivity—the three modes of devotional practice. The meditative character of the work is confirmed by a passage which occurs towards the end of the preface, modifying the initial concept of a *traitté*: '...que je peusse en ce faisant par quelques sainctes meditations loüer nostre Dieu souverain et tout bon.' (p. 34.)

This was in 1577.[2] Since 1575 Desportes had been including religious

---

[1] Cf. *ibid.* pp. 36–7.
[2] This was the publication date; but according to the preface, the poems were written in 1568–9.

poems—*stances* and sonnets—in his collections of poetry; the largest group to date also came out in 1577, and contains a sonnet with this quatrain:

> Seigneur, d'un de tes cloux je veux faire ma plume,
> Mon encre de ton sang, mon papier de ta Croix,
> Mon subject de ta gloire, et les chants de ma voix
> De ta mort, qui la mort éternelle consume.[1]

Elsewhere, Desportes formulates his programme for religious poetry according to the usual 'rivalry' commonplaces (this same sonnet begins with a rejection of profane love for sacred); but here he is proposing the Passion as a subject in its own right. His poetry is to be transformed or rather reborn by something very like meditation on the Passion; at the same time contact with the tradition of profane love-poetry is maintained through the *pointe* of the last line (which could come from the Christian tradition or from Petrarch). Desportes in fact never carried out the full implications of this programme: most of his poetry is concerned with the 'evening' themes of confession and penitence, with only a handful of sonnets on New Testament themes. In the overall economy of his work, the psalm-paraphrases clearly play a central part; and this goes a long way towards explaining why his most interesting devotional poetry is based on a pattern of themes and style which frequently recalls the Old Testament. On the other hand, as we have seen, his later prayers and meditations in prose are chiefly concerned with the Passion, and apply in abbreviated form many of the techniques of Jesuit meditation, thus providing an important link in the series of connexions between poetry and devotion.

Desportes's influence was not slow to make itself felt among the lesser poets of the Louvre circle. One of these, however, anticipated and outstripped most of his colleagues in his approach to the problem of transferring devotion into poetry: this was Jean de Boyssières, who was at one time *secrétaire de la Chambre* at the court of Henri.[2] His *Troisiesmes œuvres*, which appeared in 1579 (when even Desportes had produced very little religious poetry), include a number of *Prieres*

[1] P. Desportes, *Œuvres*, ed. A. Michiels (Paris, 1858), p. 503. On the dating of Desportes's work, and on his career in general, see J. Lavaud, *Un Poète de cour au temps des derniers Valois: Ph. Desportes (1546–1606)* (Paris, 1936).
[2] See T. Graur, *Un Disciple de Ronsard—Amadis Jamyn, 1540 (?)–1593: sa vie, son œuvre, son temps* (Paris, 1929), references to Boyssières listed in Index; and F. Fleuret and L. Perceau, *Les Satires françaises du xvie siècle*, vol. 1 (Paris, 1922), pp. 244–50.

spirituelles et sonets chrestiens, some of which come very close to poetic meditation on aspects of the life of Christ; particularly important is a set of six or seven poems intended to accompany the various stages in the taking of Holy Communion.[1] In spite of his connexion with the court, Boyssières seems to have remained attached to his native Clermont-Ferrand, and it may be that his provincial environment played a part in his precocity as a devotional poet. In many areas, the medieval *Puy* tradition had been maintained, and Clermont-Ferrand itself is in the heart of the country where this tradition originated. The poetry written for the annual competitions was as often as not religious, the themes being centred on the Virgin Mary, and thus on the life of Christ: and since Boyssières's earlier religious poetry was written before the devotional tendencies of Henri III's reign became predominant, it is at least possible that his choice of subject was determined in part by his provincial background, even if the forms he chose (the sonnet in particular) were those in fashion at court.

One other work published before 1580, Guy Le Fèvre's *Hymnes ecclésiastiques, Cantiques spirituelʒ, et autres Meslanges Poëtiques* (Paris, 1578, reprinted 1582), must have made a considerable impact on the growth of religious poetry. This collection is composed primarily of translations by Le Fèvre of a number of Neo-Latin and Italian poems, mostly of some length, and including Dante's *Vergine madre, figlia del tuo figlio*, Petrarch's *Vergine bella*, several Neo-Latin poems by later Italian poets like Sannazaro and Vida, and Du Bellay's Latin poem on the Nativity, *In Natalem Diem*. The collection as a whole is addressed to Henri III, but each poem is dedicated either to a prominent figure of the Counter-Reformation—Maldonat, Génébrard, Jacques de Billy, Geoffroy de Billy—or to a scholar or poet (Dorat, Ronsard, Baïf). The translations are followed by a group of poems by Le Fèvre himself: one of these is an *Hymne à Jesus-Christ nostre Seigneur de ses victoires et triomphes*, dedicated to Ronsard and covering nearly sixty pages, but there are also shorter poems including some *chants royaux* which attest his interest in the *Jeux Floraux*. Le Fèvre's tone is fre-

---

[1] Boyssières seems to have published at least two other collections of religious poetry: *Les Œuvres spirituelles* (Lyons, 1582), and *Sonnets sur les noms et passion de Jesus-Christ* (Paris, 1585)—the title of the latter work looks interesting, but since, according to Cioranesco, it only contains 8 fols., it is clearly not a major sequence. Unfortunately, I have been unable to discover any copy of either work.

quently learned, and the poems he chooses to translate are sometimes nearer to theological exposition than to devotional practice; nevertheless, he draws attention to the existence of a tradition (largely Italian) of serious religious poetry, and his naturalisation of foreign and Neo-Latin material must have suggested many new points of departure to other poets at court.

In the following decade, the increasingly devotional atmosphere of Henri III's reign provokes a spate of religious poems from the disciples of Desportes, from Amadis Jamyn, Joachim Blanchon, Guillaume Du Peyrat, Isaac Habert, and the young Malherbe. Significantly, Desportes's brief statement of devotional intention is echoed by more than one of these poets. Blanchon's *Priere quotidienne* (an elaboration of the Lord's Prayer) includes this tercet:

> Que de l'un de tes Cloux je choysisse ma Plume,
> Mon ancre de ton Sang de ta Croix le volume,
> Ou j'escrive ton loz hautement glorifié.[1]

Similarly, Habert's third sonnet in the *Œuvres chrestiennes*:

> Je prendray de ton chef une pointe d'espine
> Pour faire mon burin, et de ton monument
> La pierre où j'escriray ta louange divine,
> Ta grace donnera à mon œuvre ornement.[2]

Between them, the Louvre poets cover most of the themes available in the devotional context: penitence and confession in the manner of the Old Testament, analysis of the Eucharist ceremony, penitential contemplation of the Passion, meditation on Creation, and quasi-mystical invocations of divine love. Nevertheless, there is a certain lack of overall purpose in their poetry, which at times suggests a somewhat hasty adjustment to fashion rather than a considered programme for the recreation of poetry in devotional terms. A few poems—a handful of sonnets and some of the longer poems of Jamyn and Habert—show clear signs of the emergence of devotional poetry proper, and have their own independent character and value; but the general picture is fragmentary. What is important here, apart from the individual achievements, is the fact that devotion and poetry have become linked

---

[1] J. Blanchon, *Les Premieres œuvres poetiques* (Paris, 1583), p. 187.
[2] I. Habert, *Les Trois livres des Meteores avecques autres œuvres poëtiques* (Paris, 1585), *Œuvres chrestiennes*, fol. 2.

in the context of court society, a society renowned (at least among its Calvinist critics) for its self-indulgence, its love of profane pleasures as well as for its devotionalism. The example of this court no doubt had a substantial influence on the formation of provincial circles, and in many respects it prefigures the fashionable devotional society of the early seventeenth century.

Meanwhile, the Calvinist poets had been far from inactive. Although the religious drama, founded by Bèze and continued by Des Masures, had been flourishing for some time, their first major contribution to religious lyric poetry was the anthology of *Poèmes chrestiens* published at Geneva in 1574.[1] This collection includes a number of extended poems, largely penitential and closely linked with the Psalms, by Montméja, Tagaut, Bèze and others, and a cycle of odes and sonnets by Goulart. One of the more interesting of the longer poems is Montméja's *La Solitude*, recommending solitary meditation and implying a progression from penitence to divine love:

> Quand Solitude est avec nous,
> Nous pouvons lors à deux genoux,
> Sans nuls tesmoins, sans nulle fainte,
> Invoquer ta majesté saincte,
> O Dieu: implorant tes bontez
> Pour laver nos iniquitez.
> Alors de nulle hypocrisie
> Nostre pensee n'est saisie,
> Car l'homme ne nous apperçoit,
> Nul, fors que le ciel ne nous voit.
> C'est alors que pleure et lamente
> L'ame, en son malheur gemissante,
> Ornant tous ses meilleurs desirs
> De vrayes larmes et souspirs,
> Et devant toy, Pere celeste,
> De son amendement proteste.
> Par toy, Solitude, nos cœurs
> Sentent les divines ardeurs
> Brusler nos pensees mauvaises,

---

[1] On the question of the Protestant attitude to style, both in poetry and prose, with reference particularly to Bèze, see M. Richter, 'La Poetica di Théodore de Bèze e le Chrestiennes Méditations', *Ævum*, 38 (1964), pp. 479 ff. See also the same author's 'Philippe du Plessis-Mornay: un aspetto del manierismo poetico protestante', in *Contributi dell'Istituto di Filologia moderna*, Serie francese, 3 (Milan, 1964), pp. 1 ff.

> Comme en ces ardantes fournaises
> La chaume est fait en un moment
> La proye du chaud element.   (p. 36.)

Here, a concept of devotion is being stated explicitly in poetry; and the application of this concept is strikingly illustrated by two other poems in the collection. The *Meditation chrestienne* of a certain A.I.[1] is a carefully structured poem which takes certain natural phenomena as a starting-point for meditation:

> Quand j'apperçoy ce grand flambeau des cieux,
> Cacher sous l'eau ses raiz loin de nos yeux,
> Et que la nuict sur les mortels s'avance:
> Lors à penser aux tenebres je vien
> De mon peché inique et ancien,
> Qui de mon bien m'oste la connoissance.   (p. 78.)

The night of sin is redeemed by the sun of grace; then follow similar antitheses in terms of winter and summer, autumn and spring, and the final stanza brings together the three parallels:

> Donques de moy rien sortir je ne vois,
> Qu'obscurité, froid et mort chasque fois,
> De nuict, d'hiver, et de malheur suivie.
> Mais j'ay pour jour, pour esté, pour beautemps,
> Ta grace seule, o Seigneur, dont j'attens
> Incessamment clarté, chaleur et vie.   (p. 79.)

Similarly, *Le Voyage de la montagne*, a much longer and more loosely organised poem by one E.D.P., recounts a day's expedition into the mountains made by the poet and a few friends: each episode of the walk is considered in terms of its religious significance. Such poems suggest that a simple, direct and personal form of meditation may have been common among Calvinists, contrasting with the elaborate devotional procedures recommended by the handbooks of the Catholics: one catches here something of the mood of Herbert, though there are certainly Catholic parallels too, as we shall see later.

---

[1] It has been suggested to me that this could be Amadis Jamyn. In certain respects the thematic and stylistic evidence would not conflict with this view: Jamyn was much concerned with meditation on the Creation, and the rhetorical organisation of the poem suggests a writer who had studied the technique of poetry as practised by the Pléiade. However, the sharp opposition between sin and grace implies a Calvinist view, and it seems unlikely either that Jamyn should write such a poem or that he should have it published in a uniformly Calvinist anthology. There is no evidence in Miss Graur's study to suggest a clandestine interest in Calvinism.

Apart from their significance in anticipating certain patterns which will soon become prevalent among Catholic poets (I am thinking here particularly of the penitential lyric), the poems of this collection show signs of a willingness to borrow some of the equipment of profane poetry. True, the poems so far quoted—Montméja's *Solitude* is an obvious case, and Tagaut has a similar manner—are sober and unadorned in style. Nevertheless, the anthology was published in the same year as Du Bartas's *Muse chrestienne*, and Goulart predicts the achievements of his colleague in the first ode of his *Imitations:*

> Quelqu'un plus docte et plus ardant,
> Sur l'arc d'une saincte Uranie,
> A nos françois ira dardant
> Les traits de ta gloire infinie. (p. 83.)

Du Bartas is not named; but one of Goulart's sonnets, combining mythological allusion, the Creation theme, and a compound participle, bears the mark of the poet whose example caused a general breakaway from the early Calvinist austerity:

> Lors que de l'Ocean Phœbus son char approuche...
> J'esleve lors mon cœur, et mes yeux et ma bouche
> A toy, qui as creé tant et tant d'animaux
> Courans-volans en terre, en l'air, et par les eaux,
> Et dessus le doux luth tes louanges je touche. (p. 147.)

Similarly, Montméja's fourth ode recommends psalm-singing in terms which are hardly reminiscent of the most severe Calvinist spirit:

> Prenez le luth, l'espinette et hautbois,
> Pour inviter les Dryades des bois,
> A resonner la douceur de ces Hymnes. (p. 9.)

Indeed, Desportes is stricter in this respect than his Protestant contemporaries: his *Œuvres chrestiennes* contain no classical imagery or allusion at all, and he admits to the heresy of which the Pléiade had been accused by some ('...les faulses louanges / De mille et mille dieux estranges / Que j'ay chantez trop follement'), and promises reform.[1]

---

[1] Ed. Michiels, p. 511. Another example of the problems posed by the 'pagan myths' is Béroalde de Verville's poem *Les Cognoissances nécessaires*. Béroalde recounts the Androgyne myth (*Les Appréhensions spirituelles* (Paris, 1583), fols. 15–16); then, in a fit of remorse, he says 'J'avois deliberé de ne me profaner / Aux fables des payans' (fol. 16). The following passage gives arguments on both sides, leaving the question unanswered: Béroalde is clearly embarrassed by it.

The same trend is continued in many of the subsequent productions of the Calvinist group. This is especially true of Poupo, who can adapt his style from the soberest tone of penitence to a rich *mignardise* or to the *emphase* of Du Bartas;[1] and at much the same time, Protestant Neo-Latin poets like Lect and Jaquemot are combining the elegances of classical Latin poets with religious subjects.[2]

Other anthologies followed the *Poèmes chrestiens*: the most outstanding are the Maisonfleur collections, in which the editorial policy is surprisingly liberal, gathering together poems by both Protestant and Catholic poets. The number of Protestant poets writing in this period, whether for the anthologies or for individual collections, is formidable—Maisonfleur himself, Sautemont, Chandieu, Du Chesne, Poupo, Odet de La Noue—but if one is thinking of an explicit connexion between meditational poetry and prose, the work of d'Aubigné, Duplessis-Mornay and Sponde is clearly crucial. For d'Aubigné (as for La Ceppède a few years later), psalm-paraphrases and prose meditation go hand in hand; while Sponde's psalm-meditations, though not directly connected with his poetry, are very much a work of literature as well as of religious reflection. Indeed, Sponde's 'discovery' of the Psalms as a source of poetic inspiration, enthusiastically described in a letter he wrote to his brother Henri in 1582 to accompany some Latin poems,[3] seems to anticipate the 'fureur poetique' of Favre; and his two series of *Stances de la Cene* are in effect short Communion meditations in verse. An equally striking connexion between prose and poetry occurs in the case of Duplessis-Mornay: not only does his *Discours de la vie et de la mort* include an *Ode* of similar material, but the Catholic Chassignet seems also to have based many of his poems on the same work.[4] The area in which Calvinist meditation can influence poetry is limited, on the whole, to the penitential themes, and it owes so much to Old Testament paraphrase that it is often difficult to see which way the influence went. But within this area, the amount of evidence available is considerable, and the level of achievement is

[1] See M. Jeanneret, 'Pierre Poupo: Recherches sur le sacré et le profane dans la poésie religieuse du xvie siècle', *Bulletin annuel de la Fondation suisse*, University of Paris, xiv (1965), pp. 15 ff.
[2] See below, p. 98, note 2.
[3] Quoted in French translation by A. M. Boase in his *Introduction* to Sponde's *Méditations*, p. xxvi.
[4] See M. Richter, 'Una fonte calvinista di J. B. Chassignet', *BHR*, 26 (1964), pp. 341 ff.

so high in the poetry of Sponde and Chassignet that a study of penitential poetry in this period must pay tribute to the Calvinist contribution.

THE PROVINCIAL POETS (1590–1613)

We have already seen that non-professional poets writing outside court circles—Billy, Marin Le Saulx—had from the outset been making a significant contribution to the development of devotional poetry; and this trend will continue and reach its climax in the next two decades. In the late 1580s, a local magistrate, Pierre Tamisier, 'President en l'election de Masconnois', was specialising in the verse-translation of devotional texts, and was thus in his own way producing some highly-developed devotional verse. In 1587 he published the pseudo-Augustine meditations, then in 1588 a series of meditations on the Penitential Psalms 'mises en vers françois, sur la prose d'un docte personnage de ce temps', together with Savonarola's meditation on Psalm 51. All these meditations are rendered in the popular six-line *stance* form; and the psalm-meditations are prefaced by a 'sonnet de l'autheur' which establishes the now familiar connexion with profane traditions:

> Dieu sera mon Phebus, mon Castalide chœur,
> Sa loy mon Helicon, son zele mon ardeur,
> Sa grace mon laurier, et le ciel mon Parnase.[1]

As well as translating prose devotion, Tamisier paraphrased in verse most of the available material in the Bible, apart from the Psalms, and in addition some medieval verse: his *Cantiques, hymnes, et prieres*, published in 1590, contain for example the Lamentations, the *Benedicite*, the *Magnificat* and *Nunc dimittis*, and the *Stabat mater*. Tamisier's work reminds one strongly of a passage from Granada, in which prayers in verse are recommended as part of the preparatory stage of meditation:

Et souvent ses (*sic*) oraisons servent mieux estans en vers, et en rithme, telles que sont plusieurs proses, et hymnes de saincts: d'autant que les parolles de Dieu ont ne sçay quelle harmonie en ce stile, lesquelles attirent avec elles plus de douceur et souëfveté pour noz ames. Ainsi nous trouvons és œuvres de sainct Bonaventure...plusieurs de tels hymnes: et d'aucuns en sainct Bernard, et grand nombre és escrits d'autres saincts personnages.[2]

[1] P. Tamisier, *Meditations chrestiennes sur les sept Psalmes de la Penitence* (Paris, 1588), liminary pieces, *non pag.*   [2] Granada, *Le Vray chemin*, fol. 178.

It seems that Tamisier was acquainted with a more illustrious president, Antoine Favre, the leading jurist of Savoy, since he wrote a liminary sonnet for Favre's tragedy *Les Gordians*.[1] This connexion is significant, for it suggests that the provincial poets were often very much aware of one another's activities, and that they felt themselves to be united in a common cause. Favre went to Burgundy in 1588, and he may well have met Tamisier on that occasion; more important, he paid several visits to Provence (notably in 1590 and 1592, when the composition of his first *centurie* cannot have been far off), and it is hard to believe that he did not meet La Ceppède and his friends there: 'Vers la fin de septembre 1590 il arriva à Nice où l'attendaient des membres du Parlement d'Aix et divers autres personnages du pays' (Mugnier, p. 123).

A year after the first publication of Desportes's prose meditations and the *Imitation des Pseaumes de la Penitence* of La Ceppède, Favre published his *Centurie premiere de sonets spirituels de l'amour divin et de la pénitence*. The title in itself is not unusual: 'amour divin' and 'pénitence' had often been associated (as for example in Blanchon's *Premieres œuvres*), perhaps by a convenient analogy with the themes of profane love, but this time, from the first page, the devotional atmosphere is unmistakable. The work is dedicated to François de Sales himself, 'Prevost de l'Eglise Cathedrale de Sainct Pierre de Geneve', and the circumstances of its conception are given in some detail:

> ... pendant mon sejour à Necy, ces mois passés vous me fistes concevoir le desir de m'esgayer dans ce champ si spatieux de la poesie spirituelle... Malaisement eussiez vous peu gaigner ce point sur mon obeissance, si vous n'eussiez attaché à vostre commandement toute l'estoffe qui me faisoit de besoing, et une bonne partie de la façon. La commodité aussi du lieu et du temps n'y servit pas de peu. C'estoit le jour feste saincte Magdeleine, guide et exemplaire des vrais Penitens: Au retour d'ouir la saincte Messe, en la chapelle des devots Peres Capuccins... En la ville de Necy, riche et peuplee de gens religieux, et lesquels animés par l'exemple d'un des plus devots et plus dignes Prelats qui vivent, ne respirent autre que la pieté.[2]

---

[1] See F. Mugnier, *Histoire et correspondance du premier Président Favre* (Paris, 1902–3), vol. I, p. 28.

[2] A. Favre, *Centurie premiere de sonets spirituels de l'amour divin et de la pénitence* (Chambéry, 1595), pp. 4–5. The phrase 'ce champ si spatieux de la poesie spirituelle' is reminiscent of the 'prairie' image of the dedication of Billy's *Livre second*. Whether or not the link is a direct one, Favre could well have read and been encouraged by Billy's work (which is after all dedicated to Magdelaine de Savoie). Billy's use of the image—and

Favre consistently avoids the humility *topos* in this dedication by attributing much of the subject-matter to St François himself:

Je ne veux ny ne doy dire que ce ne soit rien qui vaille. La dignité du subject me dementiroit, et la gentillesse de plusieurs belles conceptions, lesquelles il m'est permis de louer, non à vous, puis que pour la plus-part elles sont vostres. (p. 6.)

The implications of these passages are rich. The phrase 'm'esgayer dans ce champ si spatieux de la poesie spirituelle' suggests that poetry was coming to be considered a natural means of expression for religious thought and emotion, constituting its own 'field' or *genre*, within which a wide range of possibilities was open to the poet. Earlier religious poets (especially provincial ones) had felt the need to defend themselves against possible criticism from the 'professionals'; and their efforts to convert profane poetry often had an atmosphere of constraint—they lacked optimism and confidence. The concept of 'pleasure', too, comes quite naturally to Favre and seems to have ousted 'utility', which is taken for granted. François de Sales must have taken considerable interest in 'poesie spirituelle' if, as Favre says, he supplied a good deal of both the matter and the method. Perhaps he had written some himself; at any rate, his personal influence in the conception of a book of religious sonnets is clearly of the first importance. The final touch is added by the penitential atmosphere of 'le jour feste saincte Magdeleine', and by the association with the 'devots Peres Cappucins'—the order which recreated Franciscanism in terms of Bonaventura's mysticism.

The preface *Au Lecteur devot* (notice the addition of the adjective) gives more invaluable details. After drawing the usual parallels between sacred and profane love as poetic themes, Favre tells how he first wrote a few sonnets, which were approved by his friends (another literary circle?): 'Dés lors je pris courage, et me laissay emporter à ceste fureur poetique, jusques au dernier vers de ceste premiere centurie' (pp. 9–10).

possibly Favre's—may derive from the following passage from the *Meditationes* of the pseudo-Augustine (Migne, *Patrologia latina*, vol. 40, p. 917): 'Hujus rei gratia Scripturarum sanctarum amœna prata ingredior, viridissimas sententiarum herbas exarando carpo, legendo comedo, frequentando rumino, atque congregando tandem in alta memoriae sede repono: ut tali modo tua dulcedine degustata, minus istius miserrimae vitae amaritudines sentiam.' It is in any case interesting to establish a parallel in patristic literature for the popular 'bee' image, a parallel which might give considerable encouragement to the apologist of an attractive devotional literature. This passage appears in French translation in Guyot, *Les Meditations des zelateurs de pieté*, fol. 54, and in the extracts referred to above, pp. 20–1.

In spite of what he says in the dedication, he seems loath to part with the humility *topos*: he hopes that the content will please in spite of the 'laide forme'. What is more interesting is the continuation of this idea. If the work fails to please, he will keep his meditations

reserrees en mon ame, pour luy faire sentir plus vivement la pointe et la douceur des consolations celestes. Peut estre sera-ce mon mieux, de peur que je n'experimente en moy, ce qu'autrefois j'ay ouy dire à plusieurs grands et devots Predicateurs, qu'ilz espreuvent communement que la communication des conceptions devotes (quoy qu'elle aye beaucoup plus de merite que la meditation seule) se treuve neantmoins le plus souvent en perte, et suyvie d'une extreme tiedeur, pour ne dire tout outre refroidissement de l'esprit, à cause de ceste exhalation qui se faict, des plus vives et impatientes estincelles qui soyent en l'ame. J'espere toutefois en la bonté de Dieu, que ce feu qui commence seulement à s'allumer en moy, ne sera pas si tost esteint. (p. 11.)

Favre's poems then are meant to be used for private meditation, whether by the reader or by the poet himself; he is concerned with the publication of his poetry as a kind of 'predication', and its advantages and disadvantages for the practice of devotion; and the 'fureur poetique' has now become associated with the fervour of religious meditation. If one adds to this the fact that a group of four sonnets following the *Centurie* is entitled *Meditations preparatoires à la saincte communion*, it becomes clear that religious poetry is now being written not only to outdo profane poetry, or to 'instruct' in a more or less religious manner, but also as an appropriate means of expression of religious emotion within the pattern of private devotion. It is reasonable to assume that Favre had read many of the handbooks associated with the devotional revival and that he considered his poetry as belonging to the same atmosphere. His *Centurie premiere* comes as the first climax of a development which involves both the court poets and the provincial poets. Although his sonnets do not follow a clear-cut sequence like those of Anne de Marquets, the explicit nature of his programme suggests that the preparatory work of the 1570s and 1580s is now beginning to bear fruit: poets have become conscious of the potentialities of devotional material. Moreover, his poetry is of a much higher quality than that of many of his predecessors, exploiting with considerable intelligence the themes of penitence and the Passion in the context of the sonnet-form.

Favre continued to write devotional poetry, as the title *Centurie premiere* suggests. In 1602, he published a collection of *Stances sur la devotion de nostre Dame du Mont-de-Vic*; these are of some interest but they are overshadowed by the *Entretiens spirituels* of the same year, which add a further two *centuries*, one on the Eucharist, the other a fully-developed sequence on the Passion meditations of the Rosary. As we shall see later in more detail, this last sequence suggests a change in attitude which is significant in the light of contemporary developments of devotional taste: complexities of thought and humanist allusions are dropped in favour of a more emotive tone. One remembers in reading these sonnets that not only was Favre a close friend of St François, he will also join with him in forming the *Académie florimontane*, where he will converse with d'Urfé, writer of the 'livre de tous les courtisans'.[1]

The year 1594 had also seen the publication of Chassignet's *Mespris*. Chassignet lived at Besançon, which is not so far from Burgundy, and he too may possibly have known Tamisier. In the absence of any evidence of such a contact, however, it is wiser to emphasise his debt to Duplessis-Mornay, Montaigne and Lipsius, which suggests a relationship not only between prose and poetry or Protestant and Catholic, but also between devotion and the humanism of the late sixteenth century. At the same time, Chassignet's preface indicates that he thought of his poetry as springing from the death and destruction of the civil wars, and in this respect he is backward-looking by comparison with Favre.[2] Yet the poetry of the *Mespris* contains very little precise contemporary allusion, either polemical or elegiac: external misfortune leads the poet to inward meditation.

In Chassignet's work, the relationship between devotional prose and poetry is still somewhat tenuous, since his sources, though often precise, are not derived from the main current of devotional writing.

---

[1] See Mugnier, *Histoire et correspondance*, pp. 211–12. Cioranesco mentions a later collection, *Les Meditations spirituelles de A.F.* (*s. l.*, 1612), but I have been unable to trace this as yet.

[2] See *Le Mespris de la vie et consolation contre la mort* (Besançon, 1594), p. 12, 'Preface au lecteur': 'Je choisis un sujet conforme au malheur de nostre siecle, ou les meurdres, assassins, parjuremens, rebellions, felonnies, violemens, et seditions... semblent avoir planté l'Empire, et domination de leur desloyauté, et tandis que l'horreur de tant de carnages, et tueries fidellement rapportees à nos oreilles, me frappoit si rudement l'imagination, je conclus en moy-mesme de marcher en la piste de la mort...'.

Tamisier's pseudo-Augustine paraphrase had been an important step in this direction, but the tendency to associate prose and poetry was not explicitly realised until Henry Humbert, yet another poet from the east of France, published his *Sepmaine saincte* in 1609. This is a series of meditations on the last scenes of the life of Christ; each is divided into two parts, a prose section and a poem in alexandrine *sixains*. Humbert's programme could be prefixed to almost any Counter-Reformation devotional manual:

> J'estalle à ses yeux un tableau ou la Passion de nostre Dieu est depeinte...
> Aussy sont-ce des mysteres sacrés qui se veulent tracer avec une naifveté, qui figure plustost les simples traictz d'un zele devotieux, que les termes relevès de la biendisance. Cest une sepmaine saincte qui confere l'eternitè, une sepmaine pleine de morts qui repare l'immortalité. Que si les ravissements de ces Extases semblent trop foibles pour eslever les Ames en contemplation, elles se feront des aisles de la pieté des bons pour se porter dans le ciel.[1]

The devotional intention is if anything more explicit here than in the prefaces of Favre, and the hyperbolical terms in which it is expressed are typical of this decade in which devotion meant above all sweetness and extremes of emotion. One thus has the unique opportunity of studying in Humbert's work the relationship between a highly developed devotional prose and its poetic equivalent, although, as we shall see later, the poetry is somewhat disappointing.

The devotional sweetness represented by Humbert, and with some modifications by St François, was encouraged by the increasing feminisation of devotion which occurred towards the turn of the century; and the part played by Madame Acarie and her like in this movement was anticipated by the work of two poetesses, Sœur Anne de Marquets and Gabrielle de Coignard. Anne de Marquets had published a number of poems in the early stages of the wars of religion: these included some translations of Flaminio, which would suggest a link between Marguerite de Navarre's circle and Anne's own activities.[2]

---

[1] H. Humbert, *La Sepmaine saincte* (Toul, 1609), 'Dedication', *non pag.*

[2] Anne's first publication was a collection of *Sonets, prières et devises en forme de pasquins pour l'assemblée de messieurs les prélats et docteurs, tenue à Poissy, MDLXI* (Paris, 1566). Two years later followed the Flaminio translations, *Les Divines Poesies de Marc-Antoine Flaminius: Contenantes diverses Prieres, Meditations, Hymnes et actions de graces à Dieu: Mises en François avec le Latin respondant l'un à l'autre. Avec plusieurs Sonnets et Cantiques, ou Chansons Spirituelles pour louer Dieu* (Paris, 1568; 2nd ed. 1569). The use of the word *méditation* to describe some of these poems is a significant anticipation

Her most important work, however, the *Sonets spirituels*, remained unpublished until 1605, seventeen years after her death. These sonnets form a complete devotional sequence of 480 sonnets 'sur les Dimanches et principales solennitez de l'année', including long sections on the Nativity, the Passion, the Virgin, and the Saints; they are therefore far more advanced, in terms of the application of systematic devotional practice to poetry, than anything written in the 1570s and 1580s. The fact that the work was published so late may throw some light on the changing tastes of the period: although Ronsard had been flattering about her earlier poetry, it seems likely that the reading public during her lifetime would have been unprepared for a cycle of sonnets written within the cloister and closely reflecting the devotional habits of a nun. This, however, is only supposition, and the late publication may have been due to accidental circumstances. What is more important is that when the work finally appears, it is accompanied by a number of encomiastic poems which compare Anne to the Virgin, or lament her death in decoratively feminine terms:

> Neantmoins le bruit est, que toutes les Deesses,
> De la terre et du ciel, rompant leurs blondes tresses,
> Et se marquant de coups, te firent un convoy...[1]

Gabrielle de Coignard's *Œuvres chrestiennes* were also published posthumously, though in this instance not long after her death. This is again a substantial collection of devotional poems, including more than a hundred *sonnetz spirituels*, a paraphrase of the *Stabat mater*, some *Noelz*, a paraphrase of the Judith story which amounts to a short epic, a group of extended poems on the Passion, and a *Sommaire de sept Sermons faits par Monsieur Emond*. As will be shown later, the Passion poems are particularly important as they follow the phases of organised meditation relatively closely (though with a tendency to emphasise the narrative and emotive aspects); in fact, they seem to be

of future developments; indeed, the collection as a whole, although associated through its mystical themes with the preoccupations of Marguerite de Navarre, can be seen with the work of Billy as a prelude to the flowering of devotional poetry in the Counter-Reformation.

[1] *Sonets spirituels de feue tres-vertueuse et tres-docte dame Sr Anne de Marquet* (Paris, 1605), p. 345. For a general study of Anne and her work, see *Anne de Marquets: Poétesse religieuse du xvie siècle*, by Sister Mary H. Seiler (Washington, 1931). Sister Mary makes some useful biographical and bibliographical contributions.

based in part at least on Granada's *Le Vray chemin*. For the present, it will be sufficient to draw attention to the dedication addressed by Gabrielle's daughters *Aux Dames devotieuses*: the combination here between devotional ardour, 'felicité' and humility, and the emphasis on Gabrielle's sex, are highly indicative of the direction in which devotional poetry is moving in the 1590s:

...elle fit ce que vous lirez en c'est œuvre, avec un extreme ardeur de devotion, et quant, et quant avec une extreme felicité. Elle n'estoit ny n'avoit desiré d'estre une grande clergesse non qu'elle n'honorat les sçavantes Dames, mais elle disoit que c'estoit savoir tout, que n'ignorer point les moyens de son salut... Nous... vous viendrons icy desployer, et estaler les plus beaux ouvrages d'une Dame devote.[1]

Finally, it is worth remembering that Gabrielle's husband had been president in the Toulouse Parlement: Toulouse was renowned for its *Jeux Floraux*, and it was there, too, that La Ceppède and César de Nostredame were soon to publish their devotional poetry.

At the turn of the century, Aix-en-Provence was one of the most advanced centres of devotional activity in France. In 1600 Jean-Baptiste Roumillon founded at Aix the *Congrégation de la doctrine chrétienne*, a secular order whose chief aim was to 'catechise'; this was followed by a parallel order for women, the *Ursulines*.[2] In 1612 the original name was dropped and the order became known as the *Oratoire*, which joined the Paris *Oratoire* a few years later to become the *Oratoire de France*.[3] It thus plays a leading role in one of the most important movements of devotional reform. The secularisation of the order was so far advanced that the habit was not always worn; there was in any case no difference between the habit and the robes of a *magistrat*, a significant ambiguity when one considers that many of the Aixois devotional poets were *magistrats*. La Ceppède was himself one; at the same time he seems to have been known for his piety and

---

[1] *Œuvres chrestiennes de feu dame Gabrielle de Coignard, vefve à feu M. de Mansencal, sieur de Miremont, président en la cour du Parlement de Tholose* (Tournon, 1595) ('pour J. Favre libraire en Avignon'), pp. 3–5. An earlier edition was published at Toulouse (1594).

[2] For the history of Aix in this period, see P.-J. de Haitze, *Histoire de la ville d'Aix*, vol. IV (Aix-en-Provence, 1889). Various penitential orders also flourished in Aix in the early seventeenth century.

[3] For the history of the *Oratoire*, see Dagens, *Bérulle et les origines de la restauration catholique*; Bremond, *Histoire littéraire*, vol. III; and P. Cochois, *Bérulle et l'école française* (Paris, 1963).

charity. He was buried at the Carmelite Church, and this may have something to do with the legend that he was related to St Teresa, whose father's name was de Cepeda.[1]

Ecclesiastics figure large in the dedications and liminary poems of contemporary books of devotional poetry, particularly Paul Hurault de l'Hôpital, the Archbishop of Aix, who wrote poems in praise of Chasteuil's *Imitation des Pseaumes* and of César de Nostredame's *Pièces héroïques*.[2] If one is to judge by these liminary poems, the number of poets and would-be poets at Aix must have been considerable: Chasteuil's popular *Imitation des Pseaumes* attracted the praises of a dozen different pens, including those of La Ceppède, César de Nostredame, Paul Hurault de l'Hôpital, and François Du Périer. The *Théorèmes* were to be equally well endowed. At any given time between 1590 and 1610 there must have been up to twenty active members of the group, not to mention the ecclesiastics and others who gave the movement their approval and support without actually appearing in print. Only a few of these published their own collections of poetry, as far as one can tell from extant editions; but those who did, make it abundantly clear that devotion was their principal theme.

When the circle began to form around the figure of Henri d'Angoulême in the 1580s, there may have been a certain amount of poetic activity, but no poetry was actually published, unless one includes Malherbe's *Larmes de Saint Pierre* of 1587.[3] Chasteuil's *Prosopopee de ...Henry d'Engolesme*, published with his *Imitation* in 1595, is dedicated to Henri III (like Malherbe's *Larmes*), and both he and La Ceppède may have begun to write devotional poetry and paraphrase in the 1580s, delaying publication until the mid-1590s provided a more settled atmosphere. There is thus a period of preparation in which the key literary figures begin to assemble—La Ceppède, Du Vair, Peiresc, Malherbe—culminating in the publication of La Ceppède's *Imitation des Pseaumes de la Penitence* (together with twelve sonnets anticipating

[1] See E. Aube, 'La Poésie en Provence au temps de Malherbe', *Les Cahiers d'Aix-en-Provence* (*hiver* 1923–4), p. 23.

[2] The balance between lay and ecclesiastic is well represented by the two liminary sonnets of the *Pièces héroïques*: the second is by Claude Fauchet, 'Premier President en la Cour des Monnoyes'.

[3] For the formation of this circle, see F. Ruchon, *Essai sur la vie et l'œuvre de Jean de La Ceppède*, pp. 8–11; and R. Lebègue, 'Nouvelles études malherbiennes', *BHR*, 5 (1944), pp. 153 ff.

the *Théorèmes*) in 1594, and Chasteuil's *Imitation* (1595–7).[1] The parallel between these two works is very striking, since they were published in successive years; taking into consideration Malherbe's *Larmes*, one might call this the 'penitential' period of the Aix group. After the turn of the century, works of a greater ambition and maturity begin to appear: César de Nostredame's poems were published between 1605 and 1608, to be followed in 1612–13 by the first volume of La Ceppède's *Théorèmes*. What strikes one most about the whole group is the way in which its activities were sustained over a period of twenty years or more. The career of La Ceppède himself covers forty years, from his first meeting with Malherbe in the early 1580s to the second volume of *Théorèmes*, published in 1622; this second volume was something of an afterthought, but it shows how much momentum had been developed by the central period of activity. The unity of the period is illustrated in another way by the title of César de Nostredame's *Plainte de la Provence sur la funeste mort de feu d'illustre memoire Henry 5. d'Angoulesme grand Prieur de France, et les malheurs arrivés despuis icelle, jusques à l'heureuse et desirée venue de... Monseigneur le Duc de Guise, Gouverneur et Lieutenant General soubs le grand et victorieux Henry IIII, en Provence*: almost a generation after the death of Henri d'Angoulême, his influence had not been forgotten by the Aixois poets. Finally, it is clear that the pattern of activity in this provincial centre (which is in many respects typical of France as a whole) is based on a gathering momentum: the emergence of devotional poetry proper is anticipated at a relatively early stage, but it is only fully realised some time after the end of the religious wars, in a period when new devotional movements were beginning to take root in France.

[1] For the 1594 edition of La Ceppède's paraphrases, see V.-L. Saulnier and A. Worthington, 'Du nouveau sur Jean de La Ceppède', *BHR*, 17 (1955), pp. 415 ff. Since, according to this edition, the twelve sonnets are 'prinses de l'œuvre entier des Théorèmes de M.M.I. de la Ceppède', it seems as if many, if not all, of the *Théorèmes* as they appear in the later edition had already been written by this time. Perhaps they were circulated privately before the author decided to publish them. This fact would slightly alter the pattern of development as I have outlined it here; on the other hand it suggests that a potentiality, all but realised in the earlier years, is nevertheless held in check to some extent until the fashion for devotional literature has become fully established (as indicated earlier, the same might apply to the posthumous publication of Anne de Marquets's sequence). The full title of Chasteuil's work is *Imitation des Pseaumes de la pénitence Royalle. A treschrestien Roy de France et de Navarre Henry IIII. Par Louys de Gallaup, Sieur de Chasteuil.*

The first three books of La Ceppède's *Théorèmes...sur le sacré mystere de nostre redemption*, constituting the volume which appeared in 1613, deal with the Passion. According to the title-page, each is composed of 'cent Méditations et autant de sonnets', although the 'meditations' in prose are in the nature of a commentary on each sonnet and its sources, rather than a meditation in the devotional sense (one might contrast this with the 1594 edition, in which it is the sonnets themselves, and not the prose commentaries, that La Ceppède calls *méditations*). In fact the whole work is a long and erudite meditation in verse and prose on the mystery of the Passion, and this sense is brought out in La Ceppède's preface *A la France*, where he outlines thus his intended transformation of poetry:

> Or pour luy descoudre ses mondains habits (ou plustost habitudes) pour luy raire ses cheveux idolatres, menteurs et lascifs; j'advisay qu'on ne pouvoit mettre en œuvre un outil plus utile que le rasoir à double tranchant de la profonde meditation de la Passion et mort de nostre Sauveur JESUS CHRIST.[1]

Another passage of the preface shows the *Théorèmes* as containing the two complementary aspects of devotional practice—penitence and rejoicing, though in this case both are seen in the framework of the morning meditation on the life of Christ:

> ...apres les embrasemens de nos dernier mal-heurs, j'ay fait naistre cettuy-ci [his 'enfant', the *Théorèmes*], portant en sa main le livre du Prophete envelopé des mysteres, escrit dedans pour les doctes, et dehors pour les ignorans; contenant les plus justes et pitoyables lamentations, qui furent jamais souspirées; et les plus joyeuses et plus agreables chansons, qui furent jamais chantées: celes-là tres-propres à la douleur de nos vieux ulceres, pour detester nos pechez, qui les ont creusés; et celes-cy tres-convenables pour magnifier le doux appareil dont ce grand Chirurgien celeste les a cicatrisés: celes-là tres-utiles, pour abatre l'orgueil de nostre presumption, et graver dans nos cœurs la crainte de Dieu des armées, voyant la vengeance de sa divine Justice executée sur son propre Fils, s'estant voulu charger de nos crimes; et celes-cy tres-fortes, pour relever nostre penchante esperance, exagerant l'eternel merite de ce sang innocent si largement versé pour laver nos soüilleures...(pp. 8–9.)

It will be seen later how La Ceppède makes direct use of well-known devotional treatises as a source for many of his sonnets; but a general impression of the broad scope of his reading is given by the *Catalogue Alphabetique des Autheurs de diverse profession alleguez en cet Œuvre*

[1] La Ceppède, *Théorèmes*, 'A la France', p. 6.

which appears at the end of the 1613 edition and which includes Dionysius de Leuwis, Erasmus, Gerson, Guevara, Ignatius Loyola, Ludolphus, Maldonat, Panigarola, Ronsard, Tauler, and Vives. By the early seventeenth century, the title *méditation* (sometimes *dévote méditation*) has become common in religious poetry, sometimes replacing the more general title *prière*. It is interesting that one of the first instances of its use in this period occurs in the Protestant *Poèmes chrestiens* (the *Méditation chrestienne* discussed above). Through its subsequent use by poets such as Marin Le Saulx, Favre and La Ceppède (if not as a title, at least in prefaces), it gradually becomes established and in the anthologies of the turn of the century it appears regularly.[1] Jacques Doremet, in the *Epistre Dedicatoire* of his *Polymnie*, refers to his work as 'ce petit Enchiridion', and many of the poems themselves explicitly urge the reader to pray and to meditate;[2] Nicolas Le Digne calls his paraphrase of the *Stabat mater* a *méditation*, although it remains relatively close to the original;[3] and Hopil uses the same title in his first collection of religious poetry.[4] The popularity of the term was

[1] See, for example, Motin's *Méditation sur le Memento*, published in *Les Fleurs des plus excellens Poetes de ce Temps* (3rd ed., Paris, 1601) (N. and P. Bonfons), fols. 159–60, and in other collections; or Antoine de Vermeil's two *Devotes meditations*, published in *Le Parnasse des plus excellents poetes de ce temps ou Muses françoises r'alliées de diverses parts. Second volume* (Lyons, Ancelin, *s.d.*) and elsewhere.

[2] *Polymnie du vray amour et de la mort. Avec quelques Stances et Quatrains Spirituelz. Par Jacques Doremet, Vandomois* (Paris, 1596), p. 13. Cf. Doremet's liminary *Ode* (pp. 19 ff.):

> Car outre que la science
> Contemplative est tousjours
> La premiere en excellence,
> Donnant lumiere et secours
> A l'active, qui ne peut
> Sçavoir que ce qu'elle meut....

> Qui voudra dresser son ame
> Et la preparer aux Cieux,
> Lise ces vers que je trame:
> Il ne sera viceux:
> Et mortifiera son corps
> Avant que l'ame en soit hors.

The twentieth sonnet *du vray amour* (p. 33):

> Represente toy donc, que quand tu pries Dieu
> C'est à Dieu que tu parle, et qu'il n'est aucun lieu
> Où l'Eternel ne soit: et jamais ne te lasse
> De prier...

And the eighth sonnet *de la mort* (p. 42): 'Il faut tousjours mediter au trespas'.

[3] See the article by Vaganay referred to below, p. 187, n. 2.

[4] Claude Hopil, *Les Œuvres chrestiennes* (Paris, 1603), fols. 4 ff.: *Elegies, ou meditations chrestiennes*.

such that it was transferrred to profane love-poetry on at least one occasion, in Estienne Durand's *Méditations* of 1611.[1] 'Devotional' motifs had occasionally appeared in love-poetry, particularly in connexion with the idea of a 'hermitage': Bremond quotes three examples —Desportes, Motin and Trellon—of 'penitent' love-poets who dedicate themselves (poetically speaking) to lives of asceticism,[2] and one might add d'Aubigné's funereal retreat in the first of his *Stances*. This image is an elaboration of the 'solitude' *topos* common in Petrarchan poetry; but the devotional or penitential details seem to have been encouraged by a contemporary atmosphere, since there is little sign of them in the earlier Pléiade poetry of love.

The early history of devotional poetry in the Counter-Reformation period is to some extent obscured by the considerable volume of non-devotional religious poetry published from the 1560s onwards. Thanks largely to Ronsard and his Calvinist opponents, poetry had become involved in religious polemics, and throughout the civil wars the energies of many a minor poet were absorbed in poetic pamphleteering of one kind or another. For those who wished to encourage morality, the tradition of the versified adage or *sententia*, allied to that of the moral emblem-book, provided plenty of ready-made material: without being specifically religious, a collection like Pibrac's famous *Quatrains* could not possibly be accused of being pagan or profane. Similarly, the powerful current of apologetic 'scientific' poetry, established by Du Bartas and to a lesser extent by Guy Le Fèvre de La Boderie, would naturally tend to attract the attention of would-be poets away from lyric forms. The example of Du Bartas, who set out to exploit the equipment of Pléiade rhetoric for purposes of sacred edification, was bound to create the image of a triumphal Muse, Christian no doubt, but still accompanied by the attributes of her profane predecessor. Indeed, the authority of the Pléiade was so great that it was almost impossible for any poet to conceive of poetry in terms other than those he was familar with; and at the court of Henri III the renewed currency of Petrarchan modes was unlikely to favour the emergence of an independent manner. Many of the new minor poets claim for themselves a humble, func-

---

[1] See J. Rousset, *Anthologie de la poésie baroque française*, vol. I, pp. 74–5; this is an extract from the *Méditations*.   [2] See Bremond, *Humanisme dévot*, pp. 331–3.

tional, non-decorative style, lacking the attractions of their profane rivals; but this 'simplicity' is often not apparent in the poems themselves, or else there is merely a reduction in the quantity of devices used.[1]

These limiting factors retain some of their validity throughout the period. Nevertheless, the elements of a new programme, already detectable in the early years, eventually begin to produce concrete results in the ways we have been discussing. One of the first and the most significant sources of new material and a new manner was Biblical paraphrase, and particularly psalm-paraphrase, which provided the religious poet with a ready-made lyric form unlike those borrowed from Italy and classical antiquity, yet parallel to them and resting on a secure and venerable tradition. Partly because of these Old Testament paradigms, and partly because of the sombre mood of the day, much of the devotional poetry written between 1570 and 1595 is concerned with the themes of the evening meditation. At the same time, another pattern is beginning to take shape in the works of Boyssières, Habert, Tamisier and Anne de Marquets: the morning meditation is finding its way into poetry. This pattern is not finally clarified until rather later, for two reasons. In the first place, it implies a far more intimate relationship between poems and devotional source than does most penitential poetry; and this could only come about when the poet had become fully conscious of the potentialities of the prose material. In the second place, as we saw in the previous chapter, the development of devotional tendencies themselves follows precisely the same pattern. The Counter-Reformation in France is first concerned with penitence, with a national searching of conscience; and it is not until a generation has elapsed that the concept of a more attractive, self-indulgent devotion can begin to take root, one centred on passion and sweetness, on Christ, the Virgin, and Mary Magdalene. It is this contrast between two periods in the development of devotion and of devotional poetry that will determine the overall pattern of the following chapters.

[1] Anne de Marquets provides a good early example of this pattern; see Sister Mary Seiler, *Anne de Marquets*, pp. 60–4. Notice, once again, the image of 'viande immortelle' (*ibid.* p. 63).

CHAPTER 4

POETRY OF
SIN, SICKNESS AND DEATH.
1: THE PENITENTIAL PRAYER

THE FRAMEWORK: OLD TESTAMENT PARAPHRASE

By 1560 the tension between orthodoxy and its opponents had already been mounting for many years: Protestant martyrs had multiplied rapidly in the reign of Henri II with the institution of the *Chambre ardente*. But economically, the life of the nation had scarcely been disturbed; the security of the private individual was not threatened unless he deliberately risked it. Thus the outbreak and constant renewal of the wars of religion came as something of a shock. The ideological controversy had moved uncompromisingly into the realm of the physical, and everyone was affected, 'committed' or not; for the evils of the wars were not restricted to the carnage of battle or of massacre. Plague and famine racked the country, and the triplet 'guerre, peste et famine' became an incessant motif of prefaces, liminary pieces, and *sonnets rapportés*.[1] Treatises on how to ward off the plague appeared frequently, together with religious parallels in the form of 'prayers for times of pestilence'.[2] In the religious context, the scourges of the civil wars had an added significance: they might represent the necessary afflictions of the elect, a direct punishment for the sins of the nation, or the embodiment of man's fallen state; and both the Calvinist and the Catholic faction liked to compare their sufferings with those of the tribes of Israel.

These preoccupations soon began to be reflected in contemporary literature and art at all levels. Writers began to choose their classical models among late Latin authors—Lucan for the epic, Seneca for the

[1] See, for example, Montméja's *sonet* in *Poèmes chrestiens* (Geneva, 1574), p. 17.
[2] See, for example, N. Houël, *Regime preservatif de peste* (Paris, 1580) (also a *Traité de la peste*, Paris, 1573); Anthoine Du Four, *La Maniere de se preserver de la peste* (Lyon, 1588); and Claude Binet's *Ad Deum oratio pestilentiae tempore* (Paris, 1581).

94

drama—thus renewing the Roman civil wars and decadence in a French context; the same parallels were made in pictorial art;[1] and in 'popular' literature, the vogue of *histoires prodigieuses* attests an insatiable appetite for monsters, cosmic marvels, 'horror stories', and gruesome accounts of contemporary persecutions.[2] In religious literature, the dominant literary source was the Old Testament, which exemplifies in innumerable different ways the theme of the Fall not yet offset by the Redemption. The sequel to the Fall—the labours of Adam and Eve, the enmity of Abel and Cain—becomes one of the seminal *topoi* of the whole period: even the encyclopaedic poets (Du Bartas and his successors), who bridge the gap between Pléiade and Jesuit optimism by describing the glories of Creation, are forced to see man as the weak spot in the universe, the corrupter of the beauty of Nature. Each man repeats Adam's curse; he is born to die; labour and birth-pains are the prelude to a life of toil and misery, haunted by the image of death.[3] The Eden story, together with these accompanying themes, was versified and dramatised by several later sixteenth-century writers, Neo-Latin as well as vernacular.[4] An interesting example, taken

[1] See J. Ehrmann, 'Massacre and persecution pictures in Sixteenth-Century France', *JWI*, 8 (1945), pp. 185 ff. Ehrmann discusses parallels between Antoine Caron's paintings of the triumvirate massacres and contemporary depictions of civil war massacres (especially the woodcuts of Tortorel and Périssin, published at Geneva in 1569). Antoine Caron was for many years the official painter of Catherine de' Medici.

[2] See R. Schenda, 'Französische Prodigienschriften aus der zweiten Hälfte des 16. Jahrhunderts', *ZFSL*, 69 (1959), pp. 150 ff. Schenda quotes the *Discours entier de la persecution et cruauté exercee en la ville de Vaissy* (1562) as a 'Beispiel für Grausamkeit und politische Tagesliteratur', and places in the same category the Tortorel-Périssin collection of woodcuts. I have not seen the published thesis of Schenda, *Die französische Prodigienliteratur in der zweiten Hälfte des 16. Jahrhunderts* (Munich, 1961) (*Münchner romanistische Arbeiten*, 16).

[3] The first of the seven 'signs' of the Apocalypse (Revelation 12. 1–2) is a pregnant woman who is pursued by a dragon, takes refuge in the desert, and is saved miraculously. This symbol of the Church is used in the context of contemporary events by d'Aubigné (*Tragiques*, verse preface, ll. 165–8; *Vengeances*, ll. 150–4 and 719–21). In several of his massacre scenes, d'Aubigné describes the death of pregnant women. Although there is no close connexion between these various uses, the image is persistent in the poetry of this period and characteristically combines pathos, the sharp realisation of physical pain, and (in d'Aubigné's poem at least) a partisan opposition of innocence and bestiality. See J. Trénel, *L'Elément biblique dans l'œuvre de d'Aubigné* (Paris, 1904), pp. 46–7.

[4] See, for example, François de Monceaux, *Heden, sive Paradisus* (Arras, 1593). The Fall also provided a theme for certain Neo-Latin plays, as for example the *Protoplaste* of Zieglerus (1543), and later the *Adam exilé* of Grotius (1601): see Paul van Tieghem, 'La Littérature latine de la Renaissance', *BHR*, 4 (1944), pp. 177 ff., Pt. 3, ch. 3, pp. 347–8.

at random, is Scévole de Sainte-Marthe's treatise *Paedotrophia* (dedicated to Henri III), dealing with medical problems of pregnancy and child welfare; a discussion of the physiological aspects of birth prompts Sainte-Marthe into a complete retelling of the Eden story. Of the pains of labour, he says:

> Has autem meruit primae vesana parentis
> Ambitio poenas, et justi numinis iram.[1]

Adam and Eve are expelled from the Garden, to reap the rewards of their sin:

> Hic ubi protinus irrumpunt asperrima in illos
> Quaeque mala, et dirae circunstant undique pestes,
> Efferaque imprimis venturae Mortis imago
> Imminet, et iam tum trepidantia pectora vexat.[2]

—distress, sickness and death.

If these themes were chiefly important for didatic or moralising literature and sermons, they were also familiar to the *dévot* who wished to practise penitential meditation: only their application was different. For him, the obsession with horror was turned inward, towards the corruption of his own body, his own weight and foulness, his affinity with dust and clay.[3] If he was ill, his illness was a physical embodiment of his sin; if he was not, he felt his sin with the full force of a real sickness. This personal view of the fallen state of man had its own Old Testament paradigms in the plight of David and Job, in the sickness of Hezekiah, and (in a slightly different but still highly relevant context)

---

[1] Scévole de Sainte-Marthe, *Opera*, vol. 1 (Paris, 1616), p. 16.

[2] *Ibid.* p. 19. From the early sixteenth century, there seems to have been a tendency in Neo-Latin poetry to digress on the theme of the Fall; see Salmon Macrin's *Soter* (c. 1515), and Jean Olivier's *Pandora* (1541), both discussed by I. D. McFarlane in his article 'Jean Salmon Macrin (1490–1557)', *BHR*, 21 (1959), p. 69.

[3] Cf. Habert's eleventh *sonnet spirituel* (*op. cit.*, *Œuvres chrestiennes*, fol. 4):

> ...Nous estions tous creez pour l'immortalité,
> Mais dés que le peché rendit Adam coulpable,
> Il fut rendu mortel, nud, pauvre, et miserable,
> Et par luy nous portons l'habit d'iniquité.
> Mais je suis las d'avoir ceste robbe crasseuse
> Si long temps dessus moy, elle est orde et fangeuse,
> Je me fasche, ô mon Dieu, de l'avoir tant sur moy.
> Ainsi que le serpent sa robbe renouvelle,
> Oste ce vieil Adam, cest habit de cautelle,
> Et me couvre, ô Seigneur, d'esperance et de foy.

in the lamentations of Jeremiah; and it is these models which provide the principal point of departure for what amounts to a self-contained *genre* of religious poetry, the penitential lyric or prayer-poem.

In terms of sheer quantity, Biblical paraphrase was one of the most popular forms of poetic exercise in a period of great poetic enthusiasm and experiment. The rate of production quickened dramatically in the second half of the century, when innumerable poets of widely different styles, talents and ambitions became involved in the more or less explicit attempt to endorse or to counter the authority of the Marot-Bèze Psalter: Jean-Antoine de Baïf, Philippe Desportes, Isaac Habert, Agrippa d'Aubigné, Blaise de Vigenère, Nicolas Rapin, La Ceppède, Louis Galaup de Chasteuil, Chassignet, Bertaut, Du Perron, Malherbe...the list stretches on well into the seventeenth century. Very few of these poets paraphrased more than a handful of the Psalms (Desportes and Baïf are exceptional in this repect): the favourite choice was the seven Penitential Psalms, but many others were versified again and again— the topical *Super flumina*, for example,[1] and praise-psalms such as Psalm 104. However, if these ready-made lyric poems were the principal focus of interest for contemporary poets, other parts of the Old Testament were by no means neglected; and of those with penitential themes, the closest rival to the Psalms is undoubtedly Job, from which poets often extracted the nine *leçons des vigiles*, lessons read at the funeral service. The tradition of Job paraphrases in French goes back at least as far as the fifteenth-century poet Pierre de Nesson, celebrated for his macabre poems on the theme of death; in our period, one of the earliest paraphrases is by the Protestant Armand Du Plessis (*Le Livre de Job traduit en poesie française*, Geneva, 1552). Twenty years later, Belleau's paraphrase of the *leçons* appeared in the *Seconde journee de la bergerie*; Chassignet was to attempt a more comprehensive version which seems to have remained in manuscript form. Similarly, extracts from the Lamentations of Jeremiah were versified by Guillaume Guéroult, Jean de La Jessée and Béroalde de Verville;[2] and the prayer of Hezekiah

---

[1] F. Lachèvre (*Bibliographie des recueils collectifs de poésies publiées de 1597 à 1700*) mentions a group of ten paraphrases of the *Super flumina* which appeared in Paris in 1606 (listed in the *Catalogue de la librairie Potier* (1872), no. 1152). The authors are Marot, Desportes, Du Perron, Du Vair, Nervèze, Guinot, J. de Nostre-Dame, J. Granier, d'Hozier.

[2] For the Guéroult and Jessée paraphrases, see D. Aury, *Anthologie de la poésie religieuse française* (Paris, 1943), pp. 57–8, 61–3. See V.-L. Saulnier, 'Béroalde de Verville',

on his recovery from sickness, from Isaiah 38, was frequently paraphrased.

This current was doubled by the paraphrases of the Neo-Latin poets, whose versions of the Psalms were appearing regularly before 1550. Neo-Latin paraphrase by French poets first became popular in the 1530s (Italy seems to have taken the lead in this as in other fields): the Penitential Psalms of Jean Salmon Macrin, for example, were published in 1538. In 1556, Henri Estienne produced an anthology of psalm-paraphrases by Buchanan, Flaminio, Hessus, Macrin, and Rapicius, a sure sign that poetry of this kind was both plentiful and popular.[1] It is interesting that the Protestants, whom one associates with the effort to free the Bible from the tyranny of Latin, are almost as active as the Catholics in the field of Neo-Latin paraphrase, as witness the works of Jean Jaquemot and Jacques Lect,[2] not to mention Buchanan himself—yet another indication of the lack of any clear distinction, religious or literary, between the Catholic and the Protestant view. Of equal importance is the fact that Neo-Latin poets tend to use classical *genres* and verse-forms for their paraphrases; few of them are exclusively religious poets, and titles like Le Duchat's *Sacrorum heroum atque heroidum odae* (Troyes, 1596) are common.[3] This habit is perhaps not surprising, but it means, for example, that a psalm may have the same form as a Horatian ode, an ambiguity not without its significance for vernacular poetry. It also tends to open the door to importations of pagan material, mythological or philosophical: the convergence of Job's philosophy with the Stoic concept of constancy is implied in the

BHR, 5 (1944), pp. 209 ff., for a general study of this poet. *Les Tenebres, qui sont les Lamentations de Jeremie* were published by Guillemot in *Les Muses françoises ralliees de diverses pars* (Paris, 1599); they have a separate pagination: 1–25.

[1] See McFarlane, *art. cit. BHR*, 21 (1959), pp. 334–5; *ibid.* 22 (1960), p. 78. For a list of Neo-Latin paraphrases based on the British Museum catalogue, see J. A. Gaertner, 'Latin verse translations of the Psalms, 1500–1620', *HTR*, 49 (1956), pp. 271 ff. See also W. L. Grant, 'Neo-Latin verse-translations of the Bible', *HTR*, 52 (1959), pp. 205 ff. (intended as a bibliographical complement to Gaertner's article).

[2] Jean Jaquemot, *Lamentationes prophetae Jeremiae, variis lyricorum versuum generibus expressae* (Geneva, 1591); and Jacques Lect, *Ecclesiastes...heroico carmine a J. Lectio expositus* (*s. l.*, 1588); *J. Lectii poematum liber unus* (Geneva, 1595); *Jonah* (with Bèze's *Poemata varia*) (*s. l.*, 1599); *Poemata varia, nempe Sylvae, Elegiae, Epigrammata, Epicedia, Ecclesiastes, Jonah* (Geneva, 1609).

[3] See also above, n. 2; the *Eidyllia sacra in utrumque Testamentum* of Robertus Obrizius; the *Sacra bucolica, sive Cantici canticorum Salomonis...poetica paraphrasis* of François de Monceaux (Paris, 1587); or the *Poemata...Additae sunt lamentationes Jeremiae... elegiaco versu redditae* of Jean Rouxel (Rouen, 1600).

title of Jean-Anthoine de Thou's *Iobus, sive de constantia libri IIII, poetica metaphrasi explicati* (Paris, 1587).

Since many of the essential *topoi* of the penitential lyric, as of the equivalent prose meditations, are drawn from this Old Testament material, it will be relevant to examine them as they appear in the form of French verse-paraphrase. As there is no question here of analysing the individual literary characteristics of any given paraphrase, one may safely restrict the vast quantity of material available to certain central texts, in particular Belleau's selections from Job and the Penitential Psalms in Desportes's version. It is only fair to point out, however, that there are very great differences between the relatively straightforward paraphrase of Desportes and the intricacies of, say, Chasteuil, whose *Imitation des Pseaumes* goes far beyond the psalm-texts. Much work remains to be done in this rich field.[1]

The Psalms and many of the key passages of Job are themselves lyric poetry: the writer is involved in self-examination or prayer, as opposed to moral apostrophe in the manner of Ecclesiastes. Where the tone is penitential, the sinner (David or Job) begins by contemplating in detail his own physical and moral decay and God's avenging violence: sickness and disaster may not be a punishment for sin, but they are its outward sign. There is a characteristic Old Testament sickness, almost identical in the Psalms and in Job: the body is burnt with fever and covered with sores, the skin clings to the bones, the mouth is dry and full of ulcers. The sinner is obsessed with the smell of decay, the rotting of the body alive or dead; the words *ordure* and *pourriture* occur again and again. All this is described in direct, relatively unadorned physical detail, with few complications of syntax:

> Mes os sont pris tout le long de mon dos,
> Contre ma peau et ma chair ulceree
> En s'y collant s'est du tout retiree,
> Et ne suis plus qu'une ordonnance d'os,
> Sauf eschappé des fieres destinees,
> Monstrant la peau de mes dents descharnees.[2]

---

[1] M. Michel Jeanneret of Neuchâtel is at present completing a dissertation on psalm-paraphrase which is likely to be of considerable importance. Meanwhile, see P. Leblanc, *Les Paraphrases françaises des psaumes à la fin de la période baroque (1610–1660)* (Paris, 1960).

[2] R. Belleau, *Seconde journee de la bergerie* (Paris, 1572), fol. 7.

Tes traits vengeurs dedans moy sont fichez...
Toute ma chair est couverte d'ulceres...

De pourriture et de sang tout noirci
Coulent mes cicatrices
Pour ma folie: et courbé de mes vices
Je marche à peine angoisseux et transi...

Lieu n'est entier sur ma chair entamee...[1]

In both these passages, the description is intended to be taken literally; but to identify sickness metaphorically with sin is only a short step, already implied in the original 'pour ma folie', and brought out clearly by Desportes's own gloss 'courbé de mes vices'. In the *Miserere mei*, the connexion between vice and *ordure* is stated in the context of original sin:

Voyla, j'estois soüillé, dés que je fu receu
Dans ce val de misere:
Je me suis veu coupable aussi tost que conceu,
Et couvois le peché dans les flancs de ma mere.[2]

And the same idea, though in less explicit form, appears in Job:

Pourquoy m'as tu tiré du fond de la matrice,
Moy qui ne suis qu'ordure et que fange et que vice?
Mort nay je fusse mort, jamais œil ne m'eust veu
Chetif comme je suis...
Car si tost que je vins naistre,
L'on m'eust du ventre au tombeau
Porté comme en un berceau.[3]

These two well-known passages are the starting-point of a great deal of contemporary poetry: the commonplace of life as a 'val de misère', of the similarity between cradle and tomb, of the vain and transitory quality of human life, appear repeatedly in the Old Testament, in the penitential prayer-poems of the later sixteenth century, and, from another viewpoint, in the 'sermon' type of poem, where they become associated with all the images of the brevity of life. On the other hand, the despair which is inherent in these images of corruption and futility

---

[1] P. Desportes, *Les CL Pseaumes de David...Avec quelques Cantiques de la Bible, Hymnes, et autres œuvres et Prieres Chrestiennes* (Paris, 1604), fol. 48 (Psalm 37).
[2] *Ibid.* fol. 65.
[3] Belleau, *Seconde journee*, fol. 7. Cf. fol. 5: 'Hé! qui peut (sinon toy) rendre une chose pure, / Qui de nature est salle, et de semence impure?'

naturally provokes a prayer for recovery. The self-deprecation, the sense of uncleanness expressed in the *Miserere* passage is resolved almost at once by the 'hyssop' verse, with its imagery of washing and absolution:

> Asperge-moy d'hysope, et je verray soudain
> Ma soüillure effacee:
> Je passeray, Seigneur, me lavant de ta main,
> La blancheur de la neige en flocons amassee.[1]

As one might expect, the dominant tone of voice in this kind of Old Testament poetry is restless, often impatient: 'O Dieu jusqu'à quand ta rigueur?' The 'Lord, how long?' motif finds its way into a large number of contemporary religious poems; it is of course echoed in the wider context of the interminable civil wars. In its original setting, it may well be no more than an indirect plea for mercy; the virtue of Job lies in his refusal to rebel, in his resignation:

> Mais quand sera-ce, ô mon vray redempteur,
> Que j'auray trefve, et que de ma salive
> Je pourray sain arrouser ma gensive,
> Et l'avalant refraschir ma doleur?[2]

But even Job reasons with God; he challenges God's wisdom in allowing him to be born at all ('Pourquoy m'as-tu tiré du fond de la matrice?'); he questions God's silence:

> Ne me condamne: Il n'est pas equitable,
> Ou me declare en quoy je suis coulpable,
> Pour me juger... (fol. 4.)

And he uses the 'argument from Creation'—he is God's handiwork, 'de tes saincts doigts l'ouvrage et la facture'. Man's very abjectness and physical conditioning by God are thus used as a defence against the justice of his wrath:

> Souvienne toy avant que me damner,
> Que de limon, et de bourbe fangeuse
> Tu m'as formé et qu'en terre poudreuse,
> Apres ma mort me feras retourner. (fols. 4–5.)

Much the same questioning attitude is typical of the Penitential Psalms. In Psalm 6, the 'jusqu'à quand?' motif is followed by a common Old

[1] Desportes, *Les CL Pseaumes de David*, fol. 65 (Psalm 50).
[2] Belleau, *Seconde journee*, fol. 4.

Testament argument: God wants to be praised, but dead men cannot praise him:

> Car en la mort il n'est memoire
> De toy des vivans reclamé.[1]

In most of these passages, the questions remain unanswered, the paradoxes unresolved. The sinner finally resigns himself to the mysterious justice of God's purpose, and ends on a confident note: God will deliver him from his afflictions and from the enemies which surround him ('Tu perdras tous ceux-là qui me portent nuisance'). Confession and penitence are thus resolved in the hope of absolution.

The atmosphere of the Lamentations is somewhat different, since it contains a good deal of moral admonition:

> Triste Jerusalem, Cité desconfortée,
> Retourne toy vers Dieu, pense à te convertir.[2]

But the prophet is here addressing a whole nation which has fallen through its own corruption, and it is therefore ideally suited to the period of the civil wars: Du Vair, in a preface to his meditation on this book, warns France to contemplate herself 'dans les ruines de ce pauvre peuple Hebrieux, car c'est bien vostre vray mirouër'.[3] Moreover, the prophetic voice is counterpointed with the elegiac tone of Jerusalem herself weeping over her downfall:

> Vous tous qui passez par cette voye honteuse,
> O voyez et regardez de mon mal la grandeur,
> Ma douleur sur toute autre, est extreme et piteuse,
> Car Dieu m'a dissipée au jour de sa fureur.[4]

Indeed, many of these elegiac passages look exactly like psalm-paraphrases:

> Il ha vieilli ma chair, et ma peau deschiree,
> Mes os il ha brisez de mal et desplaisir,
> Il ha pressé sur moy, mon ame est entournee
> D'amertume et m'a faict en tenebres gesir. (p. 10.)

---

[1] Desportes, *Les CL Pseaumes de David*, fol. 5. This is also the argument of Hezekiah (Isaiah 38. 18).
[2] Béroalde de Verville, *Les Tenebres*: this is part of the refrain which appears at the end of each *leçon*.
[3] G. Du Vair, *La Saincte philosophie* (Rouen, 1603), preface to the meditation *Sur les Lamentations de Jeremie*, fol. 10.
[4] Béroalde de Verville, *Les Tenebres*, p. 3. See also below, pp. 262–3.

The framework: Old Testament paraphrase

This alternation of prophetic sermon and elegiac lament is seldom to be found in the shorter religious poems of the later sixteenth century. It does, however, provide the pattern of much of *Les Juifves*, in which Garnier blends the language of the Lamentations with that of the Penitential Psalms;[1] and Jeremiah's description of the *monde renversé*, with its horrific details—the mothers eating their children, the rivers of blood—and its pathetic contrasts between tenderness and violence, is essential to the atmosphere of *Misères*:

> Les meres dont le cœur dessus leur fruit est tendre,
> Ont avancé leur main pour cuyre leurs enfans,
> Affin de les manger las on les a veu prendre,
> Leurs petits desolez durant le mauvais temps...
> Tant de sang s'y couloit, mesme es larges espaces,
> Qu'il falloit pour passer lever l'accoustrement.[2]

At the same time, d'Aubigné relies heavily on Job for the framework story of the *Tragiques*: thus the whole range of potentialities, lyric, didactic, and narrative, of the Old Testament books was fully exploited in the literature of this period.

Such, then, is the material on which poets like Tagaut, Desportes, Bertaut and Sponde drew for much of their penitential poetry. Old Testament paraphrase establishes, in terms of French verse, a pattern of themes and metaphor; it develops a particular cast of language—violent and restless, with precise though often brief descriptions of sickness and decay; by rendering the parallelisms of Hebrew poetry, it suggests a technique of accumulation rather than of a logical syntactical development; and it imposes a roomy flexible form which can cope with all the modulations of lament, self-deprecation and prayer. On occasion, the poet may elaborate or dilute the language of the original, or he may add classical 'fossilisations' as does Chasteuil:

> Les Dires, les Fureurs qui bourrellent ma vie,
> M'ont allumé le sein, m'ont la force ravie,
> M'ont forcé dans ma fosse et fondu mon flambeau...[3]

But the amount of extraneous material he can add is limited: Desportes cannot for example exploit the prophetic symbolism of the 'hyssop' verse of the *Miserere*, or enrich the penitential tone by reference to

---

[1] See below, pp. 109–10. [2] Béroalde de Verville, *Les Tenebres*, p. 17.
[3] Chasteuil, *Imitation des Pseaumes* (1597 ed.), p. 19.

New Testament *exempla*. Thus paraphrase does not by-pass prose meditation as a background for the penitential lyric; meditation, whether in poetry or in prose, consists precisely in the augmentation of the fundamental Biblical material, and it is in the first place this augmentation and reorientation which we shall be considering in the following pages.

THE PENITENTIAL LYRIC

It will be as well to begin with a definition. For the purposes of this chapter, the penitential prayer-poem or lyric will be a poem which develops themes of self-examination, confession and penitence, without substantial reference to the Passion. The tone of the poem usually moves between a direct address to God and a first-person monologue: the poet rarely speaks explicitly to a wider audience, either to narrate or to moralise. The Old Testament is the first point of departure, while the New Testament is used mainly for its penitential *exempla*. As for the form, a typical example might contain between twelve and fifteen 6-line *stances*, in octosyllables, decasyllables, or alexandrines. Considerable variations are possible, but the outstanding feature is the long, loose development, which qualifies for a wide range of rather vague titles: *cantique, ode, stances, plainte, prière, méditation.*[1] There are a few prayers in shorter forms such as the sonnet; these will be taken into account in a later section. The form of the penitential lyric, as well as its themes, makes a parallel with the Psalms inevitable. The similarities between psalm and ode had been noticed very early both by Neo-Latin and by vernacular poets, and since psalms were often paraphrased very freely, the dividing line between paraphrase and original composition may well be none too clear, especially as paraphrases by Bertaut and others were often published as *stances* or *cantiques* with no reference to the original psalm.[2] On the other hand, the penitential prayer-poem

---

[1] The origins and definitions of these forms cannot be discussed here, and are scarcely relevant, since the poets themselves seldom make any clear distinction between them (with certain exceptions which will be noted where appropriate).

[2] In *L'Art poëtique françoys, Second livre*, ch. 6, 'Du Cantique, Chant Lyrique ou Ode et Chanson', Sebillet states that 'le Cantique François n'est autre chose que le Pséaume Hébreu ou Latin' (ed. F. Gaiffe, *STFM* (Droz, Paris, 1932), p. 143), and a page or two later, describes the *ode* as being exactly the same kind of form. Both psalm-paraphrase and ode were regularly seen in terms of a musical setting. In the *Cabinet des Muses*

is seldom merely an extended paraphrase; in the manner of a meditation, it recreates and develops its source-material by means of techniques which frequently give the impression of controlled improvisation on an established theme.

The popularity of the *genre* (if such one can call it) is not fully
established until well into the 1570s, but prayer-poems certainly
existed long before: as with much Counter-Reformation poetry, there
are foreshadowings in Neo-Latin and also in the vernacular lyric before
the Pléiade—Marguerite de Navarre's *Miroir de l'âme pécheresse* is the
outstanding example, although it would require special treatment.[1]
The Pléiade of the pre-1560 period was not much concerned with
religious poetry, particularly of the 'introspective' kind, but the few
examples which do exist are important. Since they are scrupulously
revived by the earlier anthologies of the Counter-Reformation period
(such as the *Muse chrestienne* of 1582), there is no doubt about their
validity as predecessors of the vogue created in the 1570s. Du Bellay's
two *Hymnes chrestiens* or *cantiques* are by far the most relevant
examples; although they contain a great deal of Old Testament
narration, they also develop penitential themes on the lines of the
paraphrases:

> Si je ne suys que vile pouriture,
> Tel que je suis, je suis ta creature.
>
> Coupables sommes nous, si ta severité
> Regarde seulement à nostre iniquité:
> Mais si tu as egard à la noble nature,
> Dont tu nous as ornez sur toute creature...[2]

A more transitory member of the Pléiade, Jean de La Péruse, left an
Oraison pour avoir santé; although this poem appears to have achieved
no great popularity, it nevertheless anticipates the penitential 'sickness'

(Rouen, 1619), Bertaut's *Paraphrase sur le 6e Ps.* is printed under that title and again in
a slightly different version under the title *Cantique en forme de complainte*. See also
R. Picard, 'Aspects du lyrisme religieux au XVIIe siècle', *DSS*, 66–7, (1965), pp. 58, 59.

[1] Neo-Latin: see, for example, Salmon Macrin; Professor McFarlane enumerates among
his most constant themes 'son angoisse devant la condition humaine, la conscience du
mal, le problème de la souffrance' (*art. cit.*, *BHR*, 21 (1959), p. 67). As an example from
the vernacular lyric, one might quote with Sebillet Marot's *cantique*, *Sur la maladie
de s'amye* (*Œuvres lyriques*, ed. C. A. Mayer (London, 1964), pp. 304–5).

[2] Joachim Du Bellay, *Œuvres poétiques*, ed. Chamard (*STFM*), vol. IV, p. 111; *ibid.*
vol. V, p. 408. In this edition, both have the title *Hymne chrestien*; they are entitled
Cantiques in the Maisonfleur anthology.

poem. There is no reference to the physical details of the sickness, but the 'impatience' motif, involving a struggle between *chair* and *esprit*, is unmistakable:

> Las, seigneur, je sai bien que tu m'aimes, d'autant
> Que m'envoïant ce mal, tu vas ma chair dontant,
> Et que l'affliction, en ce monde ou nous sommes,
> Est un témoin fort seur que tu aimes les hommes.
> Je le sai bien, seigneur, mais quoi? ma pauvre chair
> Impatiente au mal, ne fait que se fâcher,
> Et rebelle à ton vueil, pour le mal qu'elle endure,
> Contrariant l'esprit, toujours elle murmure.[1]

Moreover, the introduction later in the poem of the 'sacrifice' theme ('Donc je n'egorgerai ne Taureaus ne Moutons') suggests that the Penitential Psalms were uppermost in La Péruse's mind.[2]

It is perhaps surprising that Belleau wrote no penitential prayer-poems: after the Job paraphrases and the *Amours de David et de Bersabée* he must have been thoroughly steeped in the Bibilical source-material. Some of the poetry published in the *Seconde journee* of his *Bergerie* tends in this direction—prayer with considerable Old Testament reference and contemporary allusion—but no complete poems in the *genre* emerge.[3] As in other fields, it is the Protestants who are the first to publish a substantial body of penitential lyrics. The 1574 anthology of *Poèmes chrestiens* has examples by Bèze, Tagaut, Mont-méja and Goulart, and many of them may have been written earlier.[4] There is an occasional hint of Calvinist doctrine ('nous avons ce grand heur / D'estre enfans de ta grace'),[5] but otherwise the pattern is exactly the same as in the Catholic poems. When one considers the restless heptasyllables of Tagaut, his psalm-like sickness and question-ing, his use of the tones of prayer and self-analysis, it becomes very clear that Desportes and his disciples were working in a well-established *genre*:

[1] Jean de La Péruse, *Les Œuvres* (Paris, 1573), fol. 69.
[2] See Psalm 51. 16; also Du Bellay, *ed. cit.* vol. IV, p. 118.
[3] The *Amours de David* itself is a kind of short penitential epic, with comments in the manner of the Psalms ('...tant plus nostre vice / Irrite sa rigueur, plus il nous est propice').
[4] See, for example, M. Raymond, 'Jean Tagaut, poète français et bourgeois de Genève', *RSS*, 12 (1925), pp. 98 ff.
[5] *Poèmes chrestiens* (Geneva, 1574), p. 20 (from Montméja's *Prière à Dieu en temps de peste*).

Chasse-moy ma maladie
Dehors du creux de mes os...
Estein ceste fievre lente
Qui me rend sec comme bois.

Je ne trouve en moy que terre.
O que ceste chair me lasse!

Jusques à quand me plaindray-je
Du dueil que porte mon cœur?
Las! jusques à quand vivray-je
Tout abatu de langueur?...
Mes jours sont nuits tenebreuses...
Mes jours s'en vont en fumee...

Je hay ma vie et moy-mesme,
D'avoir vescu si longtemps
En tenebres, je suis blesme,
Perdant le fruict de mes ans.[1]

And yet, in spite of all this native material, the Protestant *Uranie* of 1591 will find it necessary to 'convert' poems by Desportes and Garnier to fill out the anthology.[2]

Meanwhile, on the margin of the activities of the Pléiade and their opponents, one comes across certain minor poets who anticipate later patterns, both in their use of themes and by virtue of their non-professional status. Among these is Nicolle Bargedé, whose *Odes pénitentes du moins que rien* use an unadorned style, with occasional Old Testament allusions, to express a penitential mood. The *Ode de l'autheur sur une fievre tierce de laquelle il feut malade à Paris* contains a long description of the fever, and a semi-humorous account of the visits of his friends; but towards the end, Bargedé explains his sickness in terms of sin, and moves into a psalm-like prayer for forgiveness and relief:

O dieu, mon offence patente
Me punist, et non ta rigueur,
Dont je viz en peine et langueur...
Helas Seigneur ne te recorde
De mes pechez, mais par ta grace
De ceste eau de pitié efface
Mes vices, en me regardant

---

[1] *Ibid.* pp. 58, 68, 73–4, 76. ²See below, pp. 118–19.

En glasse froid, en feu ardant,
Alteré de la pauvre bouche,
Tant qu'au pallais la langue touche
Denuee de ma salive...[1]

Some twenty years later, Sœur Anne de Marquets, a poet who was to acquire considerably more renown than Bargedé, but who was no less an 'amateur', produced her translations of Flaminio. These include a poem entitled *Pour invoquer Dieu en longue et griefve maladie*, which is based on the commonplace material of the poetry of sickness and affliction:

Ja par cinq fois la lune s'est fait plaine
Depuis le temps qu'une fiebvre inhumaine
Ronge et destruict mes membres indispos...
O bon Jesus d'un œil doux et clement
Voi mes langueurs, mon travail et tourment,
Et que ta dextre à soustenir s'appreste
Celle qui est à tomber tout preste.[2]

Sister Mary Seiler points out that one of Anne's own sonnets, *Estant malade et ne pouvant dormir*, is based on a similar theme, although here the physical reference is very limited, since the poem dwells mainly on the 'contentement' which arises from contemplation of the 'beauté', 'excellence' and 'pouvoir' of God.

Sœur Anne's example was no doubt not without its influence; and her importation of Italian material established a significant precedent. For Henri III's poets, Italy was to provide as many models as France, and for some time now Italy had been publishing religious poems of all kinds. Anthologies like the *Rime spirituali* (Venice, 1550) give pride of place to poems with a New Testament background, but there are also parallels to the penitential and sickness poem—Bembo's *Lamentatione*, for example, and prayers in verse written by Agnolo Firenzuola

---

[1] *Les Odes pénitentes du moins que rien* (Paris, 1550), fols. Hiii–Hiv. See also the last stanza of the sixth ode (fol. Ciii):

Ton destre bras tant ne descueuvre
Sa fureur que de ce tien œuvre,
Duquel as esté plasmateur,
N'ait pitié ô mon redempteur.

Technically, this collection is interesting, in that it comprises a mixture of odes, *ballades*, and sonnets; Bargedé also uses the alexandrine from time to time. Since homage is explicitly paid to Ronsard, this seems to be a very early example of 'Pléiade' influence.

[2] *Les Divines Poesies de Marc Antoine Flaminius*, p. 14. Quoted by Sister Mary Seiler, *Anne de Marquets*, p. 72.

on his sickbed.[1] Poets of a later vintage like Pagani and Tansillo were also of considerable importance in determining the direction of religious poetry in France. Nevertheless, the Louvre poets—Desportes, Amadis Jamyn, Blanchon, Boyssières, Isaac Habert—helped to expand the penitential lyric independently by paraphrasing well-known prayers and by going further afield in their choice of themes with a contemporary relevance. Verse prayers for times of war, plague and famine had cropped up at appropriate moments ever since the later Middle Ages, but at this stage the devotional atmosphere becomes more distinct through a convergence with the themes of personal sickness and confession. The sickness poem is by now coming into its own as a specific kind of variation on penitential themes, and Jamyn also has prayers for those undertaking voyages, and for the dead.

In the 1580s, religious anthologies begin to multiply, presenting a cross-section of verse from the Pléiade onwards and setting Du Bellay side by side with newer writers like Jacques de Billy and Desportes. The editorial policy of these collections may be expressly partisan, like that of the 1582 *Muse chrestienne,* or it may be as liberal as Maisonfleur's, who supports his own penitential *cantiques* with others by Du Bellay and Desportes, as well as by his fellow-Protestant Sautemont.

At about this time too, the penitential lyric was beginning to appear as a prologue, interlude, or conclusion in longer works. D'Aubigné's *Misères* ends with a prayer of 108 lines; the Old Testament 'enemies' theme is heavily stressed to suit the needs of Protestant propaganda, but apart from this, and d'Aubigné's characteristic expansion of psalm-language, the themes follow the usual pattern:

> Ne veux-tu plus avoir d'autres temples sacrez
> Qu'un blanchissant amas d'os de morts massacrez?
> Les morts te loueront-ils? Tes faicts grands et terribles
> Sortiront-ils du creux de ces bouches horribles?
> N'aurons-nous entre nous que visages terreux
> Murmurans ta loüange aux secrets de nos creux?[2]

The Prophet's monologue which opens Garnier's *Les Juifves* and states the themes of sin and suffering which are central to the play, is in many respects another of these penitential prayer-poems: the play

---

[1] *Rime spirituali. Libro secondo,* (Venice, 1550), fols. 19 and 27–32.
[2] A. d'Aubigné, *Misères,* ll. 1327–32.

opens on the familiar formula 'jusques à quand. . . ?' Here, however, the
dramatic context demands a division into two equal parts, of which the
first (lines 1–42) is a prayer, and the second (43–90) a moral apostrophe
on the same themes; there is a similar monologue in the third act of
Montchrestien's *Aman*.[1] A great deal of the poetry in *Les Juifves* (the
choruses in particular) takes the form of a meditative development on
penitential themes.

The handful of prayer-poems written by Philippe Desportes may
be used as a centre-point for the discussion of the *genre*. They have
frequently been neglected in favour of Desportes's secular work; and
they seem to me to be worth reconsidering, not perhaps because they
are more 'personal' or 'sincere' than the love-sonnets, but because the
way in which they combine emotive themes with a certain overall
structure and movement can make a fresh impact on the reader weary
of Petrarchan urbanities. Devotion and poetry have here coincided to
produce a poetic texture which is often less 'finished' than one might
have expected from Desportes, but whose very roughness can at times
invigorate. At the same time, these poems are not unrepresentative.
They were written at a time when the *genre* was well established; they
exemplify most of its outstanding characteristics; and there is an
appropriate connexion with the penitential atmosphere of the reign of
Henri III. Moreover, the name of Desportes provides an essential link
with the field of Old Testament paraphrase, and is largely responsible
for the sustained popularity of the *genre*.

Desportes appears to have written six religious poems apart from
his sonnets and his paraphrases: a *Plainte de l'autheur durant une sienne
longue maladie*, two other *Plaintes* (beginning 'Depuis six mois. . .'
and 'Des abysmes d'ennuis. . .'), a *Prière* ('Las! que feray-je?'), a
Prière en forme de confession, and an *Ode* ('Arriere, ô fureur insensée').[2]
The titles are not altogether random: the *plainte* seems to be based on
an affliction which the poet is suffering (sickness, or the death of
friends); the *prière* is primarily confessional, revolving round the
relationship of the sinner to God; and the *ode* dwells on the nature of
poetry, on the rejection of the profane for the sacred. Nevertheless,
the subject-matter of the group as a whole is relatively homogeneous:

[1] A. de Montchrestien, *Tragédies*, ed. Petit de Julleville (Paris, 1891), p. 252–5.
[2] I shall call the two *Plaintes* respectively *Plainte I* and *Plainte II*.

the *ode* will include penitential self-deprecation, the *prière* will be enriched by descriptions of physical affliction.

Like every other sixteenth-century poet, Desportes uses direct quotation as an element of composition; and an examination of the way in which the poet creates his own pattern out of these quotations will give some insight into the area in which psalm-paraphrase overlaps with the penitential lyric, and will provide a starting-point for the analysis of the poems themselves. The *Prière* is a characteristic example of the way in which Desportes reorientates his psalm-material, since it contains three stanzas which at first sight seem to be taken wholesale from Psalm 139 (*Domine probasti me*). The Vulgate text runs as follows:

Quo ibo a spiritu tuo? et quo a facie tua fugiam?

Si ascendero in caelum, tu illic es; si descendero in infernum, ades.

Si sumpsero pennas meas diluculo, et habitavero in extremis maris,

Etenim illuc manus tua deducet me, et tenebit me dextera tua.

Et dixi: Forsitan tenebrae conculcabunt me; et nox illuminatio mea in deliciis meis,

Quia tenebrae non obscurabuntur a te, et nox sicut dies illuminabitur; sicut tenebrae ejus, ita et lumen ejus.

Here are the corresponding stanzas of Desportes's own paraphrase:[1]

Où fuiray-je? ô Seigneur! où m'en pourray-je aller,
Evitant ton esprit et l'aspect de ta face?
Tu remplis tous les cieux, si j'y pense voler,
Et tout au mesme instant, si je change de place,
Je te trouve aux enfers, quand je veux devaler.

Si j'attache à mon dos le plumage divers
De l'aurore embausmée, et recelle ma fuite
Jusqu'aux bouts plus perdus des plus lontaines mers,
Ta main par tout m'attrape, ardante à ma poursuite,
Et ton bras ne me perd en l'obscur des deserts.

Quand j'ay dict: 'Pour le moins les tenebres du soir
Couvriront mes plaisirs', faulse est mon esperance;
Car la nuict à l'instant prend des yeux pour me voir:
Les tenebres, Seigneur, sont jour en ta presence,
Et le jour se fait nuict, s'il plaist à ton pouvoir.[2]

---

[1] I have recently heard from M. Jeanneret that Desportes's psalm-paraphrases were not based on the Vulgate alone; this fact may substantially modify the comparison as I have stated it, but it is likely that the differences will bear on verbal detail rather than on structural development.   [2] Desportes, ed. Michiels, pp. 523–4.

And of the *Prière*:

Cachons-nous donc, mais où pourray-je aller,
Au ciel, en l'onde, en la terre ou en l'air,
O Seigneur Dieu, pour éviter ta face?
Si je me cache en l'obscur de la nuit,
Ton œil divin par les ombres reluit,
Et tout soudain remarquera ma trace.

D'aller au ciel, tu es là présidant;
Il vaut donc mieux fuïr en descendant
Et me musser au plus creux de la terre.
Mais ce seroit redoubler mon tourment,
Car aux enfers tu as commandement,
Et jusques là tu me feras la guerre.

Soit que je veille ou que je sois couché,
Rien que je fasse, helas! ne t'est caché;
Tu me descouvre et cognois ma pensée.
Veux-je fuïr, tu me viens attraper,
Et, pour courir, je ne puis eschapper
Devant ta main justement courroucée. (p. 496.)

On close examination of the *Prière*, it becomes clear that Desportes, while adding little to the themes of the Psalm, has not followed exactly the order of the original: the 'Etenim illuc manus tua...' verse has for example been resited after a passage which recalls two earlier verses ('Tu cognovisti sessionem meam et resurrectionem meam. / Intellexisti cogitationes meas de longe'). At the same time, there is one significant addition—the phrase 'justement courroucée'. These differences regain their full importance when one considers the *Prière* as a whole. The psalm is an expression of spiritual nakedness, of God's total knowledge of man; the conclusion, which is a prayer for purification, reveals the sinner's confidence rather than his fear of God's justice ('Et vide si via iniquitatis in me est; et deduc me in via aeterna') and even the 'deliciis meis' verse does not insist on the theme of sin or punishment. The *Prière* on the other hand is full of doubt and instability; the awed resignation of the psalmist is transformed into an extreme mental anguish in the face of God's searching wrath. The first two stanzas of the poem (which are followed by those quoted above) establish this mood immediately:

Las! que feray-je? oseray-je hausser
Mes yeux au ciel, pour mon cri t'adresser,
Durant la peur qui mon ame environne?
Je suis confus, tout le sens me defaut,
Mon œil se trouble, et mon cœur qui tressaut
Me fait trembler, tant mon forfait m'estonne!
Je veux fuïr, je veux fuïr devant
L'ardent courroux de ce grand Dieu vivant,
Qui tient en main l'orage et la tempeste;
Car mon peché, qui le rend courroucé,
Merite bien que son foudre eslancé
En mille esclats me partisse la teste.

The stress on the 'courroux' of God and the sin which justifies it
explains the introduction of 'justement courroucée' at the end of the
psalm-allusion, but not the change in the order of themes. This
becomes clearer when one looks at the stanza with which Desportes
continues his poem:

Ne pouvant donc ta fureur éviter,
J'ose, ô mon Dieu! j'ose me presenter,
Palle et tremblant, à ta majesté sainte,
La veuë en bas mille pleurs degoutant,
L'ame debile et le cœur tout battant
Dans ma poitrine horriblement attainte.

The poem here changes direction. Having proved that flight is
impossible, the sinner presents himself in total humiliation and deep
disquiet to the majesty of God; whereas the psalmist continues by
considering, in the major key of praise, God's creation of his body.
Thus in retrospect, the last stanza of the psalm-allusion appears as a
final emphatic restatement of the themes of God's omniscience and of
flight; the way in which the original moves into paradoxes on the theme
of *nox-dies* would have been less suited to Desportes's overall purpose.

It is interesting that for his paraphrase Desportes should have used
the ample alexandrine metre, with few rhythmic disturbances, giving
an overall impression of symmetry and stateliness: this quality is
enhanced by decorative expansions such as 'le plumage divers / De
l'aurore embausmée', and represents an appropriate development of
the psalmist's sense of omnipresence and cosmic splendour. The *Prière*,
on the other hand, is in uneasy decasyllables; the additions never

decorate, they always point the penitential themes. In this way, the two passages represent totally different poetic interpretations of the same text; and it is the less measured, the more unstable of the two, which is characteristic of the penitential lyric.

In his reorientation of the psalm-themes, Desportes also uses the technique of augmentation which is so common in prose meditation. In *Domine probasti me*, the phrase 'manus tua' has no overtones of menace (although Desportes's paraphrase seems to imply that it has); at the same time, to anyone familiar with Old Testament literature, it could easily evoke the image of God's hand outstretched in token of wrath and destruction. It is precisely this connexion which is made in the prayer-poem; and likewise, the 'ardent courroux de ce grand Dieu vivant, / Qui tient en main l'orage et la tempeste' is derived from the overall Old Testament world-picture. Later in the poem, Desportes piles up Biblical imagery to produce an effect of extreme violence: without direct quotation, he is 'imitating' and at the same time elaborating the language of the Penitential Psalms:

> Darde sur moy la fureur de ton bras,
> Saccage moy, fay ce que tu voudras,
> Lance du ciel ta flamme estincelante...
> Desjà, Seigneur, desjà j'ay bien senti
> Sur moy, chetif, ton bras appesanti...
> Ton trait vengeur, contre moy décoché
> De son venin m'a cuit et desseiché:
> Il boit mon sang, il brusle mes entrailles:
> Je suis pressé par ton dur jugement
> D'une frayeur et d'un estonnement,
> Et sens au cœur mille rouges tenailles.   (pp. 496–7.)

These augmentations are not derived exclusively from the Old Testament. *Plainte II* contains a series of New Testament *exempla* which justify the optimism of the penitent—the good Samaritan, the lost sheep, the prodigal son. Similarly, Amadis Jamyn uses the good Samaritan motif to develop his theme of sickness and cure.[1] Thus the resolution and the consolation which the life of Christ represents for the sinner may be introduced, or at least implied, in order to give a new perspective to the themes of penitence.

Although the sickness poem can be considered as a kind of sub-

---

[1] A. Jamyn, *Le Second volume des œuvres* (Paris, 1584), fol. 10 (*En affliction*).

genre, sickness or affliction is the prevailing image in most penitential prayer-poems: indeed, some of the poetry written *en temps de maladie* by Desportes's contemporaries has less reference to physical torment than the general 'confession'.[1] As in devotional prose, the sickness is standardised on Old Testament lines: however much the poet dwells on it, the principal features remain the same—wasting, ulcers, *bouche infecte*:

> Je n'ay pas seulement du sang dedans les veines
> Pour respandre à boüillons par la bouche et les yeux...
> Les os percent ma peau, ma langue est ulcerée...
> Pour tout nourrissement j'engloutis ma salive... (p. 513.)

And insomnia:

> Depuis quatorze jours je n'ay clos les paupieres... (p. 513.)
>
> Le sommeil jamais ne me touche... (p. 493.)
>
> Las! je ne puis, je ne puis reposer! (p. 497.)

Notice, however, that this last theme is on more than one occasion developed in a way which is less dependent on the Psalms: the poet is subject to visions and hallucinations:

> Las! je n'ay clos les yeux pour sommeiller,
> Que tout tremblant il me faut reveiller,
> Espouventé de visions horribles. (p. 497.)
>
> Depuis quatorze jours je n'ay clos les paupieres,
> Et le somme, enchanteur des peines journalieres,
> De sa liqueur charmée en vain me va mouillant;
> Il est vray que l'effort du mal que je supporte
> Rend ma teste assommée, et m'assoupit de sorte
> Qu'on me jugeroit mort, ou tousjours sommeillant.
>
> En cest estonnement mille figures vaines,
> Tousjours d'effroy, de meurtre et d'horreur toutes pleines,
> Reveillent coup sur coup mon esprit agité;
> Je resve incessamment, et ma vague pensée,
> Puis deçà, puis delà, sans arrest est poussée,
> Comme un vaisseau rompu par les vents emporté. (p. 513.)

This theme is one which d'Aubigné is using, at much the same time as Desportes, for his profane as well as his religious poetry; its appearance in literature may or may not be related to a contemporary

---

[1] See, for example, Jean de Boyssières, *Les Troisiesmes œuvres*, pp. 74–5, *Prieres en Pira-mide renversees, pour un malade*, which have no details of the sickness; likewise Jamyn's *En tems de griefve maladie, op. cit.* fols. 10–11.

familiarity with plague and war-wounds, but at all events it is for Desportes a useful means of stressing the themes of agitation and mental disorientation which are uppermost in his penitential poems. Similarly, in the passage beginning 'Darde sur moy...' quoted above, the images of burning and blood are very much in the d'Aubigné manner (here the contemporary and the Old Testament backgrounds converge completely); and the rhyme *entrailles–tenailles* is one which is particularly favoured by the civil war poets. In these ways, the technique of augmentation, starting from a common set of *topoi*, can produce all manner of resonances and allow the poet to vary his material without losing sight of his central preoccupation.

The analysis of the opening section of the *Prière* gave some idea of the care which Desportes takes in constructing his poems; one will remember how he established a tone in the first stanza and developed it through an adapted psalm-quotation to the modulation at 'Ne pouvant donc...' (the *donc* is a clear structural phrase-mark). In longer poems of this kind, the poet has to cope with problems of organisation and coherence, particularly where he wishes to preserve something of the extempore nature of inward prayer. Having already seen how he overcomes the difficulty of sustaining commonplace themes without thinness or repetition, we shall therefore now consider the structure of these poems and their movement, both in a general sense and in the rhythm of the individual line. There are in fact elements of a common pattern: the opening stanzas usually consist of a direct statement of the sinner's degradation, leading into a discussion of the problems this poses and thence to a final prayer for forgiveness. The one exception is the *Ode*, which is organised around the *contr'amour* theme; this theme, together with the invocation of the Christian Muse or of a *sainte fureur*, is of course one of the most common themes of religious poetry of all kinds from Du Bellay onwards, and one is grateful that in his other poems Desportes makes no further claims of 'conversion', and, above all, by-passes the introductory *topos* ('Arriere, ô fureur insensée!... Seigneur, change et monte ma lyre...').[1] Not that the *Ode* is in itself

---

[1] Blanchon prays for a conversion in terms which are verbally almost identical with certain passages of Desportes's *Ode* (*Les Premieres œuvres poetiques*, sonnet 15, pp. 192–3; see also p. 172 and p. 181). Certain of Desportes's sonnets (notably no. 3: Michiels, p. 503) develop similar themes—the sonnet-form is of course particularly suitable for the 'anti-Petrarchan' conversion *topos*.

unsuccessful: the way in which the conversion theme is taken up later in the poem in the light of the central penitential development creates a pattern which gives the *topos* an unaccustomed depth. Nevertheless, it is as well that the other prayer-poems have a pattern of their own, and one which is closer to the devotional sequence of composition, analysis and affective prayer (though one should perhaps not insist too heavily on this similarity).

One may take as a preliminary example the *Plainte de l'autheur*, which, like Blanchon's *Plainte durant une maladie* and other sickness poems, begins with an elegiac description of the author's distress, without relation to the theme of sin; the confessional element appears later, when the poem moves into the tone of prayer. There is here a graduated intensification, leading from a physical depiction of sickness to the 'impatience' motif which provides a climax of apostrophe and questioning. Here are the first two stanzas, which take the reader immediately into the world of Job:

> Ma chair comme eau s'est escoulée,
> Et ma peau defaicte est colée
> Sur mes os pourris par dedans;
> Tout mon bien est mort en une heure.
> Et rien de moy ne me demeure
> Que la levre aupres de mes dens.
>
> Mes yeux ont tari leurs fontaines,
> Mes nuits d'amertume sont pleines,
> Mes jours sont horribles d'effroy;
> Le sommeil jamais ne me touche,
> Et la puanteur de ma bouche
> Fait que j'ay mesme horreur de moy.   (p. 493.)

The affliction is then explained, much as in the *Prière*, in terms of God's wrath:

> La main du Seigneur courroucée
> S'est en fureur sur moy poussée...

In stanza 5, the tone of the poem changes; the theme of punishment is sustained, but God is now addressed directly, and the remainder of the poem is in the form of a prayer rather than a monologue:

> Seigneur, punisseur des offances,
> On remarque ici tes vengeances
> Et les forces de ta rigueur.

From this point onward there is a constant fluctuation of position; Job-like questionings ('M'as-tu formé pour me desfaire?') culminate in an indictment of 'un Dieu trop inhumain' which is immediately revoked ('Pardonne-moy si je blaspheme'), only to be repeated in a slightly different context two stanzas later ('Je maudi la celeste grace'). This fluctuating movement reaches its climax in the last stanzas, where the elements of prayer and argument are summarised: first an invocation of God's retributive violence:

> Si ta vengeance est trop petite,
> Puny moy selon mon merite,
> Seigneur, ne me pardonne rien;
> Hausse ta main rouge de foudre,
> Et reduy tous mes os en poudre,
> Je n'attens point de plus grand bien.

And finally a contrasting plea for mercy:

> Ou si dans ta poitrine sainte
> La pitié n'est du tout estainte,
> Sauve l'ouvrage de tes mains...

In 1591, the same poem appeared in adapted form in the Protestant anthology *Uranie*; in this version, every implication that God's infliction of suffering is unjust or even questionable is systematically eliminated. The most extreme expression of Desportes's rebellion, 'Je maudi la celeste grace', is converted to the opposite meaning ('Ta grace en mon ame je sen'), and the violence of the language is throughout attenuated—the three lines beginning 'Hausse ta main...' become

> Misericorde je requier,
> Et si ta grace, ô Dieu, j'acquier
> Je ne veux point de plus grand bien.[1]

Whether or not this conversion is proof of a difference between Catholic and Protestant doctrine,[2] it demonstrates very effectively how de-

---

[1] For an accessible text of this and other examples, see R. Lebègue, 'Plagiats protestants de poésies de Garnier et de Desportes', *BHR*, 13 (1951), pp. 355 ff., and 14 (1952), pp. 334 ff.

[2] This seems to me unlikely. In the last instance quoted, the original is perfectly in keeping with the orthodox Calvinist view of man in relation to God. It is possible that the reviser is being particularly strict because he is using the poem of a leading Catholic—lines which would not have shocked him in the poetry of a fellow-Calvinist are liable to his censorship when written by a Catholic. Moreover, one can easily find instances

pendent Desportes's poem is on the emotional *agitato* of its structure; Desportes has a sense of intensification and climax, whereas the Protestant revision is slack and lifeless.

The structure of *Plainte II* is likewise determined by a movement between lamentation and a disturbed consideration of the causes of so much affliction. Two stanzas articulate this movement: the third, which establishes the central problem, the mood of doubt, and the eighth, in which an exclamatory prayer attempts to exorcise the uncertainty:

> Tu m'as posé pour butte aux angoisses ameres,
> Aux malheurs, aux regrets, aux fureurs, aux miseres;
> Mon mal n'est toutesfois si grand que mon erreur.
> Mais si, pourray-je dire en ma peine effroyable,
> Bien que je te reclame et doux et pitoyable,
> Tu me fais trop sentir les traits de ta fureur...
>
> Helas! sois-moy propice, ô mon Dieu! mon refuge!
> Puny-moy comme pere, et non pas comme juge,
> Et modere un petit le martyre où je suis;
> Tu ne veux point la mort du pecheur plein de vice,
> Mais qu'il change de vie et qu'il se convertisse;
> Las! je le veux assez, mais sans toy je ne puis. (p. 513.)

Between these two points, the 'hallucination' stanzas already quoted ('Depuis quatorze jours...') carry the feeling of disorientation to its extreme physical point. The eighth stanza terminates the central argument, but it also initiates a new development. The poet, identifying himself with various figures from New Testament parables, gradually moves into a mood of confidence: Lazarus is raised from the dead, the prodigal son is reinstated, and likewise, it is implied, the sinner will be absolved. The climax of this development and of the whole poem, following logically upon the New Testament allusions of the previous stanzas, is an evocation of the Passion and an anticipation of Paradise:

> Par le fruict de sa mort j'attens vie eternelle;
> Lavée en son pur sang, mon ame sera belle...
> O Dieu! tousjours vivant, j'ay ferme confiance

of the 'questioning' *topos* in the poetry of notable Calvinists (see above, pp. 106–7). In his article 'Calvinisme et poésie au seizième siècle en France' (*BSHPF*, 84 (1935), pp. 211 ff.), Albert-Marie Schmidt, erring in the opposite direction, actually makes of the questioning of God a Calvinist theme. See also Richter, 'La Poetica di Théodore de Bèze e le *Chrestiennes Méditations*', especially pp. 516–18; and Higman, *art. cit.*, *BHR*, 28 (1966).

The penitential prayer

> Qu'en l'extreme des jours, par ta toute-puissance,
> Ce corps couvert de terre, à ta voix se dressant,
> Prendra nouvelle vie et, par ta pure grace,
> J'auray l'heur de te voir de mes yeux face à face,
> Avec les bien-heureux ton sainct nom benissant.

This ascending movement naturally points in the direction of the Passion meditation proper; but the theme of the Last Judgement and of the resurrection of the body is reminiscent rather of the *Libera me*, which Desportes also paraphrased:

> O Seigneur, dont la main toutes choses enserre,
> Pere eternel de tout, qui m'as formé de terre,
> Qui rens par ton pur sang nos pechez nettoyez,
> Et qui feras lever mon corps de pourriture,
> Entens mes tristes cris jusqu'au ciel envoyez,
> Et prens pitié de moy, qui suis ta creature.

> Exauce, exauce, ô Dieu! ma priere enflammée!
> Destourne loin de moy ta colere allumée,
> Fay porter mon esprit par un doux jugement
> Dans le sein d'Abraham, avec tous les fidelles,
> Afin que ton sainct nom je chante incessamment
> Jouïssant bien-heureux des clairtez eternelles.[1]

One other poem, the *Prière en forme de confession*, demands analysis; it is the most closely constructed of the whole group. The opening of the poem, with its images of storm, night, mist and shipwreck, evokes an atmosphere of darkness and confusion; against this is set the intervention of God ('ton secours', 'tes rayons'), invoked and immediately granted. But with the coming of light, a new tension is set up: the sinner is now able to perceive clearly the extent of his corruption. Stanza 3 brings two more changes of position: the sinner first prays for his eyes to be covered, then for them to be opened wider, 'Pour contempler ta grace et tes grans benefices'.[2] The intuitive leaps from one theme to another in these introductory stanzas seem somewhat confusing at first sight. When one looks at the poem as a whole, however, it becomes clear that Desportes is establishing at the outset an antithesis which is to be developed in detail. Following on the theme of 'bene-

---

[1] Michiels, pp. 498-9. In this instance, augmentation of Old Testament material takes place through contact with the liturgy.
[2] *Ibid.* p. 515 (the poem begins on the previous page).

fices', stanzas 4–7 are a prayer of thanksgiving: the poet withdraws into the 'night' of his soul, illuminated by the light of God's eye, and contemplates the marvel of his creation and the world's. Certain lines, here and elsewhere in the poem, seem to echo one of the fundamental themes of mystical devotion: since each soul contains a fragment of the essence of God, the aim of the meditator is to achieve a true self-contemplation:

> Or' que tout dedans moy je me suis retiré,
> Des rayons de ton œil en ma nuict esclairé,
> Que je voy de thresors dont tu m'es favorable![1]

At all events this passage is highly affirmative; light overcomes dark, and the major key of praise and of the beauty of creation predominates. Furthermore, its place in the overall structure is carefully indicated by the last lines of stanza 7, which repeat almost verbally the lines quoted above:

> Voylà ce qu'en l'esprit je voy de ta bonté,
> Lors que ton œil divin mes tenebres esclaire.

At this point, however, the mood changes radically; the penitent sees himself in the mirror of the Law:

> Mais quand je me regarde au miroir de ta loy,
> Que dedans et dehors transformé je me voy,
> Que je trouve en mon ame et de crasse et d'ordure!
> Que mes sens corrompus sont devenus infects...

Thus two kinds of self-contemplation are contrasted to produce a maximum degree of tension: Creation is followed by the Fall. Desportes now considers in turn the corruption of his *esprit* and of his *cœur* (involving an enumeration of most of the deadly sins), and then of his sight, hearing and speech: the confessional nature of this development is stressed by the litany-like anaphora, both from stanza to stanza and from line to line ('Cet esprit...Ce cœur...Ces yeux...Mon oreille...'; 'Il a souvent bouilly...Il a senti douleur...Il a long-tans

---

[1] This theme is taken up again later in the poem:
> Cest esprit que divin tu m'avois faict avoir,
> Pour l'elever au ciel, pour entendre et sçavoir,
> Et pour te recognoistre aux traits de ton ouvrage,
> Esgaré du sentier de sa felicité,
> A choisi pour le vray l'ombre et la vanité...

couvé...Il s'est enflé...'; 'Je n'ay faict que mentir...J'ay despité le ciel...J'en ay flaté les grands...J'ay semé la discorde...J'ay souvent enchanté...'). This passage, which is the focal point of the poem, is recapitulated and concluded in stanza 17:

> Bref, chacun de mes sens, tant dedans que dehors,
> Et chacune des parts de l'esprit et du corps
> N'ont plus rien qui ressemble à leur forme premiere;
> Un seul trait de ta main n'est sur moy demeuré;
> Je suis un monstre horrible et si defiguré,
> Que de peur de me voir je fuy toute lumiere.

Notice how Desportes carefully reintroduces here the fundamental themes of light, seeing, and creation, so that the poem retains its unity as it develops. The confession proper is now concluded, although echoes of it will appear later, and there follow three stanzas of penitential weeping and lamentation. The first of these extends a hyperbole (based on a reference to Moses and the rock) by means of parallelisms which recall Hebrew verse:

> Qui du roc de mon cœur sortira des fontaines?
> Qui grossira mon chef de torrens furieux?
> Qui de larges ruisseaux m'enflera les deux yeux,
> Pour noyer mes peschez, mon angoisse et mes peines?

This is followed by a further *reprise* of earlier themes—darkness and daylight again, and the 'livre de Dieu' (the Book of Creation), provoking an apostrophe to the created world itself ('Monts, bois, fleuves, rochers, pleurez mon adventure!'). These are the only three stanzas in the poem which are not in the form of a prayer; in this way the tone is varied so that the final plea to God will have a greater impact. The concluding movement is introduced by a 'Mais pourtant...' which again clearly marks the structure; much as in the *Prière*, the sinner, having reached the lowest point of despair, decides to present himself to God and pray for forgiveness:

> Mais pourtant à mon Dieu je me veux presenter,
> Je veux, las! à ses piés tout en pleurs me jeter,
> Poussant du fond du cœur ceste voix lamentable:
> 'J'ay pesché devant toy, pere doux et clement...'[1]

---

[1] Notice how this new development echoes the prodigal son motif of the preceding stanza (J'ay deslaissé mon pere et son bien despensé, / Puis avec les pourceaux j'ay pris ma nourriture'), thus cementing the construction still further.

The last stanza brings together the themes of illumination, purification of the senses, and the proper use of *cœur*, *ame* and *corps*:

> Esclaire à mon esprit, et le conduis à toy,
> Rempli mon cœur d'amour, de confiance et de foy,
> De tous objets trompeurs mes yeux veuille distraire,
> Mon oreille à jamais soit ta voix escoutant,
> Ma bouche incessamment ta gloire aille chantant,
> Et que d'ame et de corps sans fin je te revere.

Thus a series of contrasts between dark and light, self-deprecation and praise, sin and forgiveness are in this poem developed in a relatively complex manner: themes are stated, inverted and taken up again in different contexts. At the same time, the movement is controlled by a number of tactfully inserted landmarks ('Or que', 'Mais', 'Bref', 'Mais pourtant'); these do not impose a rigid syntactical framework which would have over-formalised the progression of thought—they merely signal a change of tone.

In these poems, problems are posed and tensions are created in an emotional context which excludes any form of intellectual or theological reasoning; the restless questionings may be exorcised at the conclusion of the poem by an intuitive modulation from despair to confidence, but they are never answered in rational terms. Similarly, the tension between creation and corruption which is set up in the *Prière en forme de confession* is irreducible: the two opposing interpretations of man's nature co-exist and cannot be reconciled, in this world at least. Thus, although most of the poems conclude on an optimistic note, the optimism is by no means a final release from the sufferings of the body or the doubts of the mind. It is significant that Desportes, in the second *Plainte* and elsewhere, does not try to achieve a flight from body to soul but rather a confidence in the resurrection of his own corrupt body, 'ce corps couvert de terre', 'mon corps de pourriture'. The main preoccupation of the penitential lyric as conceived by Desportes and by other poets of his day remains an anguished awareness of sin expressed in highly physical terms, and the attempt to see this suffering in relation to God's justice; the point of departure is the extreme antithesis between God and sinner, an antithesis full of disquiet and at times of pathos:

> . . . Toy, soleil flamboyant, seul pere des lumieres,
> Moy, nuage espaissi, moite d'obscurité.   (p. 501.)

Or as Antoine de Vermeil puts it in his *Autre devote meditation*, written some twenty or thirty years later than Desportes's poem:

> Tombee à tes pieds sur ma face,
> O moy miserable Vermeil,
> Qui ne suis qu'une obscure masse
> Oseray-je prendre l'audace
> D'ainsi parler à mon Soleil?[1]

Judging by his secular work, one might have expected Desportes to underplay these effects and make his affliction as elegant as possible, but this is seldom the case. By means of the technique of augmentation, he increases the violence of Old Testament language to a point at which one is reminded of d'Aubigné; and the same applies to his descriptions of sickness, which tend to be more detailed and prolonged than in the poems of his contemporaries or successors. With this greater violence and urgency of tone goes a widening of the range of harmonies and rhythms. Desportes is famous for his ability to blend sounds in such a way as to avoid harshness and unevenness, and many lines in the religious poems reveal precisely the same skill:

> ...Et le somme, enchanteur des peines journalieres,
> De sa liqueur charmée en vain me va mouillant.

But more often the liquid l's, v's and m's give way to harsher alliterations or at least appear in a context where there is no chance of their becoming soporific:

> Les os percent me peau, ma langue est ulcerée.

Likewise, Desportes tends to break up the rhythm of the line at points of emotional tension, and this is particularly noticeable in the poems

---

[1] *Le Parnasse des plus excellents poetes de ce temps* (Lyons, Ancelin, *s.d.*), fol. 356. See also Isaac Habert, *Œuvres chrestiennes*, fol. 17; unlike Desportes's concise, finely-balanced parallelism, Habert's occupies a full alexandrine *stance*, adopting an expansive sermon-tone, full of aggressive irony:

> Quoy! oserois tu bien lever au Ciel ton œil?
> Te voudrois tu monstrer devant ce clair Soleil,
> Ce Soleil de bonté, de douceur, de justice,
> Toy noire de peché, de fraude, et de malice,
> Couverte du limon des salles voluptez,
> Et grosse du venin de mille vanitez?

written in shorter metres (octosyllables and decasyllables). Listen again to the opening of the *Prière*:

> Las! que feray-je? oseray-je hausser
> Mes yeux au ciel, pour mon cri t'adresser,
> Durant la peur qui mon ame environne?
> Je suis confus, tout le sens me defaut,
> Mon œil se trouble, et mon cœur qui tressaut
> Me fait trembler, tant mon forfait m'estonne!
>
> Je veux fuïr, je veux fuïr devant
> L'ardent courroux de ce grand Dieu vivant. . .

The disturbed and emphatic repetition of a phrase (sometimes after a brief *incise*) seems to have been a favourite device of Desportes's, at least in this poem, where it occurs six times, always underlining the restless movement:

> Je veux fuïr, je veux fuïr. . .
> J'ose, ô mon Dieu, j'ose me presenter. . .
> Tu peux, helas! tu peux me foudroyer. . .
> Tes mains pourtant, tes mains m'ont composé. . .
> Desjà, Seigneur, desjà j'ay bien senti
> Sur moy, chetif, ton bras appesanti. . .
> Las! je ne puis, je ne puis reposer!

It is only fair to say that in some of the other poems (the *Prière en forme de confession* for example), the rhythm is less urgent and breathless; the tone of lamentation and confession is more subdued and measured. Nevertheless, the overall tone of voice and movement of Desportes's prayer-poems is relatively consistent; it implies a tension, unresolved or only precariously resolved.

Much the same atmosphere is apparent in the penitential lyrics of his court contemporaries. The range of titles at once suggests the unity of intention: Blanchon produced a *Plainte durant une maladie*; Jamyn a *Confession*, an *Oraison pour le temps de Peste et de Famine*, poems written *En affliction* and *En tems de griefve maladie*, and a penitential *Ode chrestienne*; Habert various penitential *Stances* and a *Priere en forme de confession*; and Boyssières a set of *Prieres en Piramide renversees, pour un malade*. Partly because of their closeness to the Penitential Psalms, and still more no doubt because of the personal influence of Desportes, many passages in these poems seem at first sight indistinguishable from Desportes's prayer-poems:

The penitential prayer

Helas je souspire et je pleure,
Pour tant de forfaits qu'a toute heure,
J'ay commis, à lencontre toy,
Mes yeux sont aveuglez d'une Ombre,
Et le jour, m'est une nuit sombre,
Pleine de silence, et d'effroy.

Je sens les mortelles Alarmes,
Mon lict est arrouzé de Larmes,
Mes yeux ne cessent de pleurer,
Et ma chair en eau escoulée,
D'aupres des os s'est descolée,
S'il ne te plaist de m'espurer.

Ma face est si pasle et deffaitte,
Que toute semblable elle est faitte,
A cil' qui descent au tumbeau.
La rigueur enterre ma vie,
Estant pour le jourdhuy suivye,
D'ombre et de mort pour son flambeau.

Mes jours s'en vont comme fumée,
Et ma chair, toute consumée,
Seche comme fait le Tyson,
Et mon cœur fanist comme l'herbe,
Que le feneur amasse en gerbe,
Si je ne reçois guerison.

Je sens tous mes os se dissoudre,
N'ayant pour mon Pain que la poudre,
Qui ne peult mon corps substanter,
Et fais de mes larmes mon boyre,
N'ayant que la mort en memoyre,
Si tu ne veux d'icy m'oster.

O SEGNEUR, vers toy je me renge,
Voyant dessus moy tant de fange,
Je ne puis prendre mon repas,
Car la puanteur de ma bouche,
Fait que quand la viande je touche,
Mon Gozier ne l'avalle pas.

J'ay suivy pour le jour, l'ombrage,
Et pour le corps, le vain ymage,
Et le faux, pour la verité...[1]

[1] J. Blanchon, *Premieres œuvres*, pp. 181–2.

The penitential lyric

The movement here from an elegiac description of sickness to a prayer of confession is characteristic. Nevertheless, on closer examination it becomes clear that Blanchon is less skilful than Desportes at sustaining and developing the movement of the poem: indeed, he seems at times to be trying to produce a *précis* of all the best-known passages of the Penitential Psalms, at the expense of unity of tone and direction:

> Retyré du cruel servage,
> De la Tyrannie sauvage,
> Du Joug ou je suis attaché,
> Me mundant nettement d'hysoppe,
> Qu'estant devant ta saincte Troppe,
> Je sois lavé de mon peché.

> Ja la blanchissante courriere,
> A refait six fois sa Carriere,
> Despuis que j'ay senty ton fleau,
> Or comme estant ta creature,
> Aye de moy songnheuse cure,
> Et me conserve en ton Trouppeau...

> Tu mas creé à ton ymage,
> Et croy que n'aymes mon dommage,
> Car tu ne m'as ainsi portrait,
> Pour estre Autheur de ma ruyne,
> Prenant de tes mains origine,
> Et formé d'un semblable trait.   (pp. 183–4.)

It will by now be also apparent that the slackness of form is echoed in the syntax and rhythm, which, in spite of the octosyllabic metre, have neither the restlessness nor the control of Desportes's diction.

Jamyn's longer penitential poems are wider in scope than Blanchon's, and to some extent than Desportes's. Many passages are in the main-stream of Old Testament lamentation, with their questioning of God and their appeal to him as man's Creator;[1] elsewhere, however, the resonance is increased by extended references to the Passion. The *En tems de griefve maladie*, quite unlike Desportes's *Plainte...durant une sienne longue maladie*, begins with an invocation to Christ ('O

---

[1] *Second volume des œuvres*, fols. 9, 14, 15–16.

seigneur Jesuchrist seul salut des vivans').[1] It contains no description of the illness as a physical state; instead, a prayer for the 'bouclier de pieté' which protects the Martyrs, and for participation in the redemptive sacrifice of Christ.[2] Finally, envisaging the moment of his death, the poet identifies himself with the dying Christ ('O seigneur je remets mon esprit en tes mains'). Certain passages of the *Confession* are similar in tone:

> Lave moy donq, Seigneur, de ton precieux sang,
> Environne mon corps d'un acoutrement blanc
> Tel qu'est le sainct habit dont se vestent les Anges. (fol. 7.)

Here, however, there is a central section which develops the themes of man's corruption and *aveuglement*, leading to a climax in which the rotten tree of Adam is offered up for transformation and renewal:

> O celeste secours maintenant aperçoy
> Mon cœur plein de pechez, d'ulctres (*sic*) et d'esmoy:
> Qui sinon ta vertu en santé me peut rendre?...
>
> Nous sommes abatus d'un si profond sommeil,
> Que cela qui est nuit nous semble estre un soleil
> Et un aveuglement une lumiere belle...
>
> Je te donne, Seigneur, cet arbre tout pourry,
> C'est à dire ce cœur d'iniquité nourry,
> Souillé de faux propos et d'actes deshonnestes:
> Oste moy le vieil homme, arrouze moy de l'eau
> De celeste rouzée, et me fay tout nouveau:
> Je m'assure qu'en vain tu n'entens mes requestes. (fol. 8.)

Jamyn is here moving towards the rich symbolism of Passion meditation, in which the whole of the Old Testament symbolic pattern is subsumed; at the same time, through the confessional tone of the poem as a whole, and through the metaphorical identification of sin and sickness, he remains closely related to Desportes.

---

[1] The first stanza of this poem (fol. 10) reminds one of the opening of two poems by Bertaut—the *Cantique*, 'Seul espoir des humains...', and the Nativity *Cantique*, 'Soit que de votre corps vous viviez deschargés...' (Jamyn has the same 'soit que...soit que...' construction as the latter, and much the same theme as the former).

[2] *Ibid.* fols. 10–11.

The penitential lyric

Boyssières's *Prieres en Piramide renversees* are on the whole disappointing, since the syntax is often distorted almost beyond recognition by the demands of the metre. There is, however, some attempt to use the shape significantly: on one occasion at least one could say that the increasing *dépouillement* of the metre corresponds with the progress of a prayer for purification, ending with the destruction of the body and of earthly life in the single word 'finie':

Si tu me veux punir, selon mon ord peché,
Je ne puis esperer, que mon esprit, taché
De maux, d'orreurs, d'offences, et de vices,
Puisse esviter les eternels suplices,
Des Enfers: mais si ta bonté,
Eface   mon   iniquité,
Je serai bien heureuse
Pres ta main glorieuse
Que   passera,
Et que sera,
Ma vie,
Finie.[1]

A comparison with Herbert's 'shape' poems would be unkind to Boyssières; but strangely enough, like Herbert, Boyssières also knows how, on occasion, to strike a note of forthright domestic simplicity, as in this *Priere en se lavant le matin*:

En lavant de ceste Eau ma main,
Je te suplie, Pere humain,
Lave-le nette, des offences
Qu'elle a commis en mal faisant,
De tes attantes abusant,
Et m'escognoissant tes puissances.

Lavant mon visage, et mes yeux:
Seigneur, de ton sang precieux,
Nettoye-lez de leur ordure!
Rince ma bouche, par dedans,
Et rends de maux, blanches mes dents:
Qui te font a toute heure injure.

Affin que lavé, net, et blanc,
J'aille, a la mort, trouver ton flanc,

[1] *Troisiesmes œuvres*, p. 74.

Et de là, contempler ta face:
Recevant autant de repos,
Que j'ay de mal, entre les flos
Des Mers, de ceste terre basse.[1]

For a poet who, particularly in his profane poetry, shows a liking for elaborate metrical games, this is striking. It reminds one how far these court poets could adapt their style to suit the needs not only of an austere theme but also of communication to a wide audience, some of whom might not be familiar with the sophistication of profane rhetoric. Blanchon's *Plainte* is extremely easy to read, as is much of Desportes's penitential poetry: gratuitous rhetorical devices are rare. This characteristic will become still clearer later, by contrast, when Bertaut's poetry is considered; Favre and La Ceppède, too, will have a different approach.[2]

Before leaving this group, one should not forget to mention Isaac Habert, whose penitential poetry, like Jamyn's, is integrated into a wider religious view. Indeed, although his tone is very different from Jamyn's, he shares his contemporary's preoccupation with the beauty and significance of the created world on the one hand, and on the other, with the flight out of the world into the Light. In many of his poems, he exploits the antithesis between darkness and light; he thus creates a characteristic pattern which seems to be more than casually related to the Platonic ascent towards the sun, while retaining contact with the Old Testament themes of *puanteur*, pallor, and the pit. At the same time, the talent of Habert as a poet is evident in passages like the following, with its controlled modulation from doubt and despair to confidence:

Las seray-je tousjours privé de la lumiere?
Croupirai-je tousjours dedans ceste fondriere,
Triste, pasle, et tremblant, au pouvoir des malheurs?...

Qui me retirera de ceste fosse sombre
Pleine d'horreur, d'effroy, de puanteur, et d'ombre,

---

[1] *Troisiesmes œuvres*, p. 69. See also p. 62:
  Ta grace donq, soit le Ballaix
  Qui nettoye le hord Pallaix,
  Où (trop hardy) je mets ta chair divine...
[2] This whole question of style and audience will be dealt with fully by M. Michel Jeanneret in his forthcoming thesis on psalm-paraphrase.

Où Sathan me retient captif dessobs sa Loy?
Qui rompra le bandeau que sur les yeus je porte?
Qui guerira mon mal, et ouvrira la porte
Aus ennuis de mon cœur pour fuir loing de moy?

Helas! ce sera toy, ô Soleil de mon ame,
Tu viendras esclarcir ce lieu noir de ta flame...

Je voy, je voy desja la lumiere divine,
Qui chassant l'ombre espais ceste fosse illumine,
Je me sens peu à peu de ma prison tirer...

Sus donc, resveille toy mon ame paresseuse,
Veus tu tousjours dormir sur la plume otieuse,
Arrache le bandeau qui te sille les yeus,
Oste l'humeur gluant qui serre ta paupiere,
Sors de ce gouffre obscur, vien revoir la lumiere,
Y a t'il rien si beau que la clarté des Cieus?[1]

This survey, although necessarily brief and fragmentary, will give some idea of the kind of variation one may expect to find in the *genre* of the penitential lyric. The central material may be augmented by reference to the Creation, the Fall, or the Passion, or it may overlap with the themes of vanity and death which will be considered in the next chapter. Nevertheless, there is sufficient uniformity for these poems to be considered together as a related group, and this is underlined by the fact that the *genre* remains perfectly recognisable in its continued popularity beyond 1590. One is not surprised to find Chassignet subscribing to it in his *Syndereses* and in his *Oraison à Dieu Tout-Puissant*, which develops the penitential themes through a comparison with Samson and through a borrowing from *Domine probasti me*.[2] Meanwhile, the Protestant tradition of penitential *cantiques*, initiated principally by Tagaut, Bèze and Montméja in the *Poèmes chrestiens* of 1574, had continued through Maisonfleur and Sponde into the 1590s: at much the same time as Chassignet's *Mespris*, Odet de La Noue's *Poésies chrestiennes* were published. These contain among other things nine *Cantiques chrestiens*, largely penitential and concerned with affliction ('Jusques à quand, Seigneur, privé des sentiments, / Me verray-je battu de ta main rigoureuse?'); like other Protestant poets of this period —I am thinking not only of d'Aubigné but also of Pierre Poupo—

[1] *Œuvres chrestiennes*, fols. 39–40.   [2] *Mespris*, pp. 83–5, 251–3, 285–6.

La Noue tends to enrich his poetry with a substantial amount of specific reference to the contemporary situation (the wars), and to his own experience (war-wounds and imprisonment).

After the turn of the century, the new anthologies include large numbers of penitential poems, many of them anonymous; sometimes one finds different versions of the same poem appearing twice in one collection, and the overall picture is thus blurred and much in need of bibliographical clarification. As a random sample one may take the *Parnasse des plus excellents poetes de ce temps* (Lyons, Ancelin, *s.d.*), which contains a series of *Stances de feu Madame sœur du Roy durant sa maladie. En forme de priere*, a *Cantique spirituel* which closely resembles a psalm-paraphrase, and a *stance*-sequence called *Autres vers spirituels* (all anonymous), two poems by Antoine de Vermeil entitled *Devote meditation durant une maladie* and *Autre devote meditation*,[1] and a *Priere chrestienne* which appears to be a distant variant of Bertaut's 'Seul espoir des humains'.[2] Many of these poems are meditative in much the same way as those of Desportes and his contemporaries: their structure is close to the loose development of the penitential psalm, their rhythm and syntax reflect the urgency and disquiet of the prayer for healing and forgiveness:

> O Dieu je n'en puis plus, la douleur qui m'accable
> Me fait crier à toy, sois moy donc secourable,
> Modere s'il te plaist la douleur que je sens:
> Arrache de mes os ceste fievre cruelle,
> Dont l'ardente chaleur desseche ma moüelle,
> Et par des songes vains esgare tous mes sens...
>
> Mes yeux sont obscurcis, ma couleur est ternie,
> Sur ma bouche on ne voit nulle couleur de vie,
> Mes cheveux ont perdu leur lustre et leur couleur,
> Quelquefois main en main de parler je m'essaye,
> Pour te dire mon mal: mais ma langue begaye,
> Et ne peut prononcer un mot de ma langueur.   (*Parnasse*,
> fol. 343.)

The nature of the penitential prayer as a meditative *genre* is brought into sharp relief if one compares the kind of poem we have so far been

---

[1] The second of these two poems is a meditation on Creation, but the opening stanza (quoted above, p. 124) establishes a point of contact with penitential themes.

[2] The *Autres vers spirituels* also seem to bear some relation to Bertaut's poem (see *Parnasse*, fol. 353).

discussing with the penitential lyrics of Bertaut himself, which of course figure prominently in the anthologies from the turn of the century onwards. In at least one of these, the afflictions and doubts of the penitent are silenced by quasi-rational argument (strongly reminiscent of Neostoicism):

> Un cœur qui magnanime à soy-mesme commande
> Souvent fait que son mal en bien se convertit:
> Une douleur n'estant ny petite ny grande,
> Qu'autant que le courage est ou grand ou petit...
>
> La douleur a ce bien, que quand elle est durable
> Elle est aussi legere, et se porte aysément:
> Et quand son aspreté la rend intolerable,
> Sa duree est petite et passe en un moment...
>
> Armé de ta fureur je feray resistance
> Aux plus rudes assauts livrez par le malheur:
> Et pourveu que ta grace augmente ma constance,
> Je ne te requier point d'amoindrir ma douleur.[1]

But even in poems where this philosophical consolation is not invoked the tone is calm and ordered. Thematically, the *cantique* 'Seul espoir des humains...' follows the usual penitential pattern: affliction, humility, questioning, pleading, sickness and cure; the Psalms are quoted; there are fifteen alexandrine *stances* of six lines each; but yet the feeling of the poem is quite different.[2] The transformation has taken place at various levels. In the first place, the vocabulary and imagery has become more abstract, ruling out any overemphasis on the physical: Bertaut never mentions *crasse, ordure, ulcères, bouche infecte,* and his suffering is ample but not particularly urgent:

> Las! entre tant de maux qui font que je souspire,
> Je sçay bien qu'à bon droit la rigueur de ton ire
> Dessus mon chef coulpable espand tous ses vaisseaux:
> Et que ma vie estant de tes biens arrousee,
> Puis qu'ingrate elle en a la source mesprisee,
> Ton courroux a raison d'en tarir les ruisseaux.[3]

[1] J. Bertaut, *Les Œuvres poétiques*, ed. A. Chenevière (Paris, 1891), pp. 11–12.
[2] It may well be, however, that when the full history of the variants is established, Bertaut's earlier drafts will be seen to be much closer to the meditative, non-rhetorical type of penitential poem. See the thesis of T. J. D. Allott, *The Poetry of Jean Bertaut* (Oxford B.Litt., unpublished).
[3] This poem is on pp. 7–10 of Chenevière.

The third and fourth stanzas of the poem, which do achieve a certain urgency through exclamation and interrogation, lose much of their impact because of the elaborate and somewhat inappropriate circumlocution of the second stanza:

C'est pourquoy dés le poinct où l'Aube annonce au monde
Le retour du bel Astre à qui le sein de l'onde
Preste toutes les nuicts son humide sejour,
Et dés que le réveil dessille ma paupiere,
J'ouvre avec un soûpir ma bouche à la priere,
Consacrant à ton nom les premices du jour.

Verbose effects of this kind (and there is at least one other, in stanza 8) tend to distract one's attention from the devotional potentiality of the themes; and in fact the whole poem tends towards resonant abstractions from the very first lines ('Seul espoir des humains despoüillez d'esperance, / Qui de l'ame esperduë es la vraye asseurance...'). For a final—and crucial—example of this quality, one should consider stanzas 9 and 10, setting them side by side with the central stanzas of Desportes's *Plainte de l'autheur*, which develop much the same themes:

Ne vien donc point du Ciel en fureur me reprendre:
Pardonne à ceste pauvre et miserable cendre,
N'arme plus ta rigueur contre sa mauvaistié.
Si ma cause n'est juste, ô Seigneur rends la telle:
Ou m'absous par ta grace, ou permets que j'appelle
De toy plein de vengeance à toy plein de pitié.

Mais que dy-je impudent? auroy-je bien l'audace
D'en appeller à toy, sans redouter la face
De qui j'ay tant de fois le respect violé?
Le sacrilege atteint, et voisin de sa prise,
N'auroit-il point d'horreur de prendre pour franchise
Les cornes de l'autel que sa main a volé?

The immediacy of Bertaut's *volte-face* ('Mais que dy-je...?') is lost in the complex syntactical constructions which surround it; there is an air of calculation here which is not quite in keeping with the emotional tension. Indeed, the movement of the whole prayer has been rationalised, ordered by explanatory conjunctions—'C'est pourquoy', 'Mais aussi sçais-tu bien', 'Ne vien donc point', 'Toy donc', and although they are combined with apostrophe, thus simulating the tone of prayer, there is nevertheless a direct contrast with the effect of improvisation which characterises many of the prayer-poems of Desportes.[1] Finally, the syntax is tailored in broad periods to fit the unit-lengths of alex-andrine and stanza, which means that the rhythm is measured and dignified where in Desportes it is often breathless and irregular. The agitations of private devotion have with Bertaut been raised to the level of an official rhetoric; and although the poem is well-made, one is through-out conscious of a discrepancy between the subject and the tone of voice.

PENITENTIAL THEMES IN THE SONNET-FORM

The expansive material of the penitential prayer clearly demands an extended, flexible form; and largely because of its affinity with psalm and elegy, this is the form chosen by the majority of poets. The shorter, epigrammatic forms—the sonnet in particular—come into their own as a medium for the aphoristic, 'moralising' themes of vanity and death which will be discussed in the next chapter; and the penitential sonnet is often more closely related to this material than to that of the longer prayer-poems. Three or four of Desportes's sonnets come into this category (see for example nos. 1, 4, 12 and 14 in the Michiels edition). Nevertheless, the popularity of the sonnet was so overwhelming that it would be surprising if no one had attempted to transform the equivalent of a penitential psalm into a sonnet; and where it was attempted, the results are interesting if not always very satisfying.

Odet de La Noue provides a central illustration of the problems involved; the second of his three sequences of religious sonnets, entitled *Le Remede* (the other two are called *La Maladie* and *La Guerison*), contains 'en cinquante sonnets plusieurs sainctes prieres à Dieu, du pecheur affligé et touché au vif du sentiment de ses fautes'. The material he uses for this sequence is almost identical with that of the extended penitential prayer:

> Las! Seigneur, quelle fin? hé! quand cesseras-tu?
> Quand, quand verray je esteint le brasier de ton ire?
> Quand s'estanch'ra la soif qui fait que je souspire,
> Languissant apres l'eau de ta sainte vertu? . . .

[1] One should remember that the coherence of Desportes's structure does not remove the underlying tensions, but rather enhances them.

Ou si (tenant encor trop douce mon opresse),
Tu me veux recharger de nouvelle destresse,
Moy dont le moindre mal n'a son pareil ici?

(Sonnet 23, quat. 2 and ter. 2.)

Las! Seigneur, où es-tu? Las, jusqu'à quand sera-ce
Que si loin-loin de moy tu te tiendras caché?
Jusqu'à quand aveuglé dans la nuict du peché,
Ne verray-je esclairer le Soleil de ta face?...
Si quiconque te prie en toy trouve secours,
Faut-il que mon mal seul viene sans cesse pire,
Pour qui je vay criant tant de fois tous les jours?[1]

(Sonnet 33, quat. 1 and ter. 2.)

Both these sonnets end on a question which is merely a continuation of the other questions and in no way 'finishes' the poem: the structure thus becomes purely enumerative, and the organising potentialities of the sonnet-form are almost completely ignored. What La Noue has in fact done in this sequence is to replace the form of the individual sonnet by that of the sequence as a whole. The argument is carried over from one poem to the next, and the sonnet thus becomes a 'paragraph' in an extended meditation:

Mais quoy (Seigneur) si de ta main pesante
Les rudes coups me profitent si peu...
Sus, frape donc, et mon martyre augmente,
Tant qu'à la fin mon cœur en soit esmeu...   (Sonnet 24.)

Mais pourquoy veux-je voir croistre encor mon tourment...?

(Sonnet 25.)

Pour alleger le mal qui me destruit,
Un nouveau mal n'est donc pas necessaire...

(Sonnet 26; pp. 39–40.)

Although the links are not always as tightly-drawn as this, the sequence moves through phases of lamentation, despair, and 'argument' to a final resolution in which the 'remedy' is granted:

Mais ja tu m'ois, ja (piteux à mes cris)
Tu rends la force à mes foibles esprits,
Qui croupissoyent en bourbier si estrange.
Sus donc, Seigneur, tire-moi au chemin,

---

[1] Odet de La Noue, *Poésies chrestiennes* (Geneva, 1594), pp. 38 and 43 respectively.

Ne me laissant plus long temps en la fange,
Puis que desja tu m'as tendu la main.   (Sonnet 48; p. 51.)

The whole cycle is thus a penitential prayer on a massive scale; the individual sonnets have no more independence than one of a series of stances.[1]

Where the sonnet is designed as an individual unit, the problem of providing an adequate structure is more acute. Gabrielle de Coignard's fifth sonnet, 'sur le verset, Averte faciem tuam à (*sic*) peccatis meis', has the elements of a pattern: the germinal theme is stated in the first quatrain and recalled in the last line with a *reprise* in line 8:

> Destournez s'il vous plait vostre divine face,
> De ceste enormité de mon forfaict commis,
> Ne vueillez pas conter mes pechez infinis,
> Mais effacez les tous par vostre saincte grace.
> Mon corps est tout fondu comme un monceau de glace:
> Je sers de passetemps à tous mes ennemis:
> Nuict et jour je me plains je lamente, et gemis:
> Envoyez le pardon qui mes pechez efface.
> Voudriez vous bien monstrer la force de vos bras,
> Sur un corps affligé qui attend son trespas?
> Foudroyez l'orgueilleux, le mutin et rebelle:
> Regardez que mes os se tiennent à ma peau,
> Mon ame est toute preste, à descendre au tombeau,
> He! destournez voz yeux de ma faute mortelle.[2]

One could also say that there is an attempt at intensification through the themes of affliction, reaching a climax at 'tombeau' in line 13: the question and the renewed apostrophe of the tercets have a certain urgency. Nevertheless, the poem does not quite succeed in imposing its shape and its significance on the reader, partly because of the monotonous rhythms, but principally because the 'argument' is not sufficiently coherent; once again, these are the themes of an improvised meditation which can only find their own shape in a more ample form. As a further illustration, one might take Chassignet's sonnet 401.

---

[1] One should remember that this cycle is itself part of a still larger structure in which there is a planned movement from the 'sickness' (the vanity of the world and of man) through the 'remedy' (the prayers of the sinner) to the 'cure' (the 'bonté et misericorde de Dieu'), which concludes with an *action de grâces*. Odet's method is particularly interesting in that the average profane *canzoniere*, although nominally a cycle, seldom involves an organised development of this kind. It is strikingly similar to that adopted by Sponde in the four *Méditations*; see Higman, *art. cit., BHR*, 28 (1966), pp. 578 ff.

[2] Gabrielle de Coignard, *Œuvres chrestiennes*, p. 33.

Chassignet certainly knows how to put together a sonnet, and he has done his best here by using the 'jusques à quand' motif and parallelisms of syntax, but one still has the feeling that the final question is only an arbitrary ending:

> Jusques à quant, Seigneur, au milieu de la flame
> De l'infecte Sodome au hazart dangereus
> De tomber en enfer loing des murs bien-heureus
> Du renommé Segor laisseras tu mon ame [?]
> Jusques à quant, Seigneur, dans ceste Egypte infame
> Autant fertile en auls comme en oignons pleureus,
> Loing du terroir promis en tous fruis plantureus
> Me lairras tu croupir en opprobre et diffame?
> Jusques à quand, Seigneur, loing du mont de Sion
> Me feras tu languir en desolation
> En ce monde meschant ou ta gloire est fletrie?
> Quant le terme prefix est du tout escoulé
> De son banissement, le bannis exilé
> Doit il pas retourner en sa chere patrie?[1]

It will be clear by now that whereas the tradition of the love-sonnet provides a whole range of devices which can give the sonnet shape and direction (Virgilian simile, anaphora, antithesis), the poet who sets out to convert Old Testament material or the equivalent into sonnet form finds himself with few appropriate resources. For this reason, the penitential sonnet tends to move away from the material used in the longer prayer-poems; and amid all the possibilities that might suggest themselves, the most straightforward is a direct borrowing from the love-sonnet itself. The Petrarchan tradition provided plenty of examples of a penitential renunciation of profane love for sacred; and Du Bellay, like Petrarch himself, concludes his *canzoniere* with a handful of religious sonnets in which penitential themes are prominent. *Olive* 109 ('Pere du ciel...') opens with an echo of Petrarch's 'Padre del ciel...' (although even here Du Bellay bases the tercets on a psalm-allusion); and with the revival of religious poetry in the 1570s and after, sonneteers will frequently convert the commonplaces of profane love. Not, perhaps, as frequently as Vianey would have us believe;[2] but in spite

---

[1] J.-B. Chassignet, *Le Mespris*, p. 367. For similar examples of 'structureless' penitential sonnets, see, for example, Blanchon, *op. cit.* pp. 191–2, sonnets 13 and 14.

[2] See *Le Pétrarquisme en France*, ch. 4, especially pp. 293–4, 297–303.

of the ambiguity of poetic traditions, the Petrarchan affinities of some
of Béroalde de Verville's sonnets are unmistakable:

> Ha, que je vis heureux! hélas! que j'ai de peine,
> Que je sens de douleur, que je sens de bonheur,
> Que de contentement d'une amère douceur
> Par ses heureux attraits doux-aigrement me gêne.[1]

Similarly, it seems likely that a contemporary audience would have
been aware of the Petrarchan provenance of the shipwreck allegory as
it is developed in the following sonnet by Habert:

> Je vogue des long temps sur la mer der erreurs
> Triste et pasle nocher accompagné de vices,
> La chair, la volupté, les jeus et les blandices
> Poussent ma nef aux rocs des plaisirs et douleurs.
> Maintenant que je voy les prochaines horreurs,
> Les terrestres amours, les pechez, les delices,
> Qui veulent m'engouffrer dans leurs creus precipices,
> Je te prens pour mon Phare entre tant de malheurs,
> O Royne des hauts Cieux chaste et saincte pucelle
> Qui jouis du repos de la vie eternelle
> Mere de Jesus Christ (divin reparateur
> Du mortel genre humain) escoute ma priere,
> Tire de ceste mer mon ame prisonniere
> Et la conduis au port de Christ mon redempteur.[2]

The schematised allegory ('la mer des erreurs', 'aux rocs des plaisirs
et douleurs') is very much like that of Petrarch's 'Passa la nave mia. . .',
and the transference of the lighthouse image from the beloved to the
Virgin Mary is a straightforward one. Thus in this instance the pattern
of the love-sonnet and its satisfactory resolution have been borrowed
to give shape to a penitential prayer.

Other analogies with the profane love-sonnet will be considered
later, particularly in the context of the 'poetry of tears'. A different
pattern emerges where a reference to the Passion is used as a climax
and conclusion, adding a new dimension of significance.[3] Boyssières's

---

[1] V.-L. Saulnier, *Anthologie poétique de Béroalde de Verville* (Paris, 1945), p. 114. Many
of the poems of Verville (*stances* and sonnets) are closely related to the *genres* discussed
in this and the following chapter.

[2] I. Habert, *Sonnets spirituels* no. 17 (*Œuvres chrestiennes*, fol. 6).

[3] Compare the conclusion of some of the penitential lyrics discussed earlier.

fifteenth religious sonnet develops the theme of penitential weeping
and self-castigation quite independently of profane traditions:

> Larmoyez ô! mes yeux, vostre veuë lacive,
> Qui s'est tant habusee a la mondanité:
> Escrie toy ma voix, a la divinité,
> Pour avoir le Pardon, de mon Ame chetive.
> Deschire toy ma chair, frape toy chair oysive!
> Toy mesme te payant, de ta lassiveté:
> Tordez vous ô mes mains! et toy cœur de durté!
> Fends toy par le millieu, pour ta vie cattive.
> Essourde toy oreille, et vous pieds rompez vous!
> Qu'on ne voye sur moy, qu'affliction, que coups!
> Que pleurs, que cris, que sang, que peine, que misere!
> A fin que le Seigneur, que j'ay tant offencé,
> Voyant ma penitence, apaise sa colere:
> Et qu'en vain, au costé il n'ayt esté percé.[1]

At first sight, the importance of the spear-wound motif, introduced
with no great sense of purpose in the last line, seems to be limited. On
the other hand, the penitential mood is one which is much more closely
related to Passion meditation than to Old Testament lamentation: in
a sequence like La Ceppède's *Théorèmes*, this physical self-annihilation
would take on the sense of an identification with the death of Christ,
and some of Boyssières's other sonnets are in fact deeply concerned
with the Passion narrative. At the same time, the exclamatory emotion
of the sonnet is reminiscent of the *extase* of Passion contemplation rather than of the uneasiness of the Penitential Psalms. In this
context, the reference to the wounding of Christ takes on a wider
significance, resuming and transforming the theme of self-wounding
in the sonnet as a whole ('Deschire toy ma chair...', 'Fends toy par
le millieu...', 'Pieds rompez vous...'). It remains true that the allusion
of the last line is not given the relief which its importance demands;
nevertheless, the sonnet as a whole has potentialities which are lacking in many of the penitential sonnets of Blanchon or even of Chassignet.

The signs that a creative imagination is at work, imposing a new and
significant order on the available material, are still more evident in the
sonnets of Antoine Favre; and this chapter may conveniently be
brought to an end with a preliminary look at Favre's *Entretiens*

---

[1] Boyssières, *Les Troisiesmes œuvres*, p. 58.

spirituels. The Passion plays the major part in this work; but Favre's view (particularly in the *Centurie premiere*)[1] is frequently penitential, combining the tones of sermon and of inward prayer. Favre makes relatively little use of the Old Testament poetry of affliction; nevertheless the eighty-ninth sonnet is based firmly on the *Domine probasti me* theme, and will provide a good starting-point:

> Où fuirai-je, ô grand Dieu, du courroux de ta face!
> Si ton sceptre estoit tel que de noz potentats,
> Je pourrois m'enfuyant loin de tous tes estats
> Mespriser de tes mains la plus fiere menace.
> Mais, las! en quelque endroit que ma crainte me place,
> Soit que je vise au ciel, ou en terre, ou plus bas,
> Je voy ce bras vengeur qui devance mes pas,
> Pour s'opposer au vol qui me porte à ta grace.
> Helas, puis qu'il faut donc que je sois veu de toy,
> Permets du moins, permets que ne monstrant que moy,
> Je cache mes pechez dont ta fureur s'irrite:
> Mais comment à demi pourroi-je estre caché?
> N'aiant plus rien en moy qui ne soit tout peché!
> Voi-les, mais teints du sang qui ta mercy merite.

The psalm-allusion, although more than just a germinal idea, is treated very freely, particularly where the image of God's avenging arm is developed (in lines 7–8) into a vision of divine justice sealing off the sinner's access to grace. The sense of despair is thus deepened by the perception of what amounts to a paradox: God the avenger is opposed to God the giver of grace; at the same time, the paradox is expressed in physical terms, and the potency of the Old Testament image is increased rather than diluted. The tercets move further away from the Psalm as the awareness of sin becomes more and more explicit. Unlike Desportes's presentation of himself to God, which is full of pathos, Favre's contains an intellectual element—the conscious realisation that sin is inseparable from the body, that the body (or at least his body) is all sin. Meanwhile, the emotional force of the quatrains is sustained through the urgency of the prayer ('Permets du moins, permets...')

[1] In the ensuing analysis, all the sonnet-numbers given will refer to the *Centurie premiere*; the text quoted from will be that of the *Entretiens spirituels*, but the sonnet-numbers are the same in this edition as in the 1595 edition, where only these first hundred sonnets are published, plus four sonnets on the Communion and two odes.

into the final surrender of 'Voi-les...' In this way, the questions, the changing attitudes ('mais...mais...'), the repeated lamentations all move forward to a more painful sense of exposure (echoing, perhaps, Adam's guilty awareness of being naked), which is then resolved in the modulation of the last line. The reference to the Passion here is clearer and more emphatic than Boyssières's, and carries the weight of the sonnet, completing the emotional pattern and at the same time deepening the significance of the poem: the body of Christ, covered in blood, redeems the guilty nakedness of Adam, and the way is opened to the God of grace.[1]

Favre's devotional material is extended and enriched by a humanist imagination which can give his poetry a tone very different from that of Desportes and his circle. The most striking example of this is his use of the philosophical-scientific notion that the universe is based on a circular or spherical form, which is echoed in the shape of the soul and in the circular movement through which extremes can meet, as God and man meet in Christ. This theme occurs frequently in Favre's poetry.[2] One of its principal variants, the concept of a centre towards which all things move, provides the overall shape of sonnet 46, developing the devotional 'spiritual combat' between body and soul in terms of two opposing centres:

> Quel combat sens-je en moy de mes deux plus fidelles!
> Mon corps pestri de bouë, et de terre vivant
> Ne cherche rien que terre, et tousjours va fuyant
> Comme à son premier centre aux enfers plus rebelles.
> L'ame tout au rebours prenant du ciel ses esles
> Tousjours contre le ciel va son vol eslevant,
> La son centre elle voit, et plus viste que vent
> Penetre jusqu'à Dieu par ses flammes isnelles.
> Qui des deux combattans en fin vainqueur sera?
> Puis que juge j'en suis, l'ame l'emportera.
> Oste Ame au corps son centre, il vivra de ta gloire.

---

[1] In the following sonnet (no. 90), a similar theme of God's penetrating vision is brought to a fine conclusion:

> Ou si tu veux me voir, voy que je ne suis rien
> Qu'une matiere informe, à qui tu peux du tien
> Rendre (ren-la luy donc) pour sa forme ta grace.

[2] See for example sonnets 3, 9, 20 and 53. On the theme of the circle and the sphere in this period as a whole, see G. Poulet, 'Poésie du cercle et de la sphère', *CAEF*, 10 (1958), pp. 44 ff., and *Les Métamorphoses du cercle* (Paris, 1961), pp. 1–48.

Mais helas le peché rend la victoire au corps,
Qui porte quant et soy l'ame au centre des morts,
Pauvre sot qui te perds, perd plustost ta victoire.[1]

The antithesis between a gravitational force which pulls down the
'corps pestri de bouë, et de terre vivant' towards the 'centre des morts',
and an affective upward movement (involving images of flight and fire)
towards the centre which is God, gives the poem a powerful structure
of imagery. It is only unfortunate that Favre slackens the tension in
lines 9–10, for elsewhere he manages to find a balance between a
relatively sophisticated argument and a tone of voice which preserves
the mood of penitential meditation: the concluding line, for all its
calculated alliteration and epigrammatic construction, has the directness
of the 'inward sermon'.[2]

The use of this tone of inward apostrophe is one of Favre's most
characteristic devices. Primarily, it is a way of giving momentum to a
penitential meditation, and of invoking in the reader the required
degree of intimacy and involvement:

Hà donc, sus, leve toy, pauvrette, et puis qu'il faut
Que ton Dieu soit ton tout, d'un cœur humblement haut
Lance toy jusqu'à luy, tu verras sa menace

---

[1] For two further 'spiritual combat' sonnets, see I. Habert, *Sonnets spirituels*, no. 6 (fol. 3),
and no. 18 (fol. 6). See also Sponde's twelfth sonnet, and his *Stances* (discussed in the
next chapter). One of Chassignet's longer poems ('Sur la fragilité de la Vie Humaine
aus Ombres de Jacque Chassignet Medicin Pere de l'Autheur' (*Mespris*, pp. 129–36),
contains the following stanza, after a long passage which is for the most part a paraphrase
of Job:

> Ainsi la flame ardente
> S'envole contre-mont,
> Et la terre pesante
> Tombe au centre profond,
> Ainsi l'ame et le cors
> Souvent sont en discors.   (p. 134.)

Once again, the theme is that of the spiritual combat; and Chassignet's simple formulation clarifies the imagery of the elements (fire–spirit, earth–body) which is behind
Favre's sonnet.

[2] Favre's flexibility of tone and imagery is demonstrated by the conclusion of another
sonnet (no. 45) which emphasises the conflict between an upward and a downward
movement through the image of Jacob's ladder:

> Mais que ferai-je helas! mes pechez si pesans
> M'empeschent de monter. A l'aide Anges puissans,
> Haussez moy. Garde, ô Dieu, que le tout ne renverse.

Cf. also the conclusion of sonnet 43 ('Autrement tu seras semblable à ce qu'il peut /
Remplir le Paradis: toy l'enfer, miserable!').

> Preste à te foudroier. Ne recule pourtant,
> Mais par pleurs, par sanglots va luy representant
> Le prix de ton salut ja payé pour ta grace.   (Sonnet 22.)

The mood here (where he is addressing his *âme*) is coaxing, flattering, persuasive; but it can easily become more aggressive:

> Pauvret! à qui jadis l'estre fils de famille
> Au Palais plantureux d'un pere si puissant,
> Donnoit, avec le nom, le credit de l'enfant,
> Qu'as tu fait, qui n'as plus ny coque, ny coquille?
> Que veut dire l'horreur de ce sac qui t'habille,
> Et la gland que tu prens pour ton mets plus plaisant,
> Mets que les pourceaux vont à ta faim refusant,
> Jaloux qu'en leur moisson ell'ait mis sa faucille,
> A ton pere iras tu? quel pere te voudra?...   (Sonnet 24.)

At this point one is moving into an area in which sermon and meditation overlap and at times become almost indistinguishable, and one is reminded of similar ambiguities in prose literature as well as of Favre's own remarks on the connexions between the two 'tones'. Indeed, in one of the group of sonnets which are concerned with the *sac noir* of penitence, inward meditation is reached through the sermon-tone proper:

> Ce n'est d'un sac mouillé visages hypocrites,
> Qu'il faut masquer son front aux pieds du Dieu vivant...
> Mais contre qui parle-je? Hé! ne suis-je celluy
> Qui feignant d'aimer Dieu, me mocque plus de luy?...
> D'un sac noir desormais je m'envelopperay,
> Mais par pleurs, par sanglots, ce sac je moüilleray,
> D'un sac ainsi moüillé, Dieu veut bien qu'on se couvre.
>
> (Sonnet 92.)

Many of the first *centurie* of sonnets exploit to the full the attacking manner of the preacher; but these will be considered in their proper place in the next chapter.

When one reads certain penitential sonnets of this period, one has the feeling that to speak of a 'meditational sonnet' would amount to a contradiction in terms. The compactness of a sonnet and the free movement of a meditative prayer would seem to be mutually exclusive, and the poetry of the Old Testament is unquestionably more at home in the expansive universe of d'Aubigné's *Tragiques* or even of Garnier's

Juifves than in the enclosed, self-conscious art-form of the *canzoniere*. Yet the phrase can apply to Favre. The sonnets of the *Entretiens spirituels* suggest a special mode of meditation which relies on exploration in depth rather than extended improvisation. They combine an element of intellectual probing with a wide range of imagery and above all with a diction which can give the poem emotional momentum; the image and the tone of voice create a unity and a direction which, within a very small space, put across the theological or devotional 'idea' of the poem. To use Favre's own imagery, his sonnets are circles which turn on their own centre, quite unlike the cumulative prayer-poems of Desportes or the centrifugal sonnets of Odet de La Noue. At the same time, although La Noue's sonnet-sequences fail to preserve the unity of the sonnet, the Protestant poet's concept of a continuous cycle is by no means insignificant. Indeed, it is a combination of the sonnet of meditation in the manner of Favre with the notion of a sequence which will underly the *Théorèmes*. La Ceppède writes sonnets which are meaningful as individual poems and which are at the same time part of a quasi-epic structure. Thus, in this chapter, one may broadly say that two kinds of devotional poetry have emerged. Both use the fundamental materials of devotional practice—the Old Testament background, the relationship between God and sinner, the theme of 'spiritual combat'; likewise, both use its methods—physical representation, question and argument, inward apostrophe, affective prayer. But in one case the extended form of *stances*, *cantique* or *ode* has encouraged a restless, expansive movement in which the argument is primarily physical or affective; in the other, the use of the sonnet has imposed a closed structure in which a single idea is fully analysed and worked out without necessarily losing its affective impact. In other thematic areas of devotional poetry, similar contrasts will be valid: on the one hand, César de Nostredame and Gabrielle de Coignard, on the other, La Ceppède. Thus one could already say, looking at the same pattern from a different angle, that devotion is capable of giving a new significance to the poetic forms current in the later sixteenth century.

CHAPTER 5

POETRY OF
SIN, SICKNESS AND DEATH.

2: 'VANITAS VANITATUM' AND
'MEMENTO MORI'

It is not surprising that, at a time when all forms of religious poetry flourished, the perennial themes of the vanity of life and the imminence of death should enjoy a wide popularity. Like the themes of personal affliction and penitence, they were brought into relief by the physical realities of the civil wars; and the Old Testament is once again a source of some of the most familiar material, an Old Testament represented by the moral wisdom of Ecclesiastes and Proverbs, and by the ubiquitous imagery of withering grass and flowers. However, the literature of Hebrew antiquity converges in this instance with a broader current involving the moral commonplaces of antiquity as they were formulated by the Renaissance: both Diego de Estella and the early Montaigne declare that 'philosopher, c'est apprendre à mourir', and the arguments which Seneca and others had used to reconcile man with his death are codified and popularised in all kinds of moral and religious handbooks, in prose and in verse. This somewhat abstract, gnomic presentation of man's fragility is complemented by an intensely physical concern with the corruption of the body just before death and in the tomb, often linked with an anticipation of the Last Judgement. Job contributes a certain amount to such description, but the details are more often based on the medieval meditations on death, and may attract an individual *bravura* treatment like the passage quoted from Goulart's *Trente tableaux*.[1] Both of these traditions—the abstract moral commentary and the concrete representation—appear in contemporary poetry; both may be used for inward meditation, but by their nature

[1] See above, pp. 27-8.

they are more suited to the aggressive, outward-turned meditation which is the sermon. Again, the epigrammatic nature of the sonnet (and similar forms) makes it a particularly convenient medium for communicating moral truths, especially those of the *vanitas* material. Thus whereas in the last chapter the introspective lyric and the *stance*-form were predominant, the sermon-tone and the sonnet-form will here play the principal part: this is the area in which Chassignet and Sponde are perhaps most successful, and in which Favre, too, can be outstanding.

THE 'VANITAS' TRADITION

One of the most persistent *genres* in sixteenth-century French poetry, both vernacular and Neo-Latin, is that of the short didactic poem. The demands of pedagogy, in the family context as well as in institutions, assured the circulation of *florilèges* of universal wisdom, presented in a manner which could be easily assimilated and memorised: Pibrac's *Quatrains* (and Favre's) reached a vast public, as did the parallel tradition of moral and religious emblem-books. The range of possible themes is virtually inexhaustible; but sooner or later, in every collection, one comes across the warning that worldly things are unstable, that time flies, that old age and death are imminent, and that man is worthless as dust. This theme, again, can be varied in any number of ways, depending on the particular religious, philosophical or literary slant the poet may choose—Favre's religious admonition is coupled with the language of humanism:

> Si Dieu faict chair, s'appelle ver de terre,
> Voudrois tu bien prendre un titre pareil?
> Dy que tu n'es que poudre, ains le cercueil,
> Ou le grand Rien tous ses titres enterre.[1]

Frequently, in fact, the didactic poem operates in an area of commonplace which encourages anonymity and which is best represented by the principles of selection—and the *Avant-propos de l'auteur*—of the 1582 *Muse chrestienne*, or by many of Jacques de Billy's sonnets. Nevertheless, there are certain lines of affiliation which have their own specific character, and one of the most important begins with Du Bellay's *Antiquitez* and *Songe*.

---

[1] *Entretiens spirituels*, p. 172 (one of the *Quatrains*). Cf. the liminary sonnet for Chappuys's translation of Estella, above, p. 64.

Any poet who aspired (overtly or not) to be considered an heir of the Pléiade could scarcely avoid taking the *Antiquitez* into account if he wished to comment in moral terms on the vanity of the world and the passage of time.[1] Admittedly, Du Bellay's imagery is pagan; but since Rome is being considered principally in the light of her decadence and downfall, there could be no more objection to this than to any other pagan symbol of a moral truth. The ruin of Rome has a simple physical cause in that it is part of the natural instability of the world, but even *sic transit gloria mundi* has a moral implication, and in many sonnets of this *recueil* a further cause is stated, namely pride: like the Giants of mythology, Rome rivalled the gods and brought down the anger of Jupiter on her head. This theme of *hubris* will reappear in the partisan poetry of the civil wars, where each side will use it as an accusation against the other. Furthermore, in at least four of Du Bellay's sonnets,[2] civil war is stressed as being the most corrosive of all forces, illustrated of course by the self-destroying wars of Rome herself. The violence that goes with civil war has an important influence on the vocabulary of certain sonnets; there are echoes of the *Pharsalia*, and the rhyme on *tenailles–entrailles* is going to be a favourite one during the civil war period (see above, pp. 114, 116):

> Quelle ardente Erinnys de ses rouges tenailles
> Vous pinsetoit les cœurs de rage envenimez,
> Quand si cruellement l'un sur l'autre animez
> Vous destrempiez le fer en voz propres entrailles? (no. 24.)

The *Antiquitez* thus anticipate the poetry of the wars of religion, and though Du Bellay is not the source of all poetry on these themes, he represents an important point of departure. Two other features make him in particular a precursor of the 'sermon' type of poem. In the first place, he exploits the epigrammatic potentialities of the sonnet-form in order to make a moral point with force and economy; the *Antiquitez* are on the whole reflective rather than didactic, but many of them end with a *sententia* on the lines of the emblem-poem:

> ...O mondaine inconstance!
> Ce qui est ferme, est par le temps destruit
> Et ce qui fuit, au temps fait resistance.[3]

---

[1] Similarly, the *Regrets* made a considerable impact on the satirical poetry of the wars of religion.

[2] *Antiquitez*, nos. 10, 23, 24 and 31. All Du Bellay references are to Chamard's edition (vol. II).   [3] No. 3; see also 9, 18, 20, and several of the *Songe* sonnets.

In the second place, there are a number of Biblical allusions. The 'philosophy' behind the *Antiquitez* is classical rather than Biblical, with a strong hint of Lucretius; and it is straining the evidence a little to suggest that there is a hint of the Abel and Cain story in *Antiquitez* 24.[1] But the *Songe* is unmistakably Apocalyptic in tone, and the parallel becomes explicit in sonnet 14 of this sequence:

> Ayant tant de malheurs gemy profondement,
> Je vis une Cité quasi semblable à celle
> Que vid le messager de la bonne nouvelle,
> Mais basty sur le sable estoit son fondement.

What is more important still for the sermon connexion is the allusion to Ecclesiastes in *Songe* 1—'Voy comme tout n'est rien que vanité'—and the religious tone in which the moral apostrophe continues:

> Lors, cognoissant la mondaine inconstance,
> Puis que Dieu seul au temps fait resistance,
> N'espere rien qu'en la divinité.   (See also *Songe* 2, line 12.)

Variations on this pattern of themes and form begin very early: Grévin, who follows Du Bellay more closely perhaps than anyone, uses the *Antiquitez* theme to make an occasional thrust at the Pope.[2] Although this is partisan poetry, there is now an already explicitly religious context, and the Roman material will soon be appearing as one element in the pattern of moral-religious poetry in the post-1570 period. The second of Goulart's two sonnet-cycles published in the 1574 *Poèmes chrestiens* contains a group of four sonnets entitled *Sur les portraits des antiquitez Romaines*; and one of these (no. 15 of the cycle) adds a Christian element to Du Bellay's 'Tiber' image:

> Tout ce que Rome tient de sa gloire premiere,
> C'est le Tybre coulant...
> Le temps qui mange tout, laisse un peu de matiere
> Rude, vieille et rompue, et des piliers rongez
> De sa maligne dent...
> O Dieu, quels changemens! ce qui ne semble rien,

---

[1] See V.-L. Saulnier, 'Commentaires sur les *Antiquitez*', *BHR*, 12 (1950), p. 120.

[2] L. Pinvert, *Jacques Grévin* (Paris, 1899), pp. 366–7, *Vingt quatre sonnets de Grévin sur Romme*, nos. 17–19. The *Gélodacrye* (Grévin, *Théâtre complet et poésies choisies*, ed. Pinvert (Paris, 1922), pp. 315–48) is almost as close to the *Regrets* as the *Vingt quatre sonnets* are to the *Antiquitez*. For Grévin's translations of emblematic literature, see Pinvert, *Jacques Grévin*, pp. 261–8.

> Ce qui coule et s'enfuit, brise du temps la foudre:
> Et toute grandeur tombe en ce val terrien.

Likewise, François Perrin, whose *Pourtraict de la vie humaine* was published in the same year as the *Poèmes chrestiens*, laments the corruption of the Golden Age: thanks to ambition and avarice, the world is laid open to the devastations of civil war, and the cities are deserted.[1] The same influence continues in the 1580s and 1590s with Chandieu, Sponde and Chassignet. Chandieu's thirty-second *octonaire* is in the full *Antiquitez* tradition:

> L'estranger estonné regarde, et se pourmeine,
> Par les antiquitez de la gloire Romaine:
> Il void les arcs rompus: et les arbres luisans
> Mutilez, massacrez par la fureur des ans:
> Il void pendantes en l'air une moussuë pierre
> Qui arme ses costez de longs bras du lierre:
> Et qui est ce, dit il, qui icy bas se fonde:
> Puis que le temps vainqueur triomphe de ce monde?[2]

Chandieu here develops at some length the picturesque details which had already appeared in Goulart's version but which are rare in the *Antiquitez* themselves—Du Bellay is not concerned with the appearance of the ruins as such, perhaps because he does not need to make a simple visual impact on his audience. Chandieu and Goulart on the other hand restore the Roman image to the context of the emblem-book; these are emblems which have to impose themselves on an unlearned reader by their visual interest. Chassignet will develop the theme in a way which is fundamentally similar, although the connexion with *emblemata* is less evident; in sonnet 161 of the *Mespris*, repeated imperatives are

[1] See, for example, the first *centurie*, no. 20; also nos. 17, 18, 24, 27, etc. Perrin's sonnet-cycles—which were clearly popular, since a second edition appeared in 1588—are a compendium, at times a very tedious one, of the commonplaces of 'moral' poetry in a religious context. The influence of the *Regrets* is also apparent; and the 300 sonnets are followed by the 'Antiquitez de plusieurs Citez memorables' and the 'Regrets de Fr. Perrin' (neither religious). One might compare the *Pourtraict* with Odet de La Noue's three sequences of sonnets, since both deal with the vanity of the world and man's corruption, passing to a mood of affirmation in the third sequence ('Le bien souverain de l'homme' for Perrin, 'La Guerison' for La Noue). La Noue's approach is more coherent, his progression more consistent and closer to the movement of religious meditation.
[2] All Chandieu quotations are from the anthology *Les Cantiques du Sieur de Maisonfleur* (Paris, 1586)—no. 32 is on fol. 82. This is religious poetry, not so much by internal allusion as by the *argument* which introduces the sequence: Chandieu names Ecclesiastes as his greatest predecessor on the vanity theme, and then quotes I John, 2. 15–17.

used to involve the reader in the topological aspect of the ruined Rome and thus to force acceptance of the 'moral', which is presented in the second tercet with a demonstrative 'Voila':

> Va par les carrefours des places desolees
> De l'emperiere Rome et sous les arcs bossez,
> Et dans les temples sains à l'antique dressez
> Cherches des roys deffuns les riches Mausaulees,
> Va sous les fondemens des colomnes moulees,
> Et parmi les meulons des Thermes abaissez,
> Et sous les escailliers des Theatres haussez,
> Foüilles des vieus Censeurs les cendres escoulees[.]
> Fauche parmi les os des simples laboureurs
> Les Consuls Justiciers, et les fiers Empereurs
> Pesle mesle sont mis sous la tombe fatale[.]
> Voila le vray miroir ou se doivent mirer
> Ces ceurs (*sic*) ambicieus, pour y considerer
> Que la mort aus plus grans les plus pauvres egale.

The disintegration of Rome's greatness, and even more of her great men (as in this last sonnet), naturally suggests a further theme which goes back through Villon and the Middle Ages to classical and Hebrew antiquity: the *Ubi sunt?* commonplace. Montméja uses it, and Chassignet;[1] and Jaques Doremet, in two consecutive sonnets, develops it with an irony which reminds one that many a preacher must have seized on it as an ideal means of attacking his audience:

> Ou sont tous ces pompeux, ces amateurs du monde,
> Qui avant peu de temps estoient avecques nous?
> On ne voit plus rien d'eux que les os tout dissouz,
> Terre, ilz sont retournez en la terre profonde.
>
> Où est leur grand estat? où sont les escuyers?
> Où les forts Orateurs? où les Satrapes fiers?
> Où sont les potentats et les vieux Capitaines?
> Ce n'est plus rien, que poudre...[2]

All this imagery evokes the world of pagan Rome, and much of the other material used by the *vanitas* poets is drawn from a similar back-

---

[1] Montméja, *Ode* 1, in *Poèmes chrestiens* (Geneva, 1574), p. 3 ('Ou sont ces Cesars glorieux...? / Nous avons leurs noms retenus, / La Terre en a humé les cendres'); Chassignet, *Mespris*, sonnet 21. See E. Gilson, 'De la Bible à François Villon' and 'Tables pour l'histoire du thème Ubi sunt?', in *Les Idées et les lettres* (Paris, 1932), pp. 9 ff., 31 ff.

[2] *Polymnie du vray amour et de la mort*, p. 51. All the Doremet sonnets quoted in this chapter are from the *Mort* sequence.

ground. On a literary level, one might quote for example the famous Horatian *locus* of the rustic who waits for the river to flow away before he will cross: both Perrin and Goulart use the image in contexts which bring out its moral sense.[1] Indeed, Perrin's *centuries* are full of classical *exempla* and other such allusions: admonishing the reader to know himself, he refers to the Delphic oracle rather than to the Christian tradition (*Seconde centurie*, sonnet 10). Similarly, for his philosophical arguments, Chassignet is known to have made extensive use of Lipsius, Duplessis-Mornay and Montaigne.[2] However, in most poetry (and even prose) of this kind, only the broader commonplaces of classical learning are exploited; the moral argument is taken out of the structure of its original philosophical context and standardised. In spite of his borrowings from Lipsius, Chassignet is hardly a 'Neostoic'; and the argument of the fourty-fourth sonnet of the *Mespris*, for which Richter has found precise sources in Duplessis-Mornay, is on much the same level as the list of 'accidental deaths' in sonnet 142, which is a commonplace set of *exempla* appearing both in Montaigne and in Sponde's third *Méditation*.[3] Chassignet fails in his 'philosophical' sonnets because he is unable to adapt serious thought to the needs of a poem: his arguments always have the air of imported fragments.

In the *Antiquitez* tradition, the moral argument always emerged from, and was dependent upon, a physical or historical reality. Similarly, in the broader current of *vanitas* poetry as a whole, the poet will most often try to make his point by drawing on a stock of common imagery. In the penitential lyric there is essentially only one image, that of sickness or *ordure*, with its accompanying images of healing and washing; or on a more general level, the contrast between darkness and light. The poet has no need to demonstrate or explain: he describes and reflects, often at length; and although in the course of his reflection he may come across paradoxes and antitheses, he is not using them to arouse someone else's attention. The *vanitas* poet is in a very different situation. For him, the image must convey a single moral truth which

[1] See Perrin's first *centurie*, no. 42; Goulart's *Suite des imitations*, book 2, no. 26 (in *Poèmes chrestiens*, 1574).

[2] See A. Müller, *J.-B. Chassignet*, pp. 19, 22; M. Richter, 'Una Fonte calvinista di J. B. Chassignet'; and Roy E. Leake, Jr., 'Jean-Baptiste Chassignet and Montaigne', *BHR*, 23 (1961), pp. 292 ff.

[3] Montaigne, *Œuvres*, pp. 83–4; Sponde, *Méditations*, p. 103; cf. Goulart, *Trente tableaux de la mort*, p. 29.

would otherwise be lost in abstraction; he may elaborate it or not to suit his purpose, but it is always one parallel among many possible parallels, since in most cases it operates on a purely figurative level. As a result, one of the most characteristic techniques is the accumulation of small, undeveloped images, as in the sonnet of Favre which concludes his first *centurie*:

> Mon aage ainsi que vent d'heure en heure s'envole,
> Ou comme la fumee qui se dissipe au vent,
> Ou comme d'un oyseau, qui gaigne le devant,
> L'ombre sans yeux, sans pieds, sans air, sans aisles vole.
> Ou comme un trait: qui fend la campagne d'Eole,
> Ou comme l'eau, qui va la mer mesme bravant,
> Ou comme une vapeur sur les eaux s'eslevant,
> Ou d'un songe frivol l'ombre encor plus frivole.

The rapid succession of images is here an essential part of the significance of the poem: they disappear almost before they have had time to take shape. Chandieu, who uses much the same images—sea and sand, wind, flower and wave, rivers and streams, water, arrow and wind, and so on[1]—seems to have been particularly interested in effects of sound and rhythm, experimenting with line-lengths, repetitions and alliterations, always to give added point to his theme; and the evocation by rhythmic means of sudden, rapid movement is one of his favourite devices:

> La beauté soudain passe, et eschappe à tes yeux:
> Tu ois, puis tu n'ois plus le son melodieux...
>
> Quel monstre voy-je là...?
> Je le voy: Je l'ay veu. Qu'estoit-ce donc? Le Monde.[2]

The second of these two examples is taken from a poem which develops a single image allegorically, in the manner of an emblem-poem. Several of the *octonaires* are of this kind: 'C'est un arbre que le monde...', 'Le monde est un jardin...' (nos. 33 and 34), or again no. 30: 'Orfevre, taille moy une boule bien ronde, / Creuse, et plaine

---

[1] See, for example, *octonaires* 4, 5, 19, 25, 28.

[2] *Octonaires* 12 and 46. See also no. 5:

> Vous fleuves et ruisseaux, et vous claires fonteines,
> De qui le glissant pas
> Se roule roule en bas...

One should recall that Chandeu's *Octonaires* were set to music by both Claude Le Jeune and Paschal de l'Estocart; see G. Reese, *Music in the Renaissance* (New York, 1959), pp. 384, 390. Reese points out Le Jeune's technique of word-painting in his vocal music.

de vent, l'image de ce monde...'. Whichever technique is used, a schematised visual framework is provided in order to pack the maximum amount of moral significance into a short space: each detail could be given its gloss, and each contributes to the compressed, epigrammatic sense of the whole.

Further examples of the *vanitas* imagery and its integration into the movement and structure of the poem will be considered later, when the sermon poem is discussed in its own right. It is already becoming clear, however, that the demands of an emphatic, outward-turned argument are producing—in the hands of the more talented poets at least—a special kind of rhetoric involving imagery, rhythm, and the economy of an epigrammatic argument; the flat, moral statement which is so tedious in Pibrac's *Quatrains* can in this way be imbued with life and significance. On the other hand, the *vanitas* themes do find their way occasionally into non-didactic, penitential poetry. In one of Habert's sonnets, a characteristic list of images provides the momentum for a statement of the 'uselessness' of God's wrath given the sinner's total abasement:

> Comme l'herbe fauchee on me voit desseicher,
> Comme un flambeau je vi du gain de mon dommage:
> Mais quoy je ne vi pas las! je meurs, car mon aage
> Fuit plus viste qu'un trait ne part au descocher.
> Veux tu contre une paille, ô Seigneur, te fascher?
> Helas! je ne suis rien qu'une ombre et qu'un nuage,
> Que le songe d'un songe, et qu'un leger plumage,
> Que sert de ta fureur tant de traits delascher?
> Je suis pauvre pecheur, tu és Dieu de clemence...[1]

Sonnets spirituels, no. 5. See also Desportes's *Prière* (ed. Michiels, p. 496):

> Tu peux, helas! tu peux me foudroyer:
> Mais que te sert de ta main desployer
> Encontre moy, qui ne suis rien que poudre?
> Tu es tout grand, tout juste et tout puissant;
> Je ne suis rien; et, en me punissant,
> Tu pers, Seigneur, et ta peine et ton foudre.

> Me chastiant, tu te rens poursuivant
> Contre un festu qui est poussé du vent;
> Tu veux monstrer ta force à un ombrage,
> A un corps mort, à un bois desseiché,
> A un bouton qui languit tout panché,
> Et au bouïllon enflé sur le rivage.

For two further examples of *vanitas* sonnets in a penitential context, see Chassignet's *Mespris*, sonnets 413 and 428.

Habert has here succeeded in creating a unity of tone and purpose. Frequently, however, the two different tones of voice—the penitential and the 'moral'—can be seen to coexist in a single poem. Desportes's twelfth *sonnet spirituel* begins in general terms ('...Tout est vent, songe et nue et folie evidente') and then in the tercets moves into a tone of personal penitence:

> Las! c'est dont je me plains, moy qui voy commencer
> Ma teste à se mesler, et mes jours se passer,
> Dont j'ay mis les plus beaux en ces vaines fumées;
> Et le fruict que je cueille, et que je voy sortir
> Des heures de ma vie, helas! si mal semées,
> C'est honte, ennuy, regret, dommage et repentir.
>
> (Michiels, p. 507.)

And Favre's hundredth sonnet, of which the quatrains have already been quoted (above, p. 153), uses the first person throughout, but ends with a generalised moral:

> Arreste-le, ô bon Dieu, qu'il ne s'eschappe ainsi,
> Pour me donner le temps d'impetrer ta mercy,
> Non, ne l'arreste pas, un instant peut suffire.
> Mais avance l'instant, qui tant d'heur me donra,
> Puis l'autre instant soudain, qui mes jours finira,
> Le reste n'est que mort: fol est qui la desire.

This dual aspect may justify itself in terms of an increased richness. In Favre's poem, the final phrase has the weight of a truth which emerges from personal reflection; Desportes's, too, is carefully drawn together by the parallelism of the last line with the eighth, and by the strategic placing of 'ces vaines fumées', so that the personal sense of vanity resumes and intensifies the *sententia* of the quatrains. However, such poems are exceptional; and they themselves demonstrate sufficiently that the *vanitas* tradition and moral generalisation are virtually inseparable.

This section may conveniently be concluded by a reading of Favre's ninety-fourth sonnet, which exploits the *vanitas* commonplaces in an unusually complex and probing manner. The tone of this poem is perfectly ambiguous: it is ostensibly an inward-turned apostrophe, the poet addressing his own soul; but it is equally an admonition, challenging the reader directly and involving him from the first line: 'Croupiras-tu tousjours en ceste terre basse. . .'. The movement of the poem is at times rather awkward, but the imagery of hollowness and of an imminent collapse, stressed by the resounding assonance of 't'accrase, et te fracasse', is finely worked out; and the compact identification of the sinful soul with the windy emptiness of the world in lines 9–10 ('ton vuide', 'ta terre') is one of Favre's most memorable ideas:

> Croupiras-tu tousjours en ceste terre basse,
> Ame, qui tant te plais de vivre en liberté!
> Attens-tu que le monde avec sa vanité
> Tombant dessus ton chef t'accrase, et te fracasse!
> Voy que, comme une nef, te passant il se passe,
> Ses fondemens plus seurs croulent à ton costé,
> Encor veux-tu de luy prendre l'eternité,
> N'est-ce un passage affreux des malheurs qu'il te brasse?
> Ne vois tu que ses vents dont tu te veux enfler
> Dedans ton vuide enclos font ta terre trembler?
> Eschange avec le ciel son terroir plein d'espines:
> Lors m'esprisant (*sic*) les biens qu'il feint de te donner,
> Tu vivras toute à Dieu, et sans point t'estonner
> Quand le ciel tomberoit, tu verras ses ruines.

THE VISION OF DEATH

The *vanitas* poet—Perrin or Chandieu—often speaks of death, but he scarcely lingers on its physical results; and Chassignet, whose poetry alternates between warnings of vanity and descriptions of death, tends to maintain a distinction between these two different approaches to what is fundamentally the same theme. Likewise, although the poetry of death may be penitential, and may at times recall the penitential lyric, there is a different emphasis: sickness and death are here symbolic not of sin as such, but of the fragility of human life; and if Job and Jeremiah are still important sources, the Old Testament poetry of sickness and lamentation nevertheless plays a less central rôle. Like their predecessors in the field of prose meditation, Chassignet and some of his contemporaries will try to represent directly and at close quarters the state of the body at death and after, the *gourmandise* of the worms and the evil smell enclosed in the coffin. Since their aim is thus to provoke meditation on death as a physical reality, they will use all their resources in an attempt to shock and horrify; and once again, their tone of voice will most often be aggressive, outward-turned, like that of the preacher.

The history of the horrors of the tomb as a poetic theme is often considered—particularly since Huizinga's *Waning of the Middle Ages*— to have reached its climax in the fifteenth century, in Villon and Pierre de Nesson; but the theme is nevertheless endemic to the Christian tradition, from the Church Fathers through the medieval masters and Latin poets to the sixteenth century and beyond. Appearing at the peak of Pléiade enthusiasm in the 1550s, Ronsard's *Hymne de la mort* characteristically rejects the physical terror of death as being a product of ignorance;[1] but it suggests at the same time that the 'worms and skeleton' view of death, although perhaps not a theme of serious literature, was still highly popular, sustained no doubt by the *ars moriendi* and by the 'dance of death' motif in visual art. The atmosphere of Ronsard's own *Derniers vers* is already very different, both in the amount of detail given and in its personal application:

> Je n'ai plus que les os, un schelette je semble,
> Decharné, denervé, demusclé, depoulpé...
> Je n'ose voir mes bras que de peur je ne tremble...
> Mon corps s'en va descendre où tout se desassemble...[2]

The restlessness and despair are balanced by a mood of serene resignation, or by a resolution in terms of the resurrection of the spirit; yet there is a real attempt to convey the horror and corruption of the dying body. As is well known, it is from one of these last lines of Ronsard that Chassignet apparently took the material which he developed in his 125th sonnet; the same adjectives describe a corpse:

> Mortel pense quel est dessous la couverture
> D'un charnier mortuaire un cors mangé de vers,
> Descharné, desnervé, où les os descouvers,
> Depoulpez, desnouez, delaissent leur jointure...

Ronsard limits his details, subordinates them to the theme of a nostalgic leave-taking; Chassignet attacks an imaginary audience with what

---

[1] See *Œuvres complètes*, ed. Laumonier (*STFM*), vol. VIII (Paris, 1963), p. 167. See also M. Bensimon, 'Ronsard et la Mort', *MLR*, 57 (1962), pp. 183 ff.

[2] *Œuvres complètes*, ed. Laumonier (Paris, Lemerre, 1914–19), vol. VI, p. 6 (this edition is quoted from since the more recent one in *STFM* is still incomplete).

amounts to a 'composition of place' for a meditation on death. A year or two later, Jacques Doremet published the following sonnet, based on the same allusion to the *Derniers vers*:

> Homme chétif! pourquoy donc à toute heure
> Ne te dispose et ne t'appreste-tu?
> Regarde toy, comme estant abbatu
> Ja par la faux de la mort toute seure,
> Tu sçais fort bien qu'il faudra que tu meure,
> Et que tu sois de ton corps dévestu,
> Qui tout dissouls restera sans vertu,
> Et sans que veine entiere luy demeure.
> Bref tu seras un Squelette raclé
> Tout dénervé, dépoulpé, démusclé,
> Sans mouvement, sans yeux et sans paupieres:
> Ton test seché n'aura plus que les dens
> Sans forme, tel que ceux qu'on voit dedans
> L'ample pourpris des fameux cimetieres.   (*Polymnie*, p. 44.)

This example shows, incidentally, how Ronsard's influence could establish a pattern even through a handful of poems published posthumously; on a more general level, it illustrates the standardisation to which such 'concrete' description, no less than the *vanitas* imagery, is susceptible. Sponde will echo Villon; and still more interesting, because it demonstrates a connexion between poetry and prose meditation, is Claude Hopil's exploitation, in his *De l'heure de la mort*, of the Damian-Granada description of the dying man quoted in chapter 2:

> Une pasle couleur esvanouit son teint,
> Cet œil est demy clos, et cet autre s'esteint,
> Son estomach panthois en vain, en vain s'efforce
> De pousser son haleine, et son cœur est sans force,
> Ses poulmons sanglottans, et son ciflet noué
> Monstre que le gosier est du tout enroué:
> Mesmes il ne peut pas, tant sa vigueur est mole,
> Exprimer par ses mains une seule parole,
> La langue est retenuë, il se sert en son lieu
> Des levres du penser pour parler à son DIEU.
> Les nerfs sont retirez, les membres se roidissent,
> Tous les sens sont perdus, et les dents se noircissent,

La vertu luy defaut, et ne peut repousser
Un extreme souspir pour sa mort annoncer.[1]

This unity of tradition corresponds broadly to the way in which the penitential lyric repeats and develops the manner of Old Testament lyric poetry.

The reorientation of common material to create an individual and significant pattern can take place on various levels. What strikes one most at a first reading is the degree of physical evocation which is achieved. Hopil expands his sources with all kinds of details of his own invention—the 'poulmons sanglottans', the 'ciflet noué'—and he even attempts to convey rhythmically, through the repetition of 'en vain', the difficulty of breathing. Chassignet in particular visualises death for his reader by means of an extraordinarily rich vocabulary, reinforced by a concentration of sound-values, of strong vowels and consonants:

> . . . et les muscles divers
> Servent aux vers goulus d'ordinaire pasture[.]
> Le ventre deschiré cornant de puanteur
> Infecte l'air voisin de mauvais senteur,
> Et le né my-rongé difforme le visage. . . (*Mespris*, no. 125.)

Most of these poems have an air of generalisation in so far as the poet is describing the common fate of man rather than a specific instance; and as we shall see later, a preaching tone is often used precisely to give the sense of a personal contact. Other means of 'localisation' are however open to the poet: Chassignet, for example, in a sonnet of penitence, imagines himself as an *anatomie*:

> Que feray-je, Seigneur, si ta presence amie
> Se retire de moy? veu que les mieus nourris
> Sont les mieus consumez devorez et pourris
> Sous le silence coy de la tombe ennemie?
> Je me presente ici comme une anatomie
> Le ceur (*sic*) sans battement, la bouche sans souris
> La teste sans cheveus, les os allangouris,
> L'œil cavé, le né froid, et la face blesmie.
> Pour avoir pris la vie en trop grande seurté
> Je suis tombé, Seigneur, en ceste malheurté,
> Nageant entre la peur l'esperance et le doute. . .[2]

[1] Hopil, *Les Œuvres chrestiennes*, fol. 16. See above, p. 42.
[2] *Mespris*, p. 224. This sonnet is not numbered.

Similarly, he will describe in detail his own illness ('Malade je couchois sur la chambre devant. . .'), and then draw from it a generalised truth ('. . . la peine, et l'ennuy nous suit jusqu'au trespas').[1]

All these poets integrate their physical description into an argument of some kind, although the fascination with death on a sensual level may well monopolise the poem: something of this kind happens in Doremet's sonnet, where the 'lesson', itself a very elementary one, is stated briefly in the second line and then forgotten. Hopil's *bravura* passage is followed by a somewhat pedantic 'moral':

> (Chrestiens) si ceste mort est un sault necessaire,
> La meditation est un frein salutaire
> Pour dompter les desirs de nostre infirmité,
> Qui se laisse emporter à toute vanité.
> Pensons bien à la mort, n'attendons sa venuë,
> La mort est trescertaine, et son heure incogneuë. . .
> Il faut que nos pensers vers le ciel s'acheminent,
> Et l'accez de la mort nos pasles sens ruminent,
> Qui medite en sa mort ne redoute ses coups.[2]

Chassignet himself tends on occasion to set an abstract argument side by side with an evocation of death without sufficiently integrating the two elements; and Motin's *Méditation sur le memento homo* is neatly constructed on a narrative plan, but disappoints by the thinness of both its description and its moral ('Pense mortel à ceste rage, / Et tu ne pecheras jamais').[3] For a more complex approach one must turn once again to Favre, although physical death is not one of his most frequent preoccupations:

---

[1] *Ibid.* no. 60. The phrase 'his own illness' ought perhaps to be modified, since this sonnet is modelled on a passage from Duplessis-Mornay (*Discours de la vie et de la mort*, ed. Richter (Milan, 1964), p. 61). Compare the list of illnesses in sonnet 18, which, though detailed, is not linked to any specific circumstance and culminates in a general 'moral': 'Entre tant de douleurs l'homme encore ne veut / Se guerir par la mort'. The description of personal sickness in certain poems of this period, being in no way related to the Old Testament sickness, is perhaps better considered in this context than in that of the penitential lyric; see for example Pierre Poupo, *La Muse chrestienne*, book 1 (Paris, 1590), sonnets 7 and 8; Gabrielle de Coignard's thirty-first sonnet; and Boyssières's fourteenth religious sonnet (*Les troisiesmes œuvres*, p. 58), although the description here is less specific. Ronsard's *Derniers vers* are again relevant. See also above, p. 115.

[2] The physical description itself occurs late in the poem, and is preceded by 'abstract' reflection on death and by prayer (of little interest).—Notice, however, that Hopil recalls the Ignatian technique of meditation in the penultimate line of this quotation.

[3] Published in Rousset's *Anthologie de la poésie baroque française*, vol. II, pp. 116–18.

The vision of death

Voy le lict de ta mort ô ame miserable,
Voy le piteux estat où t'a mis ton peché,
Pourquoy n'as-tu desja, soigneuse, recherché
Contre un si traistre mal, un secours favorable?
Mais quel remede, helas, te sera proufitable,
Si tu tiens l'ennemy dans toi-mesme caché?
La grace de ton Dieu du seul odeur faché,
Veut un vase tout net pour demeure aggreable.
Vomy ce vieil poison, et pleure s'il te deult,
Que si ton estomac foiblet vomir ne peut,
Fay que ce mesme odeur en toy face miracle.
C'est le poison qu'il faut en antidot broyer
Pour tes pleurs, quant et luy, à Dieu mesme envoier,
Broyant tout en son sang, fay Dieu le theriacle. (Sonnet 77.)

This poem, like many of Favre's, is rather confusing at first sight. Nevertheless, it takes ideas from a number of widely differing domains and binds them together in the attempt to make a significant statement; the result, for all its intricacy, is a coherent and purposeful whole. Contact with the reality of death is made simply and economically in the first line; but instead of developing this germinal idea by a display of horrific details Favre passes immediately to a metaphorical level. Death is identified with mortal sin, and the remainder of the poem develops the problem of a 'remedy', exploiting the metaphor and its significance in an increasingly complex manner. The second quatrain takes up a problem which we have already met in another of Favre's sonnets (see above, p. 141): man's sin is so much a part of him that he is sealed off from the grace of God; how then can grace cure him? The 'enemy' (sin, death, or the devil) now becomes the 'vieil poison', an image for original sin which suggests the serpent in the Garden of Eden and all the consequences of the Fall, while remaining perfectly consistent with the imagery of the poem as a whole; and the last four lines work out the theological problem of grace and original sin through the metaphor of the poison and its 'antidote' or *theriacle* (a specific for the cure of snake-bite). If man is unable to cast out his sinful nature, which excludes him from grace, he must, by a 'miracle', grind down the poison and mix it with tears to produce its own antidote (the reference here is presumably to a primitive version of the immunisation theory): man confesses his sinful nature to God, and by the act of penitence, may be absolved. However, such absolution would be impossible but for a further 'ingredient': the blood of Christ, into which both the sin and the tears are mixed, thus making God himself the antidote.

This sonnet combines meditation on death with a consideration of the problems of sin, grace, penitence and the Passion; it uses imagery from the *ars moriendi* tradition, from the Bible, and from medical theory; and yet it is thoroughly coherent. At the same time, the emotional movement is sustained by demonstrative imperatives and questions ('Voy..., Voy..., Pourquoy..., Mais quel remede..., Vomy..., Fay..., Fay...'); and if one modifies the punctuation slightly by placing a semi-colon after 'envoier', the last line emerges as a clear and balanced conclusion.

In Granada's sequence, the Wednesday meditation on death is followed on Thursday by a consideration of the Last Judgement; likewise, after a description of death and a funeral procession, Motin makes his reader imagine how his soul will appear at the Judgement, 'Toute tremblante et desolee'.[1] The theme is however relatively rare in the poetry of this period. One of Bèze's early Latin poems was a *Descriptio poetica Supremi Judicii* (1539);[2] but in French poetry, it does not seem to appear until the last decades of the sixteenth century, and even then it usually takes a somewhat fragmentary form. Desportes uses it as a conclusion for his *Plainte II*, remodelling the *Libera me* which, together with Revelation itself, is a major source of its literary expression (see above, pp. 119–20); Chassignet's seventy-ninth sonnet reflects on the resurrection and beatification of the body, but does not refer to the Last Judgement as such; and Favre imagines God's judgement of his sins taking place in the present:

> Herissez mes cheveux d'une frayeur non feinte,
> Tremblez—mes pieds pesants, fend toy mon traistre cœur,
> Apprehendez pour moy d'un si juste Seigneur
> L'horrible jugement qui me pasme de crainte...
> O Dieu, si contre moy tu viens en jugement
> Balancer mes forfaits, quand seras-tu clement? (Sonnet 96.)

Doremet comes closer than any of these to a vision of the last day, again drawing on the *Libera me*:

---

[1] Rousset, *Anthologie*, vol. II, p. 117.
[2] Published and discussed by F. Aubert, J. Boussard and H. Meylan in *BHR*, 15 (1953), pp. 164 ff., 257 ff. ('Un premier recueil de poésies latines de Théodore de Bèze').

The vision of death

A tout ce que je fais, ou que je dis, je pense
Ja la trompette ouyr sonner terriblement,
Qui dit: Levez vous Morts, venez au jugement. . . .
O Dieu fai moy pardon, à fin que sans ahan
Partant d'ici, je puisse estre au sein d'Abraham
Par tes Anges porté, pour te louer sans cesse.

(*Polymnie*, p. 52.)

But this is a subject which properly demands extended, even epic, treatment, as d'Aubigné demonstrates. *Jugement* combines many of the elements of meditational method, although they are projected on to d'Aubigné's vast canvas: a wealth of detailed imagination of the physical scene; a long section of theological analysis (lines 329–660); a prayer invoking the divine justice by way of introduction; and a mystical conclusion in which the senses are transfigured and the soul united to God.[1] Furthermore, the tone of the sermon plays a prominent part, since there is a vigorous passage of invective against sinners. Chassignet's *Mespris* ends with a poem called *Le Dernier Jugement*, based on Revelation (*Mespris*, pp. 385–92); it is introduced by a prose passage which brings out the moral aspect of the scene, and, once again, invective against the 'goats' becomes the focus of attention:

L'Autheur deliberé de finir et parachever son livre par une breve description de la fin et consommation de l'univers, nous a voulu representer en ce poeme, tiré pour la plus part des escritures saintes, les ravages de tant de miseres qui lors abymeront les hommes, tellement attachez au cordeau de leurs sales voluptez, que marchandant les bras croisez avec le tems et la fortune une venteuse chimere de plaisir et seureté, se verront plustost couvers du deluge des calamitez, fleaus, infortunes et tormens ordonnez pour la juste punition des meschans. . . ils seront contrains à la fin de pendre au gibet de la vengeance divine, et comme boucs puans et lascifs separez du troupeau des brebis debonnaires trebuscher en la maison ou perpetuellement gronde le tintamarre des pleurs et grincemens de dens, qui sera d'autant plus d'occasion aus bons et vertueus qui se seront tenus reglez parmi tant de debordemens de louer d'un Cantique eternel la justice de ce grand et incomparable Roy qui de vases vils et abjets les ayant fais vaisseaus d'honneur et de gloire les ensaisinera de la possession de son royaume eternel.

[1] Unfortunately, a proper analysis of *Jugement* cannot be undertaken here, since this could only be done in the context of the *Tragiques* as a whole (the same is true of d'Aubigné's whole manner of treating death, which is clearly related to the material discussed in this chapter, but which involves a large number of extraneous considerations). Also, owing to its late publication, it had no impact in the period we are dealing with; but cf. also Saint-Amant's *Le Contemplateur*, which includes a visualisation of the Last Judgement.

Although this introduction speaks of the 'wailing and gnashing of teeth', the poem itself does not consider the torments of Hell (or the delights of Paradise); and in fact the Friday meditation on Hell is conspicuously absent from the poetry of this period—the only instance which comes to mind is a brief allusion in Motin's *Memento* poem. There are a number of possible reasons for this. In the first place, no poet of the authority of Ronsard, Desportes or Bèze had ever set a precedent for a poetry of Hell-fire. Secondly, there was no secular parallel from which a poet might draw ideas and images; there is no doubt that the thematic pattern of Chassignet's *Mespris* was much influenced by contemporary philosophical treatises on death. Finally— and this is perhaps the most important reason—there was no Biblical source-text which could be paraphrased and thus transferred into the poetic tradition.

The vision of death is itself a less common theme than one might be led to think. Certainly it is a significant aspect of poetic creation in this period; but some of its most important effects concern epic and dramatic literature, where other poetic influences of a non-religious character are prevalent. In 'lyric' poetry, it occurs from time to time as one element of a wider complex of themes: even the *Mespris* concentrates one's attention less on the description of death than on abstract argument, sententious generalisations, and *vanitas* imagery, although it is naturally the violent, concrete poems which strike one at a first reading. Moreover, a rich, sensual vocabulary is not the only means of making a physical impact on the reader; when one speaks of the 'concrete' or 'realistic' manner of Chassignet or Sponde, one may be reacting rather to the tone of voice of the poet than to the physical imagery as such. It is this tone of voice which will be the subject of the next section, and which is I think the most significant general characteristic of all the poetry discussed in this chapter.

THE VOICE OF THE PREACHER

The direct influence of the sermon on literature in the later sixteenth century is difficult to assess, partly because little attention has been given to written sermons as a potential literary source, and partly because the sermons which were written down and published can only constitute a minute and probably unrepresentative fraction of those preached. There is nevertheless no doubt that in this period the preacher had an essential and indeed a very difficult part to play: theology and politics often went hand in hand, and no one was immune from suspicion of heresy. He would thus have been the focus of public attention; and anyone who set out to write religious poetry would be likely, consciously or not, to use ideas or ways of speaking which he had heard from the pulpit. In some cases—Chandieu, Bertaut, Du Perron—the poet would himself have given sermons. The renewal and importance of the sermon in the sixteenth century is perhaps best represented by the Calvinist *prêche*, which may well be a source of d'Aubigné's invective, and of the more controlled 'preaching' of Chandieu and Sponde. On the other hand, the techniques of the sermon were equally familiar to Catholics, and would have been emphasised, not only by the example of the Protestants, but also by the growing popularity of devotional method and by the propaganda programme of the Jesuits and Mendicants; thus the parallels between Sponde and Chassignet are perfectly comprehensible.

The refinements of the funeral oration as Saulnier describes it must represent an extreme, if not an exception;[1] but the *genre* has characteristics which are nevertheless suggestive: 'L'Oraison funèbre est bien fille de l'âge de la Ligue, fille de la Contre-Réforme. De là qu'elle tend au sermon, pour confusément que ce soit' (p. 131). In the first place, it draws extensively on the commonplaces of the *vanitas* tradition: the themes enumerated by Saulnier include the *vanitas vanitatum* itself, the life of man as a 'collection d'incidents éphémères', 'fleurs qui se fanent', 'pourtraict de la vie humaine' (pp. 140 ff.). Where death is evoked, it is seen only in general terms as being horrific: '"O cruelle mort! malheureuse, funeste, calamiteuse, digne des larmes de la France, de l'Europe, de toute la terre, et du ciel mesme, s'il en estoit capable!"' (p. 143). This elegant invective corresponds to the abstract arguments on the subject of death that one finds for example in Chassignet; and the same is true of what Saulnier calls 'les mouvements pseudo-paradoxaux du "mort non mort"' (pp. 150–1). At the same time, the speaker had to make an emotive impact on his audience, and his rhetoric would include 'mouvements de pathétique grammatical, interrogatif ou

[1] V.-L. Saulnier, 'L'Oraison funèbre au XVIe siècle', *BHR*, 10 (1948), pp. 124 ff.

exclamatif' (p. 151). These techniques can of course be explained by reference to rhetorical method alone; but the art of preaching is in any event largely a specific variant of persuasive rhetoric, and even a less elevated cleric than Du Perron would have learnt his rhetoric and used it to give urgency and immediacy to his message. The principal difference is that whereas a court audience would expect to be addressed with a certain propriety and respect, an ordinary congregation might well be subjected to irony, sarcasms, and a down-to-earth if not violent vocabulary.

The point of these observations is not to prove a direct connexion—for which evidence is lacking—between poetry and the sermon, but rather to provide a background against which the character of a certain kind of poetry will emerge more clearly. Moreover, although this character can be defined most conveniently in the context of the themes of vanity and death, it is fundamental to much devotional poetry; owing to the ambivalence by means of which a sermon can become a personal meditation and vice versa, the preaching tone can be used as an element of the penitential poem or of the contemplation of the Passion.[1] In the ensuing discussion, the examples will be such that no *a priori* distinction need be made between an 'inward' and an 'outward' application; the flexibility of the sermon tone will consequently be implicit throughout.

The rhetoric of the sermon poem is a rhetoric of the second person: an audience is always implied. The very first sonnet of Chassignet's *Mespris* establishes this cardinal relationship with the reader:

> Vous quiconque allechez des voluptez charnelles
> Que vous humez, gloutons, en ce cors terrien,
> Ne pouvez sans horreur dissoudre le lien
> Qui detient en prison vos ames criminelles...

Where this audience is addressed directly, it is always on the most general level—*mortel, mondain, pécheur, homme chétif*—allowing the poet to summarise his theme and at the same time to establish an emphatic and aggressive manner; deprecatory adjectives can be added at will ('Mortels insensez', 'Magnifiques mondains'). As the primary

[1] It is rare in the penitential lyric, but as we have seen, it occurs frequently in the penitential sonnet (see above, especially pp. 143–4). The point will be illustrated again later, in the context of 'life of Christ' poetry.

aim of the preacher is to capture attention, to involve the imagination of the listener, he will accompany these vocatives with imperatives which spotlight a specific point, often a physical reality: 'Voy le lict de ta mort ô ame miserable'; 'Mortel pense quel est dessous la couverture / D'un charnier mortuaire un cors mangé de vers'. This corresponds to the imaginative effort which the *dévot* is encouraged to make in the composition phase of meditation. Similarly, interrogatives will be used to give momentum to what would otherwise be flat statement:

> Dieu qui le fait l'achepte, Et pour qui? pour nous tous:
> Mais quand? de jour en jour: comment? veillant sur nous:
> Moy las! qui pers tant d'ans, qu'auray-je donc à dire?
>
> Pecheurs impenitens, qui forgez à toute heure
> Contre un Dieu si clement maint peché tout nouveau...
> Qu'attendez-vous? La mort? Ha! vous estes ja morts.
> Voulez-vous mieux mourir? Il est temps de renaistre.[1]

In the second of these quotations, there is a strong element of irony, a scathing, aggressive tone, which is one of the most common effects of rhetorical question in the sermon poem. It can be supported by a number of other devices. In these poems of Favre, as in many of Chandieu's or Chassignet's, the clipped phrases and broken rhythms create emphasis and at the same time a mood of impatience, a mood which recalls the Sponde of the *Méditations*, or the Goulart of the *Trente tableaux*:

> Qu'as-tu? pauvre amoureux, dont l'ame demy-morte
> Souspire des sanglots au vent qui les emporte.
> N'accuse rien que toy. Ton mal est ton desir...
>
> Arreste: ô Mondain, où cours tu?
> Escoute, enten la voix de la vertu.
> Las! il passe outre: il court apres ce monde...[2]

Similar effects of emphasis are produced by alliteration and assonance, a device used in particular by Favre; as we have seen, it plays a

---

[1] Favre, *Centurie premiere*, sonnets 63 and 57 respectively. The 'le' in the first line of the first quotation refers to 'time'. See also sonnets 24 and 94 (above, pp. 144, 156); and Chandieu's forty-sixth *octonaire* (above, p. 153).
[2] Chandieu, *octonaires* 23 and 47. See above, pp. 35–6.

prominent part in his twenty-fourth and ninety-fourth sonnets. But Chassignet too will use it, setting the tone of a whole sonnet with the contemptuous alliteration of 'Tu trottes':

> Tu trottes et discours par les lieus perilleus
> Et te plains de chopper, tu marches et chemines
> Parmi les barbillons des mordantes espines
> Sans vouloir dechirer tes vestements drilleus...
> Miserable mondain...
> Pourquoy t'estonnes tu des accidens humains...?[1]

The 368th sonnet of the *Mespris* begins with an insistent and ironic 'Toy seul...', and develops through an occasional alliteration into a full-scale bombardment based on a repetition of the word *monde*; Chandieu's thirteenth *octonaire* is constructed wholly on alliterations and repetitions of *vie, mort,* and *monde*. Such poems are evidently designed to amaze the reader with their rhetorical virtuosity, which is often excessive; but the central mood of admonition remains perfectly clear.

The culmination of the preaching manner, within the context of the themes of vanity and death at least, is straightforward invective, where the tone is raised to shouting pitch, and the vocabulary becomes violent: Chassignet addresses his 371st sonnet, not to the usual 'mortels' or 'mondains', but to the 'Hydropiques enflez que la dypsade mord'. The insistent manner is now replaced by a technique of accumulation: a list of injurious adjectives or nouns is thrown at the 'audience' in rapid succession:

> Enfleure d'un tombeau, cloaque de vermine,
> Pasture de Serpentz, taniere de la mort:
> Oses tu desployer ton cauteleux effort,
> Pour vouloir offencer celle qui te domine?[2]

This is Gabrielle de Coignard apostrophising the flesh; and it is interesting that this sort of invective is often inward-turned:

---

[1] *Mespris*, no. 393. See also Favre's fifty-fourth sonnet:
> Le diable tourne et vire...
> Le monde...
> Nous happe, trappe, attrape, egorge horriblement.
The first edition of the *Centurie premiere* reads: 'Le diable *gire* et vire'; in keeping with the mood of a period in which Malherbe was clarifying his views on poetry, Favre evidently felt that the original version was unnecessarily flamboyant.

[2] Gabrielle de Coignard, *op. cit.* p. 56, sonnet 95 (*Contre la chair*).

The voice of the preacher

Espargne espargne moy, et ne me fais mourir
Moy qui suis un vaisseau empuantis d'ordure,
La viande des vers, une charongne impure
Nourriture du feu...
Que suis je miserable en ceste mer bouillante?
Chetif que deviendray je? un vase de fiente
Un pot de pourriture, infet de puanteur
Aveugle, pauvre, nud, inconstant, et menteur
Endurant chacque jour mille peines funebres
Jusqu'a tant que mes yeus soint sillez de tenebres
Have, palle, et plombé de peine et de souci
Ignorant son entree et son issue aussi
Miserable et mortel dont la vie importune
S'evanouit plustost que l'ombre de la lune
Croit comme fait la fleur, qui fleurit maintenant
Puis fanit tout soudain, et meurt incontinant.[1]

Miserable pecheur, o! pecheur miserable,
Crie, crie, merci, las! crie incessament
Misericorde, a Dieu, que j'ay si grandement
Offencé, par ma vie: helas! trop detestable!
Laid, puant, et infet, je me suis fait l'estable,
A loger sans respect, tout ce que le gourmand,
Le paillard, et l'oisif, loge en l'entendement,
Si rempli de pechez, que les rives de sable,
Animal plain d'ordure, et tout partout souillé:
D'offences entaché, de vices tout rouillé,
Magasin de tous maux, riviere d'amertume!
Leve les yeux au Ciel, de tenebres voilez,
Et du flambeau de foy, tes offences consume:
Affin que de bien-faits, tes costez soient aislez.[2]

[1] Chassignet, *Mespris*, pp. 176–7. This is part of a long poem entitled *De la Misere de l'homme, et fragilité de la vie humaine*; in spite of its title, it is primarily a penitential prayer:

Tu vis, et je suis mort, tu es la medicine
Moy le pauvre malade, aveugle je chemine
Par l'obscur de la nuit, et tu es la clarté...
Reprouverois tu bien l'ouvrage de tes mains?...
Pardonne au serviteur qui pressé de ton ire
Ose à si grand Seigneur descouvrir son martire. (pp. 175–6.)

It is therefore an interesting example of how the various different *topoi* of sin, sickness and death can be combined.
[2] Boyssières, *Les Troisiesmes Œuvres*, p. 76, sonnet 16.

Finally, a passage of invective by Doremet, illustrating the sermon commonplace of the body fattened for the worms:

> Pourquoy attises-tu si curieusement
> Et engraisses ta chair de chose precieuse,
> Ta chair laquelle en bref dedans la tombe creuse
> Les vers devoreront en puant aliment?...
> Oses-tu bien mal-caut l'Ame tousjours vivante
> Moins priser que le corps, qui n'est qu'une prison
> Et sans ame n'est rien que charongne puante?[1]

I have quoted these passages at some length, and from a variety of different poets, to demonstrate the popularity of this manner, which is not the province of Chassignet and Sponde alone. But they are worth quoting for their own sake: they have a verve, a sense of movement, a challenging tone, which is often lacking in the didactic poetry of the sixteenth century, and which, for all its roughness, is a refreshing contrast to the insipidity of Desportes's love-sonnets or the heavy-handed rhetoric of Bertaut. They use material which is for the most part standardised, and stock devices of rhetoric; but they create a momentum, they conscript the reader's attention—and this is true not only of the last passages quoted, but also of a high proportion of the sermon poems of Favre, Chassignet and the rest. In the *Mespris*, it is this type of poem which stands out, reinvigorating the contemplation of death and even the sententious abstractions; the ninety-eighth sonnet takes the *vanitas* imagery, adds an occasional detail, and gives it a physical impact:

> Qu'est-ce de vostre vie? une bouteille molle
> Qui s'enfle dessus l'eau...
> Qu'est-ce de vostre vie? un tourbillon roüant,
> De fumiere à flos gris, parmy l'air se joüant
> Qui passe plus soudain que la foudre meurdriere.
> Puis vous negligerez dorenavant le bien
> Durable, et permanent, pour un point qui n'est rien
> Qu'une confle, un mensonge, un songe, une fumiere.

Once again, the urgency is produced by the repeated ironic questions, on which the whole structure of the sonnet is based; it is the balance between these questions and their answers, together with alliteration,

---

[1] *Polymnie*, p. 49. Compare once again the end of the passage quoted from Goulart (above, p. 28).

assonance, and the emphatic list of the last line, which establishes the restless, challenging tone of the preacher. Hence the 'physical impact' of the sonnet is a function not so much of the images themselves as of rhythm and tone.

THE 'STANCES ET SONNETS DE LA MORT' OF JEAN DE SPONDE

Sponde's poems on death demand individual treatment for two reasons. In the first place, they have a sustained quality and at the same time an ease of manner which are lacking in his contemporaries; even Favre, in spite of his analytic approach and his dexterity with the preaching tone, tends to be unrelaxed and at times tortuous. Secondly, the *Stances et sonnets* illustrate in a very coherent way how the penitential and sermon *genres* can complement one another while retaining their own individual character, thus drawing together some of the threads of the last two chapters. At the same time, Sponde was immersed in the atmosphere of prose and verse meditation through his affiliation with Protestant literary circles in both France and Switzerland; thus he remains characteristic of his age.

If Sponde chose death as his subject, it is not that he intended, in either the *Stances* or the sonnets, to paint a detailed portrait of the horrors of death. The only hint of such a portrayal occurs in the first stanza of the eleventh sonnet, where the vocabulary is pale beside that of Chassignet:

> Et quel bien de la mort? où la vermine ronge
> Tous ces nerfs, tous ces os? où l'Ame se départ
> De ceste orde charogne, et se tient à l'escart,
> Et laisse un souvenir de nous comme d'un songe?[1]

It is the *vanitas* imagery which dominates the atmosphere of the sonnets; and the same is true, to a certain extent, of the *Stances*. Neverthe-

---

[1] I quote from Boase's edition of the *Méditations*, which also contains the first extant text of the *Essay de poèmes chrestiens*. The *Stances* will be quoted from the same edition (pp. 181–5). It seems necessary to counter the view, based on very little evidence, that Sponde's conception of death is 'concrete', 'physical', 'realistic'; see for example Glauco Natoli, *Figure e problemi della cultura francese* (Florence, 1956), *Il distacco dalla Pléiade*, II: 'La poesia amorosa e religiosa di Jean de Sponde.' Natoli uses phrases like 'realismo crudo' (p. 111), 'fisico orrore', 'realismo macabro', 'elemento orrido e sensibile della morte', 'espressioni crude,...materializzate' (p. 113), etc.

less, the longer poem is best considered as a penitential lyric, albeit an unusual one. The *stances*-form is the same as that used by Desportes and his circle for the majority of their poems; and the central theme is introspective and penitential. The Old Testament provides the theme of 'Thou has created me', and the questioning that goes with it:

> Et puis si c'est ta main qui façonna le Monde,
> Dont la riche Beauté à ta Beauté responde,
> La chair croit que le Tout pour elle fust parfaict:
> Tout fust parfaict pour elle, et elle d'avantage
> Se vante d'estre, ô Dieu, de tes mains un ouvrage,
> Hé! deffairois-tu donc ce que tes mains ont faict?

Similarly, there are echoes of the Old Testament in stanza 14 ('J'ay bien veu sauteler les bouillons de ton zèle...'); and there is an initial statement of the *taedium vitae* theme, although not in terms of the Biblical sickness:

> Je m'ennuye de vivre, et mes tendres années,
> Gémissant sous le faix de bien peu de journées,
> Me trouvent au milieu de ma course cassé.

The later part of the poem includes an invocation of God's liberating wrath, the themes of suffering and cure, and a fluctuation between questioning and resignation.

In one of the penitential lyrics discussed earlier, these passages would have become elements of a development recalling that of a penitential psalm. With Sponde, the total atmosphere is much further from the Old Testament. At its best, the penitential prayer-poem is urgent and restless: Sponde deepens this urgency by increasing the tension between body and soul, between earth and heaven. The dialectic is established immediately in the opening stanza, with its contrasts between the illusory light of the world, the darkness of death, and the brilliance of the other life, and becomes the mainspring of the whole poem.[1] The poet's *taedium vitae* and the desire of his spirit to attain to

---

[1] Cf. Rousset's 'trois éclairages', in his article 'Les images de la nuit et de la lumière chez quelques poètes religieux', *CAEF*, 10 (1958), pp. 58 ff. For a detailed interpretation of the *Stances*, see A. Pizzorusso, 'Le *Stances de la mort* di Jean de Sponde', in *Studi in onore di Carlo Pellegrini*, Biblioteca di Studi Francesi, 2 (Turin, 1963), pp. 193 ff. I have recently read a dissertation submitted in 1963 for a Doctorate of Philosophy in the University of Michigan entitled *The Poetry of Jean de Sponde: A Critical Evaluation*, by

celestial beauty are counteracted by 'quelque chose qui gronde, / Qui faict contre le Ciel le partisan du Monde', and this clear-cut division attracts the broadest possible images: light and dark (stanzas 1, 15, 16), water and fire (stanza 5). The confessional element remains implicit, but the theme of sin is just beneath the surface in all the references to the world and the flesh—the pride of the flesh that dares to challenge God (stanza 11), the heaviness of the flesh that weighs down the spirit (stanza 13), the darkness of 'ces relants abysmes / Que tu noircis sans fin des horreurs de tes crimes' (stanza 15). It is in the context of this life and death struggle that one has to see the conventional 'questioning' motifs, and also the final resolution, where the poet surrenders himself to God's will in a prayer taken from the broadest area of philosophical and religious tradition: 'Appren-moy de bien vivre, afin de bien mourir'.

In order to convey this *combat spirituel* between flesh and spirit, Sponde brings into play an unusually wide range of tones of voice. The elegiac description of the poet's predicament (as in stanzas 2–6) is developed by apostrophes both to his *Esprit* and to God; and these varying attitudes allow a movement between reflection, admonition, exhortation, exclamation, interrogation, and affective prayer. The poet does not dramatise himself as either Flesh or Spirit, but remains at least partly independent, observing, analysing, warning, and praying for a resolution; and at one point the arguments of the poet and of the flesh seem to merge, till suddenly the independent judgement intervenes and dramatically reveals the arguments as false:

> Sans ton ayde, mon Dieu, ceste chair orgueilleuse
> Rendra de ce combat l'issuë périlleuse,
> Car elle est en son règne, et l'autre est estranger...
>
> Et puis si c'est ta main qui façonna le Monde...
> Hé! deffairois-tu donc ce que tes mains ont faict?
>
> Voylà comme l'effort de la charnelle ruse
> De son bien pour son mal ouvertement abuse...
> Viens donc, et mets la main, mon Dieu, dedans ce trouble...

Laura G. Durand. This seems to me to have a number of valuable things to say, particularly on points of interpretative detail; and Miss Durand's general view of the sonnets coincides in certain important respects with my own (see pp. 93, 107, 108 and 158 of the thesis).

Ne crain point, mon Esprit, d'entrer en ceste Lice...

C'est assez enduré que de ceste vermine
La superbe insolence à ta grandeur domine...

Thus the implication of 'La chair *croit* que le Tout pour elle fust parfaict' is brought out;[1] the rational faculty becomes arbiter of the spiritual combat, deciding on the validity of the opposing claims.[2] One has the feeling here of an intellectual control, a certainty of judgement, whereas in Desportes's sickness poem, which has a similar *volte-face*, there is no 'superior voice' to exorcise the instability and fluctuation.

This dramatised analysis of a fundamental tension excludes any substantial reference to physical corruption, to the penitential *ordure* or sickness. At the same time, the tendency towards apostrophe results in the grafting on to the penitential prayer of some of the devices of the sermon poem. Large sections of the poem are in effect a sermon preached by the poet to his soul, and even elsewhere there are passages which would fit perfectly well into the atmosphere of the sonnets:

> J'ay veu comme le Monde embrasse ses délices,
> Et je n'embrasse rien au Monde que supplices.

> Ce Monde qui croupist ainsi dedans soy-mesme,
> N'esloigne point jamais son cœur de ce qu'il ayme,
> Et ne peut rien aymer que sa déformité.

Several of the images are from the *vanitas* stock—*verre, roseau, poudre, fumée,* 'Ton Mal, c'est ton prison', 'Ce vivre est une mer'; and these, together with lines such as 'Tout se haste, se perd, et coule avec ce Temps' and the *mort-vie* paradoxes of stanza 19, remind one that Sponde's prose meditations frequently have the character of a *vanitas* sermon.

---

[1] Compare this passage from one of Duplessis–Mornay's meditations: 'Hé! Seigneur, jusques à quand? Seigneur, ainsi parle ceste chair: pardonne-lui. Et lui semble qu'elle a bien dit. Et là dessus le Diable desploye ses argumens' (*Meditations chrestiennes*, p. 11).

[2] Cf. A. Levi, *French Moralists*, pp. 123–4; Sponde's *Stances* do in fact seem to imply a 'trichotomist psychology' which 'is inevitably associated with the combat in the neo-stoic moralists, in the *Banquet* commentary as well as in Erasmus, Charron, and du Vair'. The Platonic 'ascent' also seems to be implied in Favre's 'spiritual combat' sonnet (above, pp. 142–3; see also Habert, above, pp. 130–1); although Habert's view is based rather on the simple duality of soul and body. See also Higman, *art. cit. BHR,* 28 (1966), pp. 579–80, for Sponde's technique of representing an argument as if he agreed with it, and then refuting it.

The 'Stances et sonnets de la mort' of Jean de Sponde

The mingling of *genres* in the *Stances* has certain potential disadvantages. Owing to the epigrammatic tendencies of sermon poetry, the individual *stance* often becomes a unit, with its own image and *pointe*, a short poem with all the characteristics of the short poem:

> Quelle plaine en l'Enfer de ces pointus encombres?
> Quel beau jour en la nuict de ces affreuses ombres?
> Quel doux largue au destroict de tant de vents battu?
> Repren cœur, mon Esprit, repren nouvelle force,
> Toy, mouëlle d'un festu, perce à travers l'écorce,
> Et, vivant, fay mourir l'escorce, et le festu.

Here the accumulation of miniature images has a strong syntactic link with the previous stanza; but stanza 20 is scarcely connected with 19, and is only continued in 21 by a verbal echo:

> Je sçay bien, mon Esprit, que cest air, et ceste onde,
> Ceste Terre, et ce Feu, ce Ciel qui ceint le Monde,
> Enfle, abysme, retient, brusle, estreint tes désirs:
> Tu vois je ne sçay quoy de plaisant et aymable,
> Mais le dessus du Ciel est bien plus estimable,
> En de plaisans amours, et d'aymables plaisirs.
>
> Ces Amours, ces Plaisirs...

This concentration of two obtrusive rhetorical devices within a single stanza tends to choke the development of the poem, and there is a real danger that at these points the sequence will lose its overall momentum and become a series of loosely integrated fragments.[1]

In the sonnets, the apostrophe is for the most part externalised: Sponde is addressing an imaginary congregation. Admittedly, sonnet 10 is an internal colloquy, with an apostrophe to the soul; the seventh sonnet begins with a personal predicament and ends with a general moral; and in sonnet 9, there is a personal application after eleven lines in the full sermon style. Nevertheless, the tone is relatively uniform throughout; and the prayer of sonnet 12, which is an epilogue to the whole sequence, is in keeping with the normal pattern of a sermon— instruction is followed by a prayer for aid in carrying out the lesson. Most of the sonnets are in the full *vanitas* tradition: reminders of

---

[1] See also the following passage:
> L'Esprit qui n'est que feu de ses désirs m'enflamme,
> Et la chair qui n'est qu'Eau pleut des Eaux sur ma flamme,
> Mes ces eaux-là pourtant n'esteignent point ce feu.

death and the frailty of life, images of impermanence, variations on the *mort-vie* paradox, epigrammatic developments and so on. The influence of Du Bellay is less immediately clear than in some of Sponde's contemporaries, but it is implied in the theme of *orgueil* and its accompanying images:

> Je voy ces vermisseaux bastir dedans leurs plaines
> Les monts de leurs desseins, dont les cimes hautaines
> Semblent presque esgaler leurs cœurs ambitieux.
> Géants, où poussez-vous ces beaux amas de poudre?
> Vous les amoncelez? Vous les verrez dissouldre:
> Ils montent de la Terre? Ils tomberont des Cieux.   (Sonnet 3.)

And one senses the satirical tradition of the *Regrets* behind the *être-paraître* theme of sonnet 9:

> Et qui sont ces valets, et qui sont ces Seigneurs?...[1]
> Ces masques desguisez, dont la troupe folastre,
> S'amuse à caresser je ne sçay quels donneurs
> De fumées de Court...

It is only when one has seen how much in these poems belongs to tradition that one can begin to define Sponde's manner: in the famous sonnet 'Mais si faut-il mourir', for example, the images in themselves are scarcely either 'original' or 'physical'. As a list of *similitudes*, it is like any number of similar lists in both prose and poetry, in Chassignet's 'Qu'est-ce de vostre vie...', in Favre's 'Mon aage ainsi que vent...', in Habert's 'Comme l'herbe fauchee...', in the prose meditations quoted in chapter 2 (above, pp. 45–6), or in Du Perron's funeral oration on the death of Ronsard: 'L'homme est une fueille d'automne preste à choir au premier vent, une fleur d'une matinée, une ampoule qui s'enfle et s'esleve sur l'eau, une petite estincelle de flamme dans le cœur, et un peu de fumée dans les narines'.[2] Parallels of this kind—some apparently very precise, although to speak of 'sources' would be dangerous on such common territory—could be multiplied almost endlessly, both for this sonnet and for most of the others. In fact the overall pattern of imagery is very much like that of the emblem-

---

[1] In connexion with this line, cf. Gilson's quotation from a sermon attributed to Augustine (*Les Idées et les lettres*, p. 15): '...Respice sepulcra, et vide quis servus, quis dominus...' The 'Respice sepulcra' theme is also highly relevant to Goulart's *Trente Tableaux*.

[2] Quoted by Saulnier in 'L'Oraison funèbre', p. 143. Note the verbal similarities between the bubble image here, in the Chassignet and Favre sonnets mentioned, and in the Desportes passage quoted above, p. 154, n. 1.

book: the eighth sonnet is essentially an emblem-poem, constructed on the mainstream *similitude* of the arrow, and even the less familiar images like the 'verd de la cire' and the 'huyle de ce Tableau' of sonnet 2 would not surprise one if one found them in a collection of *emblemata*.

On the other hand, Sponde has at his disposal a number of techniques for bringing well-worn material to life. Sometimes he uses a single rich word—often a verb—to enliven an otherwise commonplace vocabulary: *hâleront* in sonnet 2, *pantelle* in sonnet 4, *saboule* in sonnet 10. More often, however, he will rely on sound-effects; but unlike some of his contemporaries, Sponde does not over-indulge in alliterations and repetitions. He introduces them where they are required for emphasis, to give edge and impact to the tone of voice: one reason why sonnet 2 is so successful is that the alliterations are so bold and yet economical: 'Ce beau flambeau qui lance une flamme fumeuse', 'Ces lyons rugissans je les ay veus sans rage'. Likewise, *pantelle* and *saboule* are supported by alliteration, so that their impact is not isolated: 'Pantelle en la poictrine', 'saboule / Le Sablon';[1] and the potentially overpowering repetitions of *vie, mort, mortels* in the first sonnet are at least partially relieved by the play on other words (*thrésors, maisons, remors, souvenir, accuse–excuse, oubly*). Finally—and this is one of his favourite devices—Sponde will strengthen his nouns with demonstratives. He is of course not exceptional in this respect among either poets or prose-writers: the demonstrative is an essential element of sermon technique. But Sponde uses it with unusual liberality, and at the same time with great incisiveness. Its function is principally to specify an idea or image, to focus attention on it: thus the flowers, the bubble, the torch, the waves, and the other images of sonnet 2 are presented to the reader with an immediacy and a potency which most lists of this kind have lost through over-use. Furthermore, the demonstrative can impose a tone of irony, of contempt, of aggression: the sceptres and thrones of sonnet 4, the *valets* and the *Seigneurs* of sonnet 9, are held up for scorn and ridicule. Thus with a single device, Sponde can produce both the actuality and the attack which he needs in order to hammer home his point.

These characteristics, in isolation, might produce an occasional out-

---

[1] In both cases, the effect is increased by the rhythm.

standing phrase or line, but it is their integration into the dynamics of a whole poem which really matters; and in this respect, Sponde is unrivalled among his contemporaries. Take for example the way in which the accumulation of images in the second sonnet is organised. The even, incisive tone of the quatrains is succeeded by an intensification: the prophet of doom demonstrates his point by referring to his own (and his audience's) experience; the first person singular is specific, and at the same time general and even apocalyptic. Thus when the last half-line echoes the first, it comes at the peak of a crescendo in which the ironic apostrophe 'Vivez, hommes, vivez' takes on its full force. Chassignet's ninety-eighth sonnet has impetus, and is neatly and emphatically rounded off, but its structure has none of the potency of Sponde's. In certain respects, this sonnet stands in isolation: there are no others with this degree of cumulative imagery. But accumulation of one kind or another is often fundamental to the structure of Sponde's religious sonnets—if not of images, then of questions: nos. 4, 9 and 11 all depend on insistent questioning, alternating with sections of analysis. One of the most common patterns throughout the sequence is the movement from apostrophe (interrogative, imperative, or at least vocative) which states the problem, through an elaboration in terms of images (nos. 2 and 4) or rhetorical devices (no. 5, lines 6–7), to a final apostrophe. In this way, the symmetry of the sonnet-form can be preserved and used significantly, allowing a variation in tone of voice.

With Sponde, as with Chassignet, the menacing tone of the preacher often provides the momentum of the sonnet. Sponde, however, goes much further than Chassignet in creating a rhythmic disturbance within the pattern of the alexandrine, alternating short and long units, and frequently disregarding the metrical unit. This kind of disturbance usually occurs at the beginning of the sonnet, demanding the reader's attention and setting the tone and pace:

> Pour qui tant de travaux? Pour vous? de qui l'haleine
> Pantelle en la poictrine et traîne sa langueur?

> Et quel bien de la Mort? où la vermine ronge
> Tous ces nerfs, tous ces os? où l'Ame se départ
> De ceste orde charogne...

The description of death here, although verbally undistinguished, comes alive with the broken rhythm and the demonstrative repetition of 'Tous ces nerfs, tous ces os'. In both cases the sonnet opens abruptly, even elliptically, again arousing the reader and drawing him directly into the atmosphere. Similar effects occur elsewhere: the use of the conjunction *et* or *mais* in sonnets 2, 10, and 11, implying that the argument has already begun; the exclamatory 'Ha!' or 'Hélas!' (nos. 3 and 5); or the short, isolated phrase immediately repeated of sonnet 9: 'Qui sont, qui sont ceux-la...'.

Once this aggressive tone has been established, Sponde can exploit the symmetries which the epigrammatic sonnet-form offers. Whereas the symmetries of the *Stances* tended to isolate individual passages and thus fragment the poem, in the sonnets they make the argument compact and incisive. The symmetrical crescendo of sonnet 2 or the ternary movement of 12 are the clearest examples, but there are many others. The most characteristic technique is the use of verbal and rhythmic symmetries to reinforce one another: although it may occur at any point in the sonnet, its main function is to provide a conclusion:

> Mortels, chacun accuse, et j'excuse le tort
> Qu'on forge en vostre oubly. Un oubly d'une mort
> Vous montre un souvenir d'une éternelle vie.   (no. 1.)

> Géants, où poussez-vous ces beaux amas de poudre?
> Vous les amoncelez? Vous les verrez dissouldre:
> Ils montent de la Terre? Ils tomberont des Cieux.   (no. 3.)

> Mais pourquoy ce souci? mais pourquoy cest effort?
> Sçavez-vous bien que c'est le train de ceste vie?
> La fuite de la Vie, et la course à la Mort.   (no. 4.)

In effect, this is a development of the familiar epigrammatic conclusion, but it is in many cases fertilised by contact with the preaching tone of voice, so that the epigram takes on life and movement. A poem may thus begin with a disturbed 'attack', continue with a controlled analysis, and end with an epigrammatic apostrophe. In the best Sponde there is an impressive balance, at times a dialectic, between emotional urgency and penetrating reflection, and this is the kind of characteristic one might expect from a poet who had cultivated the devotional manner.

Sponde is most at home when he is arguing, persuading, making a point; and the vehemence and brevity of many of the sonnets make an impact which the *Stances* just fail to achieve. The *souffle* which is maintained through page after page of the prose meditations is strangely lacking in the 144 lines of the *Stances*; and the prejudice which gives 'personal' poetry the advantage over 'moral' poetry is I think misleading in the case of Sponde.[1] The *Stances* have many of the elements of a great poem; the argument goes much deeper than that of most of the sonnets—sonnet 12 for example is based on a slighter and somewhat repetitive version of the spiritual combat theme. Unfortunately, however, the rhetoric is not sufficiently well fused to sustain the movement and give an impression of wholeness. This becomes particularly clear when the longer poem is read aloud, a treatment to which the sonnets, by contrast, respond extremely well. Sponde's most powerful and perhaps most characteristic style, as Professor Boase has pointed out, is the *style parlé*: but the tone of this speaking voice is neither casual nor colloquial, as *parlé* might imply, but argumentative, demonstrative, aggressive—the tone of the preacher.

There is no doubt, I think, that Sponde's greatest rival is Favre, although the Catholic poet's output of *vanitas* sonnets is small compared with Chassignet's; and it is illuminating to set a Favre sonnet next to one of the *Sonnets de la mort*. Take, for example, the fifty-third of the first *centurie*:

> Mondains tant insensez, qui tous à vau-de-route
> Courez où la fureur guide voz passions,
> Pensez-vous que la soif de voz affections
> Qui boiroit une mer, s'abbreuve d'une goute?
> Dites, quand vous auriez le ciel, la terre toute,
> Et tout ce que l'enfer a de tentations,
> Pourriez-vous assouvir de voz ambitions
> Ceste faim, qui rien tant que sa fin ne redoute?
> Arpentez l'infini de l'ame, et si son lieu
> Tant il est spacieux, est capable d'un Dieu,
> Ce qui est moins que Dieu vous peut-il satisfaire?
> Ha! puis qu'en vous formant le triangle luy pleut,
> Croiez qu'un monde rond, pour grand qu'il soit, ne peut
> De vostre ame remplir tout le triangulaire.

The argument is, as usual, relatively complex. The passions, or worldly affections, have an infinite thirst which the world is unable to satisfy;

---

[1] Professor Boase prefers the *Stances*, partly on these grounds (*Méditations*, 'Introduction', pp. clvii–clviii).

only God can fill the 'triangle' of the soul.[1] The analogy is not a mere play on words, or a clever trick: it conveys a serious theological statement about the relationship of man to the world and to God, which is explained carefully and logically. Sponde's eleventh sonnet, 'Et quel bien de la mort?', is based on a comparable theme, that of the relationship of body and soul before and after death (the first stanza has already been quoted):

> ...Ce Corps, qui dans la vie en ses grandeurs se plonge,
>   Si soudain dans la mort estouffera sa part,
>   Et sera ce beau Nom qui tant partout s'espard,
>   Borné de Vanité, couronné de Mensonge.
>   A quoy cest Ame, hélas! et ce corps désunis,
>   Du commerce du monde hors du monde bannis?
>   A quoy ces nœuds si beaux que le Trespas deslie?
>   Pour vivre au Ciel il faut mourir plustost ici:
>   Ce n'en est pas pourtant le sentier raccourcy,
>   Mais quoy? nous n'avons plus ny d'Hénoch, ni d'Elie.

Although the thought of this sonnet is not on the level of a simple generalisation, Sponde is not concerned with a systematically developed argument: his point—that the body must die, that the bonds of body and soul must be painfully torn apart—is made elliptically and allusively. His tone is attacking and ironic, but it has at the same time a light touch, an ease of movement, particularly in the tercets; and it is precisely this taut, economical diction which Favre is unable to match. Favre's manner, with its interrogatives and imperatives (notice particularly the 'Dites' of line 5), is clearly conceived in terms of the need to communicate a truth: it is earnest and pressing. But there are too many dependent clauses, and the rhythmic groups are uncomfortably balanced, with the result that the tone remains earnest, and even a little pedantic.

[1] Favre is perhaps referring to the three Augustinian powers of the soul (memory, cognition and love) which correspond to the persons of the Trinity; this does not explain the explicitly geometrical nature of the image, but cf. Augustine's treatise *De quantitate animae*. See also the following *quatrain*, from the series which follows the *Entretiens spirituels*, but which may well have been written earlier than the sonnet in question:

> Le monde est rond, l'ame triangulaire,
> Comment pourroient mille mondes remplir
> L'ame, qui est capable de tenir
> Celuy, qui peut mille mondes deffaire? (*Entretiens spirituels*, p. 180.)

Neither Sponde nor Favre is a great poet; both have sufficient personality to make them memorable. Although Sponde may indeed be the better of the two, he has received as much attention as he deserves while Favre is seldom mentioned (partly, no doubt, because his poems have not yet been made widely accessible); and it might well be that some would prefer Favre's broader range and his intellectual imagination.

We have now come far enough to be able to make an initial review of some of the broader patterns of devotional poetry. In the first place, it has been shown that the poetry of penitence, vanity and death can effectively be seen against a background of devotional prose. The precise contacts between prose and poetry are in themselves significant; but what matters most is that the general analogy should be valid, and that individual poems should respond to an analysis conceived in devotional terms. Without suggesting that each (or even any) poet was setting out consciously to write according to the methods of meditation, one can legitimately consider a high proportion of this poetry as putting into practice the three devotional modes—physical, analytic, and affective. The physical imagination of the penitential poets was nourished by the Old Testament world of irreductible adversity, by the devotional tradition which is itself often based on the Bible, by the *ars moriendi* with its sharply visualised woodcuts, by the skeletons and death's heads of church art, and by the contemporary environment of war and plague, in which wounds, high fever, and the sight of corpses were everyday occurrences. In turn, the physical predicament, in an age when theological problems had moved out into society at all levels, gave a special urgency to reflection on the nature of body in relation to soul, or of one's sin in relation to God's grace. Often these problems are presented in a simple, generalised way; but they are always real problems, whereas the rhetoric of love-poetry may be concerned with an argument which is at several removes from reality. Finally, the meditations of both the *imagination* and the *entendement* naturally give rise to all manner of emotional tensions: the uneasiness of the sinner who is uncertain of his salvation, or the urgent, demanding attitude of preacher to congregation, of poet to reader. Whether they occur within the enclosed structure of the sonnet or the more flexible form of *cantique* or *ode*, these modes are in the best poems complementary, and may indeed be inseparable. They renew and revitalise the structures of secular rhetoric, so that the sonnet or the *stances*-sequence can become a specifically devotional medium. At the same time, the traditions of profane poetry and of secular humanism may be exploited in order to enrich the thought of the poem, or to capture the attention of a cultivated lay audience. Naturally, one could not claim that a sudden upsurge of devotional consciousness transformed all religious poetry of the later sixteenth century: the renewal is uneven and fragmentary, and as in any period and any *genre* there are countless poems which are trite, repetitive, badly-constructed. Nevertheless, certain poets are beginning to think in a new and interesting way which is only partially determined by the influence, diverse as it is, of Ronsard and the Pléiade; and César de Nostredame, La Ceppède, and Favre himself will take this process still further in their meditation on the life of Christ.

CHAPTER 6

POETRY OF THE INCARNATION AND REDEMPTION.

1: THE DEVOTIONAL SONNET— FAVRE AND LA CEPPÈDE

The chronological development of poetry connected with the life of Christ is relatively clear-cut. The first period, the period of preparation, corresponds with the reign of Henri III, and is represented by the Louvre poets, who are on the whole not concerned with producing an extended sequence. At this stage there is an Italian influence which, if not all-pervasive, nevertheless accounts for many of the sonnets of Desportes and Jamyn; by 1570, the life of Christ had already been for some time an important theme of Italian verse and prose literature.[1] Meanwhile, at Aix-en-Provence, the circle of Henri d'Angoulême was laying the foundation for the future achievements of the Aixois poets. That contact between these two worlds of court and province was sometimes established is illustrated by Malherbe's *Larmes de Saint Pierre*, based on Tansillo and dedicated to Henri III not long after Malherbe's stay at Aix; but the contact is a tenuous one, and there will soon be a clear distinction between the 'professional' poet and the provincial amateur. In the 1590s, the pattern is already very different: within the space of two years (1594–5), La Ceppède appears in print, announcing the *Théorèmes*; Gabrielle de Coignard's poetry is published, with its highly-developed longer poems on the life of Christ; and Favre's *Centurie première* appears, containing a handful of mature Passion and Eucharist sonnets which anticipate not only the *Entretiens*

[1] See. J. Vianey, *Le Pétrarquisme en France*, pp. 303–7; Vianey lists Italian sources for fourteen of the eighteen *sonnets spirituels* of Desportes, and for Jamyn's *Du glorieux martyr Sainct Sebastien* and *Pour le jour de la Passion*. For Italian verse on the life of Christ, see, for example, the *Scelta di rime spirituali* mentioned by Vianey, or the earlier *Rime spirituali* (Venice, 1550).

spirituels but also the *Théorèmes* themselves. In 1594 too, the Calvinist Odet de La Noue publishes a long devotional poem on the Passion, a sure sign of the change of atmosphere; but the period of full realisation begins with the new century. In the 1602 edition of the Maisonfleur-Valagre anthology, Malherbe's *Larmes* are accompanied by a quantity of tear-poems by other poets; and in the same year, Favre's *Entretiens spirituels* were published, followed in 1605 by Anne de Marquets's *Sonnets spirituels*, the first two major sonnet-cycles in French on themes connected with the life of Christ. Thereafter follow Humbert, César de Nostredame, and La Ceppède's *Théorèmes*; and the extent of the development becomes clear when one compares César's *Perles* with Malherbe's *Larmes*, the *Théorèmes* with the sonnets of Desportes or Boyssières, or Favre's *Entretiens* with his own *Centurie première*. This is a movement towards completeness, towards the integral conception of a devotional poetry with its own range of themes and styles; and although there are parallels in the poetry of penitence and death, it is nevertheless striking that most if not all of the major works of devotional poetry in the post-1600 period are concerned with the life of Christ. The narrative sequence of the events of Easter week imposes a continuity and a coherence which is lacking in the penitential cycle; at a more profound level, the life of Christ resumes and resolves the history of man, and is central to the whole emotional, moral and theological outlook of the *dévot*. Hence the difference between the *Théorèmes* and a work like Chassignet's *Mespris*, which, although compendious, still gives the impression of being fragmentary. It is not that Chassignet owes more to secular traditions, poetic or otherwise, since these are evident too in La Ceppède and even in Anne de Marquets: one feels rather that he has not fully considered the problems of writing poetry in terms of the practice of devotion; and if the popularity of religious poetry had declined after 1595, the case for defining poetry as 'devotional' in this period as a whole would be greatly weakened. Finally, as we have already seen, the development towards an integral poetry of the life of Christ is also due in part to the changing historical and moral climate, and an analysis of this poetry will indicate the prevalent religious sensibility which determines its character.

The unity of this and the following chapter is based on a number of factors. After an introductory section dealing with paraphrase and with explicit connexions between poetry and prose, this chapter will be mainly, though not exclusively, concerned with the sonnet and the sonnet-sequence. In this field, Favre and La Ceppède are clearly the major figures; and the two poets are comparable not only because they are both *magistrats* as well as poets, but because their conception of the sonnet is close to that of a 'devout humanism'. In their meditation on the mysteries of the Passion, intellectual analysis, often involving thought and imagery from secular sources, is an essential element, and medieval and Renaissance patterns are closely interwoven. At the same time, they illustrate between them the widest range of devotional modes, from simple narration to a prayer enriched by the techniques of 'identification' and of analysis. The next chapter, by contrast, will stress the longer forms, in which there tends to be a greater elaboration of narrative detail; the dominant mode will there be affective, sometimes to an extravagant degree; and the connexions with profane literature will bear rather on love-poetry and the *roman sentimental* than on humanist traditions.

TOWARDS A POETRY OF THE LIFE OF CHRIST

Just as the poetry of penitence is best approached through Old Testament paraphrase, so the emergence of a poetry of the life of Christ owes much to paraphrase of medieval hymns. The popularity of these hymns as a subject for paraphrase was considerably less than that of the Psalms or of Job; no Calvinist would be likely to translate into French verse the *Stabat mater* or the *Iesu corona virginum*, and therefore no rivalry was set up between the two confessions. Moreover, a poet influenced by Pléiade humanism would naturally be tempted to imitate the poetry of David, the Biblical Orpheus, rather than that of the medieval Fathers, however venerable. Nevertheless, the hymns made their impact. Tamisier and the Jesuit Michel Coyssard published substantial collections of hymn-paraphrases; both Desportes and Jamyn produced versions of a handful of hymns;[1] and new paraphrases continue to appear regularly beyond the turn of the century in the antho-

---

[1] Desportes's *Hymne des saintes vierges et martires* appeared in 1598, and his *Hymne de Saint-Sixte* and *Hymne de Sainte-Agathe* in 1603. Jamyn's *Parafrase du Veni creator spiritus* and *Parafrase de Christe qui lux es et dies* appeared in his *Second volume des œuvres.*

Towards a poetry of the life of Christ

logies and elsewhere.[1] Of all the hymns, the *Stabat mater* is the only one which attains a certain popularity: there are versions by Du Peyrat (1587), Tamisier (1590), Coyssard (1594), Gabrielle de Coignard (1595), Nicolas Le Digne (1600), César de Nostredame (1606), La Ceppède (1613), and in 1624 by Henry Humbert.[2] Despite the relative scarcity of such paraphrases, it is likely that the medieval hymns played an important part in determining the themes and imagery of Favre, La Ceppède and many of their contemporaries. They would have been familiar with them through the liturgy, into which many had been absorbed: Aquinas' Vespers hymn for the feast of Corpus Christi, *Pange lingua gloriosi corporis mysterium*, the much older *Pange lingua* of Venantius Fortunatus, which together with the *Vexilla regis* of the same author was used as a Maundy Thursday hymn, or the *Stabat mater* itself. These poems, which represent one of the most characteristic forms of medieval devotion (the *Stabat mater* is a product of Franciscanism), transmitted the traditional symbolism of the Passion to the sixteenth century in a simple and eloquent manner; and the same is true of the symbolism of the Virgin, embodied in the three *Stella maris* hymns and in the *Salve regina*, which had provided subjects of meditation for Bonaventura and which were used for the same purpose in the Counter-Reformation by Coster and no doubt the *confrérie* in general.[3]

The *Stabat mater* paraphrases constitute a central example of the development of poetry on the life of Christ, not only because of their frequency, but also because of the intrinsic interest of the hymn as a way of representing the Passion. It has all the pathos of the Mary-

[1] E.g. Du Perron's *Pange lingua* and *Vexilla regis*; an anonymous *Hymne des Innocens* in Ancelin's *Parnasse* (fol. 344); La Ceppède's *Stabat mater* and *Vexilla regis*.

[2] For an accessible text of the paraphrases by Du Peyrat, Coyssard and Le Digne, see H. Vaganay, 'Un sonnet italien peu connu; quatre traductions du *Stabat Mater* au XVIᵉ siècle', *RB*, 21 (1911), pp. 393 ff. The fourth paraphrase given by Vaganay is that of Pierre Doré, one of the most popular devotional writers of the mid-sixteenth century (see above, pp. 7, 8, 38): it appeared at Paris in 1540 in the *Image de Vertu*, and provides an interesting stylistic contrast with the later versions.

[3] See above, p. 49. Coster's *De cantico Salve regina* also contains meditations on the *Ave maris stella*; a pseudo-Bonaventuran treatise, *Les Meditacions du glorieux saint Bonaventure sur le salve regina*, was translated by Gerson and published under this title at Poitiers(?) in 1490 (?), and at Paris in 1530 (?). See R. Tuve, *A Reading of George Herbert*, *passim*, for the importance of medieval hymns in the formulation and transmission of devotional commponplaces in the English context. For the text of the hymns themselves, see C. Blume and G. M. Dreves, *Analecta hymnica medii aevi*, 51 vols. (Leipzig, 1886–1908); or for a convenient selection, *The Oxford Book of Medieval Latin Verse*, ed. F. Raby (from which most of my quotations are taken).

187

Christ relationship at its most painful moment; it has a certain physical immediacy; and it is a fervent prayer for redemption through the suffering of Christ. Furthermore, the parallel between the physical agony of Christ and the spiritual agony of Mary establishes a model for the 'identification' or 'sympathetic suffering' which the contemplator of the Passion must achieve. The French poets are relatively restrained in their paraphrases: the Jesuit Coyssard, whom one might have expected to elaborate the text in the manner of Counter-Reformation devotional technique, is the most literal of translators—scarcely a word is added or taken away; and even César de Nostredame's *Larmes de la saincte Vierge* has none of the richness and detail of, say, his *Marie dolente.*[1] Thus there is nothing in French like Crashaw's *Patheticall descant upon the devout Plainsong of Stabat Mater Dolorosa,* which runs to 110 lines and which is so free as to become almost an independent poem.[2] Nevertheless, where the original is reworked or expanded, the results can be interesting. Du Peyrat adds only one stanza to the ten of the hymn, but unlike his contemporaries he uses the alexandrine, and the light texture of the medieval lines gives way to a massive dignity. The style is established from the first line with the addition of a broad rhetorical period:

> La Mere du Sauveur qui racheta le monde,
> Qui d'un rien façonna l'air, et la terre, et l'onde,
> Estoit pres de la Croix...[3]

It is true that there are moments at which the development has a distinctly devotional ring. The simple concrete references to the Passion story in stanza 4 of the hymn are greatly augmented and given added pathos:

> Ell'a veu le doux fruit de sa pucelle couche
> Humer le fiel amer qu'on luy offre à la bouche,
> Et que pour le peché commis par nos ayeux
> Il mouroit innocent plein d'horribles ulceres,
> Elle l'a veu souffrir mille douleurs ameres,
> Et mille coups de foüets sur son corps precieux.

---

[1] The *Marie dolente* will be discussed in the next chapter. Since this poem is partially based on the *Stabat mater*, it is clear that paraphrase and free composition provoke totally different stylistic reactions from César.

[2] See Martz, *The Poetry of Meditation*, pp. 115–17.

[3] Du Peyrat, *Hymne de la Trinité, avec quelques sonnets spirituels* (Paris, 1587), fols. 13–14 (this reference covers the whole poem).

And the physical image latent in 'cruce hac inebriari' is underlined: 'Enyvre moy du sang qui couloit de la Croix'. But these expansions are unadventurous when one compares them with a later paraphrase like that of Henry Humbert, which, although strictly speaking outside our period, is an excellent example of the way in which a Counter-Reformation poet can add to the straightforward medieval imagination:

> Enyvré des torrents qui d'une source vraye
> Ruissellent de son flanc,
> Faicts que pour son amour je ne sois qu'une playe
> Toute rouge de sang.[1]

Du Peyrat's increase in vocabulary and syntactical complexity seems more often to be due to the search for a formal eloquence, and the style of his paraphrase thus has something of the quality of Bertaut's 'devotional' poetry.

La Ceppède's developments, although not far-reaching, bear significantly on the physical and emotional aspects of the poem. The blood which plays such an important part in the devotional Passion scene is introduced in the first line ('Au pied de la Croix sanglante') and picked up immediately in an image:

> Et mille trenchans cauteres
> Alloient les vives arteres
> De son cœur entrefendant.[2]

The expansion of 'maerebat et dolebat, / et tremebat' exploits naïveté in the interests of pathos, a familiar devotional technique:

> ...La rendoient lors haletante,
> La faisoient lors tremblotante,
> Et de genoux, et de mains?

Likewise, in the prayer for identification, La Ceppède insists on the physical elements: 'crucifixi fige plagas / cordi meo valide' becomes:

> Fay que sur mon cœur soient peintes
> Fay qu'en mon cœur soient empreintes
> Les Espines de son chef...

On the other hand, the repetitive stanzas 7 and 8 of the hymn are compressed into a single stanza where the simple 'Fac me vere tecum flere' becomes a complex tear-image:

---

[1] Quoted by P. Leblanc, in 'Henry Humbert, poète lorrain', *BHR*, 18 (1956), p. 55.
[2] *Théorèmes*, vol. I, *Meslanges* (Toulouse, 1612), pp. 51–3. The *Meslanges* follow the *Imitation de la Penitence de David*, and are paginated with it.

> He! fay que je t'accompaigne
> Fay qu'aveques-toy je baigne
> De l'eau de mes yeux sa Croix.
> Fay que mes yeux dans ses playes
> Treuvent pour leurs vieilles tayes
> Un collyre à cette fois.

Behind this image, once again, is the mysterious interaction of tears and blood: the penitent, by contemplating the Passion, 'washes' Christ's wounds with his tears; and Christ's blood washes away his sins. Finally, La Ceppède's interpretation of the original hymn includes an emphasis on the wedding allegory, thus suggesting the mystical *extase* which may be the climax of Passion meditation: 'fac ut ardeat cor meum / in amando Christum Deum, / ut sibi complaceam' becomes 'qu'à ton Fils je *marie* / Mon cœur enflammé d'amour' (my italics).

These devotional characteristics are combined with a vocabulary characteristic of La Ceppède, ranging from the naïve to the erudite and including a classical allusion:

> Fay qu'allant dessous la tombe
> Sa mort soit mon Hecatombe
> Pour offrir au Dieu des Dieux.

Similarly, the reader's attention is aroused by unexpected combinations of words ('Fay que son Gibet m'enyvre'), although it may also be irritated by the introduction of obtrusive word-games. Much the same features appear in the *Vexilla regis* paraphrase, but in greater concentration: the choice of the alexandrine in place of the original octosyllabic line allows an elaborate treatment. The impression of density is created not only by the wide and at times unexpected vocabulary, but also by bold syntax, by repetitions and *reprises*, by hyperbolical images and word-games:

> Les cornetes du Roy, volent par la campaigne,
> La Croix mysterieuse éclate un nouveau jour,
> Où l'Autheur de la chair, de sa chair s'accompaigne
> Et fait de son Gibet un Theatre d'Amour.

> ...Il tend ore ses mains tend ses deux, (*sic*) pieds aux cloux,
> Tandis les cloux d'amour cloüent dans sa poitrine
> Son cœur tout amoureux, qui s'immole pour nous.

> ...tu balances ce Corps
> Qui nos pechez balance. En toy sont nos revanches,
> Tu reprens sa reprinse au Coursaire des morts.[1]

Two lines of the fifth stanza give a clue to much that is central to
La Ceppède's Passion poetry. The image of a beautiful Cross, clothed
in a royal purple, is supplied by the hymn itself: 'Arbor decora et
fulgida, / ornata regis purpura'; La Ceppède seizes it and adds an
extravagant series of verbs:

> Arbre brillant et beau, que la pourpre Royale
> Pare, orne, vermillonne, enlumine, enrichit...

The colour and light of the visual image are intensified, while the sound-
values are enriched by strong alliteration and by the *martellato* effect
of the rhythm. This rich, flamboyant beauty, in which the blood of
Christ is transformed into a royal purple, is one of the dominant themes
of the first volume of *Théorèmes*; and as in the devotional manuals, it
is often enhanced by a violent contrast with the ugliness of the suffering
and the insults. There is the same decorative effect, though in a less
developed form, in Desportes's paraphrase of the *Iesu corona virginum*:

> En deux leur bande est separee,
> Dont l'une porte le lys blanc,
> De roses l'autre est reparee,
> Que teint le pourpre de leur sang.[2]

It is thus that the medieval vision of the Passion finds its way into the
poetry of the Counter-Reformation, where it is given a greater pomp
and brilliance.

The *Pange lingua* of Fortunatus, though rarely paraphrased, must
have been well known to all the poets we are considering; and it is one
of the oldest and most fundamental meditations in verse on the life of
Christ. Like the *Vexilla regis*, it is a hymn to the Cross, which is seen
as the 'trophy' of the victorious Christ; the triumph over death and sin
is symbolised by the image of the two trees:

> Pange, lingua, gloriosi proelium certaminis
> et super crucis tropaeo dic triumphum nobilem,
> qualiter redemptor orbis immolatus vicerit.

---

[1] *Meslanges*, pp. 50–1. For an interesting stylistic contrast, compare this paraphrase with
Du Perron's.
[2] Desportes, *Les CL Pseaumes de David*, fol. 197. See also the *Hymne des Innocens* mentioned above, p. 187, n. 1.

De parentis protoplasti fraude factor condolens,
quando pomi noxialis morte morsu corruit,
ipse lignum tunc notavit, damna ligni ut solveret.[1]

The central section of the poem is a summary of the life of Christ. The Nativity is represented briefly, and then the Passion is evoked by a list of the instruments of suffering:

Vagit infans inter arta conditus praesaepia,
membra pannis involuta virgo mater adligat,
et pedes manusque crura stricta pingit fascia. . . .
Hic acetum, fel, arundo, sputa, clavi, lancea;
mite corpus perforatur; sanguis, unda profluit,
terra pontus astra mundus quo lavantur flumine.

César de Nostredame will use precisely the same listing technique, although at far greater length, in two of his poems, and several other poets summarise Christ's life from the Nativity onwards in a single sonnet.[2] Du Perron's paraphrase of this hymn is simple, remaining close to the original; but he adds an interpretation of the Christchild's tears, and the diminutives of the Nativity stanza are in keeping with an age in which the sentimentalisation of the cradle scene was common:

Enfant il gémit en la créche,
Aux pleurs pour nos pechez contrainct,
La Vierge qui ses larmes seche,
De langes amoureux l'estreint,
Et ses pieds et mains tendrelettes
Serre d'estroittes bandelettes.[3]

The later *Pange lingua*, also paraphrased by Du Perron, lays the foundation for a rather different kind of poem. The celebration of the Last Supper provokes theological reflection on the mystery of the Eucharist, and Aquinas expounds as simply as possible the doctrine of transubstantiation:

Le Verbe chair, vray pain du monde
Par son Verbe fait le pain chair,
Et du vin en sang change l'onde;
Et bien qu'aux sens il ne responde,

---

[1] See also the two stanzas beginning 'Crux fidelis, inter omnes arbor una nobilis'.
[2] E.g. Boyssières (see below, pp. 219, 230), and Doremet (below, p. 222).
[3] J. D. Du Perron, *Les Diverses Œuvres* (Paris, 1622), *Poésies*, pp. 13–15.

> La foy suffit sans plus chercher
> Pour des cœurs tout doubte arracher.
>
> Que chacun donc devot s'encline
> Devant un si grand Sacrement...   (*Ibid.* p. 12.)

The miracle by which the 'accidental' nature of the bread and wine—that which is perceived by the senses—remains the same while their essential nature is transformed, is one of the central themes of Counter-Reformation Eucharist poetry; a degree of theological intricacy is almost inseparable from meditation on the Eucharist.[1] This is not to say that Aquinas' poetry is a direct source of any of the Communion poems we shall be considering later: the arguments on which transubstantiation is based are the common property of orthodox belief. Nevertheless, it is important to remember, once again, that the devotional poetry of the sixteenth and seventeenth centuries develops themes which had been the subject of some of the most famous medieval religious poetry and which had thereby entered into the consciousness of most devout laymen of this period.

The example of the medieval hymns, like that of the Psalms, provides an incentive to the writing of devotional poetry which reinforces that of the prose treatises. Furthermore, some if not all of the paraphrases elaborate their basic materials in much the same way as devotional manuals elaborate the New Testament story, though less extensively. Thus it is possible to see how far a Counter-Reformation poet, in rephrasing a familiar medieval pattern, can create a new atmosphere, adding a certain density and sophistication of language, and a taste for extravagance or hyperbole. To this extent the transformation is explicable in terms of the methods of devotion alone; at the same time, the rhetorical expansion may follow the patterns established by contemporary profane poetry. These developments are by no means incompatible, and in La Ceppède's poetry they are identified, assuming already the manner of an independent devotional poetry. Finally, it is significant that hymn-paraphrases begin to appear in greater numbers from about 1590: thus their increased popularity corresponds with the rise of poetry on the life of Christ.

Before leaving the medieval scene, it would be as well to recall that

---

[1] The *Pange lingua* should be seen in conjunction with Aquinas' other Communion poems, which have much the same characteristics (*Lauda, Sion, salvatorem; Verbum supernum prodiens; Adoro devote, latens veritas*).

the tradition of the *Puys* and other poetry of medieval origin continued to flourish in the Counter-Reformation period, even though it
had been overshadowed by the Pléiade. Such poetry may have been
looked down upon by the professional court poet; nevertheless, Du
Bartas, Guy Le Fèvre, Garnier and Pibrac all wrote for the *Jeux Floraux*
of Toulouse.[1] Boyssières too, as we have seen, may have been influenced by the religious themes and conservative forms of the *Puys*:
one of his Communion poems is a *ballade*. Many of the provincial poets
could have been connected with the *Puy* competitions, or at least
encouraged to write by them: Gabrielle de Coignard lived in Toulouse,
and César de Nostredame and La Ceppède published there. For a group
of poets who wrote explicitly in the *Puy* tradition, however, one must
turn to Douai, and in particular to Jean and Jacques Loys, whose
Œuvres poétiques were published posthumously in 1612 and 1613
respectively. To consider these works in detail would be a digression
into a poetry of little intrinsic value, but one point of interest strikes
one even on a casual examination of the collections. Although there is
no doubt as to the orthodoxy of the way in which the *Puy* was conducted at Douai (the liminary prose describes in detail both the procedure for the competitions and the rules of versification), much is said of
Ronsard: for example, the publisher says that Jean 'a esté en son temps
comme un Ronsard, pendant la naissance de la poësie Françoise en ces
quartiers';[2] language reminiscent of the Pléiade is frequent in the poems
themselves; there are sonnets as well as *chants royaux* in both collections;
and there are a number of Neo-Latin encomiastic poems at the end of
the second volume. Indeed, one could quote many passages from both
poets which have nothing obviously 'medieval' about their style, as
for example this stanza from Jean's *Cantique sur la Passion du fils de
Dieu*, which is in regular alexandrine *stances* and which has all the
attributes of a Counter-Reformation poem:

> Sus nichez vous aussy aux haliers espineux,
> Et avec la colombe aux pertuis et aux creux
> Qu'ont faict au chef de Christ les espines poignantes:
> Car mon ame, et mes sens où vouldriés mieux nicher
> Qu'aus playes de cestuy, qui vous ayant tant cher
> A blanchy par son sang voz offenses sanglantes?   (*Ibid.* p. 24.)

---

[1] See J. C. Dawson, *Toulouse in the Renaissance* (New York, 1923), pp. 9 ff., 53–63, 75–82.
[2] Jean Loys, *Les Œuvres poëtiques* (Douai, 1613), 'L'Imprimeur au Lecteur', *non pag.*

Towards a poetry of the life of Christ

This ability of the *Puy* poets to adapt themselves to changing poetic fashions is important, since it suggests that the gap between these circles and the more progressive poet, both at court and in the provinces, might be less than one would imagine at first sight; thus in this way also, traditional themes and symbols of the Virgin Mary and the Passion might in some cases have been transmitted into the newer idiom of a Favre or a La Ceppède. Finally, there is evidence that the *Puy* of Douai was actively encouraged by the *Confrérie de la Vierge*, that the connexion between the *confrérie* and Henri III's Vincennes Academy was recognised, and indeed that members of this Academy came to participate in the Douai competitions. The *Œuvres poetiques* of Jacques Loys are dedicated to 'Messieurs les Princes de la grande et honorable confrerie des clercs parisiens soubz le nom de la glorieuse et sacrée Vierge Mere'; and according to the printer, who composed the dedication, the author recognised that 'le los de sa Poësie avoit prinse sa naissance soubz le soleil de vostre honorable assemblée'. The dedication also speaks of

l'ancienne renommée de vostre honorable Confrerie, laquelle jadis voloit au pays circumvoisins (*sic*), principalement en la France, pour-ce le nom est des Clerqs Parisiens, pource que les mieux disans, et ceux lesquelz avoient gousté le miel de la langue Françoise aux Academies (prenant la Parisienne pour premiere) venoient icy étaler la richesse de leur rime, voires aucuns des vostres, ont esté mesme és villes frontieres de la France presenter leurs vers au puy, retournant chargés d'honneur. (*non pag.*)

The 'Avant-propos ou advertissement au lecteur' of the same collection is still more precise. It explains that the *confrérie* was already (in 1613) a time-honoured institution, in which the activities of the *Puy* played a central part; furthermore, it refers to the shift from the term 'Rethoriciens' to the more modern 'Poëtes', a shift which in itself reflects the influence of the Pléiade:

Convient sçavoir qu'en la ville et Université de Douay...est instituée une honorable et tres-ancienne Societé nommé Confrairie des Clercs Parisiens, Soubz le nom de la Vierge-Mere de Dieu, ayant de tout temps esté composée de venerables, illustres et rares personnages, tant ecclesiastiques, que nobles et populaires, dont le chef ou Prince se renouvelant chasque année, doit exposer pour prix aux Poëtes jadis y appellez *Rethoriciens* une Couronne, chapeau, et afficquet, ou image d'argent pour distribuer les deux premiers aux meilleurs ouvriers d'un chant Royal, au jour et sur le subject de la glorieuse assomption de leur Patrone immaculée... (*non pag.*)

Thus the *Puy*, with its age-old association with the cult of the Virgin, was renewed in the town and university of Douai by the Counter-Reformation programme of Coster and his like; while in its more specifically poetic aspect, it began at the same time to be modified by the influence of the Parisian poets and Academies.

The poetry of the life of Christ is much more closely interwoven than penitential poetry with devotional disciplines and with the central tradition of prose meditation. Chassignet is heavily dependent on prose sources, but of these only Duplessis-Mornay's *Discours* could qualify as a devotional treatise, and then only marginally. With Anne de Marquets, Gabrielle de Coignard, Favre, Humbert and La Ceppède these connexions are sharply defined, and they demonstrate a wide range of influences, all of which relate to devotional practice in the strictest sense.

Anne de Marquets's sequence of sonnets follows the pattern of a nun's private daily meditation on the festivals of the Christian year: there are often several sonnets on a single theme, and the Easter week group forms a coherent narrative cycle. The style is sober and direct, suggesting a convent piety based on a simple moral code. Many of the poems end on a *sententia* ('Car tel vit aujourd'huy qui sera mort demain'; 'qui a bien vescu ne sçauroit mal mourir'), and the lessons drawn from meditation on, say, the Nativity are moral rather than theological:

> Voyant en lieu si vil sur le foin pauvrement
> Ce grand Roy souverain, qu'enfant on emmaillote,
> Ne doibt cela servir d'un certain antidote
> Pour repousser de nous l'orgueil entierement?
> La Vierge mere aussi, qui l'adore humblement,
> Et qui par grand amour le contemple, et baisote
> Ses pieds, ses yeux, sa bouche et sa double menote,
> Nous apprend-elle pas à l'aimer ardemment?[1]

The didacticism is tempered here by an intimate, consciously feminine tone of voice which is quite unlike the sermon-tone of Chassignet or Sponde. Another of the Nativity sonnets relates the gospel scene to everyday reality; this is not a 'composition of place' on the Ignatian scale, but it implies the practical outlook of a nun accustomed to work-

---

[1] *Sonnets sprituels*, no. 36 (sonnet-numbers only will be given for Anne de Marquets).

ing with the laity who instinctively gives a simple relevance to her religious experience:

> Puisqu'on va visiter celles qui sont en couche,
> Pour les congratuler de leur enfantement,
> En esprit et par foy allons presentement,
> Voir la Vierge et son fruict, qui de si pres nous touche.
> Ne pensons la trouver en quelque riche couche,
> Ny en siege accoustré delicieusement:
> Ains à terre à genoux adorant humblement
> Son Fils que sur le foin en la creiche elle couche. (no. 49.)

As one might expect, she knows her medieval hymns: one of the sonnets begins like the *Stabat mater*;[1] similarly, it is likely that she read and utilised many of the traditional prose meditations, for the imagery and *topoi* are standard, as are the details of the Passion:

> Ce n'est ores qu'il faut que nostre ame sommeille,
> Ains elle doit par foy contempler son espoux,
> Qui comme un doux agneau seul et entre les loups
> En grand peine et tourment toute ceste nuict veille.
> L'un le poil luy arrache et luy pince l'aureille,
> L'autre luy crache au nez et le charge de coups... (no. 132.)

> ...Puis cloué sur la croix, et tiraillé de sorte
> Qu'on luy tire les nerfs, qu'on luy compte les os...
>
> (no. 143.)[2]

Anne de Marquets may at times be naïve or pedantic; but that she can command a wide range of tones becomes clear in the Passion sequence, and her language will on occasion make discreet use of literary sophistications.[3] One feels, in fact, that she is a woman of some intelligence who has deliberately chosen a manner consistent with her notion of an unpretentious yet palatable devotion: for a nun to have written a substantial quantity of poetry and to have gained a certain fame thereby was after all an achievement of some rarity.

---

[1] No. 148:
> Tout aupres de la croix estoit la Vierge mere,
> Ayant le cœur remply d'extreme affliction,
> Voyant son cher enfant plein de perfection,
> Endurer une mort si cruelle et amere...

[2] See above, p. 52. See also sonnets 34 (paradoxes of the Nativity) and 172 (Moses and the rock as a prefiguration of the Passion).

[3] See, for example, the quotation given below, p. 227.

Gabrielle de Coignard's sonnets are not presented in any special sequence, but like Anne de Marquets's, many of them are composed for Church festivals: the forty-ninth, for example, is for the festival of Mary Magdalene, the fifty-seventh and fifty-eighth 'Pour le jour de Noel'. Similarly, her habit of meditating on a *verset* of the Bible ('O vos omnes', 'Mulier ecce filius tuus') shows that she was accustomed to devotional disciplines. In some of the longer poems, however, she goes much further. The three poems entitled *Discours sur la Passion de nostre Sauveur Jesus-Christ, Complainte de la Vierge Marie*, and *La Descente de nostre Seigneur aux limbes* are in effect three sections of a single comprehensive meditation on Holy Week, from Gethsemane to the descent into Hell; each episode of the Passion story is described and analysed, then concluded with a prayer, and there is a gradual intensification of emotion culminating in the Crucifixion itself and in the identification of the meditator with the Virgin's lament. These poems will be considered in greater detail later; for the present, it is sufficient to remark that a lay poet has succeeded in producing a complex meditative poem of considerable length by following a systematic devotional method. Likewise, Favre will base his third *centurie* on 'les deux premieres Parties des admirables mysteres du Sainct Rosaire', reflecting on ten episodes of the life of Christ from the Incarnation to the Crucifixion; and his *Stances sur la devotion de nostre Dame du Mont-de-Vic* illustrate the practice of meditation on themes suggested by a local cult and place of pilgrimage.

The motives which produced Henry Humbert's *Sepmaine saincte* are clearly comparable to those of his predecessors, but his combination of prose and poetry is an innovation which suggests an exceptionally intimate contact between the devotional manual and its equivalent in poetry. The thirty-odd prose passages or *extases* do in fact read like a Counter-Reformation handbook, though they are not schematised in the Jesuit manner: the seven days of Holy Week are not separated, and the meditations themselves are loosely organised. All the principal elements of devotional procedure are there—composition, analysis, prayer—but they merge into one another, and there is no enumeration of 'points'. The only constant principle governing the lay-out of the work is the sequence of episodes provided by the Passion story. In order to convey a clear impression of these free-style meditations, and the relationship between prose and poetry within them, it will be convenient to refer to one whole *extase* with its corresponding *stances*.[1] The Flagellation episode is particularly suitable in that it exemplifies most of the main characteristics of the work as a whole, and at the same time it has all the colour and pathos which the Flagellation evokes in the Passion manuals.[2]

Humbert's description of the Flagellation (and of the other episodes of the Passion) is not romanesque;[3] there is plenty of physical detail, but no consecutive narrative—this corresponds perhaps with his own conception of the work as a *tableau*. The *extase* opens with the orthodox technique of using apostrophe to make the visualisation of the scene more demonstrative ('Approchés Ames fidelles, voyés..., contemplés..., envisagés...'). This introduces one of the major themes of the passage, the beauty of Christ obscured by blood. The first variation on the theme is a piece of hyperbolical rhetoric, highly emotional, with strong hints of the love-tradition ('beauté qui avoit accoustumé de ravir si doulcement les cœurs par les yeux'). The emotion is then intensified by a direct address to the Virgin, in which milk, blood and tears flow together in an unparalleled example of devotional pathos. The realisation of Christ's sufferings is so powerful that when their symbolical significance is introduced, it is almost lost amid the details of the Flagellation; but the address to the *bourreaux*, which at first merely helps to stress their cruelty and thus the pathos of the whole scene, gradually becomes an address to sinners in general, with the result that the 'analysis' or interpretative section is brought home with the full momentum of the 'composition'.

The *extase*, as its name suggests, is thus highly affective, bringing into play a flamboyant rhetoric ('baignés ses playes des torrents de voz larmes, afin que nous puissions revoir les astres de ces beaux yeux qui languissent de nostre amour'): one is reminded of Desportes's prose prayers, which have the same characteristics, but in a far less developed form. Extravagant or not, this prose is certainly rich and full of life: Humbert can use the devotional commonplaces with great virtuosity,

---

[1] For the complete text, see below, Appendix, pp. 310–12.
[2] See above, p. 34 (quotation from Bonaventura), for a brief but typical example.
[3] The word 'romanesque' is used, here and in ch. 7, in the sense of the French *romanesque*. I have not italicised it, since it is already becoming common in this sense in English, and since no confusion with its other meaning is possible.

and that he has an impressive sense of rhythm is demonstrated by the development on the word 'beauté', for example, or by the well-balanced antitheses of the conclusion. His main aim is clearly to 'give wings to the reader's soul', as he puts it in his dedication, and he may well have come nearer to succeeding than many of the authors of the more strictly organised devotional manuals.

It is therefore all the more disappointing to find the poetry bare and disjointed by comparison. The parallels between the *extase* and the *stances* are extremely loose: Humbert has certainly not set out to paraphrase his own prose in the way that Tamisier paraphrased meditations, and one feels that Gabrielle de Coignard's *Discours* is much closer to its devotional background than Humbert's poems. Instead of versifying his powerfully visualised introduction, he opens with two and a half stanzas in which the symbolical significance of the scene is expressed in a repetitive series of antitheses: these are hard to swallow precisely because they have little point of contact with the physical reality—the apostrophe to Pilate and the brief reference to the whips are not sufficient to replace a properly developed composition. The apostrophe with which the *extase* opens is delayed until the second half of the third stanza ('Accours à ce spectacle, ô ame criminelle'), and then dropped again till the final stanza where the 'recognition' theme appears in a context which is abstract by contrast with the prose apostrophe to Mary. In the remaining four stanzas, there are moments where the intensity of the *extase* is almost achieved: 'les verges ont rougi la neige de son flanc' is a powerful line because the alliteration reinforces the sharp contrast between red and white, and the image of the *bourreaux* being refreshed by the 'tiedes fontaines' of Christ's blood is a striking new hyperbole. But Humbert seems unable to sustain the emotional impetus, and he is too ready to wander off into abstract and irrelevant word-games: 'Celuy est le plus doulx qui est moins pitoiable', 'Ce sont morts par dedans, et doulceurs par dehors'.

By rearranging in the *stances* the themes and techniques of the *extase* he has thus frustrated any possibility of transferring the devotional *élan* into poetry. The development of the poem, the linking of the themes, is surprisingly lame; there is none of the sense of momentum and climax which makes the prose so telling. One feels that Humbert has accumulated paradoxes and antitheses because he thought that they were required by the medium of poetry, rather than letting them grow out of his impassioned contemplation of the *tableau*. He has thus not succeeded in renewing the *stances* form and revitalising the traditions of poetry by a transfusion from devotional literature; nevertheless, the *Sepmaine saincte* is certainly interesting as an experiment, and it represents an unambiguous attempt to use poetry as an element of devotional procedure, thus narrowing the gap between devotion and poetry still further.

La Ceppède set out to reproduce in poetic form 'la profonde meditation de la Passion et mort de nostre Sauveur Jesus-Christ'. He is hardly less explicit about the *estoffe* of this meditation: 'je l'ay toute choisie dans les plus loyales boutiques des plus riches et plus fideles marchands de l'Eglise'[1]—that is to say, he has selected it from orthodox Church literature. A few lines later in the same preface, he pays a tribute to the richness and the splendour of this literature by way of an 'excuse' for the shortcomings of his own work: 'ce fort drap d'or ne se manie pas aisement à tous les plis qu'on veut'. A phrase like 'fort drap d'or' scarcely evokes the style of scholastic theology, but rather the *utile dulci* of the devotional manuals, particularly those of the Counter-Reformation; and if the imagery used in this passage leaves any doubt as to La Ceppède's sources, the question is settled by his *Catalogue Alphabetique*,[2] and by the commentaries on individual sonnets: the devotional connexions are overwhelming.

Two examples from the climax of the work, the Crucifixion itself, give a precise indication of the sources and how they are used. The sixteenth sonnet of Book III describes the stretching of Christ's body to make it fit the Cross:

> On vient à la main droite; elle a eu bel à teindre
> De sang le lieu du trou: il est plus loing pourtant*
> Puis les nerfs retirez ont retiré d'autant,
> Et racourci le bras, elle n'y peut atteindre.
> Aussi tost d'une corde on commence à l'estreindre
> Puis à force on la tire, et la retire tant
> Qu'on la fait joindre au trou, où le bourreau plantant
> L'autre clou, fut pourpré du sang qu'il fit épreindre.
> De mesme au trou d'embas, les pieds demeurent cours,

---

[1] *Théorèmes*, preface 'A la France', p. 10.
[2] See above, pp. 90–1.

> Les bourreaux ont de mesme à la corde recours,
> C'est lors qu'on oit crouler cette belle structure.
> Tout ce corps se desjoint, et le dur craquement
> Des membres disloquez, et des nerfs la rupture,
> Font croire qu'on veut faire un vif demembrement.

* *Pourtant.* Toute la conception de ce Sonnet est des contemplatifs, de Ludolphe, au chapitre 48. de la 2. partie, de Guevarre au 1. livre du Mont de Calvaire chapitre 32. de Crespet Journée, 28.[1]

This brief commentary makes it plain at once that La Ceppède has not limited himself to any particular devotional manual nor indeed to any religious order: he is steeped in the whole tradition. Hence there is no question of a word-for-word transposition of sources; the *contemplatifs* already follow one another closely, and La Ceppède recreates the scene from his knowledge of the meditational corpus. Verbal parallels do of course arise frequently, not so much because he imitates any individual source but rather because the vocabulary is already standardised: for example, in the passage from Guevara to which La Ceppède refers, the pathos of the 'stretching' is increased by an apostrophe to the Virgin which is not exploited in the sonnet:

O Vierge sans pareille! ah, desconsolee mere! n'oys-tu point craquer les os de ton fils, et le froissis des membres estans desjoincts les uns des autres?[2]

The same conclusions are suggested by the nineteenth sonnet and its commentary:

> ...Au contre-coup mortel
> De la cheute du bois, l'esbranlement fut tel,*
> Qu'il n'a playe en son corps, qui n'en soit reouverte.
> Presque, presque les cloux ont my-party les mains,
> La terre d'alentour de son sang est couverte,
> Et son Test se r'attache à ses joncs inhumains.

* *Fut tel.* Ces exagerations, et circonstances hors du texte des Evangelistes sont en mille diverses façons pieusement meditées par les Peres, comme S. Bernard, saint Bonaventure, Ludolphe, Guevarre, Crespet, et autres, lesquels sans doute nous pouvons imiter supposans (comme il est raisonnable) que les executeurs de cette Tragedie, avec leurs autheurs, firent tout le plus sanglant pis dont ils peurent s'adviser pour maltraiter le Sauveur. Et notamment est-il tres-croyable, que tout ce qui est escrit en ce Sonnet, et au precedant, arriva de mesme.   (pp. 384–5.)

[1] *Théorèmes*, p. 380.
[2] Guevara, *Livre du Mont de Calvaire*, fol. 174. Guevara is perhaps the closest single model of La Ceppède's method; his colourful and emotive descriptions are followed by extensive

La Ceppède is thus composing his own meditation on the Passion, following traditional patterns and with the memory of several devotional texts fresh in his mind; medieval and Counter-Reformation authority is carefully specified for the sake of orthodoxy. But these commentaries have a further purpose which is made clear in the preface (p. 11): 'Cependant ce double travail [i.e. the provision of commentaries as well as sonnets] te relevera de la peine d'un plus long et fascheux estude, pour recueillir les passages qui te peuvent servir en l'imitation de mes conceptions.' That is to say that the reader is encouraged to return to the devotional manuals for further meditation, and perhaps to compose poetry of his own on the same themes. One could scarcely go further in the integration of poetry into the practice of devotion.

PENITENCE AND THE PASSION:

POETRY OF THE EUCHARIST

Although the phrase 'penitential poetry' has hitherto been used to describe a kind of poetry which excludes substantial reference to the Passion, it is clear that all Passion meditation is in a sense penitential, since it involves contemplation of and reflection on the redemption of man and of the individual sinner. Thus the two poetic cycles or *genres* —like the morning and evening sequences of meditation—are organically linked; the contrast between the two depends chiefly on a difference of emphasis and presentation, as is suggested by the penitential lyrics and sonnets already discussed which use the Passion, or an allusion to it, as a conclusion and resolution. Where an aspect of the life of Christ occurs in poetry of the earlier part of the period, it is frequently on this level; and the Petrarchan tradition no doubt has a part to play here, for the rejection of profane love for sacred as it appears, for example, in the Good Friday sonnets of Petrarch and Du Bellay,[1] is necessarily a penitential motif. Similarly, of those of Desportes's *sonnets spirituels* which refer directly to the Passion, one at least is based on the theme of

allegorical interpretations of all kinds, and by abundant reference to theological authorities.
[1] See above, p. 138.

wasted youth, and another is concluded by a brief allusion which recalls that of Favre's eighty-ninth sonnet:

> Je regrette en pleurant les jours mal employez
> A suivre une beauté passagere et muable. . .
> Toy qui dans ton pur sang nos mesfaits as noyez,
> Juge doux, benin pere et Sauveur pitoyable,
> Las! releve, ô Seigneur! un pecheur miserable,
> Par qui ces vrais soupirs au ciel sont envoyez.
>
> Ne tourne point les yeux sur mes actes pervers,
> Ou si tu les veux voir, voy-les teints et couvers
> Du beau sang de ton Fils, ma grace et ma justice.[1]

This tendency to isolate the penitential aspect of the Passion may in part explain the fact that the Eucharist is well represented in the earlier devotional poetry: Boyssières's Communion poems are exceptional in that they are already arranged as a sequence, but both Du Peyrat and Habert wrote sonnets on the same theme while Henri III was still on the throne, and they were soon to be followed by Doremet and Favre, and by the Calvinists Poupo and Sponde. Favre's second *centurie*, which is devoted to the Eucharist, represents the culmination of this trend. The popularity of the Eucharist theme is no doubt also due to the growth of the Counter-Reformation propaganda movement, in which the sacraments were stressed in their traditional form to counter the Protestant challenge: one of Ronsard's few contributions to the Counter-Reformation (if one excludes his polemical poetry) was a liminary piece for Auger's treatise *Des Sacremens de l'Eglise catholique et vray usage d'iceus*,[2] in which the Passion is interpreted as the source of all seven sacraments. This is in fact one of the few areas of devotional poetry in which the theological differences between the two confessions are stressed.

Meditation on the Eucharist is not an essential element of Passion meditation: in the devotional manuals, it is often treated independently. Nevertheless, anyone who reflects on this central mystery of Christian belief is likely to connect the bread and wine with the body and blood of the crucified Christ; and thus the Eucharist theme tends to lead to

---

[1] Desportes, ed. Michiels, pp. 509 and 506. For Favre's poem, see above, p. 141.
[2] This poem has been published by Henri Busson in his article 'Vers oubliés de Ronsard', *RHLF*, 59 (1959), pp. 145 ff.

contemplation of the Passion in the specific context of its power to absolve, as in this quatrain from Doremet's sequence:

> O vray sang qui coulas avec eau tout ensemble
> Du costé du Seigneur qui pour nous fut percé,
> Nettoye et lave nous de tout peché passé,
> Et avec toy aux cieux à ton corps nous assemble.[1]

The same is true of Boyssières's sequence, which develops a group of parallel themes—the red wine, the blood of Christ, the thirst of the penitent, and the need for washing. Here, as in much Eucharist poetry, certain of the physical aspects of Christ's death are exploited, in particular the abundance of blood, and the mixture of blood and water which flowed from Christ's side after the piercing by the lance. Thus the physical plane of reference is not forgotten; but the act of taking Communion is primarily symbolic, and allusions to the Passion tend to take the form of typological symbols—the water of Jordan, the fountain and the rock—to which correspond the images of the penitent's soul, the withered tree, the thirst and the pollution:

> O Clair Surgeon, vive fontaine,
> Qui ruissellant habondammant,
> Du corps du Roy du firmamant,
> Me sauvas d'Eternelle peine.
> Sang precieux, Onde Jourdaine,
> Riviere de mon sauvement,
> Faits moy reluire clairement,
> Et rends mon ame toute saine.
> Je te suplie, o! digne Sang,
> De l'arroser dans ton estang,
> Elle de maux toute poluë!
> Pour moy, las! tu t'es respandu:
> Aussi vers toy, me suis randu,
> Et a genoux je te saluë.
> (*Salut et priere au sang precieux.*)

> Je te rends graces, doux ruisseau,
> Qui du coup de la fiere Lance,
> Sortis du rocher de Clemence,
> Entre-meslé, de sang, et d'eau.

---

[1] *Polymnie*, pp. 64–5 (the sequence is entitled *Quatrains en forme de priere propre à dire, quant on fait l'eslevation du Corps de nostre Seigneur au sainct Sacrifice de la Messe*).

Faits florir ce chetif rameau,
Que l'yver poursuit a outrance,
Et de ta liquide habondance,
De Fany, rends-le verd et beau.
Precieuse et digne riviere,
Par qui nous sommes en lumiere,
Oste la soif a mon esprit.
R'afreschis mes debiles veines,
Que dans les clairtez souveraines,
De ton ancre, je sois escrit.   (*Graces*.)[1]

There is no theological complexity in these poems; but they are based on an interpretative view of the Passion, expressing itself primarily in allegorical figures: the redemptive act of Christ resumes and gives meaning to the episodes and images of the Old Testament. Thus Boyssières's hyperboles are nourished both by the physical reality of the Crucifixion and by the rich store of allegories laid down for the most part in the Middle Ages. Similarly, Du Peyrat associates the eating of the Eucharist bread with Adam's tasting of the apple, a symbolic parallel as fundamental as that of the 'two trees':

Comme le premier homme ayant gousté du fruit,
Qui estoit defendu par la bouche eternelle,
Decheut incontinant de la vie immortelle,
Dieu changeant sa lumiere, en une obscure nuit:
Ainsi faut-il que ceux, que ce pere a produit,
Mangeans le pain sacré que Dieu livre au fidele,
Retournent à la vie immortellement belle,
Et au repos, qu'Adam par sa faulte a destruit.[2]

And in his second sonnet on this theme, Du Peyrat gives a list of Old Testament figures of the Eucharist:

C'est la manne du ciel, que Dieu faisoit descendre
Aux Peres des desers, qu'ils cueilloyent tous les jours
Hor-mis quand le sabbath revenoit à ses tours:
C'est, cest agneau paschal, que l'on ne peut comprendre.

[1] *Troisiesmes œuvres*, pp. 64–5.
[2] Du Peyrat, *Hymne de la Trinité*, fol. 7, sonnet no. 4. The tercets embellish this frame-work of allusion by a reference to the 'celeste Ambrosie', 'pasture des Anges', and by a psalm-quotation ('Mon ame dit David, comme foin s'est flestrie, / Pour-ce que de manger ce sacré pain j'oublie').

C'est le pain qu'Abraham fit cuire soubs la cendre...
C'est ce rayon de miel (ô merveilleux discours)
Qui fit soudain la veuë à Jonathe reprendre.
C'est, cest arbre vital, que l'eternel jadis
Planta dans le milieu du terrain paradis:
C'est du pain, et du vin ceste devote offrande,
Que fit Melchisedech à son trois-fois-grand Dieu...   (no. 5.)

Boyssières's sonnets are both prayers, in which the symbolism is set in motion by an affective tone; Du Peyrat's, on the other hand, are primarily explanatory, and as such are characteristic of much Eucharist poetry, where the object is to unfold a 'mystery'. Thus as penitential poetry, this is very different from the penitential lyric: the tone is more didactic, with few uncertainties or emotional fluctuations; and the analysing faculty becomes predominant, using a consciously symbolic language. Prayer and internal colloquy, where they occur, often depend on this 'instructive' tone:

> Esleve toy mon ame, adore ton Soleil...
> Maintenant il luy plaist en ce sainct appareil
> De descendre du Ciel pour laver ton offence
> Et pour te substanter d'une pure substance
> Il se donne à toy mesme, ô don à nul pareil.
> Ce vin realement en son sang propre il change,
> Et ce pain en sa chair, boy donc mon ame et mange...
> Seigneur de ces douceurs mon ame rassasie
> Et me faits par ton corps vivre eternellement.[1]

This theological emphasis can result in a poetry of some complexity. One of the Neo-Latin 'hymns' paraphrased by Guy Le Fèvre is a Eucharist poem by Vida (dedicated by Le Fèvre to Maldonat) in which the doctrine of the real presence, stated briefly by Habert and by the *Pange lingua* of Aquinas, is expounded at length; a short extract will indicate the tone:

> Rien n'est changé dehors, ains en semblance pure
> Demeure aux accidents leur premiere figure
> Si bien qu'en apparence elle pourroit tromper
> L'œil louche de l'esprit, et le faire choper
> Lors que la seule espece, et que des fruicts l'image

[1] Habert, *Sonnets spirituels*, no. 23 (fol. 7).

Se represente aux yeux, et au sens en nuage
Christ est pourtant dedans, et y tient lieu sans lieu
L'unique tout-voyant et non voyable Dieu.[1]

In such poems, the theological argument is presented in sufficient detail to suggest a direct reaction to Protestant doctrine; Vida's poem, as it appears in Le Fèvre's collection, is a symptom of the propaganda war. The Communion poetry of Poupo, though hardly militant, is controversial in the same sense. Poupo is at pains to stress the chasm which divides flesh from spirit: Christ must not be drawn down to inhabit the 'limon sensuel'; the Eucharist is a sign of faith, a 'festin mystic':

En ce festin mystic où ton Sauveur t'appelle,
Sacrement successif de l'aigneau passager:
Pour te donner soy mesme à boire, et à manger
N'imagine Chrestien une repeu charnelle.
Ce celeste aliment de substance immortelle,
Qui de pauvres humains en dieux nous peut changer:
Est donné pour nourrir l'esprit franc et leger
Du limon sensuel, à la vie eternelle.
Comme donc l'oyseau tire à mont vers son gibier,
Leve le cœur en haut bien loin de ce bourbier,
Où le Seigneur ta foy, non ta bouche convie.
Christ est monté es cieux pour nous tirer à soy,
De le tirer à nous s'est (*sic*) renverser la foy:
La chair ne sert de rien, l'esprit seul vivifie.[2]

Similarly, Sponde makes a clear distinction between the spiritual and the carnal banquet, and states explicitly that the physical act is merely the visible sign of a higher mystery:

Embrasse estroictement ce Corps brillant de gloire,
Embrasse-le, mon Ame, et à force de croire
Mange-le tout entier, comme tu doibs manger,
Hume ce sang vermeil respandu de ses veines,
Et remporte du Ciel des espreuves certaines
Que j'en suis domestique et non pas estranger.

---

[1] Guy Le Fèvre, *Hymnes ecclésiastiques*, fol. 142. Vida also gives several lists of Old Testament figures of the Eucharist (see *ibid.* fols. 144 and 147). It will be apparent that Vida's liking for intellectual analysis, in this poem at least, corresponds with Le Fèvre's own manner.

[2] Poupo, *La Muse chrestienne*, Book I, sonnet 34 (p. 18). Poupo wrote a number of sonnets on the Eucharist, in particular the sequence on pp. 14–19 (nos. 28–36), but also nos. 45–6, pp. 151–2.

Penitence and the Passion

> Or cependant qu'au Ciel ceste double substance
> Saoule l'avidité de ta ferme asseurance,
> Avec le fruict entier de ce sainct Sacrement:
> Icy mon foible corps beaucoup moins que toy digne,
> N'en prend visiblement que le visible signe,
> Mais il prend tout par toy comme invisiblement.[1]

That Sponde, whose religious poetry is usually far from polemical, should specify his theological position is indicative of the unusually analytic character of Communion poetry; when one reads a passage of this kind, one is made very aware of the rarity of theological discussion —say, of the doctrine of grace—in the devotional poetry of a period of great religious controversy.

Sponde wrote two long poems on the Communion, so that even the passage quoted is not extensive when it is seen in its proper context. If there is any consistent theological colouring in these poems, it is of a more general kind, one which coincides with Sponde's overall character as a poet. There is no display, no extravagance; there is certainly emotion, both in his argumentation and his scornful apostrophe, but any kind of pathos would be foreign to his manner. The Communion ceremony demands the austerity of penitence, and because it is a 'mystery' it also demands intellectual effort: both these characteristics suit Sponde's style very well. The *Stances de la Cene* are indeed in many ways similar to the *Stances de la mort*, particularly as the long first section is a penitential apostrophe to the soul ('Mon Ame, couvre-toi du sac et de la cendre'). This passage is a preparation for the act of Communion itself as expressed in the stanzas quoted ('Embrasse estroictement ce Corps...'): thus the theological exposition is brought home by the emotional momentum acquired in the prelude. At this point the poem becomes a prayer, taking up the paradox by which Christ dwells in and gives life to the sinner who has 'murdered' him; a brief struggle to understand this mystery is followed by a resignation to incomprehensibility:

> Mais, hélas! mon Sauveur; Mais quoy? faut-il encore
> Que je mange ce corps, ce Sainct corps que j'adore?
> Seray-je son meurtrier, seray-je son tombeau?

---

[1] For this poem, see Sponde, *Méditations*, ed. Boase, pp. 171–5; for Sponde's second Communion poem, see *ibid.* pp. 176–80: here too there is a strong hint of Calvinist doctrine ('C'est ce repas, où Dieu ce jourd'huy vous appelle, / Ce repas immortel pour vostre Ame immortelle').

> Ou bien ce corps mangé retiendra-t-il sa vie?
> Esprit de vérité, pour brider mon envie,
> Sille mes yeux ouverts d'un modeste bandeau.

The rapid changes of tone, coupled with a questioning, analytic manner, are unmistakably Spondian; while the liking for a sermon-like apostrophe on the lines of the death poems is easily reconcilable to the didactic manner of Eucharist poetry. In one stanza of the first poem, the voice of the preacher is explicit, singling out the elect who are alone worthy to receive the sacrament:

> Prophane, esloigne-toy d'un si sacré mystère,
> Mais, ô vous, qui des saincts portez le charactère
> Venez avecques moy, Mignons, dans ce sainct lieu,
> Vous, espoints du désir d'une éternelle vie,
> Beuvez tous ce Nectar, mangez ceste Ambrosie,
> Nul ne vit qui ne vit en la table de Dieu.

This opposition between 'Prophane' and 'Mignons' provides the whole movement of the second poem, where the manner of the sermon is followed throughout: an aggressive address to the 'goats' (corresponding to the penitential opening of the first poem) leads to a much longer discourse to the 'Agneaux', culminating in the introduction of the Communion theme itself; and the poem ends with a ten-line prayer.

In both poems, meditation on the Eucharist results in an interpretation of the Passion, juxtaposing the Fall and the Redemption. Sponde's presentation of the Passion includes some direct physical description:

> Tu sentis les effrois de son aspre disgrâce,
> Quand les grumeaux de sang ondoyoient sur ta face...
> Quand les clous en la croix blémissoient ton visage,
> Quand le fer de ton flanc tiroit le sang et l'eau...

But in these few details there is no pathos, no mention of Christ's beauty, no painful elaboration of the suffering. The Passion is grim and austere: all the emphasis is on the symbolic drama, which Sponde sees, in the first poem, as the working out of the Father's anger on the Son:

> Alors pour nous aimer, Dieu le prit comme en haine,[1]
> Et pour nous soulager, te donnant nostre peine,
> Le vaisseau de son ire en toy fut espanché.

[1] 'le' is presumably a misprint for 'te'.

This interpretation gives a structure and an emotional impetus to what is otherwise conventional enumeration of the phases of man's redemption; the paradox of the drama has a potency which most poetic paradoxes of this period (including many of Sponde's) have entirely lost:

> Dieu te quitta luy-mesme en l'ardeur de son ire,
> Et tu t'allas cacher jusques dans le tombeau.[1]

In the second poem, more emphasis is given to the Fall: the eviction of Man from Eden (and Sponde paraphrases it as if it were his congregation who had been evicted) is described at some length. At first, the degree of detail of this passage seems surprising; one expects to move on to the Passion after a rapid allusion to the Fall. But Sponde wants to press home the sinful nature of man, to make clear to his listeners the plight they would be in were it not for the death of Christ. In this way he prepares a *volte-face*, a typically Spondian modulation. Having dwelt on the hopelessness of man's situation, he changes his tone with an abrupt 'Mais quoy?', and demonstrates in less than half as many lines how the Passion transforms the hopelessness into salvation; and the power of the demonstration is reinforced by the demonstratives of which Sponde is so fond:

> Les ruisseaux de ce sang estouffèrent ces flammes...
> Bref, ce corps vous fournist d'une douce pasture
> Pour les pointus chardons qu'avortoit la nature:
> Ce salutaire sang, au lieu de ce poison,
> S'espandit dessus vous, et vous fust pour boisson.[2]

This development, with its sharp contrast between perdition and salvation, is unmistakably Calvinist. At the same time, Sponde is not concerned merely with expounding Calvinist doctrine: he uses his theology, as in the other poem, to provide a powerful rhetorical structure. Thus the Fall, the Passion, the Eucharist, and the doctrine of election which is implied by the distinction between 'goats' and 'sheep', are woven together to form a highly persuasive poem.

---

[1] Contrast, for example, the following stanza (from the same poem):

> C'est ores, mon Sauveur, qu'il me vient en mémoire,
> A quel prix tu gaignas ceste belle victoire,
> Qui des torrents d'Enfer nous tira dans le port:
> Il te fallut hélas! mon Dieu, chercher toy-mesme
> A noz extrêmes maux ce seul remède extrême,
> Et toy-mesme mourir pour meurtrir nostre mort.

[2] This passage is, once again, very much in the figural tradition.

These poems have much in common with other Eucharist poetry—the association of the Eucharist wtth the Passion, the juxtaposition of Old and New Testaments, the tendency towards an analytic, expository manner—but they are exceptional in their length, since other French poets nearly always use the sonnet for this theme. They are also most interesting as a further example of Sponde's style: they deserve the closest study, and it is strange that they should have been almost totally neglected in the assessment of Sponde's poetic achievement.

Favre, whose second *centurie* is the most substantial collection of Communion poems in this period, was clearly concerned, like his predecessors, to maintain the Catholic doctrine of the real presence: several of the sonnets condemn those who are unable to believe in transubstantiation, and this is not surprising when one considers how important the continuation of the propaganda war could be in a region so close to Geneva. Thus the tone of instruction and persuasion is again much in evidence:

> Meschant qui ne crois pas que la toute-puissance
> Qui de rien te crea sur son propre portrait,
> Qui te soustient sans toy, puisse quand il luy plait
> Separer l'accident de sa propre substance.
> S'il change l'eau en vin, si sans changer l'essence
> Des plus ameres eaux, plus douces il les faict...
> Qu'est-ce qui peut encor te faire contester
> Qu'il ne puisse du corps l'accident escarter?[1]

As one might expect, Favre's analytic mind is attracted by the mysteries of the Eucharist, and interprets them through a wide range of images and arguments. He uses the figures of the Old Testament (manna, David dancing before the Ark, the Ark of Noah and the Ark of the Covenant), and the incidents of the New Testament (the publican, the woman with the flux of blood); but he draws too on non-Biblical thought and imagery. The tenth sonnet begins with an allusion to manna as a figure of the Eucharist (dealt with at greater length in the preceding sonnets), and continues with the miracle of Christ's presence in the Wafer; here Favre introduces the commonplace humanist image of 'le Tout', reinforcing it with an implicit comparison between the circular form of the Wafer and that of the universe:

[1] *Entretiens spirituels, Centurie seconde,* no. 15 (p. 59) (sonnet-numbers only will be given for this sequence).

> Pain descendu du ciel, quoy que pestry de terre,
> Pain de vie, et vivant, mais veritable corps,
> De celuy qui se dit le premier né des morts,
> Qui contiens en ton peu plus que le Tout n'enserre.
> Pain qui sçais enyvrer, et sans vin, et sans verre,
> Quiconque va baisant de ton cercle les bords...

The later part of the poem reintroduces the manna theme; the taste of the Eucharist bread surpasses that of manna because it appeals to the 'senses of the soul', not to the physical sense of taste; but the taste of sin has corrupted the senses and turned the living Christ into a source of death for the sinner:

> Quel goust est celuy là, qu'en te mangeant je sens,
> Sinon tel que le font de mon ame les sens?
> Quelle manne pourroit à mon goust plus complaire?
> Si mes pechez, helas! ne l'avoient tant foulé,
> Qu'à ma mort j'ay plustost ceste vie avallé,
> Sans que leur goust maudit m'ayt oncques sçeu desplaire.

This sonnet has a fault characteristic of Favre: the density of thought seems to clog the movement of the poem, so that the rhythm of the last lines, instead of clarifying the principal idea, obscures it. Line 13 in particular, which has the elements of a powerful elliptical statement, is spoilt by the rhythmic emphasis on *plustost*, which distracts attention from the parallelism of *mort* and *vie*. Similarly, the twenty-sixth sonnet, which is based once again on the miracle of the macrocosm enclosed in the microcosm, has an awkward conclusion:

> Ce corps qu'ores tu vois, ja fait Dieu nourricier,
> Qui dans si peu de rond se cache tout entier,
> N'est-ce un autre abregé de bien autres merveilles?

One of the major themes of the sequence is of a penitential order: how can the corrupt body of the sinner house the body of Christ? This question had already been posed in the four sonnets entitled *Meditations preparatoires à la saincte communion* which concluded the *Centurie premiere*,[1] and it is one which is central to Eucharist meditation. Favre is above all concerned with the problem of how sin can be absolved when it has taken root in the sinner, and one is often reminded of the eighty-ninth sonnet of the first *centurie*, where the same theme

---

[1] *Entretiens spirituels*, pp. 103–5.

appears.[1] The fifteenth sonnet suggests a characteristic answer: just as the physical appearance of the bread and wine is 'accidental' and can be separated from its transformed substance, sin too is accidental and can be separated from the soul (for the early part of this sonnet, see above, p. 212):

> Mais las! où fuyras tu, si le champ te demeure!
> Si de l'ame il ne peut separer le peché,
> Où pourras tu (pauvret) si bien estre caché
> Que sauf son accident ta substance ne meure!

Sin can thus be destroyed without the damnation of the soul.[2] Sonnet 47 develops the theme in greater detail, proposing a solution which is fundamentally similar, although it is expressed in different terms:

> Mais comment Seigneur Dieu, mais pour ta residence
> Voudrois tu bien choisir un si sale palais,
> Plus destruit, plus infect, que si ton corps jamais
> Ne l'avoit honoré de sa saincte presence!...
> Je suis ce publiquain, indigne de te voir
> Et plus indigne encor d'oser te recepvoir
> Si par toy le salut à la maison n'arrive!
> Reçoy donques premier en ta grace mon cœur,
> Loge le tout en toy, lors il pourra sans peur
> Mourant en toy, loger en sa mort ta chair vive.

This is a prayer for the absolving grace which must precede the taking of Communion. The heart, or affections, is offered to God, and will thus surrender its earthly, physical life and become in its turn a fit lodging for the living Christ; in other words, by the combined action of faith and grace, the corrupt nature of the meditator is cast off and the soul prepared for the Eucharist. This complete self-surrender which results in absolution is taken up again elsewhere; sonnet 17, for example, argues against the fear and 'pride' of the soul which draws back from the sacrament, doubting its power to purify:

> Mais pourquoy trembles tu pauvre ame pecheresse
> Si ton Dieu, ton Sauveur t'ordonne d'approcher
> De ce sacré banquet, où l'on vit de sa chair,
> Puis que dez si long temps la famine te presse!

---

[1] See above, p. 141.

[2] See also no. 88 ('...soy donc celeste pain, / Ruine à mes pechez, mais à moy medecine!').

And sonnet 98, resuming the mystery of man's creation, of the Passion
and of the Eucharist, is a prayer for participation in the love which
motivates God's liberality:

Qui suis-je, ô Seigneur Dieu, mais que fus-je avant qu'estre
En l'abisme infini de ton eternité,
Pour qui tu deusses ja semondre ta bonté
D'apprester les tresors d'un si digne, et grand Estre!
O amour! ô amour! Un tel Dieu se soubmettre
A pastir, à mourir pour ma meschanceté,
Et par sa mort m'ayant de la mort rachepté
Se donner vif en pain, pour de sa chair me paistre!
Me faisant tant de biens ne veux tu rien de moy?
Et que puis-je t'offrir si je ne l'ay de toy!
Que veux tu donc, mon cœur? rien plus? qu'encor il t'aime:
Las! quant au cœur je l'ay: mais si froid, qu'il n'est point
Capable d'un tel feu, si tu ne fais que joint
Au tien, ton sang boüillant l'eschauffe tout de mesme.[1]

These sonnets of penitence and faith are the most impressive of the
sequence, since they combine a theological structure with a strong
affective impulse. The tension and disquiet of a crucial meditative
problem are established at the outset by broken rhythms, *reprises*, and
the persistent, questioning 'mais'; intensified—particularly in sonnet 98—by exclamation and by an intimate colloquy with God; and
resolved by a prayer which draws on the imagery and argument of the
sonnet as a whole. Even the metrical disorder of the second tercet of
sonnet 98 is justified in part, not by any emphasis of the meaning but
by the sense of an emotional momentum which it provides: the poem
ends with an upsurge of the affections.

The predominant tone of this *centurie* remains didactic. At times the
desire to analyse and explain results in an over-complex argument which
strains the sonnet beyond its capacity. Nevertheless, the poetry of the
Eucharist as conceived by Favre gives a foretaste of Passion meditation

[1] See also no. 56, where the ecstasy of the stigmatised St Francis is described in mystical
terms:

Quelle fust ceste ardeur qui te fit exstatique,
Quand ton ame glissant hors de soy peu à peu,
S'abisma dans la mer de l'amour, qui a sceu
Faire qu'un Dieu soit mort, et de mort tant inique!

The poet then compares this experience with his own devotional weakness in the context of the Passion.

proper: the unresolved restlessness of the penitential lyric is finally overcome by reliance on faith, and by progress (through analytic reflection) towards participation in divine love. Similarly, the Eucharist poetry as a whole, with its preference for the sonnet and its use of the figural tradition for the interpretation of the Passion, is a convenient prelude to the Passion poetry which will be discussed in the remainder of this chapter.

THE DEVOTIONAL SONNET

The rigid separation of the phases of meditation into the three modes of composition, analysis and prayer is an artificial device which seldom occurs in devotional prose: the methodologists of the Counter-Reformation only make this kind of distinction for clarity of exposition. One should therefore not expect a similar categorisation in devotional poetry. However, that the modes correspond to a real and significant mental and literary procedure is undeniable, provided one takes into account the flexibility and overlapping which occur at every turn; and much devotional poetry does in fact respond very well to analysis on these lines.

Take, for example, the *Théorèmes* of La Ceppède. At first sight there is no organisation beyond the narrative grouping into 'books' of 100 sonnets; within these broad units, the various aspects of meditation seem to appear at random. This is partly the case: La Ceppède prefers free meditation. On the other hand, some kind of pattern does emerge if one thinks in terms of the meditational sequence, a pattern which involves groups of up to twenty sonnets, although the group is often much smaller. The first sonnet or sonnets in the group carry the narrative forward, or describe a scene: this is the composition. Then follow a number of sonnets explaining the meaning of the episode, comparing it with a parallel episode in the Old Testament, using it as a text for a brief 'sermon' or for a prayer. The act of Crucifixion is described and commented upon in a large group of this kind. Sonnets 10–19 of Book III cover the narrative from the *despouillement* of Christ to the moment when the jolt of the Cross as it falls into place renews his agony (see above, pp. 201–2). Then in sonnet 20 there is a sudden change of tone: in La Ceppède's own words, this is a 'Raport des principaux points de la Passion à l'ardante amour de Dieu envers nous, comme des effects à leur cause'. This last phrase underlines the poet's intention to explain the events just described; and his explanation takes the form of a devotional commonplace, used also by Granada in his 'analysis' of the Passion:

> ...L'amour a ces haliers à son chef attaché:
> L'amour fait que sa Mere à ce bois le void pendre:
> L'amour a dans ses mains ces rudes cloux fiché:
> L'amour le va tantost dans le sepulchre estendre.[1]

The sonnet ends with an apostrophe to the faithful soul which is developed in the following sonnet: 'Apostrophe à l'ame fidele, ou à l'Eglise, sur les tourmens que Jesus-Christ endure pour elle, avec semonce particuliere de se venir loger aux logettes de la pierre mystique de son corps.' The reference to the 'pierre mystique' introduces the traditional symbolism of the Passion, thus developing the interpretative view of the scene, while the tone of apostrophe sustains the emotional movement of the meditation. Sonnet 23 consists entirely of allegorical parallels of the Cross from the Old Testament ('...raport de l'Autel des parfums, du Serpent d'Airain, du Pressoir de la Vigne, et de l'Eschele de Jacob, à la Croix'), and this symbolism is continued for the remainder of the group (to sonnet 31), becoming at times relatively complex. But the tone is varied in one of the later sonnets (25) by a prayer based on the symbol of the tower of David:

> Belle Tour de David, forte de deux remparts,
> Où pendent mille escus: à toy de toutes parts
> Accourent les mortels. He! soy donq ma retraite.
> Tu brises aujourd'huy les portes des Enfers,
> Fay que ta sainte Image en mon ame pourtraite
> Brise ainsi quelque jour, ma prison, et mes fers. (p. 394.)

And the concluding sonnet of the group (no. 31) is wholly a prayer to the Cross, seen as the tree of Nebuchadnezzar's dream:

> ...Et fay qu'à ce grand jour, qui te verra brillante,
> Dans les plaines d'azur, ta lumiere drillante
> N'épouvante mon ame, aux pieds de ce vaincueur. (p. 403.)

It would be impossible to reduce the whole of La Ceppède's verse meditation to a series of sonnet-groups of this kind: but the pattern is

[1] *Théorèmes*, pp. 385–6. See above, p. 35.

clear enough to be significant. In effect, it is one way of carrying out
the double devotional programme of the preface: '...j'ay fait naistre
cettuy-ci, portant en sa main le livre du Prophete envelopé des mysteres,
escrit dedans pour les doctes, et dehors pour les ignorans'.[1] The colourful
narrative and the simpler 'explanations', together with occasional
pieces of moral advice, are intended for the *ignorans*, the more complex
and learned symbolism for the *doctes*. There is a very wide range in the
tone of La Ceppède's sonnets, from the naïve to the obscure, and these
tones are seldom mixed: one may find a simple image in one of the
composition sonnets, but there is seldom a leap from straightforward
narrative to dense symbolism within a single poem. Thus, adapting the
devotional modes to his own purpose and retaining their flexibility,
La Ceppède nevertheless exploits the different functions of imagination, intellect and emotion.

Favre's technique is rather different, chiefly because he avoids detailed narrative and description for their own sake. Thus most of the
sonnets of the third *centurie* take the composition phase for granted,
as in the first of the Flagellation sonnets, where the *donc* refers back to
an imaginary description of the trial:

> L'Arrest donc est donné, qu'en la fleur de ton aage
> Il faut mon doux Jesus que tu meures pour moy...

Whereas La Ceppède will frequently use a whole sonnet purely for
descriptive purposes, Favre's physical details are in most cases the
framework for an interpretation. However, Favre's practice varies
according to the theme of his meditation. As we have seen, the Communion sonnets provoke a predominantly analytic mode, and the same
is true of the *Stances sur la devotion de nostre Dame du Mont-de-Vic*;
the Rosary sonnets, on the other hand, are far more affective, the
thought less complex, and pathetic detail plays an important if not
independent part. This suggests that Favre is consciously adapting the
style of his devotion to the tradition within which he is working: he
will deliberately avoid the complex thought and imagery of which he
is so fond in order to remain faithful to the simple devotional practice
of the rosary. Once again, a different texture of style is produced by
the way in which certain devotional modes are emphasised at the expense of others.

[1] 'A la France', p. 8. (See above, p. 90.)

La Ceppède's first object, then, is to make his reader relive each episode, using familiar language and indicating time and place:

> Ces barbares en fin lassez de garroter
> Cil qui monstre tousjours une face plus douce,
> Le sortent du jardin d'une roide secousse:
> Le mettent sur ses pieds, le pressent de troter...
> Environ la minuict cette troupe inhumaine
> Repasse le torrent, et le Sauveur emmeine
> Parmi les cris, les fers, la fange et les caillous. (I, 95, p. 185.)

This simple, almost naïve tone is often reinforced by brief, staccato sentences, which convey the dramatic impact of the events:

> Le Tribun prend la teste, et conduit sa Cohorte[.]
> Maint fifre, maint tambour anime le Soudart...
> Tout au tour les Sergens font un double rempart.
> Tout marche en ordonnance. On arrive à la porte.
>
> (II, 100, p. 343.)

This device is particularly useful in a sonnet-sequence, where the poet has to compress his narrative into a comparatively small space; one might compare a sonnet by Boyssières in which several episodes of the Passion are considered within a few lines:

> En fin apres avoir fait goute à goute espandre
> Ton sang: mourir en Crois: là piteusement randre
> A ton pere l'Esprit: et mis dans un tombeau...[1]

The closest parallel to La Ceppède's tone in such passages is however Anne de Marquets's use of brief, unpretentious narration:

> Puis ce traistre Judas detestable entre tous,
> Leur vient dire, messieurs, que me donnerez-vous,
> Et je le livreray entre vos mains sans doubte? (sonnet 124.)

> Luy donc portant sa croix le peuple le convoye,
> Les principaux des Juifs remplis d'inimitié,
> De rage, de fureur, d'estreme mauvaitié,
> Vont la teste levee et tressaillent de joye. (no. 143.)

These poems, by their very simplicity, aim at a dramatic involvement in the scene portrayed. As in the prose treatises, this involvement is

---

[1] *Troisiesmes œuvres*, p. 51 (sonnet 1).

deepened by the technique of 'identification': La Ceppède and his contemporaries will tell the story in the first person, as if they were actually present:

> Qui m'ouvrira les rangs? Qui me fendra la presse
> Pour t'approcher, Seigneur? pour endosser ta Croix?
> Pour (joinct à toy) gravir d'une prompte alegresse
> Sur la crouppe où ton cœur va rendre les abbois?
>
> (III, I, p. 351.)[1]

Similarly, they will use the devotional 'colloquy', addressing Christ, or the Cross, or Mary: the effect in every case is to heighten the emotion and the intimacy, so that the affections are aroused from the very beginning of the meditation. The emphasis given to the rôle of Mary as a spectator and participant of the Passion is here essential; Gabrielle de Coignard exploits all the pathos of the 'Mulier ecce filius tuus':

> Haussez vos tristes yeux, ô Vierge nompareille,
> Dressez vostre regard sur la sanglante Croix,
> Oyez de vostre fils la douleureuse voix,
> Qui d'un son gemissant resonne à vostre oreille.   (sonnet 114.)

And Favres varies what is essentially the same theme:

> Ah! Vierge cache toy, retire toy de grace,
> Pour ne voir tant de maux que souffre ton cher fils,
> Qui lié, garotté par la rage des Juifs,
> Ne monstre rien que sang pour lustre de sa face![2]

Conversely, La Ceppède and Favre apostrophise Judas, or the Jews, or the executioners:

---

[1] See also Gabrielle de Coignard's fifty-eighth sonnet (*Pour le jour de Noel*): 'Je voy le fils de Dieu, dans la loge champestre, / Plié dans ses drappeaux...'; similarly La Ceppède's apostrophe to his soul (II, 100): 'Sors apres luy mon ame, et t'endosse son bois...' Favre makes explicit the theme of the 'inward eye' (*Entretiens*, p. 163, *Crucifiement*, 4):

> Doncques esleve toy ma pauvre amt (*sic*) atterree,
> Et si tu n'as encor perdu tout sentiment,
> Ouvre les foibles yeux de ton entendement,
> Voy la chair de ton Dieu, tout-par-tout deschiree.

Cf. Anne de Marquets, sonnet 132.

[2] *Entretiens*, p. 144, *Flagellation*, 3. See also *Visitation*, 5 (p. 115), *Coronation*, 10 (p. 154), *Crucifiement*, 13 (p. 167). La Ceppède dwells less on this aspect of the Passion (but see III, 12, 17, and 61 *et seq.*). Favre's *Stances sur la devotion de nostre Dame du Mont-de-Vic*, as well as his Rosary sequence, suggest a special involvement in the cult of the Virgin Mary.

Traistres, cruels bourreaux, d'où vous vient ceste audace
D'oser impudemment, d'oser mettre la main
Sur le corps de mon Dieu, et d'un foet inhumain
Diffamer ce qu'il a de douceur, et de grace![1]

One is thus reminded again and again of the rich effects produced by Humbert, and by his predecessors throughout the devotional tradition, through an apostrophe which allows a total imaginative realisation of the Passion, and which can at the same time lead to prayer or to interpretative reflection.

One other feature of the composition procedure is central: the description of Christ himself. In meditation on both the Nativity and the Passion, the usual technique is to insist on a series of paradoxes, which in the case of the Passion may be purely visual, as in the famous 'Ecce homo' sonnet of La Ceppède (II, 70, p. 304):

Ces cheveux (l'ornement de son chef venerable)
Sanglantez, herissez, par ce couronnement,
Embroüillez dans ces joncs, servent indignement
A son test ulceré d'une haye execrable.
Ces yeux (tantost si beaux) rébatus, r'enfoncez,
Ressalis, sont helas! deux Soleils éclipsez,
Le coral de sa bouche est ores jaune-pasle.
Les roses, et les lys de son teint sont flétris...[2]

Christ is throughout referred to in terms of extreme sweetness and gentleness—'un doux agneau', 'un simple Aignelet innocentement doux'—so that where his beauty is deformed by blood, suffering and *crachats*, the pathos is intensified. Since Christ suffers physically through his human as opposed to his divine nature,[3] the consideration of Christ on the Cross, or as a child in the manger, naturally provokes a further series of paradoxes which, though intimately related to the act of visualisation, imply a simple and fundamental interpretation of the scene, or at least an awareness of its mystery. Two sonnets of Doremet enumerate the paradoxes of God incarnate:

---

[1] *Entretiens*, p. 145, *Flagellation*, 5. Cf. *Théorèmes*, I, 44, 91; also Chassignet, *Mespris*, p. 250, where Chassignet compares himself with the executioners in a penitential passage.

[2] Cf. Favre, *Entretiens*, p. 154, *Coronation*, 10.

[3] See Favre's *Coron.*, 10: 'c'est bien luy tousjour / Qui ne peut comme Dieu souffrir nul impropere'.

Celuy que (*sic*) a fait l'homme, ô miracle! s'est fait
Homme: et le Roy des Cieux vient succer la mammelle:
Le pain vivant à (*sic*) faim, la lumiere immortelle
Dort, et sans point mourir, meurt le Seigneur parfait...

Le Sainct chef redoutable aux esprits angeliques
Est poinct par l'espesseur d'une aspre cruauté:
Le visage passant tous hommes en beauté
Est souillé du crachat des gosiers Judaiques...
Clouees sont les mains qui formerent les Cieux:
Et la bouche enseignant les propos precieux
Est abbreuvee en fin de boisson tres-amere.[1]

The interpretative element becomes explicit where the vicarious nature
of the sacrifice is explained: starting from the simple paradox that
Christ dies so that man shall live, a whole series of correspondences can
be elaborated:

Que vois-je en ceste Croix! la mort qui vivifie,
Les playes de mon Dieu, pour les miennes guerir,
Un sang pur, et naif, pour mon ame blanchir,
Un monde de crachats, qui les ords mondifie...
Une extreme, et grand soif, qui va nous enyvrant,
Un despouillé tout nud qui nous va rechauffant,
Deux bras clouëz au bois, qui deslient mes cordes...

Il est donq monté, belle, au gibet ordonné
Pour vous faire monter à son Throsne supreme,
Il a son tendre chef de ronces couronné,
Pour ceindre vostre chef d'un brillant diademe...
Il vuide ores de sang son corps livide, et bléme,
Pour le prix dont prodigue il vous a rançonné...[2]

At this point, we are moving into the realm of analytic meditation,
which may pick up the descriptive details and explain their significance
as in the examples just given, or use other devices such as the 'question
and answer' technique. An imaginary dialogue, in which the meditator
himself supplies the answers to his questions, is a convenient way of

---

[1] *Polymnie*, pp. 33–4. For further Nativity paradoxes in sonnet form, see Favre, *Nativité*,
7 (p. 122); Anne de Marquets, sonnet 34 (see Tuve, pp. 36 ff. and 53–4, for this and
parallel themes in the medieval tradition· also above, p. 52). For Passion paradoxes,
see Favre, *Crucifiement*, 12 (p. 167), and La Ceppède, III, 64.

[2] Favre, *Crucifiement*, 12; La Ceppède, III, 21, p. 387. Cf. also III, 20; Anne de Marquets,
sonnet 161; similarly, Boyssières's two sonnets summarising the life of Christ within
an interpretative framework.

making a point clear, although the 'problem' may not be a complex
one:

> Et quel mot? Qu'il soit fait, mais par qui prononcé?
> Par la Vierge. Et comment? D'un cœur humble...
> Mais tu veux te rendre homme. Et pour qui? pour des hommes:
> Quels hommes? Ennemis de ta divinité...[1]

In the second of these sonnets, the dialogue is conducted with Christ
himself, so that the analytic technique is connected with that of intimate
participation in the mystery of the Passion; and it is by this device that
La Ceppède masks his didactic purpose in a sonnet of relative complexity:

> Vous parlez Syriaque, ou vulgaire Hebraïque,
> Grec, et Latin ensemble, en cette humble oraison.
> Pourquoy cela, mon Christ? ce n'est pas sans raison:
> Tous vos faits, tous vos dits, ont un sens heroïque...
>
> (I, 30, p. 72.)

As we have already seen, the interpretations of the Passion which
this devotional rhetoric is designed to make more accessible vary widely
in intellectual depth, from simple moral *sententiae* to the complex figural
patterns of, say, La Ceppède's Crucifixion sonnets.[2] Fundamentally,
however, most of such analysis is based on the attempt to grasp the
allegorical or symbolic significance of every aspect of the episodes
described. One of Favre's Flagellation sonnets derives a moral allegory
from the scene: the *cordes* represent *pechez*, the *bourreaux* are *vanitez*,
the *colonne* is the 'durté de mon cœur', the 'fleuve de sang' is forgiveness; and the sonnet concludes:

> ...ren-moy la charité
> Pour corde, pour bourreaux, un remord effronté,
> Pour colonne, ta croix, pour sang, l'eau de mes larmes.   (p. 146.)

It will be apparent that Favre only partially 'invents' his allegory to
provide a moral: the correspondences between blood, tears and forgiveness are universal and permanent, as is the parallelism between the

---

[1] Favre, *Incarnation*, 6 and 1 (pp. 110 and 107). These two poems are far removed from
Favre's complexity in the earlier sequences: occurring at the beginning of the Rosary
sequence, they immediately set a tone which is less demanding intellectually, although
still inclined towards enquiry.

[2] Compare, for example, La Ceppède's III, 23 with his III, 59, or with the moral *sententiae*
of Anne de Marquets (see above, pp. 196–7).

Flagellation and the Crucifixion. Thus the interpretation is theological as well as moral; it is based on the mysterious unity of all the articles and episodes of the Passion. Similarly, Favre interprets the seamless robe as a symbol of the flesh with which the Word is 'clothed'.[1] Such parallels are closely related to the figural tradition itself, in which the life of Christ, and the Passion in particular, is seen as the central point of an immutable order, both historical and transcendental: the Incarnation illuminates the history of man and resolves the prophetic allegories of the Old Testament, as La Ceppède states explicitly in a sonnet which interprets the 'Consummatum est':

> Son œuvre est achevé: son Pere est satisfait,
> Tout ce qui devoit estre a produit son effet:
> En luy sont accomplis tous les divins augures.
> Il nous a dechiffré tous les Tableaux secrets,
> La verité succede à l'ombre des Figures:
> La vieille Loy fait place à ses nouveaux Decrets.[2]

There is no need here to dwell at length on this tradition, since it has already been discussed in the context of Eucharist poetry; and the article referred to analyses the question in some detail. However, certain observations are essential. In the first place, while La Ceppède is particularly fond of figural symbolism (for reasons which will become apparent shortly), most of the poets considered in this and the following chapter use it instinctively: one could without much difficulty compile a concordance of symbols from these poets which would demonstrate the community of the tradition and at the same time

---

[1] *Flagellation*, 3 (p. 144). The first quatrain of this rich sonnet (quoted above, p. 220) is a physical and emotive prelude to the analysis of the remainder:

> Las! ce n'est plus celuy qui voulut en ta race
> Prendre ce corps doüillet de ton sang plus exquis,
> Ces deux habillements, ô Vierge que tu fis
> Et au Verbe, et au Corps, vois-tu qu'on les defface?
> Ceste robbe qui fust une de toutes parts,
> Dans peu d'heures sera le joüet des soudars,
> Mais son corps ja des-ja tout par tout se deschire:
> Bon Dieu, qui le croira, le Verbe estre faict chair,
> Et souffrir que les foets la puissent escorcher,
> Sans que pour tant de coups seulement il souspire?

[2] III, 79, p. 475. This sonnet is quoted also by Ruchon in the introduction to his selection, and by A. R. Evans, Jr., in his article 'Figural Art in the *Théorèmes* of Jean de La Ceppède', *MLN*, 78 (1963), pp. 279 ff. This article is a suggestive one; it also gives some useful bibliographical indications.

provide a useful basis for considering the individual styles and theological bias of the poets concerned.[1] In the second place, the symbolic
pattern has certain focal points which have an enormously rich allusive
potentiality: however often they are used, these *topoi* are always
capable of further variation. Perhaps the most fundamental of all is the
complex series of associations between the rock struck by Moses,
giving forth a fountain which enabled the Israelites to survive in the
desert; the body of Christ, struck by the lance and giving forth blood
and water; and the tears of the penitent. Anne de Marquets's 172nd
sonnet is characteristic as an expression of the *topos* itself and also of
Anne's carefully explicit manner of exposition:

> Moyse print sa verge, et frappa le rocher
> Dont il feit sortir l'eau pour le peuple Hebraïque,
> Qui sous luy traversant le desert Arabique,
> De grand soif et de chault se sentoit tout secher:
> Ainsi Dieu a frappé son Fils unique et cher,
> Qui est la pierre vraye, et le rocher mystique,
> Pour nous ouvrir la source heureuse et deïfique,
> Où tout fidelle doit refrigere chercher.
> La maison de David, c'est à dire l'Eglise,
> A qui ceste fontaine avoit esté promise,
> Puise en icelle l'eau, et le sang precieux,
> Qui lave le pecheur de toute chose immunde,
> Qui repoulse la soif des vanitez du monde,
> Et qui d'enfer esteint le feu pernicieux.

There is here a further allusion: Christ is the cornerstone of the Church
(just as St Peter, representing Christ, will be the rock on which the
Church is built); and La Ceppède uses a similar range of symbols in
his apostrophe to the faithful soul or the Church:

> Il souffre patient qu'à ce jour on fabrique
> Des logettes pour vous dans la pierre mystique
> De son corps, et sa voix vous semond d'y venir.
> Belle, venez y donq, vostre Espoux le commande:
> Et pour tant de bien-faits dont il veut vous benir,
> Donnez-luy vostre cœur, c'est tout ce qu'il demande.[2]

---

[1] For example the figure of the 'brazen serpent' (with which Moses cured the Israelites in the desert) is found in Anne de Marquets (sonnet 167), in Favre (*Crucifiement*, 3, p. 162), in Chassignet (*Mespris*, sonnet 431), and in La Ceppède (III, 23).
[2] III, 21, pp. 387–8. This theme is also related to the blood and sweat of the Agony in the Garden (see Favre's sequence on this episode, esp. nos. 4 and 10, pp. 139 and 142),

The word *mystique*, as it occurs in both these sonnets, has the sense of a 'mystery' or symbol, a hidden truth which can be partly if not fully understood by the intellect. The presentation and interpretation of these figures is however an essential preparation for an experience of self-identification with Christ and his love which is of a mystical order. It is not by accident that La Ceppède uses the image of the 'pierre mystique' in the context of a love-allegory deriving from the Song of Solomon, or that this sonnet is preceded by one in which love is emphasised as the motive of the Passion. At the culmination of the Crucifixion meditation, the *dévot* is crucified with Christ;[1] his soul, like the Church, becomes the bride of Christ; he takes refuge in the wounds; and, surrendering his earthly life, he offers up his 'heart' to God. The full implications of such an experience are not exploited by any of these poets, as they are, for example, by St John of the Cross: nevertheless, the mystical language is used by La Ceppède, Favre and Anne de Marquets to suggest a climactic moment of their meditation.[2]

La Ceppède's use of Biblical symbolism is matched by a wide range of figures drawn from pagan antiquity.[3] In a footnote to the second sonnet of the first book, he justifies his use of mythological allusion; having called Christ 'Alcide non feint' in the sonnet itself, he comments on the phrase thus: '*non feint*, garantit ce vers du fabuleux mensonge: n'estant point illicite de parler ainsi en Poësie et de Chrestienner les fables. Ainsi lisons-nous en meint autheur Chrestien, le vray Jupiter, le vray Apollon, le vray Neptune' (p. 24). La Ceppède is here, and throughout the *Théorèmes*, carrying on the tradition of syncretism which reaches its height in the Renaissance, but which has its roots in the earliest Middle Ages. In later Renaissance poetry, it is best represented by the 'encyclopaedic' poetry of Du Bartas and Guy Le Fèvre. One should however not forget Ronsard's *Hercule chrestien*, which, although relatively narrow in its intellectual scope, implies precisely the same viewpoint as La Ceppède's; this poem was written fifty-eight

and to the weeping of the rocks at Christ's death (Favre, *Centurie premiere*, no. 12). Guevara (*Livre du Mont de Calvaire*, fol. 285) refers the *logettes* in Christ's body to the rooms, window and door of Noah's Ark.

[1] See Anne de Marquets, sonnet 165: 'Voila comment il faut qu'elle [l'ame devotieuse] se mortifie, / Et qu'avec son espoux elle se crucifie...'

[2] See Anne de Marquets, sonnets 161 and 176; for Favre, see above, p. 215, and below, pp. 233–4.

[3] See Evans, *MLN*, 78 (1963), pp. 285–6.

years before the *Théorèmes* were published, but it was given a new
lease of life in the 1580s by the Catholic anthologies, and its influence
seems to be attested by the existence of a similar work by d'Aubigné.[1]
The occasional use of mythological images and the like occurs in much
devotional poetry: Anne de Marquets, whose style is relatively unadorned, introduces it at the moment of Christ's triumph, a significant
connexion:

> Il est ores vainqueur du monstre de peché,
> Il a tué de mort la cruelle Chimere,
> A brisé les Enfers, et du cruel Cerbere
> Il a le triple chef sous ses pieds escaché. (no. 157.)

La Ceppède is far more systematic. Not only does his whole topo-
graphy rely heavily on myth (Heaven is 'l'Olympe', Hell 'l'Erebe' or
'l'empire Avernal'; Satan is 'Pluton' or 'le Prince Stygieux'); his
conception of the unity of history, illustrated by his liberal use of
Biblical figures, is extended by such allusions to include classical
antiquity. The Passion of Christ is an epic, subsuming Virgil's epic
(which itself reflect Homer's): as is well known, the *Théorèmes* begin
with a transposition of 'arma virumque cano'. It is an epic in the
narrative sense, in that it tells a story in a rich language designed to
evoke a physical reality; but more important still, it has all the significance of an epic interpreted as a moral and transcendental allegory.
Christ is prefigured by all the heroes of the pagan world, just as he is
prefigured by the prophets of the Old Testament: 'Tous vos faits, tous
vos dits, ont un sens heroïque' (see above, p. 223).[2] In this way, the
Théorèmes are proposed as a 'definitive' work, gathering together all
the principal strands of history, literature and theology at the focal

---

[1] Ed. Réaume and de Caussade, vol. II, pp. 226 ff. Both Ronsard and Pontus de Tyard
were familiar with the syncretist thought of the Florentine Academy, and with the
mythological allegories associated with it—on which see E. Wind, *Pagan Mysteries in
the Renaissance* (London, 1958)—and the tradition was carried on by Guy Le Fèvre and
by Baïf's Academy (see Yates, *French Academies*). La Ceppède's *Catalogue Alphabetique*
includes Pico della Mirandola. The basic study of the mythological tradition in the
Christian era is of course J. Seznec's *La Survivance des dieux antiques* (London, 1939);
on the Hercules myth, see M.-R. Jung, *Hercule dans la littérature française du xvie
siècle* (Geneva, 1966), esp. ch. v.

[2] It is important to remember that the concept of Christ's death as a 'triumph', with its
accompanying classical connotations, was already to be found in the medieval hymns,
especially perhaps in Fortunatus: see the *Vexilla regis* ('praedam tulitque tartari');
also the opening of the *Pange lingua*.

point of man's destiny. Such a conception is not foreign to devotion: in a mind nourished by a humanist education and by the view of history expounded by Augustine in the *Civitas Dei*, meditation on the mystery of the Passion could legitimately lead to an attempt to reconcile the different realms of human experience.

No doubt there is some discrepancy between the ambition and the achievement. La Ceppède may often sound pedantic, particularly to modern ears, and even obscure: but the allusions would have been more familiar to a contemporary audience, and La Ceppède explains many of them in his commentaries. Moreover, if one compares the *Théorèmes* with the psalm-paraphrases of La Ceppède's colleague Chasteuil,[1] or even with some of Favre's more complex sonnets, it becomes clear that any obscurity is superficial. Favre's attitude is very like La Ceppède's in certain respects: although he uses little humanist allusion in the Rosary sequence,[2] and although none of his work suggests the same systematic programme, his syncretist view of religious experience as involving certain significant aspects of humanist learning is based on the same premises and traceable to similar sources.

The third aspect of devotional rhetoric, the incitement to emotional involvement and prayer, is already apparent in many of the quotations given above. A sequence which consisted purely of third-person narrative and instruction would scarcely be devotional: the affections are required at every stage in the contemplation of the Passion, since all meditation is in a sense a prayer. Composition is accompanied by the admiration or tears of the meditator, by his involvement in the scene, and by his apostrophes and prayers to Christ or Mary; an understanding of the meaning of the scene contemplated provokes further prayer, as in the sonnets where La Ceppède combines analytic figures with affective apostrophe; and the progress towards a mystical experience implies an intimate blend of symbolic analysis with a receptive emotional state. In his Rosary sequence, Favre is often explicitly concerned with the problem of animating the affections; in the last of the Nativity sonnets, he considers the relationship which ought

---

[1] In Chasteuil's *Imitation des Pseaumes de la pénitence Royalle*, meanings are derived from 'les 7 accouplemens des 22. lettres Acrostiques en l'Hebrieu' (see, for example, pp. 4 and 20).

[2] It is significant that in *Crucifiement*, 8 (p. 165), Favre introduces his favourite theme of *circonference* without developing it into a full-scale image.

to exist between meditation on the mysteries of the Incarnation and emotional response:

> Quand je vay meditant d'une ame moins distraite
> Ces mysteres tant hauts du Sauveur incarné,
> Soit comme ja conceu, soit comme desja né,
> D'où se faict, que mon cœur point de larmes n'en jette?
> Est ce, que le plaisir de voir ce, qu'il souhaitte
> Le rende esperdument plus joyeux qu'estonné?
> Ou que pour estre trop à la chair addonné
> Il ne puisse à l'esprit faire si douce feste?
> O cœur diamantin! Si ce n'est de douleur,
> Pourquoy d'amour au moins n'esprains tu quelque pleur?
> Quel subject de pleurer aux ames plus devotes!
> Si pour nostre salut il daigne naistre ainsi,
> Est il pourtant moins juste? He! d'où vient donc cecy,
> Qu'il tremble, et pleure ja? N'est ce, helas, pour mes fautes![1]

This poem crystallises a tendency which underlies all the devotional poetry of Favre, La Ceppède, Anne de Marquets and many of their contemporaries: the rhetorical devices they use (*descriptio*, apostrophe, prosopopeia and the like), whether derived from profane or sacred rhetoric, are brought into contact with an urgent desire to move the reader, and presumably with the poet's own emotional responses. If one couples with this the fact that in many cases the object is to achieve the highest pitch of emotion, it will be evident that the potentialities of this particular combination of devotion and poetry are very great.

It will by now be clear that one cannot talk of these poems in terms of emotion alone: the affections are defined by the physical or interpretative context in which they arise. Significant results are thus produced by a convergence of at least two of the devotional modes, and the best poems may well involve all three. Moreover, we are here considering the sonnet or sonnet-sequence as a specific medium for devotion: the real achievement of Favre or La Ceppède can only be discussed in terms of whole poems. The sonnet is of course used by many lesser poets for contemplation of the life of Christ, but again

[1] See also *Retrouvement*, 6 (p. 134):

> Devots consolez vous, si par fois Dieu retire
> Ses consolations, quand plus vous le priez
> Qu'il vous soit favorable...
> Meditez avec moy la Vierge, qui souspire
> Son propre fils perdu...

and again, the potentialities of the form are not properly realised, no doubt because the poetic art tends to be a secondary consideration for the religious poet: a list of descriptive details, a series of paradoxes, will often fill a whole sonnet, without the organising power of a central idea.[1] Favre and La Ceppède may themselves err in this direction; but it is significant that these two 'analytic' poets choose the argumentative shape of the sonnet as their principal medium, and in their better poems show an awareness of what this medium is capable of.

Two earlier poets, Boyssières and Poupo, give a foretaste of the devotional sonnet at its height. One of Boyssières's Passion sonnets has already been considered (above, p. 140), another quoted in part (p. 219); in the latter poem, the compressed narrative, already couched as a prayer, is resolved by a prayer for salvation through the identification of the sinner with the sacrifice:

> Faits que pour moy, Seigneur, ta Passion soit bonne:
> Et que ton Sang, ta Mort, et ton poignant Chapeau,
> Me serve de Ruisseau, de Vie, et de Couronne.

The parallelism of the last two lines, following the suspended, one-sentence syntax of the rest of the poem, fixes the symbol of the Passion in a solemn, immutable order which has nothing to do with the over-worked symmetries of, say, the *mort-vie* paradox. In Boyssières's fifth sonnet, several episodes are again enumerated, this time spanning the whole life of Christ, from conception to descent into Hell:

> Helas: que ta servy, de demeurer neuf mois,
> Dans le sain virginal, de ta piteuse Mere,
> Naistre si pauvrement, souffrir tant de misere,
> Te rendre si petit, toy, Roy de tous les Roys.
> Helas! que t'a servy, d'avoir par tant de fois
> M'enseigné le chemin, pour aller vers ton Pere,
> D'endurer une mort, des morts la plus amere,
> Honteusement pendu, au feste d'une Crois.
> Helas! que ta servy, de causer tant de peine,
> D'avoir fait si souvent perdre la douce alleine
> A ta mere, en voyant te moquer, tourmenter.
> Et bref: que t'a servy, encore de dessendre
> Jusqu'en bas aux Enfers: Bon Dieu pour m'acheter?
> Puis qu'a si bon marché, je me tourne revendre.[2]

---

[1] See, for example, Doremet's two 'paradox' sonnets (*Polymnie*, pp. 33–4).
[2] *Troisiesmes œuvres*, p. 53.

Here again, the structure and symmetry of the sonnet are syntactical: a series of rhetorical questions leads up to the last line, where the penitent explains why the sacrifice has been useless. This penitential ending derives considerable force from the accumulation of pathos in the previous thirteen lines; and the whole meaning of the Passion is summed up in the word *acheter*, only to be immediately transformed into the ironic *revendre*—another symmetry which is an integral part of what the sonnet is about.

Some years later, Goulart's admirer Pierre Poupo produced a sonnet which is much closer to Boyssières, Favre or La Ceppède than one might have expected from a Protestant:

> Voila mon Redempteur, pour payer mon offense
> Estendu sur le bois. Miserable pecheur!
> Devroi-je pas au moins crucifier mon cœur
> Cause de ce tourment, par triste repentance?
> Te suffisoit-il pas, ô thresor de clemence!
> M'adresser par ta bouche à un sentier meilleur,
> Si tu ne l'esmaillois d'une vive couleur
> Par ton sang respandu en si grande abondance?
> Voyant ton digne corps ouvert en tant d'endroits,
> Perse mon ame, ô Dieu! du vray sens de ta croix,
> Si que de part en part tes b[l]essures je porte,
> Blessures en nous deux d'effect bien different:
> Car elles t'ont occis, pour estre un restaurant
> De nouveauté de vie en ma charongne morte.[1]

The opening 'composition' is followed immediately by a penitential application, involving the 'crucifixion' of the sinner and leading to a prayer ('Perse mon ame...') which is based on the same theme and which is reminiscent of the 'crucifixi fige plagas...' of the *Stabat mater*. This theme thus provides the dominant direction of the sonnet: it is then expanded in the second quatrain, where Poupo emphasises the colour and quantity of Christ's blood, less obsessively than Favre or La Ceppède, but sufficiently to provide a point of comparison. Finally, the wounds of Christ are represented in the second tercet as giving life to the sinner's corpse: thus the parallel between the sinner and Christ is prolonged in an antithesis essential to the concept of a vicarious sacrifice.

[1] Poupo, *La Muse chrestienne*, Book II, sonnet 77, p. 170.

Poupo's sonnet thus explores a single theme in a controlled and explicit manner. Although it is primarily a first-person meditation, it involves the reader from the outset by the sermon-tone of the demonstrative 'Voila...' and of 'Miserable pecheur...'; and it combines a simple realisation of the physical Passion with reflection and with an emotive application of its significance. The twenty-third sonnet of Favre's *Centurie premiere* has certain features in common with this poem. It begins with a second-person attack in the full sermon manner, carrying the movement without a break to the end of the second quatrain:

> Magnifiques mondains qui de voz mortels peres
> Apres leur jour venu faites ouvrir les corps,
> Feignans de ne scavoir d'où procedent leurs morts,
> Effects du seul peché, misere des miseres,
> Elevez voz esprits à plus divins misteres,
> Voiez morte la vie, et dittes quels efforts
> Ont meurtri l'immortel, le plus fort des plus forts,
> Qui n'avoit ni peché, ni part en noz affaires.
> L'anatomie est faite, et le coup ja donné
> Dans le flanc jusqu'au cœur, m'en fait moins estonné,
> Voiez le cœur ouvert par la lance pointue,
> Voiez quel feu d'amour brusle encor au dedans,
> Ne cherchez de sa mort autres motifs plus grands,
> Ny de la vostre aussi, si ce coup ne vous tue.[1]

Favre's tone, unlike Poupo's, is far from subdued, indulging in insistent alliterations, paradoxes and Biblical superlatives: and the rhetorical *souffle* is powerful enough to justify devices which might elsewhere seem hackneyed or contrived. But the impact of the poem does not rely exclusively on sermon-rhetoric. The familiar 'Magnifiques mondains' leads directly into an unusual and provoking image drawn from medical science: Favre juxtaposes scientific 'curiosity' with theological explanation, and in doing so he creates a rich and highly individual field of allusion.[2] Poupo's parallel between the *charongne* of the

---

[1] The sermon-tone is used regularly in poetry on the life of Christ: it is once again a means of increasing the emotional participation of the meditator. See also Favre's *Coronation*, 8 (p. 153) ('Mondains, mondains, mondains, qui de la gloire vaine / Faites si grand estat... / Venez cest homme voir...'); Du Peyrat's seventh *sonnet spirituel* ('Sur le Crucifix'); and many others, including the 'inward sermon' of Poupo's sonnet.

[2] Guevara uses the same image, but fails to develop it, introducing the theme of the 'two trees' in order to explain the meaning of the 'anatomie': 'Ah corps! qui souffres une si estrange anatomie, comme peux-tu vivre une seule heure. Les medecins font de pareilles

sinner and the body of Christ is thus deepened both by the topical
nature of the image and by its physicality; similarly, the association of
the piercing of Christ's body with the intellectual act of analysis, a
fundamental concept already present in Poupo's tenth line, takes on
the character of a 'metaphysical' conceit when Favre sees the spear-
thrust as an exploratory dissection of Christ's 'anatomy'. Finally, with
a characteristic modulation, Favre rearranges his theme to allude to the
imitative crucifixion of the sinner, who must die unless he participates
in the Passion.

The elaborate working out of a single image in this fine sonnet has
a unity of impact which does not exclude a high degree of allusiveness:
and the same could be said of sonnet 12 of the *Centurie premiere*, which
integrates the figural images of the weeping rocks, the tears that become
blood, and the Red Sea, or of sonnet 40, which will be considered later.
As usual, Favre may overload an already complex pattern: in sonnet 68,
for example, which analyses the relationship between the literal and the
figurative nails, the wounding of body and soul, the effort required to
find the meaning is not compensated by intellectual penetration. Nevertheless, if this sonnet is a failure, it is an impressive one, a failure on the
part of a poet who is capable of sustained and intricate thought and who
uses the framework of the sonnet in an attempt to elucidate this thought.

As we have already seen, the tone of the Rosary sequence is gentler,
the imagination less intellectual. Questions are posed, symbols analysed,
allusions multiplied; but the relationship between the sinner and
Christ, and in many cases the Virgin, is more intimate, the emotion
more direct. These characteristics become immediately apparent if one
compares one of the last of the Crucifixion sonnets with the poems we
have just been looking at:

> Soubs cet arbre de vie arreste toy, mon ame,
> Si tu cherches repos, savoure ce fruict doux,
> Qui pend devant tes yeux, bien qu'il soit plein de coups,
> Voy quel bon suc en sort quand la lance l'entame.
> Icy tu peux ceuillir (*sic*) la myrrhe que la Dame

incisions et deschiquetures sur les corps ja morts. Et pourquoy fait-on ceste cy sur toy,
ô douloureux Jesus estant encore en vie? Cyrille sur S. Jean dit. Non sans grand mystere
Jesus Christ observa en souffrant tout ce que le premier homme avoit fait en pechant.
Car comme Adam estendit la main à l'arbre pour en cueillir le fruict, aussi le second
Adam estendit la sienne en la croix, afin qu'elle y fust attachée: tellement que Jesus
Christ porta en son martyre les pas et traicts du peché d'Adam' (*Livre du Mont de
Calvaire*, fols. 171–2).

> Sentoit tomber des mains, et des doigts de l'espoux,
> Mais niche toy plustost dans le creux de ces trous
> Ouvert, pour y cacher ce que tu as d'infame.
> Le sang de tes pechez par le sien effacé
> Ne creindra la fureur de ton Dieu courroucé,
> Mais garde, qu'avec toy tes vices je ne porte:
> Pose les soubs la Croix, quitte doncques ma chair,
> Ou la portant en haut, appren de l'attacher
> Si bien à ceste croix, qu'ell' en demeure morte.[1]

The theme of self-crucifixion which concludes the sonnet is much the same as that of the earlier poems; but it emerges from a context in which the healing effects of the Passion—its 'sweetness'—are predominant. The lance brings forth a 'bon suc', the 'blood' of sin is already effaced in Christ's blood, the fear of God's anger is cancelled, and the separation of body and soul involves little torment or conflict. The *dévot* is here at an advanced stage in his contemplation of the Passion: the problems posed by his sinful nature are almost overcome, and he begins to use the language of mysticism. Beneath this suave exterior, the accumulation of allusion which gives the poem much of its richness is managed with Favre's customary care. The first quatrain develops the symbol of the new tree of life and its beneficial fruit, in which the tree of Adam is absorbed and transformed: the fruit is 'battered' but its virtue is none the less great (the conceits of *coups* and *lance* here are almost as daring as those of the *anatomie* sonnet). Lines 5–6 introduce an entirely new symbol, taken from the Song of Solomon: but unlike so many other Passion sonnets, where the transition between one figure and the next is abrupt if not arbitrary, Favre weaves the two images together by the word *cueillir*, which prolongs the fruit image, and by the sensual impression of liquid sweetness which is common to both. The theme of mystical marriage, once alluded to, is then modulated into that of the sinner hiding in Christ's wounds: there is no explicit sexual connotation here, but La Ceppède, too, instinctively associates the concept of the bride and bridegroom with that of the wounds as a refuge (see above, p. 225), and this suggests that the psychological overtones of both images are profoundly linked. Favre does not exploit this pattern of symbolism further in the tercets: nevertheless, it provides a tonality which gives a special emphasis to

[1] *Crucifiement*, 7, p. 164.

the soul's abandonment or crucifixion of the flesh. The logic of this poem is thus more emotional and sensual than that of the earlier sonnets, but the pattern is nevertheless controlled and articulate: the distance between the *vie* of the first line and the *morte* of the last has been carefully measured.

Favre's sonnets, even those of the Rosary sequence, are self-contained, and, with a few minor exceptions, independent of one another. They each focus attention on one aspect of the mystery of the Passion, and deal with it exhaustively within their confined space. With La Ceppède, as we have already demonstrated, one is much more conscious of a sequence. Many of the sonnets of the *Théorèmes* are thus nourished by their context in the meditation as a whole, and lose something of their richness when seen in isolation. This is not to say that, like Odet de La Noue, La Ceppède tends to make the dividing line between any two sonnets arbitrary: the structure of each poem is usually conceived in its own terms, and is not left 'open'. However, since La Ceppède may use a whole sonnet for physical description or narration, one may in such cases be left with the feeling that this is only a prelude, a preparation for reflection and analysis, as it would be in meditation proper. Take, for example, sonnets 67 and 70 of the second book. In both poems, the principal aim is to evoke a sense of horror at the revilement inflicted on Christ:

> He! voyez que le sang, qui de son chef distille
> Ses pruneles détrempe, et rend leur jour affreux.
> Ce pur sang, ce Nectar, prophané se mélange
> A vos sales crachats, dont la sanglante fange
> Change ce beau visage en celuy d'un lepreux.[1]

The structure in each case is enumerative, rather than argumentative or explanatory; and the antithesis which resumes no. 67 operates on a purely physical and emotive level. No doubt they are both striking poems in their own right; but it would be unwise to overlook their dependence on the sonnet which in each case follows. La Ceppède calls 68 a 'Correction de l'Autheur de ce qu'il avoit dit au precedent Sonnet, avec un rapport moral de la salive, et de la fange, qui guerit l'aveugle-nay, au meslange du sang de Jesus-Christ decoulant de sa teste, avec les crachats dont les Soldats avoient couvert sa face'; it counter-

[1] II, 67, p. 301; for II, 70, see above, p. 221.

balances and completes the composition of 67 with an interpretative argument, modulating systematically the descriptive details through metaphor and Biblical figure; sonnet 71 fulfils a similar function for 70. Favre might have compressed the same material into a single sonnet, producing a greater density but perhaps straining the structure: La Ceppède does not forget that he is writing in sonnet-form, but he will compromise, often successfully, between the unit and the sequence.

Where two or more sonnets of the *Théorèmes* are closely knit together, they may be in the same 'mode', descriptive or analytic (as in the descriptive sequence III, 10–19); but the overall impression given by a reading in sequence is that of an ever-changing tone. Thus the two pairs just considered are made up of contrasting units: since they are thematically inseparable, there is no risk of fragmentation. Similarly, in I, 91–5, the bonds of Christ are considered from a number of totally different but mutually supporting points of view. In this way, thanks to La Ceppède's adaptation to poetry of devotional method, an organic unity is combined with broad scope and great flexibility; furthermore, a single effect (physical pathos, accumulation of figures) can be prolonged over a whole sonnet, a technique which could well be fatal to an isolated poem. This characteristic leads one directly to a consideration of what is perhaps La Ceppède's principal talent, the creation of a highly adaptable and forceful poetic diction. It is this, I think, which makes the *Vexilla* paraphrase such a striking poem, and which may be in part responsible for the recent popularity of La Ceppède as compared with Favre. The sheer verbal inventiveness of the 'Ecce homo' sonnet, its unexpected juxtapositions, raise the commonplace Passion *descriptio* to a level at which it can move and excite the reader; and in such passages, La Ceppède may enrich the effect still further with sound-values: the last three lines of II, 67 (see above) contain an impressive display of assonances. Similarly, in III, 23, a flamboyant, almost exotic tone is produced by the close proximity of Hebrew proper names and words bordering on neologism. Indeed, this taste for unexpected word-combination may at times give a false impression of intellectual complexity, particularly no doubt to the modern reader: in spite of its unfamiliar texture, the last sonnet mentioned is perfectly accessible if one has a minimal knowledge of figural symbolism. This is again unlike Favre, whose surprise effects work on an intellectual

rather than a verbal level, and whose diction is often his weakest point.
La Ceppède is seldom elegant in the manner of a Du Perron, but
whether he is elaborating the pathos of Christ's death, expounding a
simple moral or symbolic interpretation, or giving a display of humanist
rhetoric, his language is well adapted and syntactically controlled,
hitting the reader hard and with precision. For further examples, one
could turn to many of the narrative sonnets, or to the uncomplicated
emotion of Mary's lamentation, where the movement in the tercets
from theological assurance to human grief creates a fine minor cadence:

> Avecques Noëmi, cette chetive Mere
> Aux Dames de Salem disoit je vous suply,
> Ne me dites plus belle, ains m'appelez amere:
> Le Seigneur a mon cœur d'amertume remply.
> Les plus griefves doleurs peintes sur le reply,
> Des vieux siecles passés reduites en sommaire,
> Auprés de ma douleur, ne sont qu'une Chimere.
> Voicy ton Prognostic, ô Vieillard, accomply.
> De la mort de mon Fils naist la ferme esperance
> Du salut des humains: j'ay fidele asseurance
> Que sa mort de la mort le rend ores vainqueur.
> Mais son corps qui s'expose à ce martyre extreme
> Est à moy, c'est mon sang, il m'est plus que moy-mesme[:]
> Ce qu'il souffre en son corps, je le souffre en mon cœur.
>
> (III, 61, pp. 449–450.)

There is no doubt that the success of this diction depends on the
fact that each sonnet has its own individual tone, that La Ceppède does
not ask too much of any one poem: structure and language are intimately linked. It is the same cast of mind which results in the predominantly explicit theology of the sequence as a whole. La Ceppède's
manner of exposition is expansive; instead of drawing his arguments
together into a confined space like Favre, he will develop them dis-
cretely and at leisure. The allegory of sonnet 53 of book II, one of
those which comment on Christ's white robe, is carefully explicit:

> Appren de ce manteau dont il est revestu,
> Que son cœur n'aime rien que la blanche vertu,
> Que son Ame, et son Corps sont parez d'une sorte.
> Le blanc, pur, simple, égal, sans teinture et sans art
> Figure l'innocence. Et ce Christ qui le porte
> Egal, simple, innocent, vit sans tache, et sans fard. (p. 286.)

The details added to the basic parallel are synonyms which make comprehension still easier, whereas Favre will progressively increase the complexity of the metaphorical structure, leaving the reader to puzzle out the meaning. Thus, too, La Ceppède constantly points out that each action has a symbolic significance, making apparent the link between the figurative and the literal planes: 'ô Symbolique fange', 'Tous vos faits, tous vos dits, ont un sens heroïque', 'La verité succede à l'ombre des Figures'; and the prose commentaries bear out this inclination to the full. Where Favre's imagination tends towards metaphor, La Ceppède's is often allegorical: and while it may be a post-Symbolist prejudice to give the advantage to metaphor, there are times when Favre's thought can be more penetrating. La Ceppède's sonnets on the Agony in the Garden (i, 24–34) consider the humility of Christ (drawing from it a moral precept), then the allegorical significance of the three languages and the triple prayer used by Christ: the tone is frankly didactic. Favre, in a parallel sequence, dwells on the spiritual combat between soul and body, and in a magnificent concluding sonnet, applies the same meditative themes to his own fear of death and damnation:

> Voiant de mon Sauveur l'ame tant angoissee
> Lors qu'il suë le sang, de douleur, et d'esmoy,
> Je prevoy ja ce jour, où la mort, où l'effroy
> Des enfers combatra ma pauvre ame oppressee!
> Quand je seray sans poulx, ma force terracee,
> Mes esprits sans esprit, les Diables contre moy,
> Pauvre ame où fuiras-tu? s'il ne combat pour toy,
> Ou si de son amour il ne te rend blessee!
> Anges que faites vous, qui retenez ce sang,
> Que sa saincte sueur va sur terre versant!
> Souffrez que son amour une goute m'en baille!
> Ah! bening Redempteur, n'auras tu lors pitié
> De qui te couste tant, si ja ma mauvaistié
> Te faict entrer pour moy dans ce champ de bataille! (p. 142.)

The imagery of battle, flight, wounds and blood is here woven fully into the texture of the poem; and the paradox of lines 7–8, the conceit of the concluding lines, seem to go deeper because they are presented elliptically, with no explicit 'commentary'.

Nevertheless, La Ceppède has great resources of style. From time to time, his meditation culminates in a sonnet which, exploiting all the devotional modes, forms a focal point: and at such moments, the imagery may fuse into a concise yet fertile pattern, still related to the surrounding material, but constituting a whole and rounded poem in its own right. A localised example occurs in I, 44, where an invective against Judas in the sermon manner is concluded with an admirable double metaphor, illuminating the idea of the previous three lines without laborious explanation:

> Ha! lasche je voy bien cette munificence,
> Excedant le pouvoir de ta recognoissance,
> Te rend ce bien-facteur desormais odieux.
> Ton cœur est un crapaud, qui les fleurettes change
> En son mortel venin: c'est un monceau de fange
> Qui s'endurcit au jour du Soleil radieux. (p. 120.)

One is however inevitably drawn to the full-scale universal symbolism of La Ceppède's 'white' and 'red' sonnets (II, 54 and 63). The first of these justifies the preparatory didacticism of the preceding sonnet (see above) by exploring in full the potentialities of the material there established; the second descants on the central *topos* of Christ's blood and its symbolic colour in the context of the robe of purple. Both have been admirably analysed by Dr de Mourgues;[1] but as a final example of what the devotional sonnet can do in the framework of Passion meditation, it is illuminating to set the 'red' sonnet beside a poem of Favre on a similar theme (*Centurie premiere*, 40):

> Ame rouge de sang pour tant d'enormes vices,
> Qui t'ont ja tant de fois meurtry cruellement,
> Veux-tu survivre à toy pour mourir seulement?
> Meur plustost par l'horreur de si sanglans supplices.
> Lave toy par les eaux de tes larmes propices,
> A fin que tes pechés soy't blanchis promptement,
> Avant que de ton Dieu le sanglant jugement
> Sur ta mort immortelle empourpre ses justices.
> Mais pour changer le teint de pechés si sanglans,
> Pleure larmes de sang, ils seront faits tous blancs:
> Hà que dis-je? je faux, de rouge est la livree,
> Ton sang n'est plus vermeil, tant il est tout pourry,
> Pren donc de celuy là de l'agneau favory,
> Chez le grand Assuer' nul autre n'a l'entree.

[1] *Metaphysical, Baroque and Précieux Poetry*, pp. 52–3.

Aux monarques vaincueurs la rouge cotte d'armes
Appartient justement. Ce Roy victorieux
Est justement vestu par ces mocqueurs gens-d'armes
D'un manteau, qui le marque et Prince, et glorieux.
O pourpre emplis mon test de ton jus precieux
Et luy fay distiller mille pourprines larmes,
A tant que meditant ton sens mysterieux,
Du sang trait de mes yeux j'ensanglante ces Carmes.
Ta sanglante couleur figure nos pechez
Au dos de cet Agneau par le Pere attachez:
Et ce Christ t'endossant se charge de nos crimes.
O Christ, ô sainct Agneau, daigne toy de cacher
Tous mes rouges pechez (brindelles des abysmes)
Dans les sanglans replis du manteau de ta chair.

(*Théorèmes*, p. 297.)

In Favre's poem, the starting-point is the colour and abundance of
blood, a theme already used by the devotional masters in all its symbolic
connotations.[1] The word *sang* (or *sanglant*) occurs six times; words
connected explicitly with the colour red (*rouge*, *empourpre*, *vermeil*)
four times; and the two references to white point the contrast in a
manner which is again common in devotional treatises. At key points
the use of these words is extremely bold, investing an abstract with
colour:[2] one almost overlooks the fact that 'le sanglant jugement...

[1] See above, pp. 28, 53-5; also Favre, *Centurie premiere*, no. 12; and Marin Le Saulx,
Theanthropogamie, p. 130, sonnet 182, which, as an early example, should be quoted:

Encor que le pourpré de mon rouge manteau
Egalle pour le moins la couleur rougissante,
De ceux qui ont foullé la grappe gemissante,
Dessous leurs pieds trempez dedans son sang nouveau:
Quoy que j'aye mouillé de sang, ainsi que d'eau,
Mes vestements molets, et ma dextre puissante
Ait trempé dans le sang sa darde punissante,
De ceux qui captivoyent mon fidele troupeau:
Si ne suis-je pourtant de rien moins agreable,
Moins doux, moins gracieux, moins beau, moins delectable
A celle qui sous pieds a le monde soumis.
Qui sçait pour tout certain que j'ay pris ceste peine,
Pour elle qui de maux et d'ennuis toute pleine,
Ploïoit sous la mercy de ses fiers ennemis.

This sonnet represents the reply of Christ to his 'Espouse', who, as in the Song of
Solomon, has justified her dark skin (p. 130, sonnet 181). Thus it also illustrates how
themes from the bridal allegory and from the Passion can be juxtaposed, suggesting
further variants of the figural method.

[2] The opening phrase, 'Ame rouge de sang', establishes the embryo of theme and image
in much the same way as Donne's 'Oh my blacke soule'.

empourpre ses justices' is a tautology, so obsessive is the image. La
Ceppède uses precisely the same technique, both in his insistence on
blood and redness (tears of blood and bloody sins), and in the combination of abstract and concrete.[1] Thematically, however, the symbol of
the purple robe gives a different emphasis to La Ceppède's poem,
prefiguring Christ's triumph and thus referring to the central 'epic'
theme of the sequence: the poem opens in a major key closer to the
Vexilla regis than to Favre's inward dialogue. This difference in
tonality is deepened by the manner of argument. La Ceppède establishes
a mood through direct explanatory statement (contrast Favre's initial
metaphor), followed in the second quatrain by a prayer which elaborates
the theme of the purple dye: there is no complex logical progression
here, merely a juxtaposition of two focal ideas, related by a universal
image. Similarly, the 'tears' of this second quatrain provoke by
association the penitential development of the tercets, where La
Ceppède characteristically makes his allegory explicit by the word
figure. The accumulation of allusion, of metaphorical significance,
which reaches an extreme concentration in the prayer of the second
tercet, is thus brought about without any obtrusive play of the intellect:
the syntax is clear and measured, the structural divisions symmetrical.
By contrast, Favre's sonnet is tense and contorted. In the quatrains, the
insistence on imagery of blood is doubled by the paradoxes on *mourir*;
and the logical continuity is expressed through a series of subordinate
clauses. The meaning is here straightforward enough, but the syntax
is unrelaxed—rightly, perhaps, since it indicates the mental conflict of
the penitent. In the tercets, the complexity increases at once with a new
conceit: to combat the blood of sin, the tears must become blood,
paradoxically resulting in the white of purification. With the mention
of whiteness, a rapid series of modulations begins: red, not white, is
the proper 'livery' of the penitent who contemplates the Passion (as it
is for La Ceppède); but the sinner's blood is corrupt, so he must borrow
Christ's. The progression of thought here is highly elliptical, although
based on a logical progression: the one weak link is the leap from white
back to red, which is not fully supported by the movement of the

[1] See Ruchon's *Introduction*, p. 24 n. 1; Ruchon refers to d'Aubigné's use of the same
technique. See also Favre's 'le sang de tes pechez' (above, p. 234), and Marin Le Saulx's
fifty-ninth sonnet (*Theanthropogamie*, p. 69), which includes the phrases 'le sanglant
de mon vice', 'ta rouge cruauté', and 'ma noire injustice'.

penitential argument. The last line of all adds yet another unexpected dimension from the figural tradition; whereas La Ceppède widens his significance in his concluding lines, Favre makes the mistake of 'localising' the argument in an image which fails to resume the central themes of the sonnet.

La Ceppède's sonnet remains, I think, the more satisfying poem, but it is none the less important to have recognised that the material and even the mode of thought on which it is based could produce parallel results in other poets—in Favre, and to a lesser extent in Poupo and Boyssières. The position is very much like that in other Renaissance poetry, where several independent poems may be created on the basis of a common source: one remembers for example Du Bellay's 'Ores qu'en l'air' (*Olive*, 45) and Ronsard's 'Or que Juppin' (*Cassandre*, 127), which share the same Petrarchan theme and the same classical allusions without their distinction as individual poems being in any way impaired.

If the rhetoric of meditation on the life of Christ is designed to induce in the *dévot* a high pitch of emotion at every stage of his contemplation, if *larmes* and *extase* are the sign of a true devotion, the rhetoric of the sonnet imposes a structure and thus a control which are fundamental to the poetry of Favre and La Ceppède. Within the schema of meditation, emotion is of course counterbalanced and nourished by analysis of the theological mysteries: the same combination is encouraged in poetry by the use of a form which implies a strict discipline. There is no doubt, I think, that the qualities of Favre's poetry are bound up with the mode of thinking of a man accustomed to the techniques of meditation: but he is nevertheless a poet who reacts to the specific problems posed by his chosen form. Likewise, the richness of the *Théorèmes* is due in part to the ever-present physical plane of reference, to the urgency of the moral and theological problems, to the inexhaustible emotional resources of the spectacle and its meaning; it is due in part also to La Ceppède's own mastery of language; but it is inconceivable without the special function of the sonnet in concentrating attention on each point and thus encouraging the emergence of the fine 'focal' poems. A similar process will take place in the more expansive poetry of César de Nostredame, but the resulting devotional style will be quite different: in this way, poetry becomes not a mere imitation of devotional technique but a new and powerful extension of its range.

CHAPTER 7

POETRY OF
THE INCARNATION AND
REDEMPTION.

2: THE SENTIMENTAL AND
THE ROMANESQUE

When one turns from the poetry of La Ceppède to that of his friend and compatriot César de Nostredame, one enters an entirely new devotional atmosphere. Certain themes and modes of development remain constant; but there is a clear divergence between the sensibility and imagination of the two poets. Whereas La Ceppède prolongs the Renaissance dream of a universal framework of thought, drawing together the types and symbols of the pagan and the Biblical world, César de Nostredame's taste is characterised by a liking for sensual representation and for emotional indulgence. Behind this contrast lies a broader pattern which involves the changing tastes of a whole generation: each poet is typical of a period in which devotional poetry reaches a highwater mark, but while La Ceppède looks back to an ideal which has already lost much of its impetus, César de Nostredame mirrors the taste of a generation eager for an easy and accessible devotion. For this reason, the present chapter will dwell on the 'poetry of tears', a poetry in which, freed from the control imposed by theological and moral problems, the imagination and the affections are allowed free play, and in which narrative and decorative visual effects begin to predominate. First, however, one must return briefly to devotional prose, and see how its romanesque potentialities could be developed.

The sentimental and the romanesque

ROMANESQUE ELEMENTS IN DEVOTIONAL PROSE

Consider this scene from Granada's representation of the procession to Calvary:

Le Vierge donc va pres son fils, desirant de voir en soy quelle force est ce que luy estoit la douleur: elle oyt de loing le cliquetis des armes, le bruit du peuple ay (*sic*) acourant, le cry des sergeans, et bruit de trompettes qui publioient sa sentence. Elle voit soudain la splendeur du fer des lances et halebardes, veoit par le chemin la trace du sang espandu de son fils, qui luy monstroient assez par où il avoit passé.[1]

In the attempt to involve the reader, he dwells on minor colourful details, evoking the noise and movement of the procession, the brightness of the weapons, and finally, amid the confusion, the trail of blood left by Christ himself. Coster, writing a generation later than Granada, elaborates the scene still further; first the executioners,

en apres une grande troupe d'hommes suivant legerement, comme c'est la coustume, pour occuper et se saisir des lieux eminens et commodes à veoir le spectacle, desquels les uns s'esclattoient de rire, les autres crioient et tempestoient avec cris et huees, et plusieurs vomissoient et desgorgeaient plusieurs blasphemes en irrision et mocquerie de Jesus Christ: puis suivoient les cohortes et la troupe de soldatz, et au milieu d'eux deux larrons liez de cordes, et apres eux l'enfant Jesus griefvement chargé...Sa face estoit meurtrie, couverte de flegmes, de crachat, de sang et d'ordures: les mains et les piedz n'avoient autre apparence sinon d'un sang vermeil comme rose, et comme une chair descouverte de peau et sanglante, une couronne d'espines poingnoit et picquoit son chef, couvroit et cachoit son visage...Considere 2. qu'aussi tost que le Seigneur fust passé, la mere, qui le suivoit avec les aultres femmes, veit les goutes de sang qui s'estoient escoulees du corps sacré de son filz.[2]

The violence implicit in Granada's rendering is here brought to the foreground, preparing the pathos of Christ's appearance as 'l'enfant Jesus' (a phrase which already suggests a 'feminised' devotional attitude). Furthermore, the traditional elements of the scene are rephrased in a way which stresses action and movement: the passage is dominated by the pairs of verbs, supported by similar doublets of nouns, of adjectives, and even of whole phrases. Indeed, apart from the Jesuit classification into *points*, this passage looks exactly as if it came from a

[1] *Le Vray chemin*, fols. 53–4.
[2] *Cinquante meditations*, pp. 218–20.

roman—the *roman sentimental* of the Passion. Even the reflective pauses which alternate with the narrative take on this character, stressing the emotional reactions of the principal figures: what did Mary and Christ feel when they looked at each other on the road to the Cross? At this point, the interpenetration of the devotional and the romanesque is reinforced by an ambiguous use of the traditional love-imagery. Christ's love for mankind is the principal motive force behind the Passion; the mutual love of Christ and Mary provides much of the pathos of the Calvary scene; and the *dévot* himself must become suffused with divine love if his meditation is to be effective—Bonaventura's 'devout soul' contemplates the Flagellation with the intimacy and emotional involvement of a lover: 'O ame amoureuse contemple le doux Jesus flagellé, ainsi nud et tremblant de froid. Regarde le de pres d'une intime et amoureuse tendresse, et le considere delicat, tres noble et innocent qu'il est tout nud fouëtté, sanglant et ainsi cruellement deschiré' (*Meditations*, pp. 212–13). When Granada depicts the 'silent dialogue' between Christ and Mary on the way to Calvary, he uses what is essentially the same tradition: '...ces deux lumieres du ciel se regardent l'une l'autre, et s'outrent reciproquement les cœurs avec les yeux, et blecent leurs ames passionnees avec leurs veuës'.[1] But there is one major difference here: Granada's use of hyperbole makes a parallel with the language of profane love inevitable, and this ambiguity will become still more apparent in contemporary poetry. From the early seventeenth century, devotional practice is designed more and more for women,[2] so that the allegory of Christ the lover and his beloved is taken more and more literally. At the same time, the cult of the Virgin Mary begins to be rivalled by the popularity of Mary Magdalene, with whose appearance the number of possibilities for romanesque developments multiplies rapidly, as we shall see when we come to César de Nostredame.

[1] *Le Vray chemin*, fol. 54. See also Alonso de Madrid, *La Methode de servir Dieu*, p. 283; Henry Humbert, above, p. 199, and below, Appendix, p. 310, and Humbert's *Sepmaine saincte*, pp. 160–4 (*Jesus parla aux femmes qui se lamentoient aprés luy*), especially pp. 163–4: 'Voz yeux et les siens enveloppés de nuages, enflés des pluyes de voz larmes, s'entre-rencontrent souvent sur ce chemin, et vos œillades mutuelles, les interpretes d'un amour reciproque, sont des sagettes amoureuses qui font des bresches dans vos ames languissantes de douleur et d'amitié...'

[2] One thinks of Madame Acarie, of 'Philothée', of Jeanne de Chantal—'le sexe dévot', to use Bremond's phrase (*Humanisme dévot*, vol. I, p. 47; cf. vol. II, pp. 36 ff.). See above, pp. 85–7.

In this way, the formal meditation converges with the devotional *roman* which is to be so popular from the turn of the century. Bremond speaks of Richeome, in his *Pèlerin de Lorette*, 'soudant...un roman aux *Exercices* de saint Ignace';[1] conversely, Gustave Reynier gives a place to the *roman pieux* in his history of the origins of the *roman sentimental*:

Le grand réveil du sentiment chrétien qui se manifeste si nettement au commencement du XVIIᵉ siècle (œuvres charitables et œuvres de propagande, couvents qui se rouvrent, congrégations nouvelles, etc.) a donné naissance à une nouvelle sorte de roman: le roman pieux. Il s'annonçait par l'allégorie mystique de P. Joulet, *Les Amours Spirituels de Psiché* (1600), qui n'est guère qu'un recueil d'élévations et d'hymnes ferventes, et aussi par la conclusion dévote de certaines nouvelles...En 1608, de Nervèze publie *La Victoire de l'Amour Divin soubs les Amours de Polidore et de Virgine*.[2]

In 1603, Nervèze had produced *Le Jardin sacré de l'âme solitaire*, which draws a parallel between divine and earthly love,[3] while in 1605 there appeared a *Recueil des traictez spirituels de l'éloquent Nervèze*; so it is clear that this 'éloquent Nervèze' was able to write within five years and with no problems of transition a number of works ranging from the devotional treatise to the *roman pieux*. Similarly, François de Rosset, whom we shall find translating Aretino's devotional narratives, also rendered Ariosto, Cervantes, monastic works such as the Carmelite Juan de Jesus-María's *Discipline claustrale* and *L'Instruction des novices*, and La Puente's famous *Guide spirituelle*; while in 1604 he published *Les XII beautez de Phyllis, et autres œuvres poétiques*.

Such combinations make it clear that the theme of sacred and profane love plays an important part in the convergence of devotion and literature in the first decade of the seventeenth century, and that it is intimately connected with the resurgence of the *conte* and the *roman*. Once again, as in the days of Marguerite de Navarre, the *Symposium* is a source of religious reflection and literary entertainment;[4] and the parallel

[1] Bremond, *Humanisme dévot*, p. 31. Bremond has a chapter on the *roman dévot*, dealing with Camus and other authors writing outside our period. He quotes an interesting passage from Camus's *La Pieuse Julie* of 1625, in which an episode is recounted in what is unmistakably the devotional 'composition' technique (*ibid.* pp. 286–8).

[2] G. Reynier, *Le Roman sentimental avant l'Astrée* (Paris, 1908), p. 353.

[3] See Bremond, *Humanisme dévot*, pp. 337 ff.

[4] See *ibid.* p. 379: 'Ce discours de Diotime, des livres de dévotion le commentaient à l'usage des simples fidèles. Dans le *Traité de l'amour de Dieu* par le P. Fonseca, traduit en 1604, se trouve tout un chapître sur "l'amour de la beauté humaine".' Bremond also discusses the part played by the growing cult of the Magdalene in the Platonic context.

with Marguerite de Navarre is not a wholly accidental one, for the *Heptaméron* was not published till 1558, and its influence was in part responsible for the growth of the *roman sentimental* and thus of the *roman pieux*. Reynier's phrase 'la conclusion dévote de certaines nouvelles' would fit the *Heptaméron* perfectly well—one thinks, for example, of Parlamente's story on the first day, where an attempt at human love ends in the cloister. Furthermore, there is a resemblance between the atmosphere of Marguerite de Navarre's circle, with its emphasis on a devout 'feminism', and the society of the early seventeenth century. Indeed, it is possible to see the later period as a renewal of the impulse underlying the contemplative literature of Marguerite de Navarre and her circle in the context of a new literary taste and a broadened concept of devotion.

A further illustration of the connexions between the two periods is provided by the fortunes of Aretino's works in French translation. Toffanin sees Aretino as a precursor of Counter-Reformation literature:

Con l'intuito dei grandi orecchianti, l'Aretino sentì giunta l'ora della poesia biblica...e fu in certo senso un precursore: subito dopo dilagheranno quei poemetti religiosi, delizia della controriforma, nei quali i fatti biblici son vaghezziati come, prima, quelli del mito classico. Si consentirebbe a un pregiudizio estetico opponendo che l'Aretino descrive in prosa la Strage degli Innocenti e la conversione della Maddalena, laddove il Marino ed Erasmo da Valvassone la descrivono in ottave.[1]

In his choice of subject-matter and his use of prose Aretino is thus a devotional writer using literary means: his liking for narrative is attested not only by his *Humanità di Christo* (a romanesque account of the life of Christ), but also by his *Genesi* and even his prose paraphrase of the Penitential Psalms, each of which is preceded by a passage giving the 'background story' and providing an overall continuity. The epithets used in the title of the first French translation of the *Humanità* —'divinement descripte, et au vif representée'—remind one that Aretino was also famous for his rich descriptions and unusual images, which the second dedication of the *Humanité* (to Marguerite de Navarre) describes thus:

...le non trivial sentier par ou l'Aretin conduict *l'Humanité de Christ*, est tant difficile a tenir pour les torrens, et brisées de son inacoustumé parler, avec les nayfves graces, phrases, et merveilleusement bien adaptées

---

[1] G. Toffanin, *Il Cinquecento* (Milan, 1965), p. 311.

comparaisons, desquelles, comme un pré estoillé de diverses fleurs, embellit
tant son verdoyant, et guay cheminer, que cela le peult, s'il y a riens qui le
puisse faire surnommer divin, et moy rendre fort craintif et maussade.[1]

The Italian originals of the three works so far mentioned, and of
*La Passione di Giesù con due can̄ȥoni, una alla Vergine, et l'altra al
Christianissimo*, were in François Ier's library;[2] a French version of the
psalm-paraphrases appeared in 1540 (*Les Sept pseaulmes de la pénitence*,
at Lyons), and of the *Genesi* in 1542 (*La Genèse avec la vision de Noë*,
also at Lyons). A new translation of the *Humanità*, by Pierre Delarivey,
was to appear in 1604, and François de Rosset's version of the *Salmi de
la Penitentia* in 1605; since the preface of the latter work announces
that it is 'le fameux Aretin qui parle', Aretino had evidently not been
forgotten. Editions of his secular works had appeared occasionally in
the later sixteenth century, as for example the popular *Miroir des
courtisans* from the third *Giornata* of the first part of the *Ragionamenti*
(Lyons, 1580): Aretino would certainly have been read at the court of
Henri III, where Italian influence was particularly strong. This work
appeared again at Paris in 1595 under the more explicit title *Histoire
des amours faintes et dissimulées de Lais et Lamia...où sont descouvertes
les falaces et communes tromperies dont usent les mieux affectées courtisanes
de ce temps à l'endroit de leurs amis* (this edition also contains Du
Bellay's *Vieille courtisane*). The apparent lack of translations of
Aretino's religious works between the 1540s and the first decade of the
seventeenth century suggests that Aretino remained *fameux* for his
secular works: it also underlines the character of devotional interests at
the turn of the century, especially as the new translations were presumably intended for the same audience as the *Histoire des amours
faintes* (or Rosset's *XII Beautés de Phyllis*). This character is evoked
unambiguously in the dedication of the Penitential Psalms (to Madame
Jacqueline Du Bueil, Comtesse de Moret):

Mes Muses reduites à la Penitence de David, soit par l'ingratitude de ce siecle
present, ou bien qu'elles tirent cest accident malheureux de leur propre

---

[1] *Trois livres de l'Humanité de Jesuchrist: divinement descripte, et au vif représentée par
Pierre Aretin Italien. Nouvellement traduictȥ en françois* (Lyons, 1539), dedication,
non pag.
[2] *La Passione di Giesù* (Vinegia, 1535), 'Rel. aux armes de François Ier' (Bib. Nat. catalogue); *I Sette Salmi de la Penitentia di David* (Vinegia, 1536), 'Rel. aux armes de Fr.
Ier'; *Il Genesi* (Venice, 1538), 'Rel. de la bibliothèque de Fr. Ier'; *I Quattro Libri de la
humanità di Christo* (Venice, 1539), 'Rel. aux armes de Fr. Ier'.

desastre, vous viennent offrir le tesmoignage de leur repentance: Elles sont
repentantes (Madame) de n'avoir encores semé le Ciel de la gloire de vos
louanges, et remply l'univers de l'estonnement de vos merveilles. Mais elles
jurent par leur Apollon de faire si bien...que vous n'aurez point subject
d'envier la Beauté qui fit jadis armer l'Europe contre l'Asie.

This is followed by a series of *Stanses* ('à la même'), of which the
following four lines are typical:

> Deux miracles nouveaux paroissent sur la terre,
> Mon Prince et la Beauté qui charme ses espris:
> L'un porte sur son front les lauriers de la guerre,
> L'autre dedans ses yeux les foudres de Cypris.[1]

To explore further the prose of a period in which narrative fiction
establishes itself once and for all as a major literary *genre* would be
an undertaking far beyond the limits of the present study. Nevertheless,
it will already be clear that the sacred and the profane have here
mingled—at times inextricably—to produce a definable literary
character: elegant and courtly on the one hand, earnestly devout on
the other, the taste of the age inclines towards both decorative narrative
and the dual register of love.

THE POETRY OF TEARS

One of the first extended poems on the Passion to appear in French
during the reign of Henri III was a translation by Guy Le Fèvre of
Sannazaro's *De morte Christi Domini ad mortales lamentatio*. This
Neo-Latin poem, which was first published in 1526, was Sannazaro's
most celebrated Christian Latin poem after the *De partu Virginis*. It
represents an early stage in a tradition which was to be of great
importance in Italy, for the combination of a Virgilian style with
Christian themes as practised by Sannazaro and by his contemporary
Vida anticipates the epic poems of Tasso: and there are some elements
of a parallel movement in France.[2] In this way the Neo-Latin poets,

---

[1] *Les VII Psalmes de la Penitence de David*, trans. Fr. de Rosset (Paris, 1605), 'Dédicace',
etc., *non pag.*
[2] See, for example, the Neo-Latin poetry referred to above, p. 98; also Macrin and
his debt to the Neo-Latin Christian poetry of Italy (I. D. McFarlane, *BHR*, 21
(1959), pp. 67–9, 314–15, 324 ff., 336 ff.); and Du Bellay's *Poemata* includes a Latin
poem on the Nativity entitled *In Natalem Diem*. The use of *La Christiade* as a title
by Jean Loys (see above, p. 66) recalls Vida as well as the epic programme of the

both Italian and French, laid a foundation on which the Counter-Reformation vernacular poets might build. The *Lamentation aux hommes sur la mort de nostre Seigneur Jesus Christ* is of course accompanied in the *Hymnes ecclésiastiques* of Guy Le Fèvre by many other poems, and it would be unwise to attribute to it any direct influence in the shaping of the poetry of the coming generation; nevertheless, it has certain characteristics which will soon become widespread in French religious poetry. In the first place, it dwells on the physical and emotive aspects of the Passion, combining an exclamatory devotional manner with an elaborately worked style:

> D'Olympe le grand Roy gist or' palle et deffait...
> Aux grands cloux donne lieu meinte beante playe,
> Et sur les bras plombez le sang se caille et raye,
> Ah chef, indigne d'estre d'espines poingt,
> Perruque mesme au Ciel venerable en tout point
> Et qui fut tant de fois environnée et ceinte
> De la noble couronne, et de clairs Astres peinte!
> Ah poitrine beante! ah de cruelle main
> Belle barbe arrachée! ah le corps tant humain
> Meurtry de tant de coups, membres plus froids que glace!
> Donc estes vous ces piedz jadis tous pleins de grace
> Coustumiers de marcher les Astres et les Cieux
> Les manoirs empirez, et les hauts toits des Dieux,
> Qui avez enduré douleur continuelle.
> Et les coups enfoncez de la pointe cruelle.
> Et avez arrousé la terre et durs rochers
> De gros bouillons de sang, et de grumeaux si chers?
> Donques ne tremble point, donc n'est de peur troublée
> De tous hommes mortels, l'ame trop aveuglée?[1]

Pagan allusion is extensive, and no attempt is made to justify it on a symbolic level: Sannazaro is not afraid to use his talent for the marine eclogue in the context of the death of Christ:

Pléiade; and the same background is clearly also relevant to the epic intention of La Ceppède's *Théorèmes*. For another possible Italian model, see Chariteo's narrative poem *Pascha*, which reappeared in the Venice *Rime spirituali* and which would certainly have been known by many French poets. This is a vernacular poem, and not specifically Virgilian; nevertheless, its manner is very similar in certain respects to that of the poetry to be considered in this chapter. It contains for example a description of Mary at the tomb of Christ, against the decorative background of a spring landscape, and indulges in hyperbole ('Affrena gli occhi, occhi non gia: ma rivi'); later, Christ's descent into Hell is described through the metaphor of Orpheus and Eurydice.

[1] *Hymnes ecclésiastiques*, fols. 153–4.

The poetry of tears

Et quoy ne vid on pas la rage de la mer...
Lors que le bleu Triton des cavernes marines
Tirant son moite chef, et de bouche et narines
Enflant sa Conque torte en feist ouyr le bruit
Sur les flots sonoreux de la mer qui s'enfuit
Entonnant aux nochers d'une voix fort horrible
Que le Pere, le Roy, l'Ouvrier et Dieu paisible
De nature estoit mort?...   (fol. 154.)

There is here no provocation to thought: the reader's attention is directed to the rhetorical colours, to the eloquence of the declamation, so that the devotional mood is one of self-indulgence rather than of solemn meditation.

There is no doubt that Sannazaro's poem appeared in France at a critical moment. The *Hymnes ecclésiastiques* were printed in 1578 and 1582; three years later the religious poems of Isaac Habert were published, one of which was a *Lamentation sur le corps de nostre Seigneur Jesus Christ*. If the similarity of the title could easily be accidental, the poem itself frequently reminds one of Sannazaro's manner; and its seems likely that Habert, who as a 'scientific' poet was closely related to Guy Le Fèvre, might have taken a particular interest in the *Hymnes ecclésiastiques*. Habert's preoccupation with the beauty of the created world—again characteristic of his wider interest in natural phenomena—moves him to open his poem with a passage in which the reader is urged to pass from 'meditation on the creatures' to a self-afflicting contemplation of the Passion:

...Si le Soleil sortant hors de la porte d'or
De rayons couronné, et si la nuit encor'
Ardante de flambeaus, si la belle lumiere
Aus rais d'argent qui fait mouvoir l'eau mariniere:
Si tous les Elements, si toutes les saisons,
Leurs tresors differents, leurs fleurs, et leurs boutons,
Leurs odeurs, leurs espics, leurs liqueurs, leurs fruictages,
Autre-fois vous ont fait eslever vos courages
A contempler un Dieu qui seul de rien a fait
L'emerveillable corps de ce monde parfait,
Tournez icy vos yeus, ô mortels miserables,
Que vos cueurs soient dolents, vos ames pitoiables,
Et vos sens attristez, pleurez mortels pleurez,
Remplissez l'air de cris, pleurez et souspirez...[1]

[1] *Œuvres chrestiennes*, fols. 31–2.

251

Although the meditation on nature is presented as an earlier stage in the devotional progression, it is nevertheless dwelt on with some rhetorical indulgence. Here, as elsewhere in his poetry, Habert is concerned with exploiting in a religious context all the attractions of a sensual poetry made current by the Pléiade; and, what is more important for our present discussion, he establishes a parallel between the riches of nature and the physical aspect of the Passion, so that one is hardly surprised to find that the portrait of Christ himself is painted with the elegant similes, the rich vocabulary and sound-values, and the rhetorical gestures of a Du Bellay or a Ronsard:

> Comme l'on voit un Lis par l'orage froissé
> Avoir le chef terni jusqu'en terre abaissé,
> Ou comme on voit le teint d'une rose fleurie
> Se flestrir et gaster si tost qu'elle est cueillie,
> Ainsi nostre Sauveur à la crois attaché,
> Tout pasle, et tout plombé, pend pour nostre peché.
> Voiez humains, voyez la couronne d'espine
> Qui luy perce le chef, d'où sort l'humeur pourprine
> Qui luy baigne sa chair, voyez ses pieds percez,
> Ses mains, et son costé, et ses cheveus froissez.
> Pleure inferme nature, et toy ô monde pleure,
> Pleurez Cieus, pleurez vents, pleurez tous à ceste heure
> Et toy cœur pleure aussi, si tu n'es un rocher...[1]

Neither of these poems is in narrative form: they are both static 'portraits' of Christ on the Cross. Nevertheless, they are sufficiently long to develop in full the sensual and affective aspects of the Passion. Whereas the sonnets considered in the previous chapter isolated a single theme (the crown of thorns, the quantity of blood, the travestied beauty of Christ) or compressed several episodes into a few lines, Sannazaro and Habert are unconcerned by the economy of structure. On the other hand, unlike the longer Eucharist poems of Vida or

[1] *Œuvres chrestiennes*, fol. 32. The following passage develops the familiar antithesis of the Passion in a similar tone:

> Ses mains qui ont tiré du Cahos effroiable
> Tous les quatre Elements, qui ont la terre stable
> Sur les eaus appuiee, ont souffert du tourment,
> Ses pieds qui cheminoient dessus le Firmament
> Sont clouez à la crois, ô plaies pretieuses,
> O sang trois fois sacré...

Sponde, the two Lamentations use their unconstricted space not for theological analysis or instruction but for an expansive rhetoric which makes constant and overt concessions to profane poetics. Thus they are highly accessible to an audience which would be temperamentally unsuited to any asceticism of style or of moral purpose.

It is in precisely this context that it is most profitable to consider Malherbe's *Larmes de Saint Pierre*. It first appeared in 1587, two years after Habert's religious poetry; it is derived explicitly from the Italian tradition of which Sannazaro was a principal founder; and it will become increasingly popular in the following decades, provoking a quantity of analogous poetry and no doubt influencing the conception of César de Nostredame's devotional verse. Malherbe's theme is penitence, but the *Larmes* is quite unlike the Old Testament penitential poetry of Desportes: St Peter is the penitent, and the poem treats in detail an episode in the story of the Passion, concluding with the coming of dawn on Good Friday. An elegant courtly tone is established at once with a 30-line introduction in which Malherbe rejects profane subjects and pays compliments to Henri III; thereafter, the poem proper begins on a narrative reference: 'Mais le coq a chanté'. There are not many events in the poem; nevertheless, its movement is articulated by a number of similar references: '...du Sauveur il se veid regardé...La place lui desplaist...Il part...Il chemine tousjours...Il arrive au jardin...(Il) remarque les endroits...La nuict s'en va...Le jour est desja grand'. This narrative progression provides a framework for the central affective developments, which include three speeches: the eyes of Christ 'speak' to Peter, reproaching him for his betrayal, and Peter himself has two monologues, one a kind of penitential prayer, the other a eulogy of Christ's footsteps. The highly formalised direct speech of these passages closely resembles the eloquence of Christ's silent dialogue with Mary in the devotional handbooks, particularly as the theme of love provokes a wealth of hyperbole and conceit in which the connexions with profane love-poetry are unmistakable. Malherbe's manner, like Sannazaro's and Habert's, is based on the desire to flatter the reader's palate, to solicit the tears of devotion by means of an elegiac sweetness. Hence the digression into a pathetic account of the Massacre of the Innocents, descanting on the lilies and roses of the medieval martyrs' hymns;

hence too the closing description of dawn, which disguises the distress
of Good Friday in an elegant display of rhetorical colours:

> Ce furent de beaux lis, qui mieux que la nature,
> Meslans à leur blancheur l'incarnate peinture,
> Que tira de leur sein le cousteau criminel,
> Devant que d'un hyver la tempeste et l'orage
> A leur teint delicat peussent faire dommage,
> S'en allerent fleurir au printemps eternel...
>
> L'Aurore d'une main en sortant de ses portes,
> Tient un vase de fleurs languissantes et mortes;
> Elle verse de l'autre une cruche de pleurs,
> Et d'un voile tissu de vapeur et d'orage
> Couvrant ses cheveux d'or, descouvre en son visage
> Tout ce qu'une ame sent de cruelles douleurs.[1]

The type of taste (both religious and literary) implied by this poem is
remote from that which determines Malherbe's later work, as many
critics, including Malherbe himself, have pointed out; but it is at least
equally foreign to the *Théorèmes*, and Favre's poetry is only occasionally touched by it.

None of the poems so far discussed in this section is fully and overtly
related to devotional practice proper. For such a connexion one must
turn to a poet who is less concerned with profane poetics and a courtly
audience than with systematic meditation on the life of Christ. Gabrielle
de Coignard's set of poems on the Passion deals continuously with the
progression of events from the Agony in the Garden to the Harrowing
of Hell: it also appears to be based on Granada's *Vray chemin*, since
the principal meditative developments are much the same, and there
are passages in which Granada is echoed verbally:

> Elle voyoit ses pas empraints dessus la place,
> Et son sang precieux qui luy monstroit la trace,
> Elle entendoit le bruit, et rumeur de ses gens,
> Oyoit les cliquetis des armes des sergens,
> Puis voit haut eslever les picques, et les lances,
> Qui à son pauvre cœur estoient dix mille trances...

---

[1] Malherbe, *Poésies*, ed. P. Martinon (Paris, *s.d.*), pp. 211 and 217. On this poem, see
G. Allais, *Malherbe et la poésie française* (Paris, 1891), pp. 113–39, and R. Lebègue,
'*Les Larmes de Saint-Pierre*: poème baroque', *RSH* (1949), pp. 145 ff.

The poetry of tears

Là de dueil ses flambeaux (pour l'estat languissant,
Du plus divin flambeau) vont s'entresblouyssant;
Leur bouche avoit perdu leur parole divine,
Mais les cœurs affligez parloyent en leur poitrine.[1]

Gabrielle has here reorientated the presentation of her material, sub-
ordinating the narrative details to Mary's discovery of Christ's tracks
and subsequently to her emotional reactions; she also omits some of
Granada's references to light and noise. However, this may be partly
due to the demands of her verse-form (her skill as a poet is somewhat
uneven, as the blurred image of the *flambeaux* also suggests); and elsewhere she dwells at length on the visual scene and on the physical
actions of the participants. Old Testament figures are frequently adduced
to demonstrate the significance of the scene envisaged, and there are
passages in which the theological or moral 'message' is brought out,
but this analytic aspect is secondary in the overall economy of the
work. In particular, the descent from the Cross, the Pietà and the
embalming are described so carefully that they become the focal point
of the whole meditation, a fact which is not without its significance
when one remembers that similar scenes will capture the imagination
of César de Nostredame.[2]

Gabrielle's interest in description and narration is paralleled by her
evident inclination towards pathetic emotion. Her representation of
the silent dialogue between Christ and Mary is far more extensive than
Granada's; and the sufferings and lamentations of the Virgin absorb
much of her attention throughout the sequence, as is suggested by the
fact that she devotes a whole section to the *Complainte de la Vierge*.
From the beginning of the sequence, the 'âme amoureuse' of the meditator is exhorted to affective contemplation and thence to tears:

Ha! combien de douleurs, d'angoisses, et travaux
Enduroit le Seigneur pour effacer nos maux.
Mon ame esleve toy, voy son sacre (*sic*) visage,
Qui chasse de ton cœur tout tenebreux nuage,

---

[1] *Œuvres chrestiennes*, pp. 181–2 (from the *Discours sur la Passion*). See above, p. 244.
See also *ibid.* pp. 171, 172–3, 184–5, which are comparable with Granada, *Le Vray
chemin*, fol. 45, and with the passages referred to above, pp. 35 and 31 respectively.
Compare also the extract given below in the Appendix with *Le Vray chemin*, fols. 66–70
(esp. fols. 67, 'Je ne te verray...', to 68,'...consoler'; 68, 'Ay-je peché...', to 69,
'...benissent avec eux').
[2] See below, Appendix, pp. 312–19; also pp. 327–8.

Contemple la clairté, et lumiere des cieux,
Qui donne au clair soleil son lustre gracieux,
Ces beaux yeux amoureux, et sa face admirée
Estre pour nos pechez toute deffigurée,
Et le sang ruissellant sur les herbes, et fleurs
Abondamment meslé du crystal de ses pleurs.
  Quel sentiment as tu ô mon ame assoupie,
Voyant souffrir ton Dieu lumiere de ta vie?
Car si en cest endroit tu n'as compassion,
De l'extreme douleur de son affliction:
Si luy suant le sang pour laver ton offence,
Tu n'espans de tes yeux larmes en abondance,
Je pense que ton cœur est plus dur que le fer...[1]

Furthermore, as will already be apparent from this passage, the blood and tears of Christ are readily associated with decorative stylistic effects, involving the grass and flowers of the surrounding landscape.[2] Thus the emotional effect of the meditation is on such occasions defined in a special way: Gabrielle is showing, in embryo, a taste for *mignardise*, for a mingling of elegiac emotion with a natural setting full of grace and sweetness. She seldom exploits this mode to the full: her style suggests a sober, if not hostile, attitude to profane poetics. Nevertheless, there is at least one passage—an extension of the Pietà—in which she makes a wholly unambiguous use of the 'style doux-coulant' so popular with admirers of the Pléiade, associating it once more with a highly affective and feminine devotion.[3] Here the hyperbolical description of the tears of the Virgin and her companions, the extended simile, the diminutives (*avettes*, *fleurettes*), the constant emphasis on *douceur* (*gracieux*, *doucement*, *douceur*, *douces*), compose a mood in which the outraged body of Christ is contemplated not for moral or theological profit, but for the sake of the emotional indulgence,

---

[1] *Œuvres chrestiennes*, pp. 158–9. This passage is from the Gethsemane meditation, which opens Gabrielle's Passion cycle.

[2] See also, for example, *ibid.* p. 162:

> ...Estant ceste peau saincte en cent pars deschirée,
> Dont le sang ruisseloit sur l'herbe colorée...
> ...la clarté mesme a perdu sa lumiere,
> La gloire est tourmentée, et l'honneur despouillé,
> Et...ce beau miroir de larmes est souillé:
> La fontaine d'amour de sang est colourée,
> Et la mesme beauté y est deffigurée.

[3] See below, Appendix, p. 317.

and indeed the delight, of the reader. Thus, although she is isolated (geographically at least) from the poetic taste implied by Malherbe's *Larmes*, and although she has evident affiliations with the main current of devotional practice, Gabrielle nevertheless prefers a devotional style which is far from ascetic, and in which a certain ambiguity of emotional experience is, no doubt unconsciously, maintained.

When Gabrielle de Coignard's poems were published (posthumously), Odet de La Noue had just produced his *Poésies chrestiennes*. Among these is a *Discours meditatif sur la semaine de Pasques* which, as its title suggests, is an extended and continuous meditation on the Passion.[1] Indeed, it ranges more widely, prefacing the Passion meditation proper with an account of the Fall and then of the Incarnation. The reasons for this are probably associated with La Noue's Calvinism: the juxtaposition of the Fall and the Redemption stresses the relationship between man's corruption and Christ's gratuitous sacrifice (although the poem does not make this point explicitly). La Noue's account of the Passion follows the same pattern as that of contemporary Catholic poetry, although his sober, masculine approach tends to exclude extremes of pathos, no reference being made to the physical beauty of Christ. On the other hand, at moments of crisis, his poetry assumes a rhetorical richness which can scarcely be dissociated from profane rhetoric, even if it is not exactly *doux-coulant*.[2] Indeed, it is interesting to notice that he here combines a declamatory lamentation, not unlike that of the *oraison funèbre*, with the aggressive tone of the sermon ('Mais quoy?...Quoy donc? Pleurerons-nous?...'). Such poetry proves above all that the *genre* of narrative and affective Passion poetry was already widely diffused in the early 1590s, widely enough to determine, in part at least, the manner of a Protestant poet.

When the anthologies begin to appear at the end of the century, the

---

[1] This poem begins with an interesting comment on meditation in general (*Poésies chrestiennes*, p. 250):

> Si ne faut-il croupir tousjours en mesme ordure,
> Mais au moins quelquefois forçant nostre nature,
> Mediter en ce Dieu qui est nostre secours,
> Puis que nous ne pouvons le faire tous les jours.

To meditate on God is to 'force one's nature', since man's nature is totally corrupt: hence it cannot be a regular daily exercise, as the Catholic teachers recommend; and the subsequent reference to the Fall reinforces this point.

[2] See below, Appendix, pp. 319–21. For the use of profane rhetoric by Calvinist poets, see above, pp. 78–9.

success of Malherbe's *Larmes* is attested not only by their frequent publication, but also by the efforts of minor poets to follow in Malherbe's footsteps: as we saw earlier, the Valagre anthology of 1602 prints a group of tear-poems together with Malherbe's own. Of these, at least two are based explicitly on Italian models: *Les Larmes de Jesus-Christ, imitation de T. Tasse* by Doudemare, and *Les Pleurs de la Vierge, mesme imitation*. Tasso's poems have much the same demonstrative and emotive impact as, say, Gabrielle de Coignard's, as in this 'Pietà' from *Les Pleurs*:

> Ce corps qu'elle remire en l'œil de sa pensee
> Sur son foible giron paslement estendu,
> Cette main qu'elle tient cruellement percee,
> Ce bras vuide de sang, ains tout sanglant rendu,
> Ce front encores ceint du bandeau qui l'oppresse,
> Et ces deux pieds outrez, et ce coup en ce flanc,
> Tirent ores ses pleurs avec plus de destresse
> Que l'espine et les cloux ne tirerent leur sang.[1]

The other poems in the group are all concerned with related themes: they include a long penitential contemplation of the Passion entitled *Les Larmes de la Magdaleine*, together with three *Sonnets d'elle mesme*; a series of *stances* on *la saincte Croix* and another on *le jour de la Passion* (the latter by Crampon); and the *Larmes* of one M.D.I. This last poem indicates how far the habits of devotion had been assimilated by the aristocracy, since it consists of a defence of penitential weeping placed in the mouth of a duke who is mortifying himself in a desert wilderness. The poem ends thus:

> Ainsi pleignoit au creux d'une grote sauvage
> Les beaux lis de son sein de cailloux meurtrissant,
> Un Duc qui desireux du celeste heritage
> Alloit les faits de Dieu jour et nuict benissant.   (p. 424.)

The image is no doubt hyperbolical, like the whole setting of the poem, and is based on the 'solitude' *topos* which is rapidly becoming popular in a devotional context;[2] nevertheless it is important that the second

---

[1] *Les Cantiques du Sieur de Valagre . . . En cette dernière edition ont esté adjoustées les Larmes de Jesus Christ, les Pleurs de la Vierge, les Larmes de S. Pierre, de la Magdeleine, et autres œuvres chrestiennes* (Rouen, 1602), p. 339. The repeated demonstratives are also reminiscent of the pseudo-Augustine meditation in Tamisier's paraphrase (see above, pp. 53–4).

[2] See also the *Stances sur la saincte Croix, ibid.* pp. 341–3. For an early Calvinist use of this theme, see above, pp. 76–7; and for a general study in a Spanish context, see K. Vossler, *Poesie der Einsamkeit in Spanien*, 3 vols. (Munich, 1935–8).

line, with its decorative pathos, should be applied not to Christ himself or to a martyr, but to a contemporary, and presumably a layman.[1] The ramifications of the pattern established in this chapter are wide; and most of them imply a deliberate exploitation of the area in which profane and sacred overlap, both psychologically and stylistically. The pattern naturally includes a wealth of sonnets, and, although we are here concerned chiefly with the more generous *stances* and couplet forms, it will be relevant to quote two characteristic examples of sonnets from different settings. The first is the Magdalene sonnet of Desportes (Michiels no. 15, p. 508):

> De foy, d'espoir, d'amour et de douleur comblée
> Celle que les pecheurs doivent tous imiter,
> O Seigneur! vint ce jour à tes piés se jetter,
> Peu craignant le mespris de toute une assemblée.
> Ses yeux, sources de feu, d'où l'Amour à l'emblée
> Souloit dedans les cœurs tant de traits blueter,

---

[1] It seems likely that 'M.D.I.' could stand for 'Monsieur de Joyeuse', i.e. Henri or Frère Ange de Joyeuse, the *mignon* turned Capuchin (see above, pp. 10, 12 n. 1). Having in 1592 obtained dispensation from his brother François, Cardinal and Archbishop of Toulouse, to return to public life, Henri 'repented' in 1600 and entered holy orders once again. His sermons of the same year, preached at Paris, seem to have made a considerable stir, which may explain the existence of the *Larmes*. The impact of one such sermon is recorded in a somewhat different mood by d'Aubigné's Baron de Fæneste: '... sur tout je fus conberti par un sermon que fit Pere Ange à Paris, le Judi-Asolu: il conta la Passion tant pitusement que je ne pus pas me tenir de plorer, ou de pitié, ou pource que je regardois attentiuement les yeux chassius de la bielle de Mersec' (*ed. cit.* vol. II, p. 589).

The following chapter consists of a parody of this sermon, in which a mock-courtly duel between Satan and Christ becomes a full-scale war (the Passion, interlarded with allusions to the wars of religion). The secular, aristocratic and military treatment of the theme satirises the exploits of 'Pere Ange' as a courtier and a participant in the last stages of the civil wars: according to the preacher, Christ has 'le courage d'un Gentilhomme de bonne maison' (p. 595). The conclusion of the sermon alludes to the devotional excesses of the Capuchin: Ange emphasizes the 'douleurs de la Passion' by comparing them with every other kind of suffering, rolls his eyes, falls into ecstatic trances, and eventually, 'transporté de fureur', nearly strangles himself with his Friar's cord. Similarly, in the preceding chapter, there is an amusing anecdote about a sermon of Panigarola (not without its relevance for the ambiguities of the 'poetry of tears'): '... Mettez en ce rang Panigarole, commençant par ces mots: *C'est pour vous, belle, que je meurs,* en appliquant ses yeux sur une galande, de l'amour de laquelle il estoit embrené et descrié partout. Il l'avoit menacee de lui faire cet affront. Le peuple tout estonné de cette entree, se rasseura quand, aprés pauses et souspirs, ce bon Docteur suivit: *dit nostre Seigneur à son Eglise*' (p. 590).

This whole section of the *Avantures du Baron de Fæneste* is interesting for the comparisons it makes between Catholic and Protestant sermon technique (especially on the use of allegory and 'fables', and the representation of the Passion: see pp. 589–90, 598).

Changez en source d'eau, ne font que degouter
L'amertume et l'ennuy de son ame troublée.
De ses pleurs, ô Seigneur! tes piés elle arrosa,
Les parfuma d'odeurs, les seicha, les baisa,
De sa nouvelle amour monstrant la vehemence.
O bien-heureuse femme! ô Dieu tousjours clement!
O pleur! ô cœur heureux! qui n'eut pas seulement
Pardon de son erreur, mais en eut recompense.

This, like most of Desportes's religious sonnets, is close to Italian models; and no doubt partly because of this influence, it uses the hyperbole of profane love in a devotional context, without any sense of a forced 'conversion': the transition from one register to another is an easy one.[1] The same is true of a sonnet by Chasteuil, which, as a recent article has shown, is a revised version of a profane love-sonnet by the same author:

Douces larmes, mais bien amoureuses perlettes,
Qui goutte à goutte, aux pieds du Seigneur arrivez,
Rozee pure et chaste, en roulant vous lavez,
Le soustien Eternel, des celestes fleurettes,
N'espargnez ce Printemps, vous sçavez ondelettes,
Qu'un sainct Amour y loge et que vous l'estuvez
Que pour vous il travaille, ainsi que vous pleuvez,
Et qu'il trempe en voz eaux, ses divines sagettes.
Clers flots, par vostre course et voz moittes replys,
En terre vous lechez, les violiers, les lys,
Qui relevent au Ciel, et vous, et voz fontaines.
Pour rejaillir en haut vous ruissellez icy,
Trainez avecques vous, le pur sang de mes vaines:
Afin qu'avecques vous, mon Ame y coure aussi.[2]

Here the *mignardise* of tears and flowers is taken so far, and the final prayer for identification so little suggests devotional contrition, that Desportes's sonnet seems almost austere in retrospect: Desportes clearly distinguishes the two forms of love, and introduces his poem with a line ('Celle que les pecheurs doivent tous imiter') which is close to moral exhortation, whereas Chasteuil indulges in the decorative abundance of the tears, and scarcely even implies the conversion of

---

[1] See above, p. 139, for the religious use of 'Petrarchan' *topoi* by Béroalde de Verville.
[2] *Imitation des Pseaumes de la pénitence Royalle* (Paris, 1597), p. 26. The article referred to is by R. Braunschweig, 'Une Source profane de la "Sainte Pécheresse"', *BHR*, 27 (1966), pp. 670–1.

Mary Magdalene. Nevertheless, the affiliation between the two sonnets is clear, and thus their differences illustrate perfectly the development of taste which will reach its first climax in the poetry of César de Nostredame.

Such poems bring up the whole question of 'conversion' in the context of the poetic love-tradition. The vernacular lyric, from its very origins, was always susceptible to changes of register: the concept of the worship and service of a mortal woman has religious overtones which make the transference from human to divine, from the courtly *dame* to Our Lady, a quite natural and even an instinctive one for the medieval poet. Indeed, one can scarcely speak of 'conversion' in such cases, unless one is thinking of the conscious movement in favour of a poetry of the Virgin Mary in the post-Albigensian era. With the coming of the Counter-Reformation, there are certainly examples of a 'forced' conversion: Malipiero's revision of Petrarch's *Canzoniere* is one of the most outstanding. But even these presuppose a religious element in the profane love-lyric, for otherwise conversion would be impossible; and the issues are seldom as clear-cut as they are with Malipiero. Jacques de Billy's nineteenth *sonnet spirituel* contains the line 'Brusle, brusle mon cœur, qui transist de froidure'; one suspects that Vianey might have labelled this line 'Petrarchan', but Billy supplies his source: 'Et ceste oraison est tiree du livre des Confessions de Sainct Augustin. Le Latin est tel, "O amor qui semper ardes, et nunquam extingueris, charitas, Deus meus, accende me".' Billy has introduced an antithesis into his poem, and this may be due to the influence of current poetic practice, but the image, even in its antithetical form, is so fundamental, so archetypal, that it could belong to any tradition, literary or religious. The 'shipwreck' image is ubiquitous in just the same way. Billy uses it in what looks like a Petrarchan manner, only to tell us that he has borrowed it from Lactantius (sonnet 5); and Desportes restores it to the context of the Flood:

> Voyant tant de grands flots et de vents s'eslever
> Pour submerger ma barque errante et passagere,
> Eussé-je, ô souverain! comme le second pere,
> Au naufrage du monde, une arche à me sauver![1]

Therefore if Desportes (or Malherbe, or Chasteuil) uses some of his profane equipment in his religious poetry, it is possible that he is

---

[1] Ed. Michiels, p. 505. See also the sonnet by Habert quoted above, p. 139.

deliberately using the universality of literary tradition rather than superficially 'twisting' the Petrarchan mode.

This area of ambiguity is further illustrated by the history of the 'O vos omnes' *topos* from Jeremiah. Dante, in the *Vita nuova*, uses it in the context of profane love, although he is clearly concerned with stressing the religious quality of his love-experience:

> O voi, che per la via d'Amor passate,
> attendete, e guardate
> s'elli è dolore alcun, quanto 'l mio, grave...

Questo sonetto ha due parti principali: chè nella prima intendo chiamare li fedeli d'amore per quelle parole di Geremia profeta che dicono: 'O vos omnes qui transitis per viam, attendite et videte, si est dolor sicut dolor meus'.[1]

The same *topos* appears in Benivieni's *Stanze in passione Domini*:

> O voi che per la via d'amor passate
> Volgete priego gli occhi, e 'l mio dolore
> Vedete il mio tormento, e contemplate
> S'in terra mai alcun ne fù maggiore.
> Vedi i miei pie, vedi le man forate;
> Le man figliuolo e i pie del tuo Signore.
> Vedi il lacero petto, e laureo crine,
> Trasfisso il capo di pungenti spine.[2]

Not only has the original apostrophe of Jeremiah been transposed into what is virtually a 'composition' of the Passion (which it traditionally prophesies); the word *amor* has also been inserted, so that the reader is consciously invited to make the connexion between this adaptation and Dante's. Thus, too, Crampon's *Stances sur le jour de la Passion*, where the phrase 'les tourmens de la rage ancienne' presumably refers to the age-old passion of love:

> Vous qui d'un prompt esprit par ce monde passez,
> Et sçavez les toumens de la rage ancienne,
> Considerez cecy, pensez et repensez
> S'il fust oncques douleur comparable à la sienne.[3]

[1] *La Vita Nuova*, ed. M. Barbi (Florence, 1932), pp. 23, 25.
[2] Published in *Rime spirituali*, fol. 186. For Benivieni's connexion with Florentine Neoplatonism and with the teaching of Savonarola, see V. Rossi, *Il Quattrocento* (Milan, 1964), pp. 373–4. Benivieni also wrote a poem in praise of Dante and the *Divine Comedy* and a dialogue on the *Inferno*.
[3] Valagre anthology, p. 351. See also the extract from Motin's *Méditation sur un Crucifix mourant* published in Rousset's *Anthologie*, vol. II, p. 140.

The poetry of tears

And in the sonnet of the *Théorèmes* which stresses love as the motive of the Passion (III, 20), La Ceppède uses the same *topos* in a way which suggests a deliberate invocation of several parallel traditions, including the courtly and the romanesque:

> Belle pour qui ce beau meurt en vous bien-aimant
> Voyez s'il fut jamais un si cruel supplice,
> Voyez s'il fut jamais un si parfait Amant.
>
> (*Théorèmes*, p. 386.)

The starting-point of this sonnet, the affective relationship between the soul (or the Church) and Christ, implies, as we saw earlier, a mystical tradition which owes a great deal to the Song of Solomon, both in its themes and in its imagery. On the authority of this book, interpreted of course in an allegorical sense, the religious poet could safely indulge in a language of great richness and sensuality, particularly as its exploitation had been central to the works of many of the medieval mystics; the fact that it was so often paraphrased in the later sixteenth century is surely due in part to this fortunate coincidence of literary potentiality with religious acceptability. Poets and writers of all kinds, both Catholic and Protestant, Neo-Latin and French, rivalled one another in versions which were more often than not accompanied by explanations, in prose or verse, of the allegory. Chassignet provided an *Allegorie des amours de Christ et de l'Eglise* with his *Amours de Salomon et Sulamite*; Bèze's Neo-Latin paraphrase and commentary were countered by Génébrard's *Canticum canticorum versibus et commentariis illustratum adversus trochaicam Theodori Beʒae Paraphrasim.*[1] As one might expect, the 'profane' associations of the tradition are particularly evident in the versions of poets like Belleau and Chassignet, who are on the whole less concerned with theology and polemics; and the style adopted by such poets and their followers was inevitably the Pléiade's 'style doux-coulant', with its intimate pastoral atmosphere. Indeed, when paraphrased by Belleau into this style, the Song of Solomon reads very much like the *Continuation des amours*:

> . . . tant est lisse et douillette
> La mollette rondeur de sa peau tendrelette.

[1] T. de Bèze, *Canticum canticorum Salomonis, Latinis versibus expressum* (*s.l.*, 1584). Génébrard's work was published at Paris in 1585. For another Calvinist version of the Song of Solomon, see Poupo's *Muse chrestienne*, Bk. III, pp. 11–43. See also Marin Le Saulx, above, pp. 71–2.

> Le miel frais espuré des ruchettes gaufrees,
> Distile, savoureux, de tes levres sucrees.
> Sous ta langue mignarde un ruisseau doucelet
> S'escoule gracieux et de manne, et de laict.[1]

Chassignet, who is usually associated with a more sombre kind of poetry, uses precisely the same manner in his *Amours de Salomon et Sulamite*:

> M'amie, tes beaus yeus, charbons d'Amour, ressemblent
> A ceus des pigeonneaus qui s'entre-mignotantz
> Se vont bec contre bec doucement baisotantz.
> Car ilz ont tant d'attraitz qu'a tous le cœur ilz emblent.
>
> Il a parlé a moi: Ça, dit il, ma mignonne.
> Il est Jour, il est jour, il se faut eveiller.
> Maintenant est passé le tems de sommeiller.[2]

In this way, the potentialities of a style developed in a profane context are released into vernacular devotion; and once again, Biblical paraphrase has been the mediator. Clearly, the implications of such a transference are considerable in the light of the shift in literary and devotional taste outlined above: the occasional *mignardise* of Gabrielle de Coignard, the sugary tears of Chasteuil's Magdalene, the whole mood of this poetry of emotion and pathetic description, must surely owe something to Belleau, if not to Chassignet, whose version is later and seems to have remained unpublished.

There is at all events a convergence of intentions here which will be fundamental to a persistent current of French poetry and prose in the earlier seventeenth century. One will find Richeome, in his *Peinture spirituelle*, describing a fly, and other insects, with such close attention and with such an evident taste for diminutives of the *jambettes* order that the influence of Belleau's (and Ronsard's) *blasons* of the 1550s and

---

[1] R. Belleau, *Eclogues sacrees, prises du Cantique des Cantiques*, published with the *Amours et nouveaux eschanges* (Paris, 1576), fols. 81, 82.

[2] J.-B. Chassignet, *Œuvres sacrez* (MS.), fols. 116, 118. At least two other mystical poems by Chassignet were enriched by importations from the Song of Solomon: *De la Felicité de l'ame sainte se partant de ce lieu* (*Mespris*, pp. 253–5) and *Le Desir qu'a l'Ame de parvenir en la Supreme Cité de Hierusalem* (*ibid.* pp. 136–9). The popularity of such poetry was of course not confined to France: see, for example, Bernardo Tasso's 'Odi dal cielo...' (*Rime spirituali*, fols. 6–9), especially the development beginning 'Deh vieni sposa mia...' (fol. 7); and the poetry of St John of the Cross, although here the connexions with the source are less direct.

1560s cannot be discounted;[1] and the devotional application of this mode was subsequently carried so far that Bremond has a whole section on what he calls *sucreries dévotes*. Surprisingly, it is a Carthusian, Polycarpe de La Rivière, whom Bremond chooses as his chief example: this is a far cry from the severity of the Cologne Charterhouse. In a passage from *Le Mystère sacré de notre rédemption*, Polycarpe addresses thus the sweet tears of devotion, imagining them as bees: 'Vous lécherez les perlettes rosines et musserez dans vos tendres cuissettes, les douceurs confites de nectar et de miel que l'amour y fait naître, que les grâces y distillent en fraîche rosée et que les Zéphirs pillotants changent en soupirs pour embaumer notre air!'[2] *Le Mystère sacré* appeared in 1621; but among his *sucreries*, Bremond also mentions *L'Antidotaire sacré* of Nicolas Salicète which was published as early as 1607. Likewise in poetry: the love of *minutiae* which one finds in the Jesuit 'encyclopaedists' (Richeome and Binet) is continued from Belleau through Chasteuil and César de Nostredame to poets like the Jesuit Jean de Bussières, whose *Descriptions poétiques* appeared in 1649, the Capuchin Martial de Brives, and Pierre Perrin, author of a collection called *Divers insectes*.[3]

The parallel made earlier between the devotional literature of this period and that of Marguerite de Navarre and her circle will by now be seen to have its limitations. In the *Heptaméron*, Marguerite makes full allowance for the limitations of human nature: divine love must be preceded by human love. Nevertheless, her hierarchy of values is perfectly clear, and her poetry—in particular *Les Prisons*—states unambiguously the problems of the soul's progress towards the love of God. By contrast, certain of the devotional writers of the later period

[1] See Bremond, *Humanisme dévot*, p. 39. Bremond also summarises a passage from Richeome's *Académie d'Honneur* in which the Pléiade's recommendation to use a rich vocabulary ('epithetes non oysifz'), and more especially *métier* words, is clearly implied (*ibid.* pp. 64–5).

[2] *Ibid.* p. 327. Like the *romans dévots* of Camus, *Le Mystère sacré* illustrates the way in which the tendencies of our period were later developed.

[3] Paris, 1645. For Perrin's *Papillon*, see Rousset's *Anthologie*, vol. 1, pp. 153–4. Rousset also includes extracts from Jean de Bussières and Martial de Brives. On the whole question of 'conversion', in the context both of love and of the description of the world, see the suggestive article of A. J. Steele, 'Conversions', in *CAEF*, 10 (1958), pp. 69 ff. For the tradition of 'meditation on the creatures' and its application in the context of English poetry, see Martz, *The Poetry of Meditation*, pp. 67 and 151–2, and Ruth C. Wallerstein, *Studies in Seventeenth-Century Poetic* (Madison, 1950), especially ch. 8. Miss Wallerstein stresses the relevance of the Song of Solomon to the history of the tradition.

are all too ready to equivocate, to flatter the need for emotional stimulus. The cult of the Magdalene may at times lead to casuistry; and the tears of penitence are inclined to become 'douces larmes, mais bien amoureuses perlettes', the tears of pleasure.

CESAR DE NOSTREDAME: POET AND PAINTER

Like Favre, La Ceppède, and many other provincial poets, César de Nostredame began to publish his poetry relatively late in life: since he was born in 1555, he was fifty when his first works of substance left the presses. He was a provincial poet in that his main interests and activities were centred in Provence; however, as he was the son of the famous Michel Nostradamus, it seems likely that he had contacts at court, and the acquaintance with Malherbe which he shared with the other Aixois writers could have given such connexions a poetic bias. In many respects, his work is a natural sequel to the *Larmes* of Malherbe and the tear-poetry of the Valagre anthology; it presents in an extreme form most of the themes and stylistic habits so far considered in this chapter, and it throws light on a number of important topics, including the relationship between devotional poetry and painting.

Among César's earliest published work is a group of eight *Cantiques a la sacrée Nativité du Sauveur du monde*, and these provide a good introduction to his devotional manner. They are in fact elaborate carols, related to the popular *noël* as well as to the Renaissance *ode*: the first has a slightly Bacchic refrain ('Iô pœan Evoé / Iô CHRIST Noé Noé'), while the refrain of the eighth ('. . . la belle Estoille qui passe / En clarté les clartés des cieux') is varied in *ballade* style to fit the syntax of each stanza; one is reminded, superficially at least, of Jean Loys's combination of medieval and Renaissance forms. The prevailing tone is that of an ingenuous pastoral: the second and fifth *cantiques* are in the form of dialogues between the two shepherds Janot and Perrot, and the presence of the shepherds throughout, with their milk and apples, induces a mood into which the Virgin, 'la pucelle clere et brunette', and her son, 'Dieu beau petit garson tout neuf', fit quite naturally.[1] The antithesis between power and infancy which is so popular a theme both in the

---

[1] The first *cantique* is reproduced below, Appendix, pp. 321–4, and will be used as the principal example of César's Nativity poetry. See stanzas 7–8 for an illustration of the pastoral tone. The *Cantiques* appear in the *Rimes spirituelles* (dedic. dated 1607).

devotional handbooks and in other Nativity poetry, is submerged in this pastoral sweetness:

> Lors ce miracle des miracles,
> Ceste image de la beauté,
> Duquel ont parlé tant d'oracles,
> Et tant de Prophetes chanté,
> Avec sa main tendre et rosine,
> Qui coule une manne' Ambrosine,
> Et qui la tempeste applanit,
> Reçevant leurs dons les benit. . .

Indeed, the analytic or reflective element of the *cantiques* is limited to a simple enumeration of the traditional symbols of the Virgin, or to a decorative speech by Mary herself on her part in the plan for salvation.[1]

However, if César is aiming at a naïve and childlike effect, his style is scarcely ingenuous: there is a calculated rhetorical richness in all these poems which is a long way from the simple piety of the *noël*. The first five stanzas of the first *cantique* (some sixty lines, excluding the refrain) contain only four brief main clauses: the remainder consists of ample subordinate clauses which have a primarily decorative function. In particular, César embroiders the image of the Virgin with repetitive and digressive descriptions of cosmic scenery, justified first by the nocturnal setting of the Nativity and then by the Virgin's own description of Creation in connexion with her 'predestination'. These descriptions rely heavily on rich rhymes, elevated vocabulary, circumlocution ('du vague Palais des oiseaux', 'la pesante machine'), and quasi-pagan reference ('l'astre Roy qu'elle adore', 'Ains que ces geantes chenues...'); but in order to harmonise his introduction with the ensuing pastoral atmosphere, César lightens the tone with an element of *mignardise* ('brunette', 'de cent cloux d'or... / Brillants comme petits crayons'). Thus the opening image of the moon, in a chariot of pearl and crystal, accompanied by 'Les petits Amours du Ciel' singing 'd'une voix de miel' announces the 'Mille petits Amours' who dance round the Christchild in stanza 7, the 'drapellets' and 'pieds potelets' of stanza 8, the 'jambelettes' of stanza 10, and the image of dawn (compared with Christ himself) which concludes the poem. It is illuminating to set the *cantique* as a whole next to Malherbe's *Larmes*, which, while more

[1] *Ibid.* stanzas 3–5; and *Rimes spirituelles*, pp. 40–1 (2nd *cant.*).

measured in cadence and less sentimental in tone, digresses both on youthful innocence and on the coming of dawn.

There is no doubt, I think, that this poem is designed to make an emotive impact which is largely dependent on visual evocation. It is as if César had combined two paintings of the Nativity. In the first, the Virgin in glory, with the world as her footstool, appears to the shepherds: she is surrounded by the jewel-like moon and stars which are reflected in the 'raiz precieux' of her eyes and face. In the second, Christ is lying in the manger, blessing with outstretched hand the shepherds who have offered their gifts; and here the portrait is done in the minutest detail. No doubt César is following the stock procedure of *descriptio* with its attendant images of snow, ivory, gold and milk;[1]

---

[1] See also the third *cantique* (*Rimes spirituelles*, p. 47):

> Voyla son poil, qui se refrise
> En mil anneaux chastains et blonds,
> A qui cede l'or, que l'on prise
> Dans Pactole aux riches sablons;
> Voila son œil, voyla sa bouche,
> Ou l'Aube se leve et se couche.

Likewise the sixth (p. 63):

> Car son poil d'or plus mol que laine
> Son front cler sans creux net et lis
> La vermeillette et blanche plaine
> De son tainct de rose et de lis,
> Son nés droict, sa petite bouche
> Entre ses yeux riants et verts,
> Font asses voir que c'est la couche
> Du Sauveur de tout l'univers.

And the eighth (p. 69):

> La perle, l'albastre, l'ivoire,
> La neige, la rose, et le lis,
> Dont la blancheur fait tant de gloire
> Pres de son blanc restent faillis...

César's Nativity poetry may be compared with Verville's *Hymne sur la nativité de nostre Seigneur et Sauveur Jesus Christ* (published with *Les Tenebres* (Paris, 1599), pp. 22–5), which combines a lengthy antithetical development with elements of narration and description; Verville, too, uses both *mignardise* and pastoral allusion:

> Ses douilletz petitz bras foibles en apparence,
> Sont les deux mesmes bras dont les cieux il voutoit...
> Il pleure envelopé de pauvres bandelettes,
> De la creche tu l'ois souspirer tendrement...
> Ses petitz yeux coulans en larmes arondies,
> Sont les sources des feus qui luysent dans les Cieux...

nevertheless, the exact position of Christ's arms and legs is indicated, and the brightness of his body is such that there is no shadow: the art of painting is 'vaincu' because it is only through shading and variation of tone that the painter can give an impression of depth and perspective. Most of César's other devotional poems are concerned with the Passion and its sequel, and in keeping with the graver subjects the octosyllabic metre of the *cantiques* lengthens into decasyllabic or alexandrine lines. In each of these poems, the Passion is contemplated in terms of one of the participants, Dymas the 'bon larron', the Virgin Mary, or Mary Magdalene. The choice of Dymas is unconventional, but he is used—just as St Peter and the penitent Magdalene are used by other poets—to demonstrate in dramatic and concrete terms the purifying effect of Christ's sacrifice on the penitent's soul. Indeed, Dymas is a model *dévot*, as well as a model penitent: his conversion is brought about by meditation, a painful inner conflict, which finally draws out the supreme prayer to a Christ present in the flesh:

> Dymas tout remply d'ombre en ceste aspre bataille
> Tire un profond souspir du fond de son entraille,
> Sa voix n'est rien que feu, toute casse d'Amour
> Si que d'une parole enflammée il s'escrie
> Souvenés-vous de moy ô Seigneur je vous prie
> Lors que vous monterés au celeste sejour.[1]

This all-consuming devotional fire and the violent emotion that goes with it appear again later in the poem, leading up to the absolution itself; the tone here is almost mystical:

> La s'arrestent à coup ses plaintes desbondées,
> La les veines du cœur desbordant par ondées
> Interrompirent l'air et casserent sa voix. . .
>
> Sa face est toute en flamme et sa bouche allumée
> Exhalle et pousse hors une sombre fumée,
> Sa voix ne sonne plus, ny ses propos bruslans,
> Son Estomac pressé d'une douleur espesse

> Possible un des bergers qui vint à l'heure mesme
> Que naissoit icy bas ce petit tout puissant,
> Sainctement transporté de cette joye extreme,
> Disoit sur son flageol l'air de semblable accent.

[1] *Dymas, ou le Bon Larron, dedié à son Altesse Serenissime de Lorraine* (Toulouse, 1606), p. 9.

Sans intervalle' aucun se rehausse et s'abbaisse,
Et violante l'air de souspirs violans.

Un grand brazier d'Amour dans son Ame s'attise,
Son desir satisfaict, et son sang le baptise,
Sa croix destruit sa mort, sa foy le rend sauvé... (p. 22.)

Thus Dymas is in a sense the first Christian martyr, the first to receive
the baptism of blood; at the same time his salvation illustrates the
moment at which the self-affliction of the penitent results in an out-
pouring of the affections.

This mimesis of an essentially austere and painful emotion seems far
removed at first sight from the sweetness of the Nativity poems:
Dymas is introduced by a sonnet in which all the grim emblems of the
Passion are compressed into a single rhetorical gesture.[1] Nevertheless
the two contrasting themes of love balance one another; and the connexion is made clear by a stanza which recalls the lost beauty of Christ
in terms of the elegiac *ubi sunt*:

Ou sont ces beaux cheveux qui pendans sus l'oreille
Vagoint de couleur brune et vivement pareille,
Puis se frisoient en nœuds et se changeoient en or,
Ou comme Amours naissans avec des aisles blondes
Les Anges volletoint et nageoint dans ces ondes
Pour separer en deux un si divin thresor. (p. 30.)

A direct source for this poem (and indeed for most of César's poetry)
might be difficult to find. However, the introductory sonnet serves as
a general 'composition', to be elaborated in the course of the poem:
after the conversion of Dymas, the demonstrative 'voyés' and 'oyés'
are used to realise the suffering of Christ himself:

Voyés comme pressé du torment qui le charge,
Au chef, aux mains, aux pieds, sur sa vermeille targe
Dans les pleurs de sa mere il augmante son dueil...

Oyés comm'il se plaint, et s'escrie à son Pere
De ce qu'il l'abandonne en tant de Vitupere
Et samble luy boucher les fenestres du Ciel.
Voyés, ô cruauté, comm'une main profane
Ayant mis une esponge au fin bout d'une canne
Porte à sa saincte bouche et la suye et le fiel. (pp. 27–8.)

[1] See below, Appendix, pp. 324–5.

Similarly, when the problems posed by the episode are briefly analysed, the familiar question and answer technique is brought into play:

> Mais comment, ô grand Juge, et comment ô grand Prestre
> Regardés vous Symon et desdaignés le traistre,
> Delivrés un Brigand et laissés l'autre aux fers?
> L'un peche de foiblesse, et l'autre de malice,
> L'un hume tous les Cieux dedans vostre calice,
> L'autre au mesme calice avalle les Enfers. (pp. 24–5.)

Thus it seems likely that César is consciously phrasing his poetry in terms of the orthodox devotional tradition, while adapting it to his own sensibility and to that of his age.

Many of the same features reappear in *La Marie dolente*, and here the overall structure of the poem is particularly clear. After a rhetorical introduction, there is a long composition section in which the crucified Christ is described in detail, with the usual contrast between his beauty and the barbarity of the torture:

> ...et ses mains et ses plantes
> (O cruauté barbare) estoint toutes sanglantes,
> Et son chef, et son front, et son corps et son flanc,
> Et sa Croix et ses cloux nageoint parmy le sang.[1]

The description of Christ is followed by a short account of the portents accompanying his death ('Le Soleil vient de flamme et la Lune de feu'); finally, to conclude the composition section, the Virgin appears. César de Nostredame has here used the opening of the *Stabat mater*, but whereas in *Les Larmes de la sainte Vierge* the paraphrase is straightforward,[2] in *La Marie dolente* it is elaborated and transformed almost out of recognition. All the pathos of the situation is exploited to the last degree: the Lamb, 'sanglante et massacrée', seeming to sleep on the Cross; the Virgin, 'esplorée, innocente et sacrée', 'pasle, descolorée', with 'pieds tramblans'; and an extravagant version of the 'tears and blood' *topos*. The last phrase of this passage, 'elle a fait ces regrets', introduces Mary's meditation, which consists for the most part of a

---

[1] *La Marie dolente. Au sieur Delsherms advocat tolosain (s.l.n.d.)* (dedication signed February 1608), p. 9. For the earlier part of this description, see below, Appendix, pp. 325–6.

[2] The paraphrase appears in *Les Perles, ou les Larmes de la saincte Magdeleine, avec quelques rymes sainctes dediées à Madame la comtesse de Carces* (Toulouse, 1606), pp. 45–9.

single rhetorical question: why should the 'heroic' life of Christ end in agony and humiliation? This one paradox, through an extended use of anaphora, gives César the opportunity for a complete summary of the life and death of Christ, reaching its climax in a *tour de force* of condensation which outdoes even the *Dymas* sonnet.[1] This, then, is the 'analysis' section: neither intellectual nor theological, scarcely even posing a problem—merely reflecting with astonishment on the extent of the sacrifice. It rephrases the elements of composition within the framework of this reflection, and is at the same time highly 'affective', since it is spoken by Mary herself, and since the paradox provokes emotion rather than thought. The emotional quality is further intensified by the conclusion of Mary's meditation, which is a lamentation involving yet another detailed description of the beauty of Christ.[2]

The poem is rounded off with a precise account of the descent from the Cross (see below, Appendix, pp. 327–8), ending abruptly on a narrative detail:

> ...Pour oindre ce sainct corps, qui dessoubs maint flambeau
> Apres estre embausmé fut mis dans ce Tumbeau. (p. 35.)

This scene, juxtaposed as it is with the lament of Mary, is in many respects reminiscent of Gabrielle de Coignard's *Complainte de la Vierge Marie*. It would in fact hardly be surprising if César had read Gabrielle's works, which were printed at Tournon for an Avignon bookseller, Jacques Favre; and he could well have known her *président* husband and even Gabrielle herself in the 1580s. What is interesting about the comparison is the way in which each poet presents the narrative details of the descent. Gabrielle tells the story at length, drawing attention in particular to the painful removal of the nails; but the object of her description is to underline the sufferings of the Virgin:

> Donc pour oster les cloux de la chair bien heureuse,
> Il y faut bien aller de force vigoureuse,
> Pour arracher les pieds d'avec les cloux pointus,
> D'un trop rude marteau faloit frapper dessus.
> Je vous prie Joseph, aussi vous Nicodeme,
> Pour l'amour du defunct dont ceste face blesme

[1] For these passages, see the extracts printed in the Appendix, below, pp. 326–7.
[2] *La Marie dolente*, pp. 28–9.

Vous attendrit le cœur d'une extreme pitié,
Et vous tient embrassez de sa saincte amitié:
Que vous frappez tout doux sur ceste playe amere,
Car decloüant le fils vous encloüez la mere...
(Œuvr. chrest., p. 199.)

Elsewhere the actions of the participants are indicated with a minimum of elaboration. César, on the other hand, is concerned with details of gesture and action for their own sake: Joseph and Nicodemus put their right foot on the first rung of the ladder, balance themselves carefully, pass the nails from one to the other, hammer the second nail from behind (i.e. from the point end), and cough and spit as they support the body. This careful use of a non-elevated language, coupled with a laborious enumeration of actions, is somewhat pedantic, especially as it has no obvious function: the passage is an anticlimax after the flamboyant pathos of the Virgin's lament. Nevertheless, it is interesting in that it suggests close observation of life rather than the reproduction of a traditional literary model. It reads like a description of a sketch in which the artist's attention is absorbed by the mechanics of composition, by the angle of Christ's body in relation to the ladders, the Cross and the two main participants, by the tensions set up in their bodies.[1]

Such passages seem to illustrate, in a highly-developed form, the technique of detailed narration as one finds it in Granada and in Coster. But César's manner of visualising people and events is not dependent on the devotional 'composition' or 'application of the senses' alone: when he describes Christ in the manger or on the Cross, he describes them as often as not with the professional eye of a painter. The two liminary sonnets for the *Pièces héroïques* eulogise his talents in the art of painting as well as poetry: Paul Hurault de l'Hôpital calls him 'excellent Peintre et Poëte', and Fauchet adds a third talent, that of lute-playing. Even without this evidence, one need only read a few lines of almost any of the poems to find César de Nostredame displaying his knowledge of painting technique. In his dedication of *Les Perles, ou les Larmes de la saincte Magdeleine*, he explains the image of tears as pearls in terms of the painter's art:

[1] Both descriptions should be compared with Guevara, *Livre du Mont de Calvaire*, chs. 55–8, with which they share a number of important details.

...Si bien que ceux qui ont quelque galante praticque avec la divine et muette Pœsie, communement appellée peinture (du don de laquelle je rends infinies graces à la nature) sçavent fort bien qu'un mesme pasle-bleu, mesme traict, mesme enfondrement, mesme faux-jour, et mesme esclat s'y doit appliquer.[1]

The *topos—ut pictura poesis—*of painting as a 'muette Pœsie' (together with the complementary idea that poetry is a 'peinture parlante') justifies the link between the two arts and enables César to talk as if his poem were a painting:

Vous y verrez, MADAME, tous les traits plus delicats de peinture, que la nature et l'art m'ont desparty, tous les mouvemens et les sursauts que l'amour et la passion m'ont fait mettre en œuvre et tous les plus beaux secrets que Phoebus et les Muses m'ont revelés. Aussi est-ce un petit tableau tout d'or et d'azur d'outre mer, avec son quadre de Perles que je vous presente de leur part. (p. 7.)

The opening of *La Marie dolente* provides an interesting variation on what is essentially the same programme:

> Meslons donques au sang, l'horreur, la plainte et l'ombre,
> La couleur de tenebre, obscure, triste et sombre,
> Et ne cherchons plus l'ordre a l'art requis et joint,
> Ou le Ciel, l'air, la Terre et les Mers n'en ont point.
>
> (*M.d.*, p. 6.)

The disorder and reversal of values implied by the death of Christ calls for its counterpart in art: the artist-poet, whose usual task is to create beauty and order, has to follow Nature and seek out horror and ugliness. One would not have been surprised to find the same four lines in the *Tragiques* of d'Aubigné, whose visual sense was also highly developed.[2]

César de Nostredame certainly portrays all the horror of the Passion, the nails and the blood; but one of his central concerns is with the beauty of Christ, to whose portrait he constantly returns. This emphasis

---

[1] *Les Perles*, p. 3.
[2] See, for example, *Misères*, lines 59–63, where d'Aubigné adapts the Pierian spring *topos* to the mood of the *Tragiques*:

> Ces ruisselets d'argent...
> Ne courent plus ici: mais les ondes si claires
> Qui eurent les sapphirs et les perles contraires
> Sont rouges de nos morts; le doux bruit de leur flots,
> Leur murmure plaisant heurte contre des os.

was undoubtedly encouraged by César's reading of the 'epistle of Publius Lentulus', for one of his poems is entitled *Le Pourtraict ou Image du Sauveur: Imitation de l'Epistre de Publius Lentulus* (published with *Les Perles*, pp. 51–5). Lentulus was supposed to have been Governor of Judaea before Pontius Pilate, and to have sent a letter to the Roman senate describing the appearance of Christ; his existence is purely fictitious, but the letter, whatever its origins, was first printed in 1474, in Ludolph the Carthusian's *Life of Christ*, a work of considerable influence. The description of Christ tallies with the earliest 'portraits', those of St John Damascene and Nicephorus, and of the 'Abgar picture'; the hair is parted in the centre, falls straight to the ears, then in curls to the shoulders; the beard is divided into two points.[1] César's paraphrase is, as usual, luxuriant, embroidering the original with colourful images:

> Sur le milieu du chef et du front net et pur
> Se partit un sentier qui leur grace recalme,
> Comm'on voit un ruisseau de cristal et d'azur
> Entre deux rangs plantés de cyprés et de palme.   (p. 53.)

Thus, although the epistle may well have provided the essential features of César's recurrent portraits, it is clear that the visual interpretation of these features is very much his own. In each case, the colours are rich and clear-cut, without *nuances*—gold, ultramarine, vermilion; and this effect is reinforced by the entirely poetic technique of using 'jewelry' images (rubies, pearls, diamonds, sapphires), and the colours of flowers (lilies, roses, carnations, violets): one should remember, once again, that the rhetorical procedure of *descriptio* is seldom far away, for the order of description almost invariably follows the 'head to feet' schema. Such passages have the character of miniatures, recreating the medieval art of manuscript illumination in the context of the Counter-Reformation: 'aussi est-ce un petit tableau tout d'or et d'azur d'outre mer, avec son quadre de Perles...' On the other hand, the descent from the Cross in the *Marie dolente* might suggest a study for a large-scale painting; and the details of light and shade in relation to colour in the description of Christ on the Cross earlier in the same poem are equally ambitious (see below, Appendix, pp. 325–6). What is lacking in nearly every case

---

[1] See below, Appendix, p. 328.

is a sense of the overall economy of the scene which is being portrayed: the virtuoso display of precise details defeats its own ends by submerging the reader's awareness of the event and its significance. In this way, even the emotive impact of the description—which is the main object of the devotional exercise—may be much reduced.[1]

If César's adaptation of painting technique to poetry is a failure on the poetic level, it is nevertheless an important illustration of the devotional practice of using visual aids to facilitate meditation. It will thus be relevant at this point to make one or two comments on this question, which is clearly fundamental if one is considering the æsthetic impact of the Counter-Reformation. In the first place, the popularity of the emblem-book, which continues the iconographical approach of the Middle Ages in a new context of increasing literacy, inevitably attracted the attention of the religious educators of the later sixteenth century. The use of an engraving to impress the reader more strongly with a given text and its meaning was another way of combining the *utile* with the *dulce*: as Praz points out, the Horatian *topos* was a commonplace of emblem-book prefaces.[2] Hence the tone in which Georgette de Montenay introduces her *Emblemes, ou Devises chrestiennes*, published at Lyons in 1571; there is more than a hint of scorn in her reference to 'ces gens desgoustés', which may reflect her Calvinist affiliation, but, like other contemporary propagandists of both confessions, she is willing to make use of all available resources to draw the masses into the fold:

> Alciat feit des Emblémes exquis,
> Lesquels voyant de plusieurs requis,
> Desir me prit de commencer les miens,
> Lesquels je croy estre premier chrestiens.
> Il est besoin chercher de tous costés
> De l'appetit pour ces gens desgoustés:
> L'un attiré sera par la peinture,
> L'autre y joindra poësie e escriture.[3]

---

[1] I have unfortunately not come across any of César's own paintings as yet; to be able to compare the visual reality with its literary counterpart would be most interesting.

[2] M. Praz, *Studies in Seventeenth-century Imagery* (London, 1939), ch. 4, 'The Pleasing and the Useful'.

[3] *Non pag.* See J. Zezula and R. J. Clements, 'La Troisième Lyonnaise: Georgette de Montenay', *L'Esprit créateur*, 5 (1965), pp. 90 ff., for a description of Georgette's life and work.

César de Nostredame: poet and painter

Georgette's claim to primacy in this field is perhaps a little sweeping, since Biblical emblem-books had been published much earlier;[1] nevertheless, her work appears at a moment of great significance, when religious literature is about to enjoy an unprecedented wave of popularity. Furthermore, the emblems themselves are far from being purely functional and schematic: indeed they are visually most attractive, superior in every way to the mediocre didactic verses which accompany them. Chappuys's *Figures de la Bible* combine in the same way, though rather more optimistically, the arts of poetry and 'painting':

Les lecteurs ont icy, par la peinture, la muette poesie, et par les stances poétiques...la peinture parlante, comme le corps et l'ame...Vous y avez le contentement de l'œil, par la naifve pourtraiture, qui n'est de moindre efficace à ce que nous pretendons, que le vers.[2]

These *Figures* must be distinguished from Georgette's *Emblemes* in that they are illustrations of Biblical episodes rather than emblems in the strict sense of the term. Moreover, the verses which accompany them operate almost exclusively on the narrative or 'historical' level: there is no complex allegorical or figural interpretation. In this respect, and because the illustrations are rich in visual detail, they may be seen as a continuation of the old picture-Bible tradition, renewed perhaps by the current devotional emphasis on 'application of the senses'.[3] Like Chappuys's *Figures*, Perrot de La Sale's *Tableaus sacrez* depict Biblical scenes. Perrot is however at pains to point out that it is not sufficient to 'contempler seulement la superficie d'une peinture', for the 'vray sujet' lies beneath the surface, and it is this that the accompanying sonnet must explain.[4] The *Tableaus* do in fact resemble

[1] E.g. Jean Mauguin, *Figures de l'Apocalypse* (Paris, 1547); G. Corrozet, *Icones historiarum veteris testamenti* (Lyons, 1547). See R. Clements, *Picta Poesis* (Rome, 1960) (*Temi e Testi*, 6).

[2] G. Chappuys, *Figures de la Bible, declarees par stances*, dedication, *non pag.*

[3] Cf. Praz, *Studies in Seventeenth-century Imagery*, p. 156: 'Thanks to their didactic properties emblems became one of the favourite weapons of propaganda of the Society of Jesus. Moreover, they seemed calculated to further the Ignatian technique of the application of the senses, to help the imagination to picture to itself in the minutest detail circumstances of religious import, the horror of sin and of the torments of Hell, the delights of a pious life. They made the supernatural accessible to all by materialising it'.

[4] P. Perrot de La Sale, *Tableaus sacrez...qui sont toutes les histoires du Viel Testament representees et exposees selon leur sens en poesie françoise* (Frankfurt, 1594), p. 7. Perrot adds a significant comment on how this 'cognoissance du vray sujet' is to be acquired:

emblems in that each has a sentensious superscription or *titre* in Latin: 'Extra Ecclesiam nulla salus' introduces and interprets the tableau of Noah's Ark amid the Flood (p. 19). These interpretations, like those of the verses, involve simple theological or moral points; but it is interesting to find that in defending his use of Latin *titres*, Perrot anticipates the possibility that the 'meditatifs' will wish to explore the sense of the tableaux more deeply:

> ...si quelqu'un trouve mauvais que j'aye emprunté mes tiltres de la boëte des anciens [many of them are classical *sententiae*], qu'il se contente, que j'ai voulu par ce moyen ouvrir la porte a ceux qui les voudroient faire Latins, *et fournir quand et quand aux meditatifs double subjet, outre le sens que je leur donne en mes vers*, comme aussi en attendant ma derniere main, que je pourrai Dieu aydant rencontrer sur quelques belles sentences francoises, sans en emprunter d'ailleurs.   (p. 13, my italics.)

These three examples, taken together, could be said to indicate an increasing emphasis on the visual aid and a simplification of the 'message'; but they are hardly conclusive. In the case of the Jesuit Richeome, however, the situation is very different. In the first place, his literary medium is prose, not verse, and Richeome was a prolific prose-writer. Secondly, his *Tableaux sacrez* rely on verbal description, since they contain no visual tableaux: it seems that in practice Richeome found literary painting more satisfactory than pictorial art itself.[1] On the other hand, in the dedication of this work to Marie de Médicis, he suggests that she should have the tableaux painted and use them as a decoration for her *cabinet d'oraison*. As Bremond puts it, 'Dans la cellule où Richeome nous fait méditer, pas une place qui ne soit ou fresque ou vitrail',[2] and it is undeniable that Richeome developed his descriptive prose by analogy with painting: consider, for example, his portrait of Elias, which reads like the description of an actual picture:

> '...et ne fault point penser, que ceste cognoissance s'acquere par longues veilles, ni par demonstrations Geometriques, moins pour scavoir toutes les sciences humaines, si les saintes et pures meditations ne s'y entremettent, lesquelles ne peuvent partir telles que d'un cœur net, et dedié a Dieu' (pp. 9–10). Thus he explicitly associates the art of interpreting *emblemata* with the need for a meditative disposition.

[1] See Bremond, *Humanisme dévot*, p. 34: 'Il disposait des premiers graveurs de l'époque, de Léonard Gaultier, par exemple, mais ceux-ci n'arrivaient jamais à le satisfaire'. The full title of Richeome's work is *Tableaux sacrez des figures mystiques du tres-auguste sacrifice et sacrement de l'Eucharistie* (Paris, 1601).

[2] *Ibid.* p. 37.

...voyez-vous son visage blesme et desfaict, et baigné de sueur froide? sa teste negligemment panchee vers la terre sur le costé, ses yeux entr'ouverts, ses bras jettez çà at là, et nul signe de respiration en la bouche, et toute la posture du corps estendu, comme s'il venoit de rendre l'esprit? (p. 299.)

Or, better still, his description of the Angel:

Le Peintre luy a faict le visage lumineux en forme d'esclair, representant par cet esclat sa nature spirituelle et subtile, sa perruque volante en arriere, est de couleur d'or; il luy a mis aussi des aisles au dos selon que l'escriture mesmes le depeinct, pour signifier la vitesse de leur mouvement. Vous les voyez estendues en l'air inegalement, l'une monstrant le dedans et l'autre le dehors, merveilleusement belles et artistement tirees. Les guidons d'icelles et les deux grosses pennes premieres sont de couleur de vert luisant, comme celuy d'un pan, les autres de mesme rang, sont entremeslees de jaune, orangé, rouge, et bleu à guise d'arc en ciel: les cerceaux et petites plumes qui revestissent les tuyaux de celles-cy, et les autres qui suivent en divers ordres, sont riopiolees à proportion des premieres; le duvet qui couvre le dos de l'aisle est comme une entasseure de menuës et petites escailles de diverses couleurs mises sur du cotton. Sa robbe c'est une estolle de fin lin brodee d'un ouvrage subtil tout autour. (pp. 301–2.)[1]

The similarity between these passages and many in César de Nostredame's poetry is striking. Taken together, they illustrate one of the central ways in which the detailed visual imagination of many writers of this and the succeeding generation might have been developed. One should remember, however, that the interaction between painting and literature is a reciprocal one: the need for more elaborate pictorial representation is provoked by devotional techniques of a literary kind, just as the movement towards a literal reading of the 'peinture parlante' *topos* encourages the development of a profuse and ornate literary manner.[2]

---

[1] Richeome's stylistic inclinations are also embodied in the title of the *Peinture spirituelle*; they are anticipated in certain respects by the prose of Aretino: 'Le Prose Sacre nacquero così: vivendo con amici pittori, l'Aretino si trovava in mezzo all'arte religiosa e, mentre, da una parte, affinava la sua sensibilità coloristica, dall'altra s'abituava a pregiare il pathos narrativo degli episodi biblici assai meglio che non avrebbe fatto tra i puri letterati...in molte pagine non si sa bene se egli descriva quadri già dipinti o voglia suggerirne ai pittori' (Toffanin, *op. cit.* p. 311).

[2] See also Goulart (my article on the *Trente tableaux*, pp. 8–9), and Humbert (above, p. 85) for connexions between style and the tableau image. One is touching here on a topic of a very broad scope. To go more deeply into it would involve many questions outside the limits of the present study, such as the impact of the Pléiade theory of concrete description and of its application by, for example, Belleau and Du Bartas.

Richeome balances his descriptions with extensive allegorical commentaries. He defines his *tableaux* as 'tables qui mettent devant les yeux, les images sacrees et figures prophetiques du mystere que nous adorons...il nous faut briefvement declarer...pourquoy Dieu a voulu qu'en la loy de nature et de Moyse, fussent couchees les figures des mysteres de la loy de grace...' (p. 2). He then goes on to define three complementary kinds of representation: 'peinture muette' (pictorial), 'peinture parlante' (written description), and allegory or mystery, which he further defines as 'contenant en soy un sens spirituel, cogneu aux gens spirituels, et caché aux grossiers' (p. 5). He also refers to the four traditional types of exposition, 'le literal ou historien qui va le premier, l'alegorique ou figuratif; qui est l'esprit du literal; le tropologique ou moral, qui forme les mœurs et l'anagogique qui monstre l'Eglise triomfante' (p. 6). All this is in keeping with the ancient tradition of Biblical interpretation, and could be reconciled with the mechanics of *emblemata*. But there is no doubt that what strikes one above all in this and other works of Richeome is the 'peinture parlante':[1] and if Richeome himself, as a religious teacher, is inclined to linger over his visual images, it is not difficult to appreciate that a layman, or a devotional poet, might be tempted to do likewise at the expense of analytic interpretation.

The gradual disappearance of the moral and intellectual structure which sustains much of the best literature of the Renaissance, and which is exemplified by the emblematic approach, is one of the most significant features of the shifting patterns of literature in this period. With it, no doubt, goes a great deal of pedantry; but it is frequently replaced by a limpness, a liking for uncontrolled effusion, which is hardly preferable. It would no doubt be unfair to compare César de Nostredame with, say, Maurice Scève, whose superiority as a poet is not a matter merely of historical context; but a more appropriate comparison is available. La Ceppède's sonnet-sequence has precisely the emblematic quality which has disappeared in César de Nostredame: his preface contains an element of austerity which is reminiscent of Georgette de Montenay, and although more than one critic has associated his poetry with visual art[2] the pictorial aspects of his meditation on the Passion are controlled and economical by comparison with

---

[1] Cf. Bremond, *Humanisme dévot*, p. 42.   [2] *Ibid.* p. 352; Ruchon, *La Ceppède*, p. 24.

César de Nostredame: poet and painter

In many ways this is an impressive poem, although it suffers from César's habitual tendency to overload his descriptions. In the tear scene, there is the same sweetness, the same use of diminutives as in Chasteuil's sonnet, but César outdoes his predecessor in richness of imagination, and manages at the same time to avoid the clumsiness of syntax which is the downfall of Chasteuil. The extravagant decoration, combined with a delicate pathos and lacking the vigorous 'intellectual' ornamentation of the Pléiade poets, can seduce a reader inclined to self-indulgence; and where the virtuoso display of colours and posed gestures is not too much in evidence, César's manner can make a powerful visual impact, as in Mary's image of the Cross,

> Le grand propheé ou son corps fut percé
> Qui tout sanglant, et tout moite de larmes
> Distille encor sous ses vermeilles armes
> Jusques à terre, ou ce grand rouge estang
> Glace les fleurs d'une lacque de sang.[1]

'Vous y verrez... tous les mouvemens et les sursauts que l'amour et la passion m'ont fait mettre en œuvre': this claim to an emotional motivation, and to a kind of improvisation, explains much that is central to César's poetry and to the age in which he lived. As he himself says earlier in the same dedication, 'C'est donc assez à propos... que je produy des Perles et des Larmes en ce sainct temps d'amour et de reformation, ou les blanches Perles de l'oraison et de la pureté, et les douces Larmes du jeusne, et du repentir doivent excellemment reluire' (pp. 5–6). This is the age of Nervèze, an age in which profane and sacred love intermingle and in which no extreme of pathos is too great. César de Nostredame is an effusive poet, and his effusions are often insipid; but his poetry is extremely rich, and at times eloquent, creating its own personality from the combined modes of devotional painting and devotional literature.

[1] See below, Appendix, p. 330. The precisely posed portrait of 'Angélique' (Appendix, p. 329) is perhaps César's most successful attempt at rendering a visual scene in words; contrast the portrait of Christ himself (Appendix, pp. 331–2), where an overloaded *descriptio* is followed by a pretentious reference to César's painting technique.

The sentimental and the romanesque

Such poetry can of course only represent one type of literary taste in the early seventeenth century, though a widespread and influential one. Favre and La Ceppède are themselves very different from César de Nostredame; but at least they share with him their provincial background and their explicitly devotional aims. Moreover, Favre's Rosary sequence and certain of La Ceppède's sonnets have affinities with the poetry of tears, although one would scarcely call them 'romanesque'.[1] Bertaut and Du Perron, on the other hand, have very little in common with the devotional poets, although each composed a handful of poems (paraphrase apart) which can be called 'devotional', and in spite of the fact that they were both of high ecclesiastical rank. The assumption that they were the joint predecessors or disciples of the later Malherbe, and that they must therefore be spoken of in the same breath, should not be accepted without closer examination; nevertheless, they both reflect a type of literary taste which is potentially opposed to the *humanisme dévot* of La Ceppède as well as to the extravagance of César de Nostredame. Potentially only: for the anthologies of the new century often include the whole range of styles in religious poetry, which suggests that the reading public was far from intransigeant in its literary preferences. It is after all not impossible for a modern reader to enjoy both Dylan Thomas and Philip Larkin, although for historians of literature the gulf which separates them will no doubt seem highly significant.

Much the same observations apply to Bertaut's *Cantique sur la naissance de Notre-Seigneur* as to his penitential poem 'Seul espoir des humains' (see above, pp. 133–5): this is devotion of the official, public variety. The theme is introduced by three declamatory stanzas, with carefully balanced syntax and a good deal of periphrasis:

> Soit que de vostre corps vous viviez déchargez,
> Soit que dans la prison où Dieu vous a logez
> Le lien de la vie encore vous enserre,
> Esprits de qui sa grace est l'espoir et l'appuy,
> Jettez des cris de joye, et chantez qu'aujourd'hui
> La mort de vostre mort daigne naistre sur terre.[2]

---

[1] See above, pp. 229, 237; also the twenty-ninth sonnet of Favre's first *centurie* (*Entretiens spirituels*, p. 15); and Marin Le Saulx's eighty-third sonnet (*Theanthropogamie*, p. 81).

[2] *Œuvres poétiques*, ed. Chenevière, pp. 1–4 (this reference covers the whole poem).

Bertaut chooses the 'outward' form of meditation, the sermon: stanza 6 begins with the familiar 'Mortel':

> Mortel, qui vois icy ton Sauveur nouveau né
> Gisant si pauvrement, n'en sois point estonné:
> Ce n'est pas impuissance, il lui plaist ainsi naistre.

But the relationship between 'preacher' and 'congregation' is never intimate: Bertaut's tone is that of a bishop addressing a royal audience on a public occasion. This sermon development includes two prayers (stanzas 10–12, 15), but since the first of them merely continues the antithetical formulations of the preceding stanzas, the change of tone is only nominal. The second prayer, which is the last stanza of the poem, is a prayer for identification:

> O! bien-heureux enfant payeur de nos rançons,
> Puis que tu nais en vain si nous ne renaissons
> Eternels heritiers de ta saincte promesse,
> Prens mon cœur pour estable, et pour creiche ma foy,
> Me comblant de tant d'heur que de renaistre en moy,
> Afin que de nouveau moy-mesme je renaisse.

Here again it is the dignity of the rhetorical period which counts, and the carefully controlled play on the theme of 'renaissance', rather than the affective impulse to renew the meaning of the Nativity. Unlike César, Bertaut avoids the physical evocation of the Christchild and his mother, apart from two lines of 'composition' in the fourth stanza: 'Le voicy qui desja souffrant pour le peché / Plore dans une creiche où foible il est couché'. Thus the antitheses which are scarcely apparent in César's *cantiques* here become the principal focus of attention.[1] Arranged as symmetrically as possible, they are designed to astonish as much by virtuosity of rhetoric as by the mystery they represent. The astonishment therefore remains abstract: there is no trace of pathos, of colour, no connexion with the literature of tears.

The phrasing and the rhythms of Du Perron's *Cantique de la Vierge* have much the same measured dignity as those of Bertaut. When Du Perron lists the traditional symbols of the Virgin, he sustains the enumeration through six stanzas, and intermingles the symbols proper with more general hyperboles; the syntax is elegantly arranged to

---

[1] 'Il commence d'estre homme, et reste tousjours Dieu', etc. See above, pp. 268–9, for a comparison between César and Béroalde de Verville; above, pp. 51–2, for the use of antithesis in Granada's Nativity meditation.

coincide with the metrical unit, so that the movement depends on parallelisms both within the couplet and within the individual line:

> C'est le palais Royal tout remply de clarté,
> Plus pur et transparant que le Ciel qui l'enserre:
> C'est le beau Paradis vers l'Orient planté,
> Les delices du Ciel, et l'espoir de la terre.
>
> C'est la myrrhe et la fleur, et le baume odorant,
> Qui rend de sa senteur nos ames consolées:
> C'est le Jardin reclus souëfvement flairant,
> C'est la Rose des champs, et les Lis des vallées...[1]

The elegant formality of these lines, like Bertaut's use of antithesis, tends to distract the reader's attention from the mysteries of typology which are so important for La Ceppède; at the same time, it avoids the sentimental intimacy of César de Nostredame's contemplation. In the opening stanzas of the poem, which describe the Assumption of the Virgin, Du Perron (like his contemporary) emphasises the cosmic splendour of the scene, the dazzling light, the radiance of the Virgin's face:

> Quand au somme mortel la Vierge eut clos les yeux,
> Les Anges qui veilloient autour de leur Maistresse,
> Esleverent son corps en la gloire des Cieux,
> Et les Cieux furent pleins d'immortelle allegresse.
>
> Les plus hauts Seraphins à son advenement
> Voloient au devant d'elle, et lui cedoient leur place,
> Se sentans tous ravis d'aise et d'estonnement
> De pouvoir contempler la splendeur de sa face.
>
> Dessus les Cieux des Cieux elle va paroissant,
> Les flambeaux estoillez lui servent de Couronne:
> La Lune est sous ses pieds en forme de Croissant,
> Et comme un vestement le Soleil l'environne.

But whereas César decorates his description with the imagery of pearls and crystal, and transforms the seraphim into Cupids, Du Perron's manner tends towards an abstraction of the 'gloire', the 'allegresse', and the 'splendeur'; the image of the cosmos in the third stanza is sober and economical.

---

[1] *Les Diverses Œuvres*, part 2, pp. 17–20 (whole poem).

Du Perron's oratory differs from Bertaut's in that it is less pretentious: the mechanics of rhetoric are seldom obtrusive. Furthermore, although his language is abstract by comparison with César de Nostredame's, he is far more concerned than Bertaut with physical reality. Eleven of the twenty-three stanzas of the *cantique* develop the theme of Mary's role as mother of Christ; there is only one allusion to the Nativity, but this in itself is closer to devotional contemplation than anything in Bertaut's poem:

> Elle luy va monstrant pour fléchir sa rigueur,
> Les mammelles qui tendre au berceau l'allaitterent,
> Dont le doux souvenir luy penetre le cœur,
> Et les flancs bien-heureux qui neuf mois le porterent.

The agony of the Passion is also realised through the Virgin—'de combien de clous son ame fut percée'—and like so many of his contemporaries, Du Perron uses the 'tears and blood' *topos*:

> Elle serroit la Croix de ses bras precieux,
> Regardant par pitié ses blesseures cruelles,
> Et respandoit autant de larmes de ses yeux
> Comme il versoit de sang de ses playes mortelles.

Nevertheless, the sensual texture of this poetry depends on rhythmic harmony and the plastic quality of the language itself as much as on explicit physical reference: the list of symbols demonstrates this very well. Du Perron never relies on luxuriance of detail or flamboyance of imagery.

The structure of the *cantique*, with its movement from the imaginative evocation of the Assumption and the life of Christ to the enumeration of symbols and thence to a concluding prayer, is reminiscent of devotional method. It seems unlikely, however, that Du Perron was consciously applying such a method. The tone of the poem remains impersonal throughout: the four lines of sermon (stanza 14) and the four lines of prayer which form a conclusion are highly formalised and are thus not designed to impel the emotional involvement of the reader. There is a ceremonial quality in the poem which detaches it from the devotional sensibility and evokes rather the ritual of official Church practice.[1] It is interesting, therefore, to find Du Perron recommending

---

[1] See O. de Mourgues, *Metaphysical, Baroque and Précieux Poetry*, p. 63.

the tears of devotion in his *Stances pour exciter à l'amour de Dieu*. This poem is based on the *topos* of the conversion of profane love to sacred:

> Amants qui souspirez tant de peines souffertes,
> Qui pleurez tant d'ennuis, de rigueurs et de pertes,
> Tant de jours en servant vainement dépensez,
> Apres une beauté mortelle et perissable,
> Tant de douteux espoirs fondez dessus le sable,
> Et tant de long (*sic*) travaux d'oubly recompensez:
> Changez tous ces regrets, ces souspirs et ces larmes,
> Quittez ces yeux trompeurs, pleins d'appas et de charmes,
> Qui rendent vostre cœur si vivement épris,
> Pour suivre une beauté du Ciel mesme adorée,
> Et concevoir un feu d'eternelle durée,
> Dont la flamme invisible éclaire vos esprits.[1]

In this respect, it is not unlike Desportes's *Ode*, although Du Perron uses the tone of the sermon rather than of the confessional. Subsequently, it moves closer to the poetry of tears of the later generation:

> Il [Dieu] veut que comme unique, unique elle [l'Ame] le serve,
> Il fait cas de ses pleurs, et les met en reserve,
> Et lors que vos pechez s'élevent jusqu'aux Cieux,
> De sa dextre irritée il laisse choir les armes,
> Se sentant surmonté par ces devotes larmes,
> Qui jamais sans effect ne sortent de vos yeux.
>
> Les larmes des éleuz ne tombent point en terre,
> L'Eternel en a soin, les recueille et les serre,
> Dedans des vaisseaux d'or, qui leur sont destinez:
> N'allez point prophanant une offrande si saincte,
> Qui peut rendre son ire en vostre endroit esteinte,
> Et vaincre les Cieux mesme à vous perdre obstinez.

It is immediately apparent, however, that Du Perron carefully avoids all the hyperbole, and the luxuriant imagery of pearls, which are so often associated with his theme. His admonition is once more explanatory rather than emotive; the language, like that of the *Cantique de la Vierge*, is sober and oratorical. Such a poem demonstrates admirably that the devotional manner is not dependent on themes alone. It is partly a matter of intention: in spite of their title, the *Stances* fail to convey the desire to record or to stimulate devotional 'affections', to 'excite the soul to the love of God' by every means available. At the

[1] *Op. cit.* pp. 115–16 (whole poem).

same time, the gradual movement towards the Malherbian conception of literary excellence is directly opposed to the requirements of devotion, and in so far as they choose a poetic medium which coincides with this movement, Bertaut and Du Perron prove that they are not concerned with the problems of devotional poetry proper.[1]

The patterns of religious poetry in the early seventeenth century are as closely interwoven as those of secular poetry. From one point of view, Desportes's successors are Bertaut and Du Perron, although they rephrase his manner to the point of transforming it entirely; from another, the poets of Henri III are already moving towards the conception of devotional poetry which will come into its own with Favre, La Ceppède and César de Nostredame. With those poets, as we have seen, certain new distinctions begin to emerge. The humanism of Favre and La Ceppède represents a view of the world and of poetry which is beginning to lose currency, while César de Nostredame already shows signs of a preoccupation with emotion which will have a wide range of applications in the seventeenth century, from the *Astrée* onwards. From the formal point of view, the long, 'improvised' poem, which develops partly through contact with Old Testament poetry and partly by analogy with the prose and verse romance, will continue to appear for another generation: Saint-Amant's *Le Contemplateur* is a good example of the way in which meditative improvisation could be applied to all manner of subjects. In fact, the themes and language of devotional poetry as they have been analysed in the last four chapters continue far into the seventeenth century, in spite of some important changes of emphasis. The poetry both of penitence and of the life of Christ will be cultivated by a host of poets, by Lazare de Selve, Zacharie de Vitré, the Carmelite Pierre de Saint-Louis, Du Bois Hus, Auvray and Pierre Lemoyne.[2] To take one example at random:

---

[1] As an extreme example of a non-devotional style applied to a devotional theme, we may here quote Malherbe's *Sur l'image d'une sainte Catherine* (*Poésies*, p. 150); this poem first appeared in 1620:

> L'art aussi bien que la nature
> Eust fait plaindre ceste peinture,
> Mais il a voulu figurer
> Qu'aux tourmens dont la cause est belle,
> La gloire d'une ame fidelle
> Est de souffrir sans murmurer.

[2] See Rousset's *Anthologie* for extracts from all these poets. The title of Lemoyne's treatise *La Dévotion aisée* reflects exactly the tone of the devotional literature discussed in this chapter.

The sentimental and the romanesque

the *Second livre des delices de la poésie française* of 1620 includes a number of sonnets by the Sieur de Meziriac, and among them is the following poem on the Flagellation:

> Que ton ame souffrit de douleurs inhumaines
> (O Mere du Sauveur!) quand tu vis detrancher
> De tant et tant de coups sa delicate chair,
> D'où ruisseloient de sang mille vives fontaines.
> En larmes tu noyas ces lumieres sereines,
> Qui peuvent d'un regard animer un rocher:
> Versant autant de pleurs qu'on luy fit espancher
> De vermeille liqueur hors de ses sainctes veines.
> Ah Seigneur! c'est assez, tu n'auras plus de sang
> Pour distiller du chef, des pieds, des mains, du flanc,
> Pour peu que desormais on t'en face respandre.
> Vierge espargne tes pleurs, où (*sic*) ton œil ne pourra
> T'en fournir au besoin, lors que ton fils mourra,
> Et pasle en ton giron tu le verras estendre.[1]

Poetry such as this—and there is no lack of it in the 1620s and the 1630s—demonstrates the coherence of the tradition and at the same time the way it is being developed towards extremes of pathos. Meanwhile, La Ceppède and Humbert are publishing further volumes of their devotional work: the more decorative tone of the second book of *Théorèmes* suggests that even La Ceppède, who was by now very old, had been affected by the new manner; and in 1623, a *Chant Royal* entitled *Pour une description d'un pourtrait de Saincte Magdelaine* by Bernard d'Aliès was entered for the *Jeux Floraux* at Toulouse,[2] another sign that the oldest traditions were being modified. At the same time, a different but related current of poetry moves into the foreground. The 'invasion mystique'—the influence of Saint Teresa and the

---

[1] *Second livre des delices*, ed. Toussainct Du Bray (Paris, 1620), p. 639. See also p. 640, *Du Couronnement d'espines*:

> Quand on vit du Sauveur le chef outreperçé
> Des poignans esguillons des Espines cruelles,
> Et le sang qui sembloit à des roses nouvelles
> Parmy ses cheveux d'or en gouttes ramassé,
> Ah! (dit la Vierge alors)...

Malherbe's St Catherine poem appeared in the same anthology. I am indebted to Miss Beverley Evans for drawing my attention to Meziriac's poems; this Meziriac must be either Guillaume or Claude Bachet, joint authors of *Chansons spirituelles* (Lyons, 1618).

[2] See Dawson, *Toulouse in the Renaissance*, pp. 40–2. The mood of this poem is in many ways reminiscent of César de Nostredame.

Devotional poetry at the cross-roads

Carmelite reform, of St François's *Traité de l'amour de Dieu*, and of a host of related works which renew the long medieval tradition of mystical contemplation—begins to provoke from poets like Claude Hopil an ambition which had only appeared in fragmentary form before the turn of the century, the ambition to describe in verse the nature of the mystical experience. Nothing emerges from this, as far as one can see at present, which can match the poetry of St John of the Cross; nevertheless, this is a rich field for investigation, and one which is clearly connected with the affectivity of the poets discussed in the present study.[1] Amid the wealth of devotional and mystical poetry published in the thirty or forty years after the first volume of La Ceppède's *Théorèmes*, it is not impossible that more 'undiscovered' poets of the stature of Sponde, Favre and La Ceppède will come to light; but I feel that it was precisely at the 'cross-roads'—the period between 1590 and 1610, when there were many tensions and much change, both in religion and in poetry—that the ground was the most fertile.

[1] For examples of mystical poetry by Hopil and others, see Rousset's *Anthologie*, under the headings *Le brouillard et la clarté* and *La lumière de la permanence*. I have recently heard that a thesis on Claude Hopil is in progress.

CONCLUSION

The emergence in the later sixteenth century of a group of related though sometimes divergent devotional styles must first be seen in a broad historical perspective. The early Renaissance in France was predominantly Christian in character; and one of its most essential preoccupations was the renewal of man's inward religious life. In this period, the devotional impetus established in the fourteenth and fifteenth centuries, by the Windesheim community in particular, began to move into the public domain: Erasmus, Lefèvre and their disciples, who owed much to the Brethren of the Common Life, took advantage of the new printing-presses to disseminate on a Europen level the notion of a *docta pietas*. From a literary point of view, Marguerite de Navarre represents the first climax of the Christian Renaissance, for in the context of a predominantly lay and courtly society, she exploited the attractions of vernacular literature in order to stress the importance of an inward religious standard; furthermore, she used poetry to describe the progress of her own meditation. Marguerite's devotional poems were not all printed in her own time, but some of them at least must have been known to her contemporaries, and her personal influence was very great; thus the psalm-paraphrases of Marot, the work of Rabelais, and perhaps even the *Délie* of Scève can in their different ways be seen as complementary to Marguerite's conception of a literature based on meditation and self-knowledge.[1] The Erasmian mood of

---

[1] There appears to be a background of devotional poetry by minor writers in the same period. See, for example, Claude Bellièvre (1487–1557), who represents both of the main devotional theme-groups with his *Le Briefz Eage de l'Homme* and his *Ecce homo*—this information is based on Charles Perrat's *Claude Bellièvre (1487–1557)*, Geneva, 1956 (*THR*, 23). The *Ecce homo* is repetitive and loosely organised, but both the themes and their presentation will be immediately familiar to anyone who has read devotional literature:

> ...on voit le sang coller
> Et ruysseller de son corps blanc et tendre...
>
> Pleurés, humeyns, ainssi que Magdeleyne
> Sa passion que checun la renomme.
> Contemplatifz, regardés: Vecy l'homme.

(The whole poem is reproduced by Perrat, *Claude Bellièvre*, pp. 150–3.) I have recently heard from Miss Jennifer Beard, who is working on Jean Bouchet, that this

Conclusion

this period was however soon disturbed. Calvin's crystallisation of the theological and political issues, and the increased severity of the ortho- dox establishment, made the Evangelist position very difficult to main- tain; with the death of Marguerite, the atmosphere at court changes, while at the same time an energetic group of poets begins to impose a poetic manner which, although not wilfully pagan, is little concerned with Christian inwardness. When, after 1560, the civil conflict draws Ronsard's attention towards specifically religious issues, he adopts the tone of militant orthodoxy rather than that of personal meditation. Meanwhile, however, the devotional tradition is continued by the Carthusians, by the Spanish and Italian Friars, and by the embryonic Jesuit movement, which will soon make their impact in France. In vernacular literature, Biblical paraphrase becomes steadily more popular, while Bèze and his colleagues institute a religious literature to counter the 'paganism' of the Pléiade. Finally, the main currents of devotional reform, carrying with them an interest in all the aspects of the tradition from the Church Fathers onwards, begin to reach a lay public throughout France, and the ground is prepared for St François and the spirituality of the seventeenth century. Thus the continued vitality of the tradition is assured, in spite of the changes implied by a comparison between, say, Erasmus and Loyola; likewise, the devo- tional poetry of the later period is a response to the same impetus which produced the meditative poetry of Marguerite de Navarre.

Given this overall pattern, the nature of the post-1570 devotional poetry is clearly subject to two main factors: on the one hand, the methods and matter provided by the devotional revival, and on the other, the primacy of the modes of writing established by the Pléiade.

is not an isolated example; there is a tradition of mixed prose and verse of a devotional nature which can be traced back into the fifteenth century. Miss Beard mentions Henri Caupain's *Le Desert de devotion* (1530?), 'an allegory aimed at inciting all who read it ("seculiers ou reguliers") to the love of God'; this work 'contains near the end "trois exclamations compassives et compassions contemplatives de devotion"—three verse passages put in the mouth of Dame Devotion on the subject of Christ on the Cross, "la vierge mere de compassion", and St John.' She also refers to Bouchet's *Triomphes de la Noble Dame amoureuse* of 1530, 'which contains several *épîtres* addressed to Christ and the Virgin Mary', and to an article on these by Marie Holban, '*Le Miroir de l'âme pécheresse* et *Les Epitres de la Noble et Amoureuse Dame*', in *Mélanges offerts à M. Abel Lefranc* (Paris, 1936), pp. 142 ff. Earlier, many of these works seem to have been written for the benefit of nuns, but Bouchet is writing expressly for the laity: the pene- tration into lay society of devotional practice is just beginning. I hope that the results of Miss Beard's research will soon become available.

The second of these factors is perhaps the more obtrusive at first sight, and since it raises important questions about the status of devotional poetry, it will be as well to deal with it at once. Indeed, one could produce evidence for the view that much religious poetry in this period is produced by a facile grafting of the commonplaces of the profane tradition on to religious themes. The allegorisation of myth and the conversion of Urania were for many poets not part of a systematic programme: if Du Bartas set out to exploit the 'dépouilles d'Egypte' theory in the grand manner, if Guy Le Fèvre prolonged the syncretist ideal, their lesser contemporaries were not always so ambitious. Ronsard and his colleagues had made the writing of poetry a highly serious occupation, and this in itself was an encouragement to the religious poet who might have been reluctant to associate his literary efforts with a frivolous and servile court poetry; furthermore, their prestige was bound to dazzle the minor poet, to make him feel that certain forms, certain kinds of language and image, were indispensable for successful poetry-writing. For the amateur, to parade the mechanical deities and fly-blown *ravissement* might seem a sure passport to poetic respectability. In the early part of the period, the wars of religion, with their demand for satire, propaganda and moralising, created a large number of these amateur poets, whose more or less religious themes were scarcely an obstacle to the use of fossilised Pléiadisms; and the same is true, in varying degrees, of many of the devotional poets. The fossilisation process is particularly evident in the sonnet, where the exigencies of the form resulted irresistibly in the use of commonplace formulations. When Goulart begins a sonnet with the line 'Lors que de l'Ocean Phœbus son char approche', the image and the phraseology are probably due to a reflex action rather than to a conscious attempt to integrate the Pléiade manner into a new situation.[1] Goulart

---

[1] See above, p. 78. See also *ibid.* Book 1, sonnet 53:

> Lors que la brune nuict charge sa robbe noire,
> Sous icelle tenant tous animaux cachez... (*Poèmes chrestiens*, p. 150.)

And sonnet 54:

> Lors que l'aurore vient des larmes de ses yeux,
> Le hasle rafreschir de la terre rostie
> Par l'ardante chaleur... (*Ibid.* p. 151.)

The apparent grouping of these sonnets according to the rhetorical device or *topos* on which they are based may be of significance, and should be looked into more closely. As Du Bartas puts it in his *Brief Advertissement* of 1584, 'La poésie est de si long

has no axe to grind over the use of profane poetic material: if he had intended to initiate a campaign for the conversion of 'pagan' poetry, he would have used mythological allusion and similar devices more often. Similarly, Jacques de Billy's *De la Beauté de l'ame fidele*:

> Plus belle encor est la voute des cieux,
> Soit quand Phebus y poursuit sa carriere,
> Et que d'un œil ardent et radieux
> Il darde en nous sa flambante lumiere:
> Ou quand Phebé, de sa lueur pillarde,
> D'un œil blaffard ce bas monde regarde.[1]

In a sonnet of the *Muse chrestienne*, Poupo conveniently summarises his own method, together with that of a hundred other poets:

> ...dés que le jour monte du bord Indique,
> Jusqu'à ce qu'il s'en voise en l'autre mer plongeant,
> Fon, refon, ba, reba, d'un marteau diligent,
> Soude, grave et poli ton labeur poëtique.
> Tu prendras le lingot au fond des saincts escrits,
> Et le traict (puisqu'ailleurs il ne peut estre pris)
> Sur Ronsard, du Bellay et l'eloquent Desportes.[2]

'Puisqu'ailleurs il ne peut estre pris': there is no suggestion of regret in this phrase; it is purely laudatory. Ronsard, Du Bellay and Desportes have laid down all the necessary formulae for poetic composition, and one can only hope to write poetry by following their example.

Many of La Ceppède's Pléiadisms have this fossilised quality: when he uses a compound such as *haut-Tonnant*, when he writes the line 'Terrasser les tuteurs du bestail porte-laine', one suspects that he is looking for a 'poetic effect'. The appearance of these words and phrases is spasmodic because La Ceppède's main task is not to produce poetic effects; he is concerned with transposing into verse a meditation on the Passion. Such profane formulae are for him a kind of exterior decoration; and this is indicated by certain of the summaries which he gives of his sonnets. Sonnet 65 of Book III, for example, he calls a 'Description poëtique de l'Eclipse du Soleil arrivé le jour de la Passion de Jesus Christ, où le Soleil est introduit parlant': significantly, the

---

temps en saisine de ces termes fabuleus, qu'il est impossible de l'en déposséder que pié à pié' (*The Works of Guillaume de Salluste Sieur Du Bartas*, ed. U. T. Holmes, etc., vol. I (Chapel Hill, 1935), p. 224).
[1] *Sonnets spirituels* (1577 ed.), p. 484.   [2] *La Muse chrestienne*, Book III, p. 58.

phrase 'description poëtique' is not used for the descriptive 'composition' sonnets, which have a quite different place in the order of things.[1] On the other hand, one is aware in La Ceppède's poetry of the ambition to reconcile the sacred and the profane, the pagan and the Christian; and it is often hard to draw a clear line between 'fossilisation' (where the stylistic *trait* is not linked with any syncretic purpose) and the deliberate merging of parallel traditions. In general, despite the cases just considered, it is wiser to stress the sixteenth-century tendency to think in terms of a community of tradition, both in thought and style. The early Christian Church had taken over many of the structures of Roman civilisation; Augustine and Jerome had exploited the philosophy and rhetoric of the pagan world in the effort to communicate Christian truth; Petrarch's conception of rhetoric had been nourished by his Augustinianism; and if the Sorbonne theologians of the later Middle Ages had minimised the importance of rhetoric, the Ciceronian and Virgilian movement of the fifteenth and early sixteenth centuries, in Italy and then in France, had demonstrated the importance of the art of rhetoric in the renewal of religious thought. For Fichet, philosophy had decayed because rhetoric had been neglected;[2] for Rabelais, clear speech was profoundly linked with self-understanding and the perception of truth; and in the *Prisons*, Marguerite de Navarre expounded the unifying power of Christian revelation in terms of all the known forms of intellectual activity, including poetry.[3] In the specific context of devotion, the parallel between the discipline of meditation and of rhetoric is already explicit in Gansfort's *Scala meditationis*, as Louis Martz has pointed out:

...these methods of meditation are in themselves adaptations of ancient principles of logic and rhetoric. This is made especially clear in one of the

---

[1] Cf. the quotation from Marin Le Saulx, above, p. 72 ('Ceste façon de parler...'). See also the *argument* of *Théorèmes*, III, 90: 'Exaggeration de la durté des ames, qui ne veulent flechir à la pitié, sur la mort de Jesus-Christ, plus dures que les pierres, et plus immobiles que la terre'. However, in the commentary of III, 19 (see above, p. 202), the word *exageration* is used in a wholly neutral sense to describe the introduction of details which are not in the Gospels, but which are nevertheless authenticated by the Fathers; it does not always have a pejorative sense in this period (see Huguet, who gives the definitions 'exprimer, dire' for 'exagerer'; Cotgrave defines 'exaggeration' as a 'heaping together', but also an 'adding of wrong unto wrong', and 'exaggerer' as to 'aggravate' and to 'augment, amplifie, increase'). See also above, p. 90.

[2] See A. Renaudet, *Préréforme et humanisme à Paris pendant les premières guerres d'Italie (1494–1517)*, pp. 84–5.

[3] *Dernières poésies*, ed. A. Lefranc, pp. 208 ff.

great prototypes of the central method of meditation practised during our period: the *Scala Meditationis* of Wessel Gansfort. . . . Gansfort's long treatise, dating from the latter part of the fifteenth century, is filled with references to the logical and rhetorical methods of Aristotle, Cicero, Raymond Lull, Rudolf Agricola, and others; his *Scala* adapts and transforms the methods of these writers for the purpose of interior 'oratory' and debate. And this is true of all the meditative treatises: all the ways of speaking and writing that a man has learned will inevitably help to form the thoughts of the 'whole soul'.[1]

At this stage, the connexion depends on form and sequence rather than on style itself. The structural aspect of rhetorical art—the point at which it is closest to logic—is retained as a discipline; but there is no suggestion that it should be accompanied by formal elegance of style. Later in the sixteenth century, however, the 'colours' of rhetoric will be exploited with increasing optimism in the devotional handbooks, so that finally the borderline between 'devotional prose' and 'literature' breaks down altogether. It is not surprising, therefore, that in the same period the intellectual humanism of Favre and La Ceppède will be accompanied by the literary humanism of César de Nostredame.

In order to examine this question fully, it would be necessary to explore in depth the rhetorical disciplines current in the later sixteenth century and see how far the sacred and the profane were interchangeable: it seems likely that at Jesuit colleges such as the Collège d'Ancien at Douai, the method of the *Spiritual Exercises* and the teaching of rhetoric were both part of the same programme. Broader parallels will also spring to mind. The famous 'application of the senses', for example, is comparable with the Pléiade interest in the 'imitation' of nature, the attempt to 'eclęrcir, exprimer e rępresanter les chosęs commę si on les santoęt'.[2] Likewise, sixteenth-century writers of all kinds shared a vast fund of *similitudes* and *figures*, drawn chiefly from the literature and encyclopaedias of antiquity and the Middle Ages, and represented *par excellence* by the popular and adaptable emblems. In such a context, poets could move freely from one register to another; without insincerity or artistic dishonesty, they could exploit the ambiguities of the love-tradition or combine Arcadia with Eden, the

---

[1] L. Martz, *op. cit.* pp. 38–9. See also Martz's Appendix on the *Rosetum, ibid.* pp. 331 ff.
[2] J. Peletier Du Mans, *Art poëtique*, ed. A. Boulanger (Paris, 1930), p. 130. See G. Castor, *Pléiade Poetics* (Cambridge, 1964), ch. 5 (especially pp. 55–61) for a discussion of the theory of 'imitation'.

Pléiade description of nature with the language of the Psalms and the Franciscan meditation on the creatures.

It is true, of course, that the authority of the Pléiade and of Du Bartas delayed the development of a poetry based on wholly devotional sources; it is also true that certain poets adopted an ascetic approach to style, avoiding as far as possible the contamination of profane poetics, and practising a deliberately humble, 'unpolished' manner. But it would be impossible to group such poets according to any simple criterion: the Calvinist poets are by no means outstanding for their austerity, except perhaps in the pre-1570 period, while Desportes, whom one might have expected to equivocate, is something of a purist in this respect. In keeping with traditional rhetorical practice, it is frequently the theme, rather than the view of the poet, which dictates the adoption of one style or another: the theme of sin and sickness attracts the language of the Old Testament; any reference to cosmic phenomena is likely to involve an element of mythology; and the relation between Christ and the Virgin, or Mary Magdalene, will be expressed in the common language of love. Furthermore, it would be facile to suggest that the 'humble', anti-pagan style is the only truly devotional mode of writing. If it is true that devotional poetry cannot be conceived exclusively in terms of a profane poetics, it is also true that the devotional imagination may legitimately absorb the scholarship and the rhetoric of humanism.

Thus if one is to show on what grounds devotional poetry may claim independence, this must be done in positive and not negative terms. The first significant fact is that few of the devotional poets work in isolation: often, they seem to share a common purpose which arises out of their religious environment, even where their styles vary widely. The poets of Henri III—Guy Le Fèvre, Desportes, Boyssières, Jamyn, Blanchon, Du Peyrat, Habert—provide the clearest early example of this pattern. In undertaking to answer the royal need for devotional material, they associate themselves with the translations of Belleforest and Chappuys, with Jacques de Billy and Blaise de Vigenère, and with spiritual leaders like Auger, Maldonat, Génébrard, and—indirectly—Borromeo. On the Calvinist side, there is the equally close grouping of writers at Geneva and Nérac, the simultaneous enthusiasm for psalm-meditation and for poetic composition both in French and Latin: the

Conclusion

ambition represented by the Geneva anthology of 1574 is sustained and developed by Chandieu, d'Aubigné, Sponde, La Noue, against an apologetic and meditative background provided by Bèze, Goulart and Duplessis-Mornay. Meanwhile, the ground is prepared for the next generation of Catholic poets. Henri d'Angoulême becomes the centre of a circle in which the dignitaries of Aix play a prominent part; Anne de Marquets is composing her sonnet-sequence; Gabrielle de Coignard is reading the devotional masters and working on her *Œuvres chrestiennes*; Tamisier is preparing his verse-paraphrases; and the sodality of the Virgin takes root at Douai, where a number of amateur poets have already associated themselves with the devotional movement. Thus, in the 1590s, a spate of devotional poetry appears, much of it already fully fledged. Along a line which runs from Mâcon through Chambéry and Aix to Toulouse, connexions are made, enthusiasms encouraged, comprehensive collections of poetry published: the key positions are held at Chambéry by Antoine Favre, friend of St François de Sales, and in the devotional town of Aix by La Ceppède and César de Nostredame, whose major works will appear after the turn of the century. Several of these groupings are as intimate as that of the Pléiade, if not more so; they only lack a manifesto, a detailed statement of purpose and method. In its place, one may adduce a wide variety of prefaces and dedications: from Jacques de Billy to Favre and La Ceppède, the intention to make poetry a means of devotion—as Granada had recommended—is repeated with increasing clarity and assurance. The vocabulary of this liminary material, of the titles of poems and collections, and of the poetry itself, is drawn more and more frequently from the realm of devotion: by the 1590s, the words *prière*, *méditation*, *contemplation*, *dévot*, *dévotion* and the like are already commonplace. Billy acknowledges the Church Fathers as his principal source, and often refers to specific models in his own commentary; likewise, La Ceppède will defend the orthodoxy of his meditations by enumerating the wide range of devotional masters on which they are based. Gabrielle de Coignard draws on Granada, Chassignet on Lipsius and Duplessis-Mornay, while Humbert writes poems to accompany his own prose meditations.

There is thus plenty of evidence of an external, factual nature for seeing all these poets not merely as casual versifiers of religious themes

301

but as participants in the preoccupation with interior worship which is fundamental both to the Reformation and the Counter-Reformation on a European level. Within the poetry itself, this evidence is mirrored by the recurrence of certain dominant patterns. The penitential prayer-poem, constructed largely but not wholly on the model of the Psalms, emerges as an independent and flexible *genre*, exploited by poets of all kinds, Catholic and Protestant, metropolitan and provincial, professional and amateur. Likewise the sermon-poem, which is particularly popular in sonnet form, but which in other contexts retains many of its salient features—the ironic, aggressive question, the use of violent description or cumulative figures. The poetry of the life of Christ, though less well-defined from a formal point of view, nevertheless has its own characteristic modes or *genres*: the narrative, descriptive mode, with its pastoral and romanesque associations, contrasts sharply with the economical and often didactic sonnet as practised by Favre and La Ceppède, who reflect primarily on the traditional mysteries and moral truths embodied in the Passion. These various *genres* are at least as distinct and recognisable as those established by the Pléiade, as the Pindaric, Horatian or Anacreontic ode, the 'Petrarchan' sonnet, the *hymne* or the *bergerie*. Each has its own range of *topoi*, of themes and images, drawn from the Bible, the Fathers, the medieval hymns, the typological tradition, and the liturgy; at the same time, the language of devotional poetry as a whole is given a wider unity by the interconnexions of the Old and the New Testament, by the modulation of the themes of corruption and purification, by the central *topos* of devotional weeping, the rock of Moses, and the blood of Christ.

It is true that this unity is that of the Christian tradition in general as it was handed down to the Counter-Reformation by the Middle Ages. Nevertheless, the way in which such commonplaces are developed is often directly linked with the procedures of devotional method. The techniques of visualising a situation, of probing its meaning through ritual images, of opening the soul to 'divine affections', are in certain poets the manifest result of the gradual evolution which culminated in the meditative treatises of the Counter-Reformation. These techniques, related as they are to those of rhetoric, offer to the devotional poet a substitute for the rhetorical procedures used by the Pléiade; whether they provide the whole structure of a poem or sequence, or whether they remain an auxiliary to profane rhetoric, they are a major factor in the emergence of a specifically devotional poetry. One of the most striking features of this poetry is the way in which it establishes contact with the physical world. If the abstractions of the professional theologians were to be communicated to the public, if individual laymen were to acquire a sense of the reality and the immediacy of the Church's teaching, such a contact had to be made: the image, which had played a central part in the medieval popularisation of religion, had to be reinterpreted in the light of a wider literacy. The early devotional masters—of whom Bonaventura is perhaps the outstanding example—had never lost their awareness of the literal nature of Christian truth: the presence of God in Creation, the historical reality of the Nativity and the Passion, the physical corruption and mortality which issued from the Fall, all these were taken in their most factual and concrete sense. The religious renewal of the sixteenth century took hold of this tradition and used it in the attempt to give religion a human content, so that, by means of meditation and prayer, the believer might penetrate (if not by-pass) the ritual of public worship and reach the truth embodied in it. Loyola replaced the image-worship of the Middle Ages by teaching men to create their own images. Thus in the later sixteenth century, 'devotion'—for both Catholic and Calvinist—involved first and foremost the physical awareness of man's body and of Christ's body; it involved, too, a sense of terrestrial and cosmic reality, the inexorable significance of height and depth, of light and dark. 'Composition' and 'application of the senses' are not merely devices for making devotion easier: they imply the need to 'incorporate' religion, to give it human and physical values, and the same need determines the high degree of physical urgency one finds in devotional poetry. Even where a description is not elaborate, where it is restricted to a stanza or a line, the use of insistent demonstratives, of bright colour, of sharp contrast or pathetic detail can give momentum to the poem as a whole; the aim is patently to involve the reader's sensual awareness, to represent the Passion or the Fall as a 'natural' event as well as a divine one. As a commonplace procedure, this kind of presentation is subject to standardisation and thus to loss of impact; it may also be abused, as in the 'picturesque' descriptions of César de Nostredame. Furthermore, it would be wrong to assume that 'imaginative devotion' belongs uniquely to the literature of this period. Nevertheless, it found its way into poetry—and other literature—at a time when the literary language is particularly rich in terms of physical reference, and it provided a powerful bulwark against the Malherbian mistrust of detailed and imaged poetry.

At this stage it will be convenient to recall the distinctions made earlier with regard to the nature and function of 'imagery' in devotional writing. On a primary or literal level, the description of a physical state (putrefaction, the Passion, Creation) is the principal object, although in religious terms any such state must have a further significance. On a secondary or figurative level, the poet may use 'figures', which have a fixed place in the hierarchy of significance (manna, the brazen serpent, the Ark), or the more casual *similitude*, which merely provides a convenient analogy (bubbles, fading flowers, a raging sea, Tauler's gibbet); the emblem occupies a place midway between these two. All these forms of imagery gravitate towards the same central truth: the world has a meaning and a purpose, which is reflected both in natural phenomena and in history. Nevertheless, the distinction between them—especially between the 'literal' and the 'figurative'—and the way in which one or the other may be emphasised, is central to the evolution of poetic and devotional style in this period. According to the theory of formal meditation, the affections (the functioning of the *volonté*) should arise both from composition (*imagination*) and from analysis (*entendement*). Thus the devotional writer will require varying degrees of intellectual participation from the reader; and it follows, too, that the descriptive language of composition will demand far less mental effort than the figures and *similitudes* which arise from analytic interpretation. No doubt, the purpose of the *similitude* or the emblem is to facilitate interpretation. Nevertheless, by contrast with the description of Hell or of the Passion, such images do not often evoke a spontaneous, 'physical' emotion: they work in conjunction with the intellect. Now the full formal sequence of meditation is seldom adhered to strictly, even where it has been a direct influence, and it often happens that a devotional writer will adopt one mode or the other. The *imagination* of Jacques de Billy, Georgette de Montenay, Duplessis-Mornay, Goulart, Chandieu, Sponde, Chassignet and Favre tends to be realised in emblematic or epigrammatic terms, and may conscript the figurative *topoi* of humanist learning. On the other hand, Richeome, Desportes (in his prose prayers and his longer poems), Gabrielle de Coignard, Humbert (in his prose *extases*) and César de Nostredame are markedly more descriptive and emotive than figurative and analytic. Such groupings are of course very approximate.

Chassignet partakes of both; some of Gabrielle de Coignard's poems are structured in much the same way as the formal meditation; and La Ceppède's range of modes is wide enough to resist grouping, although I feel that his preferences lie in the didactic and figurative direction. In such cases, it is a question rather of inclination or of a thematic bias than of *parti pris*. However, as was suggested in the last chapter, the difference of emphasis has a historical importance, in that the taste for a 'dévotion aisée' in the early seventeenth century was often met by a reduction or even an omission of the analytic element, and hence of figurative or emblematic images. It is also of some significance that the first group contains many leading Calvinists; it was after all d'Aubigné himself (quoting Henri of Navarre) who complained of the facility of a poetry which contained no intellectual structure and no emblems:

Et moy... je suis las de tant de vers qui ne disent rien, en belles et beaucoup de paroles; ils sont si coulants que le goust en est aussy tost escoulé: les autres me laissent la teste pleine de pensees excellentes, d'images et d'amblemes desquels ont prevalu les anciens. J'ayme bien ces vins qui ont corps, et condamne ceux qui ne cerchent que le coulant à boire de l'eau.[1]

Modern opinion may well agree with this view; it is at any rate important to remember (as those who have written on 'metaphysical' poetry have pointed out) that emotion may arise from thought as well as from a pathetic situation, and that Favre's ability to stimulate the reader's *volonté* is closely related to his handling of argument and image— 'nihil volitum nisi praecognitum'.

It seems likely, then, that the different modes of devotional sensibility provided an independent rhetorical framework which could be used, and in many cases was used, by the religious poets of the Counter-

---

[1] *Œuvres complètes*, ed. Réaume et de Caussade, vol. I, p. 459 (from the *Lettres touchant quelques poincts de diverses sciences*, XI). It should of course not be forgotten that the emblem-book flourished throughout the seventeenth century: one need mention only Ripa, Heinsius, or Pierre Lemoyne himself to give an idea of the prestige of emblematists in this period. However, it seems to me that, in France, literature as such—and lyric poetry in particular—became increasingly divorced from allegorical and symbolic modes of thought after the turn of the century.

Reformation and the Reformation. Other factors, apart from the influence of profane poetics, must also be taken into account—the direct exploitation of Old Testament rhetoric, the impact of sermon-technique, the development of certain aspects of visual art. But since all these are intimately related with the specific techniques of devotion, one need only give a rather broader connotation to the phrase 'devotional sensibility' to retain the validity of the proposition.

It is essential, on the other hand, to probe more deeply into this sensibility and the implications it might have for the nature of poetry. The concept of meditation, if applied directly to poetic creation, would seem to carry with it a rejection of formalism, if not of formal control: and something very like this seems to be happening in certain poems of Desportes, and in different ways in the work of Gabrielle de Coignard and César de Nostredame. La Ceppède will improvise moral interpretations of given meditative situations; while on a more general level the development of the flexible *stances*-form for the purposes of reflection and prayer is surely connected with the extempore nature of devotion. This informality might further encourage a 'personalisation' of the poetic art, since the content of the meditation would often arise from the individual circumstances in which a poet found himself. La Noue uses his own experience as an element of composition; the *Voyage de la Montagne* and Boyssières's *Prière en se lavant le matin* have a familiar, everyday point of departure; Anne de Marquets refers to her monastic occupations, La Ceppède to his profession; and amid the numerous poems of sickness and affliction, one not infrequently finds details so specific that a sickness actually undergone by the poet seems to be the main source of reflection.

However, several reservations suggest themselves at once. In the first place, although meditation was intended eventually to arise from personal improvisation, the devotional methodologists were careful to guard against dangerous 'originality' of thought: the methods are themselves formal, and the matter provided was so abundant and so highly standardised that only a poet of considerable creative powers could place it in a fully personal context. The *vanitas* imagery, the details of the Passion narrative, the sickness poems themselves illustrate the tendency of devotional writing to give way to the anonymity of tradition. Likewise, any informality of diction was likely to be inhibited by

Conclusion

the custom of borrowing stylistic elements from profane poetry, by the introduction of humanist allusion, or by contamination from the ritual language of public worship and prayer.

Thus one will find in French devotional poetry no personal statement as forceful as Herbert's *The Collar* or Donne's *Good Friday 1613. Riding Westward*. But as we saw in the case of Sponde's *Stances et sonnets de la mort*, it would be wrong to assume that lyric poetry must be 'personal' on this level. Sponde is the more impressive for the sense he conveys of a public statement: the intimacy of 'Pour qui tant de travaux? Pour vous?' or of 'Vivez, hommes, vivez: mais si faut-il mourir' is not that of an individual meditating in solitude, but of a preacher who has to approach the individual through the mass. Likewise, La Ceppède's meditation is essentially the evocation of a timeless and universal tradition, although, like Sponde's, its character is determined in the last analysis by the sensibility of an individual poet. The devotional poets are concerned less with the idiosyncrasies of personal experience than with the relationship between the individual and a universal pattern. For the *dévot*, the exercise of the *volonté* reflected the action of the Holy Ghost, the divine love which moved the universe and drew man's soul back to its Creator. Thus when Favre is deeply anxious about a sterility of the affections, an inability to respond to the objects of meditation, it is because he feels that it is essential for the individual to participate, through his own personal *volonté*, in the will of God; and it is precisely by projecting one's own personality into that of the Virgin Mary, or St Peter, or Christ himself, that the sterility may be overcome. Indeed, the devotional technique of 'identification' is based on psychological assumptions which are relevant to the interpretation of sixteenth-century poetry as a whole. The Renaissance lyric is often 'dramatic', in that the poet's voice is heard through the medium of an adopted rôle: the love-poet writes not as a lover but *as if he were* a lover, so that, through the mimesis of human passion, he may penetrate more deeply into the nature of passion itself, and perhaps participate in one of the fundamental forces of the universe.[1] Once

---

[1] The rhetorical technique of self-dramatization is discussed by R. Griffiths, 'The Influence of Formulary Rhetoric upon French Renaissance Tragedy', *MLR*, 59 (1964), pp. 204–5, 208. In mentioning the association between human love and the motive forces of the universe (the allegory of the Graces, etc.), I am thinking of the pattern of ideas analysed by Wind in *Pagan Mysteries in the Renaissance*.

again, pejorative judgements on the 'insincerity' of such an approach would be totally misplaced.

Finally, having established earlier that devotional poetry imported a great deal from profane traditions, one must ask what evidence exists for supposing that, conversely, the modes of devotional writing affected non-religious literature in the first half of the seventeenth century. This is a difficult question, and it requires far more documentation than is available at present, but one or two indications can be given. Certainly there was a very close mingling of sacred and profane from the turn of the century. This contact was not so much a question of a conscious reconciliation, as it had been for Du Bartas, and as it was for La Ceppède: it took the form rather of a convergence of two previously separate currents. In certain areas of lay society, devotion and hence devotional literature were now becoming fashionable: many poets and *romanciers* produced devotional works and secular works with little visible change of mood or intention, whereas it had previously been normal for a writer to reject his 'youthful follies' when he turned to the sacred muse. This movement carried with it a certain secularisation of religious literature: I feel that César de Nostredame's poetry, for all its overtly Christian themes, is less 'religious' than Scève's *dizains* or even than Ronsard's *Cassandre* sonnets, in that it lacks any profound sense of the relationship between the material universe and the divine. Under such circumstances, there was clearly a maximum possibility that the literary styles developed in a devotional context (the devotional rhetoric we have been discussing) would be carried over into secular literature. To be more specific, it is significant that devotional titles should begin to be given to non-religious poems; that Tristan, Théophile and Saint-Amant should sometimes base the structure of their poems on an improvisation stemming from the *imagination* or *fantaisie*; and that the love of picturesque description, of bright colours, of *minutiae*, should link César de Nostredame with Richeome on the one hand and, say, Tristan on the other.[1] One wonders, too, whether the devotional cultivation of emotional facility, and the 'literature of tears' which is derived from it, are responsible, in part at least, for the seventeenth-century interest in the nuances of emotion and in a literature which can

---

[1] Compare Odette de Mourgues's discussion of the 'Myopic or disconnected vision' of early seventeenth-century poets (*op. cit.* ch. 6, sect. 4) with Bremond's comment that 'Richeome a l'esprit myope, comme les yeux' (*Hum. dév.* p. 66).

move to tears. All this must, in the present context, remain speculation; nevertheless, it is undeniable that devotional poetry, in all its forms, raises questions which are highly relevant to the poetic creation of both the sixteenth and the seventeenth centuries.

It would be impertinent to summarise here the qualities of the leading devotional poets: literary evaluation must arise from the particularities of analysis, and is usually unimpressive in epigrammatic form. Nevertheless, it is with the poets themselves that I should like to conclude this study. They are perhaps not major poets in any universal sense, and one is sometimes aware of the gap which separates them from the best of their English equivalents, from a Herbert or a Donne. Yet this is undoubtedly a period rich in poetry which is still little known. The longer religious poems of Desportes have been almost totally neglected, although they represent an illuminating aspect of his style; and as Favre's sonnets become more accessible their qualities of seriousness, control and coherence will no doubt be recognised. This poetry, together with that of César de Nostredame and of more familiar poets such as Sponde, Chassignet and La Ceppède, has a value which goes far beyond historical curiosity; and even among the lesser poets, there is much worth reading, certainly as much as there is among the minor poets of the Pléiade. At the same time, one feels in all of them, from Jacques de Billy to La Ceppède, the impulse of the sixteenth-century religious revival. There is the sense of purpose in their work which moved the great Counter-Reformation artists; and thus, for all their limitations, they participate in a movement which changed the taste and sensibility of Europe. At this point, historical importance and intrinsic value converge. 'Deserte et ruinee est toute la terre, n'y ayant aucun, qui avec attention s'addonne à penser les choses divines', declared Granada, echoing Jeremiah;[1] and in their effort to fulfil this need, the devotional poets, Catholic and Calvinist, contributed to the evolution both of devotion and of poetry.

[1] *Vray chemin*, 'Prologue et argument de ce livre', *non pag.*

APPENDIX

SUPPLEMENTARY ILLUSTRATIONS FOR

SUPPLEMENTARY ILLUSTRATIONS FOR

CHAPTERS 6 AND 7

The following texts, which demanded quotation *in extenso*, have been grouped here to avoid interrupting the argument of the chapters concerned. The spelling, punctuation, etc., are as in the quotations given elsewhere (see 'Note on the Texts', above, Preface, p. xii); the editions used are those referred to in my text and in the Bibliography.

I. HENRY HUMBERT

La Sepmaine saincte, pp. 127–32: *Jesus flagellé*

Extase

Approchés Ames fidelles, voyés si vous pourrés recongnoistre vostre Dieu: Contemplés de pres les traicts de son Corps: envisagés ceste face ou toutes les beautés s'estoient rencontrées, ou les graces avoient estalés les plus riches meubles de leur parade, le sang qui trouve aultant de sources qu'il à de veines, nous le rend mescongnu, et les coups imprimés sur sa chair sacree ont effaces les vestiges de sa beauté: Beauté qui avoit accoustumé de ravir si doulcement les cœurs par les yeux; Beauté qui donnoit de l'amour aux esprits plus 128/ rebours. Vous sa mere tres-/pure, ses plus cheres delices, qui l'avés eslevé si tendrement, relevés nous de ce doubte qui nous tient en suspends: Asseurés nous si c'est vostre filz bien-aymé, l'unique contentement de voz yeux, les voluptés de vostre Ame. Dictes nous Mere de grace si c'est celuy que vous avés allaicté si amoureusement: Si les fontaines sanglantes qui ruissellent de tous les endroicts de son corps vous empeschent de le recongnoistre, baignés ses playes des torrents de voz larmes, afin que nous puissions revoir les astres de ces beaux yeux qui languissent de nostre amour: Ha! c'est mon Dieu, c'est mon Redempteur qui est attaché à ce pilier, et veult recevoir tant de 129/ playes pour les faire servir d'appareil à mes blessures. / Depuis la plante des pieds, jusques au sommet de la teste il n'y à point de santé en luy. Mais la tempeste de tant de coups qui se descharge dessus sa chair precieuse n'agite pas si rudement son corps que son Ame. Les foëtz penetrent jusques au centre de son cœur et le deschirent en un million de parcelles. Faictes cesser

l'orage de ces coups bourreaux passés en toutes sortes d'inhumanité? (*sic*)
Il ne reste plus de place ou vous puissiés appliquer le cachet de vostre rage.
Vous avés couvert son corps d'une playe qui se dilate par touts ces membres,
vous avés navré profondement son Ame; Est-ce pas assés pour saouler voz
cruautés abbreuvées de son sang: Repaisses voz yeux cruelz de ce spectacle
130/ qui pourroit glisser / la compassion dans les cœurs, ou jamais la raison ne
trouva la porte ouverte. Les forces de voz impietés bandées de touts les nerfs
de vostre envie, seront plustost lasches et engourdies, que la vigueur de son
courage. Toutes les peines que vous luy preparés luy sont legeres, puis-que
c'est un acheminement à nostre salut. Il est beaucoup moins offencé des
tourments qu'il endure que de voz offences; ses blessures ne luy sont pas si
mortelles que voz injures; Mais il guarit les playes de voz consciences par
celles de ses membres, reçevant la descharge de voz foëtz en son corps, et
celle de voz pechés en son ame.

131/   *Stances*

Pilate tes efforts demeurent sans puissance,
Le Sauveur s'est livré pour nostre delivrance,
Nostre eslargissement depend de sa prison.
Bruslant d'un S. desir, par sa mort il pourchasse
La vie des humains, et refuse la grace
Puis que son chastiement nous donne le pardon.

Tu faicts tomber des coups sur le Dieu de Justice
Des larrons et des serfs le foët est le supplice,
Mon Dieu pour quelle faute endurés vous ces coups?
J'ay commis le forfaict, vous portés les battures
Les playes du peché vous donnent ces injures,
Et ma punition retombe dessus vous.

Ma guarison se trouve en vostre maladie,
Vous courrés au trespas pour asseurer ma vie,
Vostre naufrage faict que j'arrive à bon port.
Accours à ce spectable (*sic*), ô ame criminelle,
Et regarde combien ta playe fut mortelle
Puis qu'un Dieu va cerchant le remede en sa mort.

De coups de foëtz sonnants, l'orage et la tempeste
N'espargne aulcunement ni les pieds ni la teste,
Les verges ont rougi la neige de son flanc.
Ainsi pour tant de coups que le Sauveur endure
Il semble estre couvert d'une seule blessure,
Qui rend le corps entier abbreuvé de son sang.

132/ Les bourreaux arrousés de ces tiedes fontaines
Que l'agneau sans macule escoulle de ses veines
Redoublent les efforts d'une sanglante main.
Celuy est le plus doulx qui est moins pitoiable
Le plus cruel effect est le plus amiable
Et le plus rigoureux est le moins inhumain.

Jesus parmy les coups sent croistre son courage
Se monstrant desireux de souffrir davantage
Bienqu'il soit martyré presque jusqu'au mourir.
Les Juifs sont espuisés et de force, et d'haleine.
Mais luy dure tousjours amoureux de sa peine
Son mal n'est si amer que doulx nostre guarir.

Encore que le foët d'une meurtriere trace
Ternisse entiérement de son lustre la grace,
Les tourments sont legers qui ne touchent qu'au corps.
Mais les coups sont des dards, donc (*sic*) l'outrageuse lame
Par les playes du corps penetrent dedans l'ame
Ce sont morts par dedans, et doulceurs par dehors.

Approchons du Sauveur afin de le congnoistre
Ce n'est pas nostre Roy, ce n'est pas nostre maistre
Si, mais il est changé à force de douleur.
Les playes qu'il recoit nous sont des ouvertures
Qui decouvrent l'amour envers ses creatures.
Ne le pouvant au corps on le congnoist au cœur.

2. GABRIELLE DE COIGNARD

Œuvres chrestiennes, pp. 197–205: from *Complainte de la Vierge Marie*

Adonc pour soulager ceste troupe attristee,
A temps il suscita Joseph d'Arimatée,
Lequel obtint pour eux congé du gouverneur,
D'enterrer le sainct corps de nostre Redempteur;
Et puis s'accompaignant du vieillard Nicodeme,
Et de tout bien pourveu alla sur l'heure mesme,
Trouver les affligez à l'entour de la croix,
Qui font gemir le ciel par leurs precieuses voix,
Portans avecques eux l'unguent aromatique,
Pour embaulmer le corps a la façon antique:
Tous deux chargez d'outilz, d'eschelles, et marteaux,
De souefves liqueurs, et delicats drapeaux,

Ayants les yeux mouillez, et la face dolente,
Ils vont voir sur le mont ceste croix eminente,
Lors tous pleins de regretz gemissantz hautement,
Regardent trespassé le Sauveur tout clement,
Ayant devant leurs yeux ses graces nompareilles,
Ses miracles divins pleins de grandes merveilles,
198/ Et le malheur prochain, qui attendoit au port
Les Hebrieux obstinez cause de ceste mort.
La Vierge et ses amis a la premiere veuë
Eurent le cœur troublé, et l'ame toute esmeuë,
Pensant que les Vieillars fussent d'autres meurtriers
Pour mettre le sainct corps en pieces et quartiers:
Mais voyant que ceux-cy venoient pour leur complaire,
Et cognoissant le bien qu'il (*sic*) desiroient leur faire,
Le bien-heureux sainct Jean avec un doux parler,
De la vierge approcha, et pour la consoler,
Madame, luy dit-il: cessez un peu vos larmes,
Et vous fortifiez de vos cruels alarmes,
Voicy ces bons Seigneurs, qui pleins de charité
Nous veullent secourir à la necessité;
Le grand Dieu tout puissant par sa douce clemence
Leur a pour nous aider donné ceste prudence,
Ils viennent bien pourveus de ce qui est requis,
A fin d'ensevelir vostre bien aymé fils.
Quelle extreme douleur deschiroit les entrailles
De ceux qui preparoient ces tristes funerailles?
Par les frequents sanglotz les voix leur tressailloient,
Et tous couvers de pleurs hautement gemissoient:
S'ils se vouloient lever sur leurs jambes tremblantes
Le cœur leur deffailloit d'angoisses vehementes:
Ils avoient le cerveau en ruisseau transformé,
Leur langue avoit perdu l'office accoustumé.
Mais considere encor, ô ame assoupie,
Qu'ils estoient lors martyrs sans esprit, et sans vie,
Voyant mort le Seigneur dont le pouvoir hautain
Distribue a chacun la vie par sa main.
Tu peux voir maintenant que le cœur qui fort aime
Vit plus en son aimé, que non pas en soy mesme,
Et puis que Jesus-Christ estoit tout leur amour,
199/ Ils mouroient comme luy mille fois en ce jour,
En ce triste destroit, et douloureux passage
Ma plume ne pourroit escrire d'avantage:

313

Mais je veux contempler dedans mon foible esprit
Les ameres douleurs que la vierge souffrit,
Quand les sages vieillards ayans reprins halaine
Monterent sur la croix, et mirent toute peine
D'arracher les fors cloux, et des pieds et des mains
De son fils trespassé pour sauver les humains.
Elle avoit de ses pleurs les joues toutes teintes,
Et son cœur virginal blessé de mille atteintes,
Son couvre-chef mouillé des larmes de ses yeux,
Ensanglanté du sang de son fils glorieux:
Et comme elle apperçoit qu'on arrache des fentes
Les cloux fichez encor es mains toutes puissantes:
Elle sent arracher son ame de son corps,
Et ce glaive poinctu luy donne mille morts.
Le sainct disciple aimé, et la triste Marie,
Soustenoient de beaux draps le divin corps sans vie,
Et puis ces bonnes gens descendent jusqu'aux pieds,
Par le sang tout caillé en la croix tout liez,
Donc pour oster les cloux de la chair bien heureuse,
Il y faut bien aller de force vigoureuse,
Pour arracher les pieds d'avec les cloux pointus,
D'un trop rude marteau faloit frapper dessus.
Je vous prie Joseph, aussi vous Nicodeme,
Pour l'amour du defunct dont ceste face blesme
Vous attendrit le cœur d'une extreme pitié,
Et vous tient embrassez de sa saincte amitié:
Que vous frappez tout doux sur ceste playe amere,
Car decloüant le fils vous encloüez la mere,
Pource que detordants les membres de son fils,
Vous faictes defaillir les siens esvanouis.
200/ Apres tout doucement le bon Joseph se charge,
De ce precieux corps que nous servit de targe,
Des traicts qui se devoient contre nous descocher,
Benin il a receu les marques en sa chair.
Quand la Vierge apperçoit la piteuse descente
De ce corps precieux, elle tend et presente
Ses deux bras langoureux laçés à l'environ,
Pour recevoir son fils en son triste giron,
Et prie ses amis, que puis que la malice
De ceux qui avoient fait ce sanglant sacrifice,
Avoit privé son cœur de pouvoir dire adieu
A son enfant aymé: maintenant en ce lieu

Elle aye les baisers d'un congé pitoyable,
Et tienne entre ses bras ce Seigneur admirable.
Puis l'ayant de la croix sur son sein retiré,
Elle embrasse le corps de playes deschiré;
Et joignant prez de soy la vie de son ame,
Un glaive de douleur son pauvre cœur entame,
Puis voyant de son fils le visage sanglant,
Elle aproche le sien de larmes ruisselant,
Sans craindre la rigueur des poignantes espines,
Qui rougissoient les lis de ses beautez divines,
Et mouillant de son sang sa face, et ses habis,
Elle lave de pleurs les playes de son fils.
O vous tous elemens escoutez la complaincte,
Les sanglots, et souspirs de ceste vierge saincte,
Elle ne peut parler tant la douleur l'atteint,
Mais dans son triste cœur muette elle se plaint,
Disant: ô mon cher fils, seul repos de ma vie,
O vigueur de mes yeux, qui es ores ternie,
O divine splendeur, et luisante clairté,
Qui as voulu tacher ce miroüer de beauté,
Quel si poignant chappeau, et couronne espineuse,
Deschire tout le cuir de ta face amoureuse,
Qu'elle lance a blessé ce cœur plein d'amitié?
(O barbare fureur) sans aucune pitié!
Voicy les sainctes mains qui par leur grand'puissance,
Resuscitoyent les morts, et donnoient allegeance
A tous pauvres chetifs, dont le pouvoir divin
Par miracle excellent transmua l'eau en vin.
Donques ils ont bien peu ces inhumains barbares
Prophaner l'honneur sainct de tes graces si rares.
Ha! mon fils, et mon sang d'où vient ce grand meschef?
Qu'elle mer de douleur me passe sur le chef?
Qui me consolera en mon triste vefvage,
Je n'auray plus aucun qui mes ennuis soulage.
Où es tu mon cher fils, mon seul contentement,
Qui à tous les mortels donnois enseignement:
Je ne te verray plus venir las, et debile
D'enseigner, et prescher aux Hebrieux l'Evangile.
Plus je n'essuyeray ta sueur en esté,
Lors que seras lassé du chemin trop hasté:
Je ne te verray plus, ô penser delectable,
Assis au pres de moy, et manger à ma table,

Me donnant le repas de ta saincte douceur,
O plaisir tost changé en tristesse, et douleur.
J'ay perdu tout mon bien, je n'ay rien a me plaire,
Il faut que desormais je vive solitaire,
O mon fils bien aymé tu ne me responds pas,
Puis qu'on t'en a privé par un cruel trespas.
O gracieux parler, ô langue nompareille,
Qui ravissoit mon cœur d'une douce merveille:
Pourquoy ne parles tu en despit de la mort,
Pour donner à mes maux quelque joye et support:
Pour adoucir un peu ceste angoisse mortelle,
Que j'ay te voyant mort d'une mort si cruelle?

. . . .

202/   O amateur benin du pauvre humain lignage,
Qui baillez a la mort vostre fils en hostage,
Vous sçavez la douleur et griefve affliction,
Qui surmonte mon cœur pour ceste passion,
Car tout autant de coups et playes infinies
Qu'a souffert ce sainct corps, autant j'en ay senties,
Et l'estoc de douleur a percé mille fois
Ce mien corps affligé au pied de ceste croix:
Mais bien qu'ores je sois la plus dolente mere,
Qui soit et qui sera en ce val de misere:
Je vous rends ô mon Dieu, mille et mille mercis
Pour mes afflictions mes peines et soucis:
Je vous loüe a jamais, soit que je vive ou meure
Pour l'amere douleur, et tourment que j'endure:
Mon cœur ne veut Seigneur que tout ce qu'il vous plait
Et qu'en tout et par tout vostre vouloir soit fait.
Le glaive douloureux qu'il vous plait que je porte,
Je le fiche en mon cœur d'une volonté forte,
Et rends pareillement graces de vos faveurs,
Pour tant d'infinis biens, pour tous les grands honneurs
Desquels j'ay herité par vostre saincte grace:
Je vous rends le depost en ceste triste place
De vostre unique fils, puis que la palle mort,
203/   Par ses traits furieux m'en a privée a tort,
Mais que pour mes travaux vous benissent les Anges,
Et mes larmes et pleurs vous servent de louanges.
     Ainsi dedans son cœur la Vierge se plaignoit,
Et le dueil des amis le sien accompaignoit.
Mais voyant que la nuict avec sa robbe brune

Avoit couvert le ciel, et ja la claire lune
Reluisoit pour servir au funebre appareil,
Reprenant a son tour l'office du soleil:
Ils prient humblement la Vierge glorieuse
De montrer au besoin son ame genereuse,
En baillant le sainct corps qu'elle tenoit serré,
Pour l'oindre, et parfumer, et puis estre enterré.
Mais elle veut garder ceste riche despouille,
Et de l'eau de ses yeux elle lave, et le mouille,
Et le tient enserré dans ses bras langoureux,
Où son cueur l'arrestoit d'un desir amoureux:
Mais a force de pleurs ceste trouppe esplourée
Receut le corps divin de la Vierge sacrée,
Se mettant tout autour de ce thresor divin,
Tout ainsi que l'on voit au gracieux matin
Se renger doucement un bel essein d'avettes,
Pour succer la douceur des plus douces fleurettes:
Ainsi le sainct troupeau autour de luy rengé,
Faisoit mille regrets sur ce corps outragé,
Regardant le Seigneur, pasle, froid, et sans vie,
Les yeux tous enfoncez, et la face ternie:
Le corps ensanglanté, rompu[,] martyrisé,
Et le sang precieux goute a goute espuisé,
Il est bien accomply ce que dit le Prophete,
Que du plus bas des pieds jusqu'au haut de la teste
Il n'avoit point en luy ny forme ny santé,
Tant inhumainement ils l'avoient tourmenté.

204/ Approche toy mon cœur, il est temps que tu ayes
Congé de ton Seigneur de contempler ses playes,
Le voila estendu sur les bras languissants
De ses tristes amis de douleur pallissants,
Soubs le sanglant autel du divin sacrifice,
Dont le piteux object t'esmouve à son service,
Va mesler les unguents, accoustrer les bandeaux,
Estendre doucement les linges, et drapeaux.
Les Anges glorieux desireroient bien estre
En ce lieu douloureux pour servir à leur maistre,
Aydans à ses amis, qui en pleurs, et souspirs,
Poserent le sainct corps, repos de leurs desirs,
Sur un suaire blanc avec grand doleance,
Afin de l'embaulmer en toute reverence.
La mere estoit au chef, la Magdaleyne aux pieds,

Le reste du troupeau aux deux costez rengez.
Puis chascun à genoux se retrousse les manches,
Espanchant ces liqueurs avecques leurs mains blanches.
Mais voyant les pertuis des sacrez pieds, et mains,
La rompure des cloux, les tourments inhumains,
La vuidange du sang, et ses beautez esteintes,
De rechef estonnez recommencent leurs plaintes:
O mon Dieu, mon desir, qui de tout as le soin,
Qui est celuy qui n'a un extreme besoin
De tes divin (*sic*) unguents pour oindre ses blesseures?
O heureux medecin de toutes creatures,
Gueris je te supply par tes sainctes douceurs
Le mal enraciné du secret de nos cœurs.
C'est toy doux Redempteur, qui les cognois, et sondes,
Comme font tes amis tes playes si profondes,
Qu'ils comblent doucement de baulmes precieux,
Destrempant ces liqueurs de larmes de leurs yeux,
Sans que l'unguent faillit aux boittes de ces dames,
205/ Ny les pleurs à leurs yeux, ny l'amour a leurs ames,
Et sans rien espargner fut oingt le corps divin,
Et sainctement plié dans un drap de fin lin:
Mais il falut porter en ceste nuict obscure,
Ce precieux tresor jusqu'a la sepulture,
   Mon ame je te pry' ne t'espouvante pas,
De voir ton Redempteur porté mort sur le bras
De ses plus chers amis; qui dressent leur voyage
Au sepulchre choisi pour leur pelerinage.
L'on porte le fils mort, la mere est au mourir,
Le reste du troupeau ne se peut soustenir.
L'Apostre bien aymé souffre une estrange peine,
Et le ciel retentit des pleurs de Magdelaine:
Les Anges estonnez regardent des hauts cieux,
Les mysteres sacrez de leur Dieu glorieux:
Tout ce grand univers regarde la merveille,
Et l'accomplissement de l'œuvre nompareille:
Tous les quatre elemens demeurent alterez,
Et d'une estrange peur les dæmons effroyez,
Voyans mourir celuy dont la mort glorieuse
Resuscitoit les morts de la tombe oublieuse.
Ne veux tu point mourir, ô mon cœur endurcy
En ce monde trompeur, ha je voy bien que si:
Va donc bruslant d'amour ce tien Redempteur suivre,

Gabrielle de Coignard

Et ne desire plus dedans ce corps revivre,
Que ce marbre gelé se fende par tronçons,
Et face rejaillir les pleurs de ses glaçons,
Que la moitie de vous garde la croix sanglante,
L'autre suive les pas de la troupe dolente,
Qui marche lentement au chemin de douleur,
Portant reverement le corps de leur Seigneur,
Avec pleurs et souspirs, qui empeschoient leurs veües
Envoyans leurs clameurs aux plus loingtaines nues.

3. ODET DE LA NOUE

Poésies chrestiennes, pp. 254–8: from *Discours meditatif sur la semaine de Pasques*

Mais qui (sans s'esmouvoir) pourroit à ceste fois
S'imaginer Jesus estendu sur la croix,
Ayant vray'ment nostre ame et nostre chair humaine,
Mortelle ainsi que l'autre et sensible à la peine,
Non un corps fantastic, comme d'aucuns ont creu,
Qui d'aucune douleur ne se peut voir esmeu?
Deux grands clous vont perçant ses paumes estandues,
Les attachant au bois: de ses playes fendues
Vont deux ruisseaux de sang courant de deux costez,
Lavement precieux de nos iniquitez.
Un tiers fleuve descend de ses plantes trouées,
Qu'un gros fer va tenant l'un sur l'autre clouees.
Son corps n'ayant soustien que sur ses rudes clous,
Panche tout, et panchant fait eslargir leurs trous.
Il n'a tendons en luy, nerfs, arteres, ne veines,
Qui ne soyent bourrellez d'un milion de geines.
Bref en telle agonie, au lieu de reconfort,
Il n'a devant les yeux qu'une image de mort.
Deux malheureux brigans, pour plus de moquerie,
Crucifiez à ses flancs lui tienent compagnie,
Qui de mesme en leur disgrace oublient leur douleur,
Pour mocquer sa misere et rire son malheur.
Les passans blasphemant lui vont hochant la teste.
Les Scribes, Pharisiens, les Prestres faisant feste,
De son affliction vont maudissant celuy,
Qui ne se sauve point et veut sauver autruy.
  O miserables Juifs! miserables gens-d'armes,
Bourreaux de nostre Christ! qui en change de larmes,

319

Dont vous devriez plorer si damnable forfait,
Alliez riant des maux que vous lui aviez fait;
Vous fustes bien cruels et d'un meschant courage
De contempler (joyeux) un si barbare outrage,
Pour qui le soleil mesme obscurcit son bel œil,
Et fut comme enfermé trois heures au cercueil.
Le voile s'en fendit: on vid trembler la terre,
Les corps morts se lever des monumens de pierre:
Tout s'esmeut, et vos cœurs plus durs qu'un diament,
N'en furent pas touchez du moindre sentiment.
    O jour vray'ment funebre entre les plus funebres,
Digne d'estre obscurci d'eternelles tenebres!
O jour! jour non pas jour, plustost espesse nuict,
Ou le soleil de vie au trespas est conduit.
Le mortel à la mort l'immortel mesme livre,
Qui s'estoit fait mortel pour l'en rendre delivre.
Ce jour la soit marqué sur tous les jours de l'an,
Pour plorer le malheur que nous acquit Adam:
Tel qu'au lieu d'y cercher en Dieu quelque remede,
Nous tuasmes celuy qui venoit à nostre aide.
    Mais quoy? ce fut ce jour source de tous nos biens,
Que Jesus Christ brisa tous les rudes liens
Du peché, de la mort, de l'enfer et du monde,
Qui nous tenoyent captifs sous un joug si immonde.
Quoy donc? pleurerons-nous? serons nous attristez,
Nous souvenant du jour qu'on nous a rachetez?

256/ C'est bien pour s'esjouir, que toutes nos ordures,
Toutes nos laschetez, noz fautes, nos souilleures,
Trouverent ce jour la lavement dans le sang,
Qui lui coula des pieds, et des mains, et du flanc.

.   .   .   .

(*The Resurrection*)

L'un s'en va desbouchant la porte du tombeau,
Pour faire trouver vray ce miracle nouveau.
Son vestement est blanc. Son regard comme un foudre
Le courage aux soldats fait tellement dissoudre,
Qu'ils tombent comme morts, les femmes en ce temps
Il r'asseure, et leur dit qu'elles voyent dedans....
    O jour, le plus beau jour que jamais on ait veu!
Jour, qui des devant jour luisoit d'un plus cler feu,
Qu'onques ne resplendit la plus belle journée,
Qu'esclaire le soleil au plus chaud de l'année!

N'estoit-il point plus clair, quand ce Dieu glorieux,
Dieu par qui ont clarté tous les flambeaux des cieux
Changea le corps mortel qu'il avoit daigné prendre,
En un corps triomphant, tel qu'il nous promet rendre?

4. CÉSAR DE NOSTREDAME

Rimes spirituelles, pp. 33–9: *Divers Cantiques, a la sacrée Nativité du Sauveur du monde, Cantique premier*

1. Cependant que la clere Lune
Va ses beaux Astres arrangeant,
Qui pour argenter la nuict brune
Ont tous pris leur robe d'Argent,
Et qu'elle' est de rayons parée
Presqu'au Soleil accomparée,
Dans son char celeste et nuictal,
Tout fait de perle et de cristal,
Que vestus d'or, et de gloire
Les petits Amours du Ciel
Chantent d'une voix de miel,
Ce bel Hymne de victoire,
Iô pœan Evoé
Iô CHRIST Noé Noé.

34 /

2. La pucelle clere et brunette,
Au teinct sans macule et tout beau,
Qui tient soubs ses pieds ce planete,
Et le fait servir d'Escabeau,
Qui couvre d'ombrage et de toiles
Mesme les plus vives estoilles,
Descouvrant les raiz precieux
De son visage et de ses yeux
En robe chaste et nymphale
Disoit adorant le fruict,
Qu'elle mesmes avoit produict,
Ceste chanson triomphale,
Iô, etc.

3. Ains que l'Aube, qui perle et dore
L'Horison d'un pourpre riant,
Et que l'astre Roy qu'elle adore
Fit son entrée en Orient:
Ains que sa robe perse'aymée

Feut de cent cloux d'or parsemée
Brillants comme petits crayons
Du Soleil et de ses rayons,
Que le soir, la matinée,
Les Estés, et les Hyvers
35 / Mesurassent l'univers,
Dieu m'avoit predestinée.
Iô, etc.

4. Avant qu'il ouvrit la grand porte
Du vague Palais des oiseaux,
Et que sa main puissante et forte
Balançast les sources des eaux;
Ains que la pesante machine
Vit rouler dessur son eschine
Le Nil, le Gange, l'Eridan,
Et qu'il eust faict de terre Adam;
Ains que la mer eust ses bornes,
Commençant de triompher,
A l'Empereur de l'Enfer
Je brisoy desja les cornes.
Iô, etc.

5. Avant que les planchers du monde
Eussent portés et soustenus
D'un art de merveille profonde
Des ces hauts collosses chenus;
Ains que ces geantes chenues,
Qui montent par dessus les nuës
36 / Avec le caucase arrogant
Allassent les Astres morgant,
Je mesjouyssoy posée
Dedans un throsne Royal,
Avec mon amy loyal,
A mon Dieu mesme espousée.
Iô, etc.

6. Au recit d'une telle histoire,
Dont les Cieux sont esmerveillés,
Et d'un si beau chant de victoire
Les pasteurs se sont esveillés,
Puis ont pris du laict et des pommes
Pour offrir au plus beau des hommes,
Et d'aigneaux tous blancs pour l'Autel

De ce bel enfant immortel,
Courans devers la contrée,
Ou ces merveilles gisoient,
Et les Anges redisoient
Ce bel Hymne à son entrée,
Iô, etc.

37 /

7. Bien tost ont veu dans une estable
Mille petits Amours danser,
Et la Vierge plus delectable,
Que l'esprit humain sçeut penser,
Adorant une creature
Telle, qu'onc ne monstra nature,
Dieu beau petit garson tout neuf
Riant entre l'Asne et le Bœuf,
Et dessus un lict de mousse,
Qu'alloit Joseph estoffant,
Ce petit Prince eschauffant
Avec leur haleine douce.
Iô, etc.

8. Lors avec grande reverence
Ils ont à genoux adoré,
Remplis de joye et d'esperance
Ce petit enfant tout doré,
Puis ont veneré d'un sainct zele
Ceste Royalle Damoiselle,
Puis ont estallés leurs presans
Avec des visages plaisans,
Puis ont admirans sa gloire
Dans ces humbles drappellets,
Baisé ses pieds potelets
Plus blancs que neige et qu'yvoire.

38 /

Iô, etc.

9. D'or est le poil de son chef alme,
Qui nouë en deux tresors pareils,
Son front est un Ciel net et calme,
Ou brillent deux petits Soleils,
Sa jouë une pomme vermeille,
Sa bouche' un Arc plain de merveille,
Ses bras, et ses doigts, et leur tour
Semblent faicts et polis au tour,

Et sur la peau tendre et neuve
De ce corps tendre et naïf
Tout de laict et de sang vif
L'envie un seul poinct ne treuve.
  Iô, etc.

10. Son œil forme un ris, ou s'abreuve
Le Ciel de merveille touché,
Son bras droict un peu se releve,
L'autre est sur son ventre couché,
Ses jambelletes sont croisées
A l'envy des Anges baisées,
Tout son corps tout clair et tout beau
Luit comm' un celeste flambeau;
En ce miracle d'ouvrage
L'Art de peincture est vaincu,
Et n'y voit l'œil plus aigu
Rien qui s'enfondre ou s'ombrage.
  Iô, etc.

11. Lors ce miracle des miracles,
Ceste image de la beauté,
Duquel ont parlé tant d'oracles,
Et tant de Prophetes chanté,
Avec sa main tendre et rosine,
Qui coule une manne' Ambrosine,
Et qui la tempeste applanit,
Reçevant leurs dons les benit
Cependant que l'Aube more
Vient de l'indique sejour
Et porte avec soy le jour
Pour adorer ceste Aurore.
  Iô, etc.

Dymas, ou le Bon Larron: introductory sonnet, *non pag.*

Envie, cruauté, rancœur, faulses Doctrines,
Conseil meschant, gent dure, implacable fureur,
Or impur, felonie, orgueil, malice, erreur,
Baisers, glaives, bastons, sacrilege, rapines,
Mespris, Buffes, souflets, roseaux, titres, espines,
Coqs, Cordages, crachats et ministres d'horreur,
Bandeaux, sceptres, bassins, tenebre, ombre, terreur,
Piliers, verges, foüets, infames, disciplines,

39 /

Trompes, cors, estandars, falots, torches, fanaux,
Cloux, escheles et croix, sentences, tribunaux,
Suye, vinaigre, fiel, marteaux, lances, tenailles,
Hebreux, Grecs et Romains, larrons, cartes et sort,
Astres, Lune, Soleil estoient aux funerailles
De celuy qui mourant fut vainqueur de la Mort.

La Marie dolente, pp. 7–35 (extracts)

L'homme dieu...
Pandoit sur un grand Arbre a trois cloux attaché:
Son chef couvert de sang, de ronces et d'espines
Panchoit sur le bras droit: ses lumieres divines
Que la mort avoit clos avoynt osté le jour
Aux flambeaux qui sont Roys du terrestre sejour:
Ses cheveux de chastaigne a flammes esblondées,
Flottoint sur son espaule esgarés par ondées,
Ou sur le plan du front: qui plus que nege blanc,

8 / Reçevoit un torrent de cent perles de sang,
Sa bouche s'entrouvroit paslement viollette,
Comme d'un coureur las, et panthelant Athlete,
Qui du laurier de gloire, et du prix resjouy
Meurt d'extreme allegresse, et tumbe esvanouy.

Ses bras droits et tendus (vrays tesmoins de ses peines)
Grossissoint leurs tendons, leurs muscles et leurs veines,
Sous l'excés de l'effort: et les cloux inhumains
Retiroint ses saincts doigts vers le creux de ses mains,
Le corps semblant un Corps d'Alebastre et de Marbre
Sur le tronq haut et droit de ce sainct et grand arbre
Se portoit sur ses mains en suspens estandu,
Et cedant a son faix n'estoit pas si tendu:
Ains composoit un creux justement vers le centre
Qui sert comme de terme et borne au petit ventre,
Enfondrant un trait d'ombre, et douce obscurité
Ou les genoux plus hauts reçeveoint la clarté,

9 / La jambe droicte et belle a la gauche couchée
D'un ombre gris et doux s'afflouyssoit touchée
Qui partoit du genoil: mais le pied relevé
Reçevant le jour plain de pourpre estoit lavé.

A la jambe senestre un' ombre un plus forte (*sic*)
Brunissoit le cristal de sa charnure morte,
Plus rude plus obscure et crue sur le gras,
Venant a s'afflouyr en descendant en bas;

Il ny avoit tendon, nerf, veine, ny partie
Qui ne fut rarement au compas despartie,
D'une juste decence au lieu propre qu'il faut,
Sans qu'on peut sur ce corps remarquer un deffaut.

10 /   .   .   .   .

Comme un peintre excellent lors qu'il couche ou qu'il
    plaque
La Romaine, Indyenne, et Florentine laque
Sur le pourpre ou le pers, le vermeil ou le gris,
L'incarnat ou le blanc d'un tableau de haut pris,
D'une seule couleur qu'il estompe et qu'il glace
De ce corps diaphane, et cramoysi qu'il passe,
Il sçait mille couleurs vivement varier,
Selon qu'a divers fonds il la vient marier:
Non autrement le sang que chasque membre verse,
Que le clou, que l'espine et que la lance perse,
Glace, varie et teint de si vives couleurs,

11 / Qu'elles font peur au vif des gemmes et des fleurs.
Le sang qui le Cristal de sa chair glace est Rose:
De la bouche glayeul: de l'ombre passeroze:
De la croix brun œillet; du poil passeveloux:
Des veines violette: et pensée des cloux.

   .   .   .   .

Ce pandant Taure croule, et Caucase et l'eschine
De la vaste, pesante, et terrestre machine
Tremble, s'esmeut [,] s'esloche, et sent craquer au fonds
Des avernes d'Enfer les Tartares proffonds.
En ce convoy lugubre et pompe funeralle,

12 / Un lamentable plaint une nuict generale,
Un crespe espouventable aux champs de l'air est veu;
Le Soleil vient de flamme et la Lune de feu,
Et des mutins Demons les trouppes desolées
D'un confus hurlement s'enfondrent aux vallées,
Aux Palais souterrains, aux lacs ords et puants
Ou sans espoir ils sont horriblement huants.
Mais la vierge esplorée, innocente et sacrée,
Qui voit ceste brebis sanglante et massacrée
Treuver tant agreable et soüefve la mort
Sur le lict de la Croix qu'on diroit qu'elle dort,
Dessus ses pieds tramblans prés de la Croix dressée,
Du glaive de douleur d'outre en outre persée,
Pasle, descolorée, escoulant de ses yeux

326

Des perles d'Oriant un fleuve precieux,
Meslant ses eaux au sang, a ses gouttes ses larmes,
A ses yeux ses regards, à son glaive ses armes,
Aux tranchans de son dœil ses cloux saincts et sacrés,
13 /　　A sa mort son Amour, elle a fait ces regrets.

24 /　　. . . . .

Bref est-ce pour avoir et par Mer et par terre
Fait d'un cœur heroique une mortelle guerre
Aux vices, aux pechez: combattu, bataillé,
Navigé, voyagé, cheminé, travaillé,
Preché, jeuné, süé, satisfaict Ambassades,
Guery, ressuscité languissants, et malades,
Bref la Mort et le Monde et Lucifer domté,
Qu'on vous a pour Trophée a cest arbre monté,
Qu'on paye ingrattement vos largesses divines
D'un sanglant diademe, et d'un chappeau d'espines,
Qu'on traite qu'on repaist ceux qui viennent du Ciel,
De verges, de foüets, de vinaigre et de fiel,
De lances et de cloux, de soufflets et de buffes,
De crachats, de bandeaux, de blasphemes, de truffes,
De Sceptres vains et verts, de titres, d'escriteaux,
De supplices, de Croix, de tronqs et de poteaux;
D'eschelles, de gibets, de vilaines potences,
25 /　　De perfides tesmoins, de meschantes sentences,
D'imposture, de cris, de trompettes, de cors,
De funeste musique et de mortels accords.
Qu'on trahit, qu'on saisit, qu'on lie, qu'on foüette,
Qu'on cloue, qu'on occit une brebis muette,
Qui simple ne dit mot quand elle voit forger
Le couteau qui la doit sur la Croix esgorger.

. . . .

32 /　　　　　　(*The descent from the Cross*)
Cepandant Nycodeme avec d'Arimathie,
Qui ont la sepulture entaillée et bastie,
Car ils furent de Christ les fidelles amys,
Pour despandre le corps deux eschelles ont mis
Au travers de la Croix: ou l'un et l'autre monte
D'une ardeur incroyable et d'une adresse pronte,
Posans le dextre pied au premier eschellon,
Et les mains aux piliers de l'eschelle selon
Que la seurté requiert, ainsi de branche en branche

Se portant au sommet d'une demarche franche,
Qui ne sent ses viellards armez de bons outils,
Et de durs ferremens à tel usage utils.

Nycodeme premier d'une forte tenaille
Arrache le clou droit, qu'il rebaise et qu'il baille
A Joseph qui le prent et qui le baise aussi,
Puis le met dans son sein, et d'un mesme soucy,
D'un tel coup de marteau pris a grande secousse
L'autre clou par la pointe et derriere repousse
Si qu'il sort tant avant dans le creux de la main,
Ou passant il a fait un trou trop inhumain,
Que bien facilement il le tire et l'arrache,
Joseph en tousse adonq et Nycodeme crache
Pour alleger ses flancs du fardeau soustenu,
Qui est de l'un et l'autre en suspens retenu.
Car un corps froid et mort qu'on soutient et qu'on charge
Sur l'espaule, et le dos a beaucoup plus de charge
Qu'un corps vif et mouvant, qui plus pront et leger
Semble en se remuant son porteur soulager...

33 /

Le Pourtraict ou Image du Sauveur, following *Les Perles,* pp. 52–4 (extracts)

Ces beaux et divins poils que le ciel mesm'à teins
D'escorce et de couleur d'avelaine un peu meure:
Sont jusques à l'oreille esgalement chasteins,
Ou mesme l'or plus beau tousjours pasle demeure.

Ceux qui tombans plus bas à flots crespés et longs
Dessus sa saincte espaule ont la couleur de cire,
Ils se monstrent espars, si luysans et si blonds,
Que la mesme lumiere esprise les desire.

. . . .

54 /

La barbe et les cheveux sont d'un mesme tresor,
Non trop vuide, ou sans poil, non trop large, ou trop drue:
Sur les extremitez se frisent en nœuds d'or,
Et du menton en bas en deux pointes fendue.

. . . .

La grace de son teint agreable et naif
De vermeil et de blanc est au ciel temperée:
Car il est composé de laict et de sang vif,
Pour faire une couleur parfaicte et moderée.

César de Nostredame

Apres l'assaut, et les combats funebres,
Ou le fier prince et l'ange des tenebres
Par CHRIST armé de son vermeil escu
Fut en duel honteusement vaincu,
Au lict Royal, contre la sepulture,
Ou ce Medor ce beau Dieu de nature
Pasle et sanglant, las et mort fut posé
Apres qu'il eust ses armes deposé.
Donnant aux vents sa tresse nonchalante,
Son Angelique esplorée et dolente
Panchoit son corps de tristesse ennuyé
Au droit genouil le bras droict appuyé,
Dedans sa main que maint Opale arrose
Portoit couché son visage de rose,

13 / Ou les desborts assemblez de ses yeux
Faisoient un lac de cristal precieux:
Qui se fendant en cent petites sources
Le long du bras tomboit à lentes courses,
Puis à boüillons argentins s'escoulant
Alloit sur l'herbe en perlettes roulant,
Pour s'aller joindre et se mesler encore
D'un moite pas aux perles que l'Aurore
Fondant en plainte et distilant en pleurs
Avoit greslé sur la robe des fleurs.
La gauche main delicatement blanche
Joincte à son bras qui sort nud de la manche
Plus blanc que neige avec ses doigts polis,
Qui font ternir l'excellence du lys,
Lasse et sans poulx s'alloit mollete et tendre
En s'allongeant sur l'autre cuisse estendre,
Qui descouvrant son pied blanc et charnu
Laissoit le dextre au genouil retenu:
Si que le ply delicat de sa robe
A l'œil subtil un seul traict ne derobe,
Tant justement on discerne au travers
Du crespe d'or, tous les muscles divers,
Ou l'or du poil qui vivement blondoye
Sans bruit aucun comme flammes ondoye,

14 / Non autrement qu'en bonasse on peut voir
L'eau de la mer sous Favon s'esmouvoir.

． ． ． ． ． ． ． ． ． ．

20 /

(*Magdalene speaking*)

Mais tout est sourd à mes complaintes vaines:
Rien ne respond que ces roches prochaines,
Sur qui mon œil contemple et void dressé
Le grand trophée ou son corps fut percé
Qui tout sanglant, et tout moite de larmes
Distille encor sous ses vermeilles armes

21 / Jusques à terre, ou ce grand rouge estang
Glace les fleurs d'une lacque de sang.

.   .   .   .

33 / (*She fails, at first, to recognise the risen Christ*)

Mais ce pendant qu'elle tremble et varie
JESUS redouble et l'appelle Marie:
Ce fut alors que ceste voix l'outra,
Et que ce mot dans son cœur penetra,
Que son cœur s'ouvre et son sang se dilatte,
Monte en sa jouë un pourpre d'escarlatte
Bruslant et vif et que presqu'espamant
Elle cogneut la voix de son amant.

Ne plus ne moins qu'on voit une bell' ame
Qu'un desir chaste et vertueux enflamme
Sous une voix d'amour et de desdain
Changer d'assiette et tressaillir soudain,
Voire approchant de l'huis et de la porte
De ce qu'elle ayme, estre pensive et morte,
Rougir, pasmer, fondre de joye en dueil
Si seulement son pied touche le sueil.

O qu'elle est ayse ayant treuvé sa joye,
O qu'elle feste, ô que de pleurs de joye
Elle respand, alors les tristes flus
De sa douleur ne vont ne viennent plus:
Elle l'œillade et l'admire et l'adore,
Le voit des yeux et des yeux le devore:

34 / Baisse la veuë et ne peut voir l'esclair
Que son œil rend si luisant et si clair,
Et l'adorant à terre agenouillée
Sa belle main de son bras despouillée
En s'allongeant tasche de l'approcher,
Mais son Seigneur ne se laisse toucher:
Ains de son doigt que toute chose avive
Touchant son front y faict la marque vive

330

Qu'on voit encor, que ny l'aage passé,
Ny mort, ny vers n'ont jamais effacé.
  Ce fut alors qu'elle fut arrosée
Non de ses pleurs, mais bien d'une rosee
Qui goutte à goutte en perles distilant
Dedans son cœur, le rendit tout bruslant:
Ce fut alors qu'elle tendit l'oreille
A ceste bouche en grace nompareille,
Qui retenoit au fil de ses devis
Tous ses esprits suspendus et ravis:
Il contoit bien de plus mystiques fables
Que ces vieux Grecs, ses parolles affables
Estoient courans d'ambrosie et de miel:
C'estoient rayons de lumiere et de ciel,
Doux ravissant, remplis d'une harmonie,
Et d'une odeur doucement infinie
Qui tiroit l'ame et fondoit tous ses sens
Dedans les cœurs des celestes accens.
  Pensons un peu de quelle vive flamme,
Et quel amour elle brusloit en l'ame:
Et quel desir agitoit sa raison
De la chasser bien tost de sa prison:
Pensons un peu comm'elle estoit ravie
De voir ainsi la fontaine de vie
Si doucement distiller en son cœur
Une si saincte et suave liqueur:
Et comme alors elle estoit attentive
A recueillir cest eau coulante et vive,
Et contempler le visage si beau
De ce beau corps revenu du tombeau.
  Autant de traitz que decoche sa face,
Luy sont autant de traitz d'or et de grace,
Chasque rayon, chascun de ses regards
Luy sont autant de brandons et de dards.
Là son amant ne tenoit plus voilée
Ne sa beauté, ny sa face estoilée,
La son poil d'or et de celeste lin
Flottoit party d'un ruisseau cristalin,
Montant du front, là ses ondes meslées
Couroient à bons sur l'espaule annelées,
Que la nature et le ciel admiroit,
Ou le ciel mesme estonné se miroit.
Là de son œil l'esclatante prunelle

35 /

36 /

Faisoit briller quelque chose plus belle
Que feu, qu'esclair, qu'estoille, que Soleil
Qui sort des eaux au point de son resveil.
Ce n'est œillet, ny rubis que sa bouche,
Car art aucun de peinture ne touche
A ces beaux Arcs d'où coulerent jadis,
Et vont coulant les eaux de Paradis.

Et bien qu'a peindre une petite image
Toute la France à ma main doive hommage:
Et que mes traits hardis subtils et flous
Facent Apelle et Tymanthe jalous,
Mon pinceau d'or qui sur sa main se jouë,
Reste confus, aussi bien qu[']a sa jouë,
Et qu'à son teint de pur laict et de sang
Qu'on voit meslé de vermeil et de blanc:
Ny mon blanc d'œuf, ou mon blanc de Venise:
Ma laque d'Inde, ou de Florence exquise:
Mon Azur d'Acre et mon bleu d'outre-mer
Peuvent son jour, ny son ombre animer.

Là mon art cede et là ma main s'arreste,
Là ceste amante attentive et muette
Tombe en extase et voit des yeux son Dieu
Qui comme esclair disparoit de ce lieu.

37 /

BIBLIOGRAPHY

No work is included which is not referred to in the text. All secondary sources referred to in the text are included. Primary sources of only marginal interest are not included here. The publication dates given are those of the editions referred to and quoted from in the text.

GENERAL REFERENCE

Cioranesco, A. *Bibliographie de la littérature française du seizième siècle.* Paris, 1959.

Cotgrave, R. *A Dictionarie of the French and English Tongues*, reproduced from the 1st ed. (London, 1611). New York, 1950.

Dagens, J. *Bibliographie chronologique de la littérature de spiritualité et de ses sources (1501–1610).* Paris, 1952.

Huguet, E. *Dictionnaire de la langue française du seizième siècle*, vols. 1–7. Paris, 1925–66.

Lachèvre, F. *Bibliographie des recueils de poésies du seizième siècle.* Paris, 1922. *Bibliographie des recueils collectifs de poésies publiées de 1597 à 1700*, vol. 1, *1597–1635.* Paris, 1901.

PRIMARY SOURCES: ANTHOLOGIES AND COLLECTIONS

Aury, D. *Anthologie de la poésie religieuse française.* Paris, 1943.

Blume, C. and Dreves, G. M. *Analecta hymnica medii ævi*, 51 vols. Leipzig, 1886–1908.

Boase, A. M. *The Poetry of France*, vol. 1, *1400–1600.* London, 1964.

Duplessis-Mornay, P. *Meditations chrestiennes sur quatre Pseaumes du Prophete David. Composees par Philippe de Mornay, seigneur du Plessis Marly. Meditation sur le Pseaume CXXVII par P. Pellisson, P. Meditation sur le Pseaume LI. traduite du Latin de Jerosme Savonarole, par S.G.S. s.l.*, 1591.

Estienne, A. *Dévot discours sur la Passion...où sont comprises plusieurs méditations recueillies des œuvres de S. Bernard, Tauler, Lansperge, Grenade, et autres auteurs.* Paris, 1582.

Fleuret, F. and Perceau, L. *Les Satires françaises du xvie siècle*, vol. 1. Paris, 1922.

Les Fleurs des plus excellens Poetes de ce Temps. Paris, N. and P. Bonfons, 1601.

333

Bibliography

Guytot, J. *Les Meditations des zelateurs de pieté recueillies de plusieurs et divers livres des saincts et anciens Peres. Avec autres Meditations prinses en la librairie sainct Victor lez Paris.* Paris, 1582 (dedication dated 1568).

Maisonfleur, E. de. *Les Cantiques du Sieur de Maisonfleur, œuvre excellent et plein de piété, auquel de nouveau ont esté adjoustez en ceste dernière édition plusieurs opuscules spirituels, recueillis de divers autheurs.* Paris, 1586.

Migne, J.-P. *Patrologia latina,* 221 vols. Paris, 1844–64.

Montméja, B. de. *Poèmes chrestiens de B. de Montméja et autres divers auteurs, recueillis et nouvellement mis en lumière par Philippes Depas.* Geneva, 1574.

La Muse chrestienne, ou recueil des poésies chrestiennes tirées des principaux poètes françois. Paris, 1582.

Les Muses françoises ralliees de diverses pars. Paris, Guillemot, 1599.

Le Parnasse des plus excellents poetes de ce temps ou Muses françoises r'alliees de diverses parts, 2nd vol. Lyons, Ancelin. *s.d.*

Raby, F. *The Oxford Book of Medieval Latin Verse.* Oxford, 1959.

Rime spirituali. Libro secondo. Venice, 1550.

Rousset, J. *Anthologie de la poésie baroque française,* 2 vols. Paris, 1961.

Schmidt, A.-M. *Poètes du xvie siècle.* Paris, 1959 (Bibliothèque de la Pléiade).

Le Second Livre des delices de la poesie françoise ou nouveau recueil des plus beaux vers de ce temps. Paris, Toussainct Du Bray, 1620.

L'Uranie, ou nouveau recueil de chansons spirituelles et chrestiennes, comprinses en cinq livres et accommodees pour la pluspart au chant des pseaumes de David. La Rochelle, J. Haultin, 1597 (also Geneva, 1591).

Valagre, Sieur de. *Les Cantiques du Sieur de Valagre…En cette dernière edition ont esté adjoustées les Larmes de Jesus Christ, les Pleurs de la Vierge, les Larmes de S. Pierre, de la Magdeleine, et autres œuvres chrestiennes.* Rouen, 1602.

PRIMARY SOURCES: SINGLE AUTHORS

Abelly, A. *Sermons sur les Lamentations du sainct prophete Hieremie.* Paris, 1582.

Alonso de Madrid. *La Methode de servir Dieu divisee en trois parties: avec le Miroir des personnes Illustres. Augmentée du Memorial de la vie de Jesus Christ: contenant sept belles Meditations pour tous les jours de la Semaine,* trans. G. Chappuys. Douai, 1600.

Aretino, P. *Trois livres de l'Humanité de Jesuchrist: divinement descripte, et au vif representée par Pierre Aretin Italien. Nouvellement traduictz en françois.* Lyons, 1539.

Les VII Psalmes de la Penitence de David. Traduicts de l'Italien de P. l'Aretin, trans. F. de Rosset. Paris, 1605.

Ariosto, L. *Orlando furioso,* ed. S. Debenedetti and C. Segre. Bologna, 1960.

Aubigné, A. d'. *Œuvres complètes*, ed. E. Réaume and F. de Caussade, 6 vols. Paris, 1873–92.

De la Douceur des afflictions, ed. F. Chavannes and C. Read. Paris, 1856.

Les Tragiques, ed. J. Plattard and A. Garnier, 4 vols. Paris, 1962 (*STFM*).

Augustine, St. *Recueil des consolations et instructions salutaires de l'ame fidele*, *extraict du volume de S. Augustin sur les Psalmes*, ed. and trans. Jacques de Billy. Paris, 1570.

(Suppositious works), *Les Meditations de sainct Augustin. Traduictes du Latin, et mises en vers françois*, trans. P. Tamisier. Lyons, 1587.

See Guytot's collection of meditations, which includes a prose version of the suppositious *Meditationes*.

Bargedé, N. *Les Odes pénitentes du moins que rien*. Paris, 1550.

Belleau, R. *La Bergerie*. Paris, 1572.

(*Les Amours et nouveaux échanges de pierres précieuses. Discours de la Vanité, pris de l'Ecclésiaste de Salomon. Eclogues sacrées prises du Cantique des Cantiques de Salomon*). Paris, 1576, title-page missing.

Belleforest, F. de. See Granada and Guevara.

Béroalde de Verville. *Les Appréhensions spirituelles, poèmes et autres œuvres philosophiques, avec les recherches de la pierre philosophale...Les Cognoissances nécessaires avec le livre de l'âme*. Paris, 1583.

Les Tenebres, qui sont les Lamentations de Jeremie. Hymne sur la nativité de nostre Seigneur et Sauveur Jesus Christ, in Guillemot's *Muses françoises* (see above). Paris, 1599 (separate pagination).

Anthologie poétique de Béroalde de Verville, ed. V.-L. Saulnier. Paris, 1945.

Bertaut, J. *Les Œuvres poétiques*, ed. A. Chenevière. Paris, 1891.

Bèze, T. de. *Chrestiennes méditations*, ed. M. Richter. Geneva, 1964 (*TLF*).

See Montméja's *Poèmes chrestiens* (above, *Anthologies and Collections*), which includes poems by Bèze.

Billy, Jacques de. *Sonnets spirituels, recueillis pour la plus part des anciens théologiens, tant grecs que latins, avec quelques autres petits traictez poëtiques de semblable matiere*. Paris, 1573.

Sonnets spirituels...Livre second. Paris, 1578.

See also Augustine, St.

Billy, Jean de. See Landsberger.

Blanchon, J. *Les Premieres œuvres poetiques*. Paris, 1583.

Bonaventura, St. *Les Meditations de S. Bonaventure, sur la Passion de nostre Seigneur Jesus Christ. Livre tres-utile et necessaire pour tous bons et devots Chrestiens, desireux de se baigner aux playes de Jesus Christ, par la contemplation de la douloureuse Passion*, trans. G. de La Brosse. Lyons, 1616.

Boyssières, J. de. *Les Troisiesmes œuvres poetiques*. Lyons, 1579.

Boyssières, J. de. (*cont.*)

Les Œuvres spirituelles. Lyons, 1582.

Sonnets sur les noms et passion de Jesus-Christ. Paris, 1585.

Calvin, J. *Institution de la religion chrestienne,* ed. J.-D. Benoît, 5 vols. Paris, 1957–63.

Chandieu, A. de. See Maisonfleur's *Cantiques* (above, *Anthologies and Collections*), which includes Chandieu's *Octonaires.*

Chappuys, G. *Figures de la Bible, declarees par stances . . . Augmentees de grand Nombre de figures aux Actes des Apostres.* Lyons, 1582.

See also Alonso de Madrid, Coster, Estella, Panigarola.

Chassignet, J.-B. *Le Mespris de la vie et consolation contre la mort.* Besançon, 1594.

Le Mespris de la vie et consolation contre la mort. Choix de sonnets, ed. A. Müller. Geneva, 1953 (*TLF*).

Œuvres sacrez de I.B.C., preface 'Au Liseur' dated 1592 (*MS*).

Chasteuil, L. Galaup de. *Imitation des Pseaumes de la pénitence Royalle. A treschrestien Roy de France et de Navarre Henry IIII.* Paris, 1597.

Coignard, G. de. *Œuvres chrestiennes de feu dame Gabrielle de Coignard, vefve à feu M. de Mansencal, sieur de Miremont, président en la cour du Parlement de Tholose.* Tournon, 1595.

Coster, F. de. *Le Livre de la Compaignie, c'est-à-dire les cinq livres des Institutions chrestiennes: Dressees pour l'usage de la Confrerie de la tres-heureuse Vierge Marie.* Antwerp, 1588.

Cinquante meditations de la vie et louanges de la Vierge Marie. Avec sept Meditations sur le Cantique SALVE REGINA, trans. G. Chappuys. Antwerp, 1590.

Coyssard, M. *Hymnes sacrez et odes spirituelles.* Lyons, 1594.

Dante Alighieri. *La Vita nuova,* ed. M. Barbi. Florence, 1932.

Desportes, P. *Œuvres,* ed. A. Michiels. Paris, 1858.

Les CL Pseaumes de David, mis en vers françois . . . Avec quelques Cantiques de la Bible, Hymnes, et autres œuvres et Prieres Chrestiennes. Paris, 1604.

Quelques prieres et meditations chrestiennes. Paris, 1603.

Doremet, J. *Polymnie du vray amour et de la mort. Avec quelques Stances et Quatrains Spirituelz.* Paris, 1596.

Du Bartas, G. de Salluste. *The Works of Guillaume de Salluste, Sieur du Bartas,* ed. U. T. Holmes, J. C. Lyons, R. W. Linker, etc., 3 vols. Chapel Hill, 1935–40.

Du Bellay, J. *Œuvres poétiques,* ed. H. Chamard. 6 vols. Paris, 1908–31 (*STFM*).

Du Perron, J. Davy. *Les Diverses œuvres . . . contenant plusieurs livres . . . non encore vus, ni publiés . . . ensemble tous les écrits mis au jour de son vivant, et maintenant réimprimés sur ses exemplaires laissez, reveus, corrigez et augmentez de sa main.* Paris, 1622 (the second part, containing the *Poésies*, is paginated separately).

Du Peyrat, G. *Hymne de la Trinité, avec quelques sonnets spirituels et un discours du S. Esprit.* Paris, 1587.

Duplessis-Mornay, P. *Discours de la vie et de la mort,* ed. M. Richter. Milan, 1964.
    See above (*Anthologies and Collections*) for the *Meditations.*

Du Vair, G. *La Saincte philosophie, avec plusieurs traitez de pieté.* Rouen, 1603.

Estella, Diego de. *Livre de la vanité du monde,* trans. G. Chappuys. Paris, 1587.

Favre, A. *Centurie premiere de sonets spirituels de l'amour divin et de la pénitence.* Chambéry, 1595.
    Les Entretiens spirituels d'Antoine Favre President D.G. Divisez en trois Centuries de Sonets. La Premiere de l'Amour divin, et de la Penitence, la seconde du tressainct Sacrement de l'Autel, la troisiesme du Sainct Rosaire. Avec une Centurie de Quatrains. Dediez a Madame Marguerite, Princesse de Savoye. Paris, 1602.
    Stances sur la devotion de nostre Dame du Mont-de-Vic. Paris, 1602.
    Les Meditations spirituelles de A.F. s.l., 1612.

François de Sales, St. *Œuvres,* vol. III, *Introduction à la vie dévote.* Annecy, 1893.

Garnier, R. *Œuvres complètes: Les Juifves, Bradamante, Poésies diverses,* ed. R. Lebègue. Paris, 1949.

Goulart, S. *Trente tableaux de la mort, ou discours chrétiens sur nostre preparation au depart de la vie presente, 2eme ed. augm. de douze tableaux. s.l.,* 1602.
    See also Montméja's *Poèmes chrestiens* (above, *Anthologies and Collections*), which includes Goulart's *Imitations* and *Suite des imitations chrestiennes* (thirteen odes and two books of sonnets).

Granada, Luis de. *Le Vray chemin et adresse pour acquerir et parvenir à la grace de Dieu, et se maintenir en icelle, par le moyen et compagnie de l'Oraison et Contemplation en la Loy et amour de Dieu,* trans. F. de Belleforest. Paris, 1579.
    Devotes contemplations et spirituelles instructions sur la Vie, Passion, Mort, Resurrection, et glorieuse Ascension de nostre Sauveur Jesus Christ, trans. F. de Belleforest. Paris, 1583.
    See also Estienne's *Dévot discours* (above, *Anthologies and Collections*).

Grévin, J. *Théâtre complet et poésies choisies,* ed. L. Pinvert. Paris, 1922.

Guevara, Antonio de. *Livre du Mont de Calvaire,* trans. F. de Belleforest. Paris, 1589.

Habert, I. *Les Trois livres des Meteores avecques autres œuvres poëtiques.* Paris, 1585 (the *Œuvres chrestiennes* are paginated separately).

Hopil, C. *Les Œuvres chrestiennes.* Paris, 1603.

Bibliography

Humbert, H. *La Sepmaine saincte*. Toul, 1609.

Ignatius de Loyola, St. *Les Vrais exercices spirituels . . . Ensemble la Guide ou Directoire pour ceux qui font faire lesdits Exercices*. Paris, 1620.

Jamyn, A. *Le Second volume des œuvres*. Paris, 1584.

La Ceppède, J. de. *Les Theoremes de messire Jean de La Ceppede . . . sur le sacré mystere de nostre redemption, Divisez en trois Livres, et enrichis de trois Tables tres-amples du sujet des Sonnets, des Matieres, et des Autheurs: Suivis de l'Imitation de quelques Pseaumes et autres Meslanges spirituels*, Toulouse, 1612–1613; photographic edition, presented by J. Rousset. Geneva, 1966 (*THR*, 80).

Landsberger (Johann Justus). *Le Manuel du chevalier chrestien*, trans. Jean de Billy. Rouen, 1609.

See also Estienne's *Dévot discours* (above, *Anthologies and Collections*).

La Noue, Odet de. *Poésies chrestiennes*. Geneva, 1594.

La Péruse, J. de. *Les Œuvres*. Paris, 1573.

Le Digne, N. *Recueil des premieres œuvres chrestiennes*. Paris, 1600.

Le Fèvre de La Boderie, G. *Hymnes ecclésiastiques, Cantiques spirituelz, et autres Meslanges Poëtiques*. Paris, 1578.

Le Saulx, Marin. *Theanthropogamie en forme de dialogue par sonnets chrestiens*. London, 1577.

Loys, Jean. *Les Œuvres poëtiques*. Douai, 1613 (this volume is bound together with the *Œuvres poetiques* of Jacques Loys, also Douai, 1613).

Malherbe, F. de. *Poésies*, ed. P. Martinon. Paris, *s.d.* (Garnier).

Marguerite de Navarre. *Les Dernières poésies*, ed. A. Lefranc. Paris, 1896.

L'Heptaméron, ed. M. François. Paris, *s.d.* (Garnier).

Marot, C. *Œuvres lyriques*, ed. C. A. Mayer. London, 1964.

Marquets, Anne de. *Sonets, prières et devises en forme de pasquins pour l'assemblée de messieurs les prélats et docteurs, tenue à Poissy, MDLXI*. Paris, 1566.

Les Divines Poesies de Marc-Antoine Flaminius: Contenantes diverses Prieres, Meditations, Hymnes et actions de graces à Dieu: Mises en François avec le Latin respondant l'un à l'autre. Avec plusieurs Sonnets et Cantiques, ou Chansons Spirituelles pour louer Dieu. Paris, 1568.

Sonets spirituels de feue tres-vertueuse et tres-docte dame Sr Anne de Marquet sur les dimanches et principales solennitez de l'annee. Paris, 1605.

Montaigne, M. de. *Œuvres complètes*, ed. A. Thibaudet. Paris, 1962 (Bibliothèque de la Pléiade).

Montchrestien, A. de. *Les Tragédies*, ed. L. Petit de Julleville. Paris, 1891.

Montenay, Georgette de. *Emblemes, ou Devises chrestiennes*. Lyons, 1571.

Montméja, B. de. See above, *Anthologies and Collections*.

Nostredame, César de. *Dymas, ou le Bon Larron, dedié à son Altesse Serenissime de Lorraine*. Toulouse, 1606.

338

Primary sources: single authors

Les Perles, ou les Larmes de la saincte Magdeleine, avec quelques rymes sainctes dediées à Madame la comtesse de Carces. Toulouse, 1606.

La Marie dolente. Au Sieur Delsherms advocat tolosain. s.l.n.d. (dedication dated 1608).

Pièces héroïques et diverses poesies dediees à Messeigneurs les Archevesques et Princes d'Arles et D'ambrun. Toulouse, 1608 (this collection includes the *Rimes spirituelles*, which are paginated separately; dedication dated 1607).

Panigarola, F. *Cent sermons sur la Passion de nostre Seigneur*, trans. G. Chappuys. Paris, 1586.

Peletier Du Mans, J. *Art poëtique*, ed. A. Boulanger. Paris, 1930.

Pellisson, P. See Duplessis-Mornay's *Meditations* (above, *Anthologies and Collections*).

Perrin, F. *Trois centuries de sonnets...Contenant le vray pourtraict de la vie humaine...Avec les antiquitez de plusieurs Citez memorables.* Paris, 1588.

Perrot de La Sale, P. *Tableaus sacrez... qui sont toutes les histoires du Viel Testament representees et exposees selon leur sens en poesie françoise.* Frankfurt, 1594.

Poupo, P. *La Muse chrestienne*, 3 books. Paris, 1590–2 (bk. III is paginated separately).

Richeome, L. *Tableaux sacrez des figures mystiques du tres-auguste sacrifice et sacrement de l'Eucharistie.* Paris, 1601.

Ronsard, P. de. *Œuvres complètes*, ed. P. Laumonier, 8 vols. Paris, 1914–1919 (Lemerre).

Œuvres complètes, ed. P. Laumonier, vol. VIII. Paris, 1963 (*STFM*).

Sainte-Marthe, S. de. *Opera*, vol. I. Paris, 1616.

Savonarola, G. *La Verité de la foy, sous le triomphe de la croix de Jésus*, trans. P. Du Mont. Douai, 1588.

See also Duplessis-Mornay's *Meditations* (above, *Anthologies and Collections*), and Tamisier (below).

Sebillet, T. *L'Art poëtique françoys*, ed. F. Gaiffe. Paris, 1932 (*STFM*).

Sponde, J. de. *Méditations avec un essai de poèmes chrétiens*, ed. A. Boase. Paris, 1954.

Tagaut, J. See Montméja's *Poëmes chrestiens* (above, *Anthologies and Collections*), which contains poems by Tagaut.

Tamisier, P. *Meditations chrestiennes sur les sept Psalmes de la Penitence du Prophete Royal David. Mises en vers françois, sur la prose d'un docte personnage de ce temps...Plus une meditation sur le Psalme cinquantiesme Miserere mei Deus, traduite du latin de F. Jerosme Savonarole, Ferrarois, et mise en vers françois.* Paris, 1588.

Cantiques, hymnes, et prieres des saincts Peres...et personnes illustres du vieil et nouveau Testament. Avec autres prieres, tirées des autheurs Catholiques. Lyons, 1590. See also Augustine, St.

Bibliography

Tauler, J. *Les Institutions divines, et salutaires enseignemens du Reverend pere frere Jean Thaulere grand Docteur contemplatif, en son vivant religieux de l'ordre de S. Dominicque...le tout nouvellement traduict de Latin en François par les peres Minimes de l'Oratoire nostre Dame de vie-Saine.* Paris, 1587.

See also Estienne's *Dévot discours* (above, *Anthologies and Collections*).

SECONDARY SOURCES

Allais, G. *Malherbe et la poésie française à la fin du xvie siècle (1585–1600)*, Paris, 1891.

Allott, T. J. D. *The Poetry of Jean Bertaut*, thesis presented for B.Litt. at Oxford, 1959–60.

Aube, E. 'La Poésie en Provence au temps de Malherbe', *Les Cahiers d'Aix-en-Provence, hiver*, 1923–1924, pp. 3 ff.

Aubert, F., Boussard, J. and Meylan, H. 'Un Premier recueil de poésies latines de Théodore de Bèze', *BHR*, 15, 1953, pp. 164 ff., 257 ff.

Bataillon, M. *Erasme et l'Espagne*. Paris, 1937.

'De Savonarole à Louis de Grenade', *RLC*, 16, 1936, pp. 23 ff.

Bensimon, M. 'Ronsard et la mort', *MLR*, 57, 1962, pp. 183 ff.

Boase, A. M. 'The Definition of Mannerism', *Proceedings of the 3rd Congress of the International Comparative Literature Association*. The Hague, 1962, pp. 143 ff.

Braunschweig, R. 'Une Source profane de la "Sainte Pécheresse"', *BHR*, 27, 1966, pp. 670 f.

Bremond, H. *Histoire littéraire du sentiment religieux en France depuis la fin des guerres de religion jusqu'à nos jours*, 11 vols. Paris, 1920–36.

Buffum, I. *Agrippa d'Aubigné's Les Tragiques; a Study of the Baroque Style in Poetry*. Yale, 1951.

Studies in the Baroque from Montaigne to Rotrou. Yale, 1957.

Buisson, F. *Sébastien Castellion: sa vie et son œuvre, 1515–1563*, 2 vols. Paris, 1892.

Busson, H. 'Vers oubliés de Ronsard', *RHLF*, 59, 1959, pp. 145 ff.

Castor, G. *Pléiade Poetics. A Study in Sixteenth-Century Thought and Terminology*. Cambridge, 1964.

Cave, T. C. 'The Protestant Devotional Tradition: Simon Goulart's *Trente tableaux de la mort*', *FS*, 21, 1967, pp. 1 ff.

Champion, P. 'Henri III et les écrivains de son temps', *BHR*, 1, 1941, pp. 43 ff.

Cioranesco, A. *L'Arioste en France des origines à la fin du xviiie siècle*, 2 vols. Paris, 1939.

Clements, R. J. *Picta Poesis: Literary and Humanistic Theory in Renaissance Emblem Books*. Rome, 1960 (*Temi e Testi*, 6).

Secondary sources

Cochois, P. *Bérulle et l'école française.* Paris, 1963.

Cognet, L. *De la Dévotion moderne à la spiritualité française.* Paris, 1958.

Coombs, I. 'Baroque Elements in Jean de Sponde's *Stances de la mort*', *EC*, 1, 1961, pp. 86 ff.

Dagens, J. *Bérulle et les origines de la restauration catholique (1575–1611).* Brussels, 1952.

Dainville, F. de. *Les Jésuites et l'éducation de la société française*, vol. II, *La Naissance de l'humanisme moderne.* Paris, 1940.

Dawson, J. C. *Toulouse in the Renaissance.* New York, 1923.

Dejob, C. *De l'Influence du Concile de Trente sur la littérature et les beaux-arts chez les peuples catholiques.* Paris, 1884.

Durand, L. E. G. *The Poetry of Jean de Sponde: a Critical Evaluation*, thesis presented for D.Phil. at University of Michigan, 1963.

Ehrmann, J. 'Massacre and Persecution Pictures in Sixteenth-Century France' *JWI*, 8, 1945, pp. 195 ff.

Evans, A. R., Jr. 'Figural Art in the *Théorèmes* of Jean de La Ceppède', *MLN*, 78, 1963, pp. 278 ff.

Febvre, L. 'Ce qu'on peut trouver dans une série d'inventaires: De la Renaissance à la Contre-Réforme', *Ann. Hist. Soc.* 3, 1941, pp. 41 ff.

Gaertner, J. A. 'Latin verse translations of the Psalms, 1500–1620', *HTR*, 49, 1956, pp. 271 ff.

Gillet, L. *Histoire artistique des ordres mendiants.* Paris, 1939.

Gilson, E. *Les Idées et les lettres.* Paris, 1932.

History of Christian Philosophy in the Middle Ages. London, 1955.

Grant, W. L. 'Neo-Latin Verse-translations of the Bible', *HTR*, 52, 1959, pp. 205 ff.

Graur, T. *Un Disciple de Ronsard—Amadis Jamyn, 1540(?)–1593: sa vie, son œuvre, son temps.* Paris, 1929.

Griffiths, R. 'The Influence of Formulary Rhetoric upon French Renaissance Tragedy', *MLR*, 59, 1964, pp. 201 ff.

Haitze, P.-J. de. *Histoire de la ville d'Aix*, vol. IV. Aix-en-Provence, 1889.

Higman, F. 'The *Méditations* of Jean de Sponde: A Book for the Times', *BHR*, 28, 1966, pp. 564 ff.

Holban, M. '*Le Miroir de l'âme pécheresse* et *Les Epitres de la Noble et Amoureuse Dame*', in *Mélanges offerts à M. Abel Lefranc.* Paris, 1936, pp. 142 ff.

Jeanneret, M. 'Pierre Poupo: Recherches sur le sacré et le profane dans la poésie religieuse du xvie siècle', *Bulletin annuel de la Fondation suisse*, University of Paris, XIV, 1965, pp. 15 ff.

Jones, L. C. *Simon Goulart (1543–1628).* Geneva-Paris, 1917.

Jung, M-R. *Hercule dans la littérature française du xvie siècle.* Geneva, 1966 (*THR*, 79).

Klein, R. 'La Dernière méditation de Savonarole', *BHR*, 23, 1961, pp. 441 ff.

Bibliography

Lavaud, J. *Un Poète de cour au temps des derniers Valois: Philippe Desportes* (*1546–1606*). Paris, 1936.

Lawrence, F. L. 'La Ceppède's *Théorèmes* and Ignatian Meditation', *CL*, 17, 1965, pp. 133 ff.

Leake, R. E., Jr. 'Jean Baptiste Chassignet and Montaigne', *BHR*, 23, 1961, pp. 282 ff.

Lebègue, R. *La Poésie française de 1560 à 1630*, 2 vols. Paris, 1951.

'Nouvelles études malherbiennes', *BHR*, 5, 1944, pp. 153 ff.

'Les Larmes de Saint-Pierre: poème baroque', *RSH*, 1949, pp. 154 ff.

'Plagiats protestants de poésies de Garnier et de Desportes', *BHR*, 13, 1951, pp. 355 ff., and 14, 1952, pp. 334 ff.

Leblanc, P. *Les Paraphrases françaises des psaumes à la fin de la période baroque* (*1610–1660*). Paris, 1960.

'Henry Humbert, poète lorrain', *BHR*, 18, 1956, pp. 46 ff.

Lemaire, H. *Les Images chez Saint François de Sales*. Paris, 1962.

François de Sales, Docteur de la confiance et de la paix. Etude de spiritualité à partir d'un choix important d'images. Paris, 1963.

Levi, A. H. T. *French Moralists: Theory of the Passions 1589–1649*. Oxford, 1964.

Mâle, E. *L'Art religieux après le concile de Trente*. Paris, 1932.

Malherbe et les poètes de son temps. Paris, 1955 (catalogue of the exhibition for the 4th centenary of the birth of Malherbe).

Martz, L. L. *The Poetry of Meditation*. Yale, 1962.

McFarlane, I. D. 'Jean Salmon Macrin (1490–1557)', *BHR*, 21, 1959, pp. 55 ff., 311 ff., and 22, 1960, pp. 73 ff.

Moore, W. G. *La Réforme allemande et la littérature française*. Strasbourg, 1930.

Mor, A. 'François de Sales e il Barocco', *SF*, 4, 1960, pp. 74 ff.

Mourgues, O. de. *Metaphysical, Baroque and Précieux Poetry*. Oxford, 1953.

Mugnier, F. *Histoire et correspondance du premier Président Favre*, 2 vols. Paris, 1902–3.

Müller, A. *La Poésie religieuse catholique de Marot à Malherbe*. Paris, 1950.

Un Poète religieux du xvie siècle: J.-B. Chassignet, 1578?–1635?. Paris, 1951.

Natoli, G. *Figure e problemi della cultura francese*. Florence, 1956.

O'Connor, M. C. *The Art of Dying Well*. New York, 1942.

Perrat, C. *Claude Bellièvre* (*1487–1557*). Geneva, 1956 (*THR*, 23).

Picard, R. 'Aspects du lyrisme religieux au xviie siècle', *DSS*, 66–67, 1965, pp. 57 ff.

Pinvert, L. *Jacques Grévin* (*1538–1570*), *sa vie, ses écrits, ses amis; étude biographique et littéraire*. Paris, 1899.

Pizzorusso, A. 'Le *Stances de la mort* di Jean de Sponde', in *Studi in onore di Carlo Pellegrini*. Turin, 1963, pp. 193 ff.

Secondary sources

Poulet, G. *Les Métamorphoses du cercle*. Paris, 1961.
'Poésie du cercle et de la sphère', *CAEF*, 10, 1958, pp. 44 ff.
Pourrat, P. *La spiritualité chrétienne*, 4 vols. Paris, 1918–28.
Prat, J-M. *Maldonat et l'Université de Paris*. Paris, 1856.
Praz, M. *Studies in Seventeenth-century Imagery*. London, 1939.
Raymond, M. *L'Influence de Ronsard sur la poésie française (1550–1585)*, 2 vols. Geneva, 1965 (*THR*, 73).
'Jean Tagaut, poète français et bourgeois de Genève', *RSS*, 12, 1925, pp. 98 ff.
Réau, L. *Iconographie de l'art chrétien*, 3 vols. in 6. Paris, 1955–9.
Reese, G. *Music in the Renaissance*. New York, 1959.
Renaudet, A. *Préréforme et humanisme à Paris pendant les premières guerres d'Italie (1494–1517)*. Paris, 1953.
Reynier, G. *Le Roman sentimental avant l'Astrée*. Paris, 1908.
Richter, M. 'Una fonte calvinista di J. B. Chassignet', *BHR*, 26, 1964, pp. 341 ff.
'Philippe du Plessis-Mornay: un aspetto del manierismo poetico protestante', in *Contributi dell'Istituto di Filologia moderna*, Serie francese, vol. III. Milan, 1964, pp. 1 ff.
'La Poetica di Théodore de Bèze e le *Chrestiennes Méditations*', *Ævum*, 38, 1964, pp. 479 ff.
Rossi, V. *Il Quattrocento*. Milan, 1964.
Rousset, J. *La Littérature de l'âge baroque en France: Circé et le paon*. Paris, 1954.
'Les Images de la nuit et de la lumière chez quelques poètes religieux', *CAEF*, 10, 1958, pp. 58 ff.
Ruchon, F. *Essai sur la vie et l'œuvre de Jean de La Ceppède, poète chrétien et Magistrat (1548–1623)*. Geneva, 1953 (*THR*, 8).
Saulnier, V.-L. 'Etude sur Béroalde de Verville', *BHR*, 5, 1944, pp. 209 ff.
'L'Oraison funèbre au XVIe siècle', *BHR*, 10, 1948, pp. 124 ff.
'Commentaires sur les Antiquitez', *BHR*, 12, 1950, pp. 114 ff.
Saulnier, V.-L. and Worthington, A. 'Du nouveau sur Jean de La Ceppède', *BHR*, 17, 1955, pp. 415 ff.
Schenda, R. 'Französische Prodigienschriften aus der zweiten Hälfte des 16. Jahrhunderts', *ZFSL*, 69, 1959, pp. 150 ff.
Die französische Prodigienliteratur in der zweiten Hälfte des 16. Jahrhunderts. Munich, 1961 (*Münchner romanistische Arbeiten*, 16).
Schmidt, A.-M. 'Calvinisme et poésie au seizième siècle en France', *BSHPF*, 84, 1935, pp. 211 ff.
Secret, F. 'Un Traité oublié de Blaise de Vigenère', *BHR*, 17, 1955, pp. 292 ff.
Seiler, M. H. *Anne de Marquets: Poétesse religieuse du XVIe siècle*. Washington, 1931.

Bibliography

Seznec, J. *La Survivance des dieux antiques*. London, 1939.

Smits, L. *Saint Augustin dans l'œuvre de Calvin*. Assen, 1957.

Steele, A. J. 'Conversions', *CAEF*, 10, 1958, pp. 69 ff.

Tapié, V. L. *Baroque et classicisme*. Paris, 1957.

Tieghem, P. van. 'La Littérature latine de la Renaissance', *BHR*, 4, 1944, pp. 177 ff.

Toffanin, G. *Il Cinquecento*. Milan, 1965.

Trénel, J. *L'Elément biblique dans l'œuvre de d'Aubigné*. Paris, 1904.

Tuve, R. *A Reading of George Herbert*. London, 1952.

Vaganay, H. 'Un Sonnet italien peu connu; quatre traductions du Stabat Mater au xvie siècle', *RB*, 21, 1911, pp. 393 ff.

Vianey, J. *Le Pétrarquisme en France*. Montpellier, 1909.

Vossler, K. *Poesie der Einsamkeit in Spanien*, 3 vols. Munich, 1935–8.

Wallerstein, R. C. *Studies in Seventeenth-Century Poetic*. Madison, 1950.

Weber, H. *La Création poétique an xvie siècle en France*, 2 vols. Paris, 1956.

Weisbach, W. *Der Barock als Kunst der Gegenreformation*. Berlin, 1921.

Französische Malerei des XVII. Jahrhunderts im Rahmen von Kultur und Gesellschaft. Berlin, 1932.

Wendel, F. *Calvin: Sources et évolution de sa pensée religieuse*. Paris, 1950.

Wind, E. *Pagan Mysteries in the Renaissance*. London, 1958.

Yates, F. A. *The French Academies of the Sixteenth Century*. London, 1947.

Zeldin, J. '*Les Tragiques* and the Baroque', *EC*, 1, 1961, pp. 67 ff.

Zezula, J. and Clements, R. J. 'La Troisième Lyonnaise: Georgette de Montenay', *EC*, 5, 1965, pp. 90 ff.

CHRONOLOGICAL SUMMARY OF PRIMARY SOURCES

Unless otherwise indicated, all dates refer to the earliest edition which I have seen mentioned. Where a different but contemporary edition has been used above, the date of this edition has here been added in brackets after the title of the work. Works published before 1570 and after 1613 are not included.

1570	Augustine, *Recueil des consolations*, trans. Jacques de Billy.
1571	Guevara, *Livre du Mont de Calvaire*, trans. F. de Belleforest (1589).
	Guytot, *Meditations des zelateurs de pieté* (1582).
	Landsberger, *Le Manuel du chevalier chrestien*, trans. Jean de Billy (1609).
	Montenay, *Emblemes, ou Devises chrestiennes.*
1572	Belleau, *La Bergerie* (including paraphrases from *Job*).
	Granada, *Devotes contemplations*, trans. Belleforest (1583).
1573	Billy (Jacques de), *Sonnets spirituels.*
	La Péruse, *Les Œuvres.*
1574	Du Bartas, *La Muse chrestienne.*
	Montméja, etc., *Poèmes chrestiens.*
	Perrin, *Le Pourtraict de la vie humaine* (1588).
1575	First appearance of religious poems by Desportes.
	D'Aubigné working on *Les Tragiques.*
	Belleau, *Les Amours et nouveaux échanges* (including paraphrases of Ecclesiastes and Song of Solomon).
1576	Duplessis-Mornay, *Excellent discours de la vie et de la mort.*
	Granada, *Le Vray chemin*, trans. Belleforest (1579).
1577	Le Saulx, *Theanthropogamie.*
1578	Billy (Jacques de), *Sonnets spirituels . . . Livre second.*
	Du Bartas, *La Sepmaine.*
	Estella, *Livre de la vanité du monde*, trans. G. Chappuys (1587).
	Le Fèvre (Guy), *Hymnes ecclésiastiques.*
1579	Boyssières, *Les Troisiesmes œuvres.*
1580	Bonaventura, *Les Meditations*, trans. G. de La Brosse (1616).
	Montaigne, *Essais.*
1581	Maisonfleur, etc., *Les Cantiques* (see also 1586).
1582	Abelly, *Sermons sur les Lamentations.*
	Bèze, *Chrestiennes méditations.*

Boyssières, *Les Œuvres spirituelles.*

Chappuys (Gabriel), *Figures de la Bible.*

Estienne, *Dévot discours* (selection of meditations).

La Muse chrestienne.

1583 Béroalde de Verville, *Les Appréhensions spirituelles,* etc.

Blanchon, *Les Premieres œuvres.*

Garnier, *Les Juifves.*

1584 Du Bartas, *Seconde Sepmaine; Brief advertissement.*

Jamyn (Amadis), *Le Second volume des œuvres.*

1585 Boyssières, *Sonnets sur les noms et passion de Jesus-Christ.*

Du Vair, *Méditations* on Penitential Psalms (see also 1603).

Habert (Isaac), *Les Trois livres des Meteores... Œuvres chrestiennes.*

Poupo, *La Muse chrestienne* (1590–92).

1586 Duplessis-Mornay, Pellisson, Savonarola, *Meditations chrestiennes* (1591).

Maisonfleur, *Les Cantiques* (including Chandieu's *Octonaires*).

Panigarola, *Cent sermons sur la Passion,* trans. G. Chappuys.

Ronsard, *Derniers vers.*

1587 Alonso de Madrid, *La Methode de servir Dieu,* etc., trans. G. Chappuys (1600).

D'Aubigné, *Meditation* on Psalm 51.

First appearance of psalm-paraphrases by Desportes.

Du Peyrat, *Hymne de la Trinité,* etc.

Malherbe, *Les Larmes de S. Pierre.*

Pseudo-Augustine, *Les Meditations,* verse trans. by Tamisier.

Tauler, *Les Institutions divines,* trans. ed. Estienne.

1588 Coster, *Le Livre de la Compaignie.*

Death of Anne de Marquets (see 1605).

Savonarola, *La Verité de la foy,* trans. Du Mont.

Sponde, *Méditations avec un essai de poèmes chrétiens.*

Tamisier, *Meditations chrestiennes* on Penitential Psalms (including Savonarola's med. on *Miserere*), verse trans.

1590 Coster, *Cinquante meditations...de la Vierge Marie,* trans. Chappuys.

Tamisier, *Cantiques, hymnes, et prieres.*

1591 *L'Uranie* (Protestant anthology).

1592 Chassignet, *MS* paraphrases of Job, Song of Solomon, etc. (preface signed 1592).

1594 Chassignet, *Le Mespris.*

Coignard, *Œuvres chrestiennes* (1595).

Coyssard, *Hymnes sacrez et odes spirituelles.*

Desportes, *Prieres et meditations* in prose.

La Ceppède, *Imitation des Pseaumes,* and 12 *Théorèmes.*

La Noue (Odet de), *Poésies chrestiennes.*

Perrot de La Sale, *Tableaus sacrez.*

1595 Chasteuil, *Imitation des Pseaumes* (1597).

Favre, *Centurie premiere.*

1596 Doremet, *Polymnie.*

1597 Poems by Bertaut and Du Perron begin to appear in anthologies.

1599 Béroalde de Verville, *Les Tenebres...Hymne sur la nativité* (in Guillemot's *Muses françoises*).

1600 Le Digne, *Recueil des premieres œuvres chrestiennes.*

D'Aubigné, *De la Douceur des afflictions* (date of dedication).

1601 First collection of poetry by Bertaut.

Les Fleurs des plus excellents Poetes, N. and P. Bonfons (3rd edition).

Goulart, *Tableaux de la mort* (1602).

Montchrestien, *Aman.*

Richeome, *Tableaux sacrez.*

1602 Favre, *Entretiens spirituels; Stances sur la devotion de nostre Dame du Mont-de-Vic.*

Valagre, *Les Cantiques* (including collection of *Larmes*).

1603 Du Vair, *La Saincte philosophie,* with complete *Méditations.*

Hopil, *Les Œuvres chrestiennes.*

1604 Desportes, *Les CL. Pseaumes* and complete religious poetry and prose.

1605 Aretino, *Les VII Psalmes de la Penitence,* trans. F. de Rosset.

Anne de Marquets, *Sonets spirituels.*

1606 Nostredame, *Dymas; Les Perles.*

1607 Nostredame, *Rimes spirituelles* (date of dedication).

1608 François de Sales, *Introduction à la vie dévote.*

Nostredame, *La Marie dolente.*

Approximate date of Ancelin's *Parnasse...ou Muses françoises.*

1609 Humbert, *La Sepmaine saincte.*

1612 Favre, *Les Meditations spirituelles.*

La Ceppède, *Imitation des Pseaumes et autres Meslanges spirituels.*

1613 La Ceppède, *Les Théorèmes* (vol. 1).

Loys (Jean and Jacques), *Les Œuvres poétiques.*

INDEX

General topics and names occurring *passim* (devotion, penitence, Calvinism, Counter-Reformation, Passion, Bible, God, Christ) and authors of secondary sources are not listed here.

Index

Index

Index

Index

Index